SLIPSTREAM

A Memoir

SLIPSTREAM

A Memoir

Elizabeth Jane Howard

MACMILLAN

First published 2002 by Macmillan
an imprint of Pan Macmillan Ltd
Pan Macmillan, 20 New Wharf Road, London N1 9RR
Basingstoke and Oxford
Associated companies throughout the world
www.panmacmillan.com

ISBN 0 333 90349 8

1 3 5 7 9 8 6 4 2

A CIP catalogue record for this book is available from
the British Library.

Typeset in 12½/15pt Bembo by SX Composing DTP, Rayleigh, Essex
Printed and Bound in Great Britain by
Mackays of Chatham, Chatham plc, Kent

To my daughter Nicola

Contents

List of Illustrations

All photographs are from private collections unless otherwise specified.

Section 1
With my father (c.1933).
My mother, a dancer in the corps de ballet (c.1917) of Diagehlev's
    Ballets Russes.
Enrico Ciccetti's class; the teacher whom all ballet dancers revered.
With my brother, Robin, and Si, my grandfather's monstrous mongrel
    (c.1929).
At Lansdowne Road, aged about eight (c.1931).
My father loved sailing (c.1930).
My father's mother, Florence Howard, with the reprehensible Si.
My father's father, Alexander Howard.
The Beacon, our family's holiday home in Sussex (c.1927).
Home Place, my father's parent's house, 3½ miles from the Beacon.
My mother with Colin, shortly after his birth (c.1932).
Edith Somervell, my mother's musical mother.
With Colin at Lansdowne Road.
A very small selection of family at the Beacon.
Peter Scott and Lady Kennet, his mother, known as K.
Peter, my first husband (1942). (copyright Fayer Camera Portraits)
After my wedding with Peter Scott (1942).
My portrait in *Country Life* (1942). (copyright *Country Life* magazine)
With Peter and K (c.1943).
Wayland, Pete's brother, drawn by Pete (1940). (copyright *Country
    Life* magazine)
Pen drawing of me, by Pete at Cowes (1942). (copyright *Country Life*
    magazine)
The naval production of *The Importance of Being Earnest* at Anglesea (1942).

List of Illustrations

Number 8 Edwards Square.

With Robert Aickman at Covent Garden. (copyright Graphic Photo Union)

At the publication of my first novel (1950).

On the *Ailsa Crag* with Robert Aickman and Anthea and James Sutherland.

Cecil Day-Lewis (c.1936). (copyright National Portrait Gallery)

Section 2

After my daughter Nicola's christening on HMS *Discovery*.

Nicola aged three.

On the *Queen Mary*, returning from New York with Pete (1946).

A. D. Peters (c.1972).

Jill Balcon and Cecil Day-Lewis, and me, at the christening of their daughter, Tamasin.

Romain Gary and his second wife Jean Seberg. (copyright Bettman/CORBIS)

Arthur Koestler. (copyright Bettman/CORBIS)

Laurie Lee (c.1955).

At Blomfield Road with Katsika, whom I'd criminally smuggled from Greece. (copyright Tony Armstrong Jones)

Kingsley Amis. (copyright Keith McMillan)

With Charlie Chaplin on the set of *A King in New York* (c.1956).

Nicola watching a rider.

In my study at Maida Vale. (copyright Gisele Freund)

With Kingsley at Maida Vale (1964). (copyright Associated Newspapers Ltd)

With the Fussells and the Keeleys in Greece.

With Rosie Plush, my first cavalier spaniel. (copyright Mark Gerson)

Sargy Man painting.

Lemmons, Hadley Common (1968).

Kingsley in his study at Lemmons.

Colin, my brother, known as Monkey.

Kingsley at Lemmons (c.1972). (copyright Fay Godwin)

Catalogue for the sale of Gardnor House (1976). (courtesy John D. Wood/Savills)

In the garden at Delancey Street (1983).

Bridge House (c.1990).

Bridge House garden in winter (c.1995).

Acknowledgements

There are various people I would like to thank. Hazel Orme has copy-edited six of my books and I would not contemplate a seventh without her. I'm also grateful to Paul Bailey and Patrick O'Connor for their help in the compilation of the biographical notes of the people who appear in the book. Selina Hastings has put up with having most of the book read aloud to her. Jeremy Trevathan, my editor and publisher, was meticulous and kind and also helped to fill in some of the pitfalls without once mentioning a spade. I'd also like to thank Jacqui Graham, who for years now has managed to make all the fringe activities of being a writer veer between being OK to downright enjoyable.

Finally, I'd like to thank Jill Day-Lewis and the Day-Lewis Estate for permission to quote Cecil Day-Louis's poem 'At Lemmons' on p. 385.

Preface

Why write about one's life? Because of the times one has lived through, the people met and known and loved? To show how interesting, virtuous, or entertaining one has been or become? Or to trace one's inward journey – whatever kind of evolution there has been between the wrinkled howling baby and the wrinkled old crone?

Writers speak of their art as being important to them as their chief means of communication with their readers. I have found that writing is often my chief means of communication with myself. I write to find things *out*, as much as, and sometimes more than, to tell them to other people. In a way, an autobiography seems to me like a household book of accounts – what has been acquired, to what purpose has it been put, was too much paid for it and did it teach you anything? How much has been learned by experience? Have patterns of behaviour and responses changed? Have I discovered where I am useful and useless, how I am nourished and starved? Have I tried to change those faults and weaknesses in me that are open to alteration? Have I learned to accept realistically what is immutable?

This sort of questioning is sometimes dubbed self-absorbed and indulgent. I think much damage has been done to people by this edict. There is a sharp line between self-absorption and taking responsibility for what and who one is. Without the latter, it's easy to assume that everything simply happens to one, and the result, an unselfish victim emerges. One needs to be *on* this fine line, not either side of it, and like every other endeavour in the world, this requires a good deal of practice.

Speaking as a very slow learner, I feel as though I have lived most of my life in the slipstream of experience. Often I have had to repeat the same disastrous situation several times before I got the message. That is still happening. I do not write this book as a wise, mature, finished person who has learned all the answers, but rather as someone who even at this late stage of seventy-nine years is still trying to change, find things out and do a bit better with them.

Cast of Characters

Richard ADDINSELL (1904–1977) Composer, pianist. Famous for the 'Warsaw Concerto', featured in the film *Dangerous Moonlight*. He composed songs for Joyce Grenfell, whom he frequently accompanied at the piano.

Barley ALISON Editor, founder of the Alison Press. She was Saul Bellow's British publisher for many years.

Michael AYRTON (1921–1975) Painter and illustrator. In the 1960s he began a third career as a novelist. His books include *The Maze Maker* and *The Midas Consequence*. Wrote monographs on Hogarth and Pissarro. His wife Elisabeth was a cookery writer.

Sybille BEDFORD (1911–) German-born novelist and biographer. Her novels include *A Legacy* and *Jigsaw*. She wrote the first biography of Aldous Huxley, who was a close friend.

Lesley BLANCH (1907–) Travel writer and biographer. Her book *The Wilder Shores of Love* was an international bestseller in the 1950s. She also wrote an invaluable cookbook, *Around the World in Eighty Dishes*.

(Herbert) Jonathan CAPE (1879–1960) Noted publisher whose career in books began as an errand-boy for Hatchards, the London bookshop. He founded the publishing house that bears his name with G. Wren Howard in 1921. Ernest Hemingway and T. E. Lawrence were among his first authors.

Pablo CASALS (1876–1973) Spanish cellist whose legendary performances of the Bach cello suites are captured on disc.

Marc CHAGALL (1887–1985) French painter and illustrator, born in Russia. Angels and demons feature in his paintings and drawings. His work includes twelve stained-glass windows for a synagogue in Jerusalem and the decorations for the ceiling of the Paris Opera House.

André CHARLOT (1882–1956) French showman and impresario who staged revues and musicals in London in the 1920s and 30s. Noël Coward and Beatrice Lillie were among his protégés.

Charles Blake (CB) COCHRAN (1872–1951) Showman who promoted boxing matches as well as revues and musical plays. He brought the illusionist Houdini to London in additon to Sarah Bernhardt and Eleanora Duse. He staged Coward's *Private Lives* and *Bitter Sweet*.

George COLE (1925–) Actor best remembered for his role as Arthur Daley, the devious used-car salesman in the television series *Minder*.

Norman COLLINS (1907–1982) Novelist and pioneer of British television. He founded Associated Television in 1955, after being controller of BBC Television from 1947 to 1950. His most famous novel *London Belongs to Me* was made into a successful film.

Ivy COMPTON-BURNETT (1884–1969) Novelist, much influenced by such classic dramatists as Euripides and Sophocles. Her novels are set in Victorian country houses, complete with servants. They are possessed of a mordant humour even as the inevitable tragedy unfolds. Her books include *A House and its Head* and *The Mighty and Their Fall*. She was made a Dame in 1967.

Cyril CONNOLLY (1903–1974) English critic and editor. With Stephen Spender he founded *Horizon*, a small literary magazine that reflected Connolly's own iconoclastic and mordant attitudes toward contemporary society. He also used his critical gifts as a long-time book reviewer for the *New Statesman* and the *Sunday Times.*

Harold CRAXTON (1885–1971) Pianist, accompanist and teacher. One of his sons, John, became a respected painter.

Clemence DANE (real name Winifred Aston) (1888–1965) Novelist and playwright, whose play, *A Bill of Divorcement*, was a huge and controversial success in the 1920s. Lifelong friend of Noël Coward.

John DAVENPORT Brilliant and belligerent literary journalist. He reviewed fiction for the *Observer.*

Frances DAY (1907–1984) Actress and singer. She played the title role in Cole Porter's *Dubarry was a Lady* in London in 1942. In the 1960s she launched a new career as a TV personality under the name Frankie Day, claiming to be her own daughter.

Sergei Pavlovich DIAGHILEV (1872–1929) Russian ballet impresario and founder of the Ballets Russes. He commissioned three of Stravinsky's greatest scores, and employed the young Picasso as a set designer.

Ruth DRAPER (1884–1956) American solo performer who wrote and acted her own brilliantly observed, and often acerbic, sketches. Her earliest admirer was Henry James and her last the singer Kathleen Ferrier.

Norman DOUGLAS (1868–1952) Author and travel writer. Worked at the British Foreign Office and as a diplomat in Russia and Italy. He published sixteen books including his only popular success the novel, *South Wind* (1917). His other books include travel writing and works of autobiography. He was always reticent about his homosexuality in his writing.

Isadora DUNCAN (1878–1927) American dancer and choreographer whose many and varied lovers included Isaac Merrit Singer, the inventor of the sewing machine.

Elaine DUNDY (real name Elaine Rita Brimberg) (1921–) American novelist, author of *The Dud Avocado*. First wife of the theatre critic Kenneth Tynan.

John FERNALD (1905–1985) Theatre director and head of RADA (Royal Academy of Dramatic Art) in the 1950s.

Romain GARY (1914–1980) French novelist, explorer and diplomat. His books include *The Roots of Heaven* and *Lady L*. He was married to Lesley Blanch and then to the American actress Jean Seberg, who committed suicide. Gary also died at his own hand.

Henry GREEN (pen name of Henry Vincent Yorke) (1905–1973) Novelist. His highly original books include *Living*, *Loving* and *Party Going*. Now regarded by many as the greatest writer of fiction in English of his time.

Joyce GRENFELL (1910–1979) Actress, broadcaster and solo performer. She achieved fame as the goofy games mistress in the film based on Ronald Searle's St Trinian's books and drawings. She toured the world with her show *Joyce Grenfell Requests the Pleasure* from 1954 onwards.

Joan HEAL (1922–1998). Actress, but best remembered for her brilliance in the intimate revues of the 1950s and 60s.

(Julia) Myra HESS (1890–1965) Pianist who organized chamber music concerts at lunchtime in the National Gallery throughout the Second World War. Her most famous recording is of a transcription of a chorale setting from Bach's Cantata No. 147, known as 'Jesu, Joy of Man's Desiring'. She made a historic recording of Beethoven's Sonata in E Major, Opus 109 in 1954. She was made a Dame in 1941.

Cast of Characters

Balliol HOLLOWAY Actor and theatrical manager at Birmingham and Stratford-upon-Avon.

Seth (real name James) HOLT (1923–1971) After a brief career as an actor, he worked as assistant editor on the famous Ealing comedies of the 1940s and 50s. (His brother-in-law, Robert Hamer, directed *Kind Hearts and Coronets*.) He then became a film director of frustrated and intermittent brilliance. His films include *A Taste of Fear* (1964) and the macabre *The Nanny* (1967) starring Bette Davis.

Ronald JEANS (1887–1973) Lyricist and revue writer who collaborated with Noël Coward on *London Calling!* in 1924. Wrote songs and sketches for popular stars of the 1930s and 40s, including Jessie Matthews.

Tamara KARSAVINA (1885–1978) Ballerina, who wrote one of the great theatrical memoirs, *Theatre Street*.

Edmund Mike KEELEY (1928?–) American translator, with Philip Sherrard, of the poems of Constantin Cavafy.

Louis KENTNER (1905–1986) Concert pianist, who regularly played at the Proms in the 1950s.

Aram Ilich KHACHATURIAN (1903–1978) Armenian-born Russian composer, who achieved popular success with his 'Ritual Fire Dance'. He wrote the score for a ballet, *Spartacus* (1954).

Terence KILMARTIN (1922–1991) Literary editor of the *Observer* for three decades. Along with D. J. Enright, he worked on a revised edition of the Scott-Moncrieff translation of Proust.

J. W. (Jack) LAMBERT (1917–1986) Literary journalist and broadcaster. Literary editor of the *Sunday Times* in the 1960s and 70s.

Benn Wolfe LEVY (1900–1973) Playwright and screenwriter. Wrote the dialogue for Alfred Hitchcock's first talkie *Blackmail*. His play *Clutterbuck* was a success in 1946. He was married to the acclaimed actress Constance Cummings.

Lydia Vasilievna LOPOKOVA (1892–1981) Russian ballerina who danced with Nijinsky in *The Firebird*. She married John Maynard Keynes, the economist, in 1925, and dedicated her life to him when he became seriously ill. She did much to promote the cause of ballet in Britain.

Ernest LUSH (1929–1988) Pianist and accompanist, notably for Kathleen Ferrier.

Olivia MANNING (1908–1980) Novelist, best known for the two trilogies *The Balkan Trilogy* and *The Levant Trilogy*, which were both adapted for television. She famously pleaded poverty and her friends were surprised to learn at her death that she was rich to the tune of several hundreds of thousands of pounds.

Denis MATTHEWS (1919–1988) Pianist and broadcaster. He gave the first performance of Edmund Rubbra's 'Piano Concerto'. In later years he was Professor of Music at Newcastle University.

Reginald MAUDLING (1917–1979) Conservative MP for Barnet, 1950–79. Chancellor of the Exchequer 1962–4, Home Secretary 1970. He resigned from the Cabinet in 1972 due to his involvement with a corrupt businessman, John Poulson, over a contract for a proposed hospital in Malta.

Carson McCULLERS (1917–1967) American novelist. First published in 1936. She married Reeves McCullers, a serviceman and aspiring writer. The marriage was a tempestuous one, marked by homosexual relationships on both sides, separations and re-unions, divorce and remarriage, alcoholism and suicide attempts. Reeves died in 1953 from an overdose of alcohol and barbituates, an apparent suicide. Carson McCullers' life was a mixture of emotional unhappiness and bad health, but with luminous talent she drew upon her empathy and experience to compose resonant, ballad-like stories about the inner lives of marginal, often physically scarred characters who were tormented by loneliness, most famously in *The Heart Is a Lonely Hunter*.

Noel MEWTON-WOOD (1922–1953) Australian pianist and composer, most admired for his interpretations of Hindemith, Busoni and Bliss. He comitted suicide following the untimely death of his male lover. Benjamin Britten's Canticle 111 'Still Falls the Rain' is dedicated to his memory.

Nina MILKINA (1919–) Russian-born concert pianist, long resident in England. She made her first public appearance in Paris at the age of eleven. She was commissioned by BBC Radio to play all of Mozart's piano sonatas in the 1950s. In her heyday she was regarded as one of the finest interpreters of Mozart.

Bruce MONTGOMERY (1921–1978) Academic and crime writer, under the pseudonym Edmund Crispin. A long-term friend of Kingsley Amis and Philip Larkin. He was a composer of film music, in particular for the *Carry On* series. He fell in love with and married Barbara Clements two years before his death.

Rodrigo MOYNIHAN (1910–1990) Painter.

Vaslaw NIJINSKY (1890–1950) Russian ballet dancer and choreographer. He was the first to dance the role of Petrushka. He danced and choreographed *The Rite of Spring*. He was diagnosed as clinically insane in his late twenties and spent many years in institutions. His *Diary* makes unsettling reading.

Ivor NOVELLO (real name David Ivor Davies) (1893–1951) Actor on stage and screen. Composer and songwriter. He became famous in 1914 with the song 'Keep the Home Fires Burning'. His script for the first Tarzan film, *Tarzan and the Apes*, is a camp masterpiece. He wrote musical comedies that ensured him a huge following, particularly with women. These include *Glamorous Night*, *Perchance to Dream* and *King's Rhapsody*.

Norman PARKINSON (1913–1990) Fashion. His photographs appeared in the British edition of *Harper's Bazaar* and throughout his long career he contributed to many publications, including *Vogue*, *Queen* and *Town and Country*. His work became famous for the liveliness, spontaneity and humour of his photographs.

William PLOMER (1903–1973) Poet and novelist. His novel *Turbott Wolfe*, published in 1926, about a mixed marriage, caused controversy in his native South Africa. He wrote the libretto for Britten's opera *Gloriana*. His poems are mostly humorous and have suffered unfairly from comparison with those of John Betjeman.

Harry PLUNKETT-GREEN (1865–1936) Irish baritone, later Professor of Singing at the Royal College of Music. He was a great advocate of song in the vernacular.

Gillie POTTER (1888–1975) Music hall comedian and broadcaster. He became famous for his monologues about the fictional village 'Hogsnorton'. His opening line was 'Hello, England. This is Gillie Potter speaking to you in English.' He first appeared on British television in the 1950s.

Patrick PROCKTOR (1936–) Painter and writer. A contemporary of David Hockney and Howard Hodgkin, he has pursued an intensely personal career, experimenting with many different techniques.

Marie (Mimi) RAMBERT (1888–1982) Ballet director and teacher, born Cyvia Myriam Ramberg in Warsaw. She studied in Paris, and moved to London in 1914. She married the playwright Ashley Dukes, assumed the name Rambert and became a British subject in 1918. One of her early pupils was Frederick Ashton. She founded the Ballet Rambert in 1934. Anthony Tudor's masterpiece *Dark Elegies*, set to music by Mahler, and *Lady Into Fox* by André Howard, are among her most important commissions.

Brian REDHEAD (1929–1994) Broadcaster and journalist, notorious for his merciless interviewing of politicians on BBC Radio 4 in the 1980s.

Henry REED (1914–1986) Poet, radio dramatist and translator from the French and Italian. Best known for his satirical poem 'The Naming of Parts' about gun duty as a soldier in the Second World War. His parody of Eliot's *Four Quartets*, 'Chard Witlow', is a comic masterpiece.

SABRINA (real name Norma Ann Sykes) (1936–) Actress, model and cabaret singer, renowned for her ample bosom. She co-starred with the comic Arthur Askey and the presenter Hughie Green on TV shows in the 1950s. She was received with great ceremony in Cuba in 1960 by Fidel Castro.

(Henry) Malcom (Watts) SARGENT (1895–1967) Conductor and organist, who first conducted a Promenade concert at the Royal Albert Hall in 1921. He was a crowd-pleaser who rarely performed contemporary music, except for works by Vaughan Williams and Walton. He was a legendary snob and was known to his fellow musicians as Flash Harry. He was knighted in 1947.

George SEFERIS (1900–1971) Greek poet, essayist and diplomat who won the Nobel Prize for Literature in 1963, Seferis is considered to be the most distinguished Greek poet of the pre-war generation of the 1930s.

Barbara SKELTON (1916–1996) *Femme fatale* who had well-documented affairs with King Farouk of Egypt, Felix Topolski and Robert Silvers, founder of the *New York Review of Books*, among many others. Her penchant was for ugly, hairy men. She married Cyril Connolly, divorced him and married the publisher George Weidenfeld. She then divorced Weidenfeld and remarried Connolly. Her memoirs *Tears Before Bedtime* (1987) and *Weep No*

More (1989) are filled with what Anthony Powell called a 'peculiarly incisive malignity'. They are also hilariously funny.

Mathew Arnold Bracy SMITH (1897–1959) Painter, famous for his female nudes and still lifes. Exhibited in Paris in 1911, and served with the Artists' Rifles and Labour Corps in the First World War. Enjoyed a large retrospective exhibition at the Tate Gallery in 1953. Knighted in 1954.

Stevie SMITH (1903–1971) Poet and novelist. Stevie Smith was born Florence Margaret Smith in 1903 in Hull, Yorkshire. She moved with her mother and sister to Palmer's Green, where they lived with her aunt. Stevie spent the rest of her life with her aunt, and worked as a private secretary. Although she had a series of boyfriends, she never married. Stevie Smith wrote six novels and nine volumes of poetry. Her first volume of poetry, *A Good Time Was Had By All*, earned her a reputation as a writer.

Nancy SPAIN (1917–1964) Journalist and novelist. Launched the magazine *She* with her long-time partner Joan Werner-Laurie. They were killed together in a plane crash, en route to the Grand National.

Sir Stephen SPENDER (1909–1995) Poet and critic. His early poetry – like that of W. H. Auden, C. Day-Lewis, and Louis MacNeice, with whom he became associated at Oxford – was inspired by social protest. A member of the political left wing during this early period, he was one of those who wrote of their disillusionment with communism. He was co-editor of the magazines *Horizon* with Cyril Connolly, and *Encounter*. Spender was knighted in 1983.

Josef or Joseph SZIGETI (1892–1973) Hungarian violinist, famous for his interpretations of the music of Bartok and Prokofiev.

Elizabeth TAYLOR (1912–1975) Novelist and short-story writer, much admired by fellow novelists. Her novels include *Angel* and

Mrs Palfrey at the Claremont, which was shortlisted for the Booker Prize in 1971. But it is as a short-story writer that she excels. The collection *Dangerous Calm*, edited by Lynn Knight, contains her best work.

Jacques THIBAUD (1880–1953) French violinist, famed for his partnership with Alfred Cortot and Pablo Casals.

Donald Francis TOVEY (1875–1940) Musicologist and critic, described by the great violinist Joachim as the 'most learned man in music who ever lived'. His *Essays in Musical Analysis* run to six volumes. Famously called Verdi's *Don Carlos* 'brass-band music'.

Tommy TRINDER (1909–1989) Music hall and radio comedian.

Derek VERSCHOYLE Publisher. Published the early writings – poetry and a monograph on John Masefield – of Muriel Spark.

Antonia WHITE (pseudonym of Eirene Botting) (1899–1980) Novelist and translator of Guy de Maupassant and Colette. Her most famous novel *Frost in May* describes her own convent upbringing. She married three times in a long life plagued by severe mental illness. Her daughters Susan Chitty and Lyndall Hopkinson have written memoirs in which she appears respectively as a demon and a misunderstood martyr.

Godfrey (Herbert) WINN (1908–1971) British actor, novelist and journalist. He began his professional career as a boy actor in the early 1920s, and his writing career with his first novel in the 1930s. As a journalist he wrote pieces for the press that emulated the style of Beverley Nichols with its sentimental whimsy. Godfrey Winn became a star columnist for the *Daily Mirror* from 1936 to 1938, and then for the *Sunday Express* from 1938 to 1942. By 1938 it was claimed that he was the most highly paid journalist in Fleet Street (where he was known as Winifred God). After the war he became established as a regular broadcaster on both the radio and the television. He died of a heart attack while playing tennis.

Francis WYNDHAM (1924–) Journalist, novelist and short-story writer. His first novel *The Other Garden* was published when he was sixty-three. It won the Whitbread Award. He was one of the founders of the *Sunday Times Magazine*.

PART ONE

I

The first thing I can remember is a dream. I dreamed I was in St Mary Abbot's church after my brother's christening. There was a tea party in the church with people standing about holding cups of tea. I was given a large plate – I needed both hands to carry it – and told to hand it round to everyone. The plate was covered by small rectangular sponge cakes with white icing, each one decorated with a crystallized violet. I longed for one, but was told I must wait until everyone had been offered the plate. Some people refused and I began to hope that there would be one left for me, but when I approached a large lady with a brown fur round her neck, she smiled kindly and took the last cake. The disappointment still pricked my eyes when I woke up.

I must have been between two and a half and three years old when I dreamed this, and it must have been the time when my parents moved from the first-floor flat in Clanricarde Gardens to a small house in Bedford Gardens, also in Kensington. I have no memory of the flat, but we stayed in Bedford Gardens until I was six or seven so I can remember some small pieces from those years.

The house was part of a terrace at the Church Street end of Bedford Gardens – flat-fronted, built of brick with pretty windows and steps leading up to the front door. There was a very small front garden in which large purple iris grew. The nursery was on the top floor – the day nursery in the front and a smaller night nursery at the back. From that back window there was a sea of chimney-pots,

3

and I used to imagine that they were the funnels of large ships waiting to take me away,

I remember little of the rest of the house; in those days middle-class children lived in their nursery quarters unless sent for at tea-time. The days were filled with long walks in Kensington Gardens when nannies would meet with Thermos flasks of Bovril, and Marie biscuits, while we were enjoined to 'play' not too far from them.

Sometimes we walked to the Round Pond and I was allowed to feed bread to the ducks. I remember clearly watching a horde of little ragged children, with a baby in a pram, fishing for sticklebacks that they put into jam jars. I longed to be with them, to have bare legs and no overcoat, no gaiters with all their buttons, and to fish with them. Once, I managed to elude Nanny and join them, but she dragged me away. 'Those children are *not* your friends.'

'They are!' I wept, but I remember thinking afterwards that *they* probably wouldn't have wanted me as a friend.

Nanny Wilshire loomed far larger in my life than either of my parents. She wore crackling aprons, smelt alternately of liquorice or pear drops, and was given to sudden rages. She told me that if I swallowed pieces of wool or cotton they'd join together and, when long enough, wind themselves around my heart and kill me. Her justice, like Portia's mercy, was an indiscriminate affair – it dropped incomprehensively from the skies: it ambushed me like a jaguar, and I endured it dazed with fear and grievance. Once she shut me in the linen cupboard, dark, hot and unbelievably frightening, because my brother Robin had cut himself on a tin motorcar when I was alone in the nursery with him. I remember shrieking with terror and pulling down all the sheets and pillowcases I could reach and stamping on them. When my noise and the damage were apparent to her, she released me and I learned my first lesson. Robin was younger, infinitely more attractive and a boy; in fact, youth, beauty, and his sex were unmistakable advantages, and beside him I felt inferior in each respect.

I don't think scenes of the linen-cupboard nature ever reached my mother's ears. Trying now to remember my parents at that time, I am left with fragments: how they smelt – my mother of China tea and sweet hay, my father of lavender water and the Lebanon cedar with which his clothes chest and wardrobe were lined, and predominating, tobacco. They both smoked, as indeed did practically all their friends. My mother had thick curly hair, but it was mostly grey, which worried me as I'd noticed that grey hair led to white, and white-haired people were so old that they might die at any minute. I'd been taught that when people died they went to Heaven, but I discovered as quickly that there was no possibility of going there alive. So if my mother died, I'd have to die too to be with her. This uncomfortable choice haunted me, at increasing intervals, for years.

We lived in the same street as my maternal grandparents, and by the time I was six, I was allowed on some Sundays to go alone for lunch with them. My grandfather would meet me just as I reached the pillar-box outside his house and, bending down, would present me with his coarse, silky white beard and faint smell that was something like sweetbriar. Then, holding hands, we'd march into the dark drawing room, crowded with a grand piano and little tables and large upholstered chairs. My grandmother, called Grannia, would be cast upon one of these, like a beautiful shipwreck. She spoiled me with a magnificent carelessness that I thoroughly appreciated, allowing me drops of wine in my water at luncheon. She would discuss the life of Christ, Communism, and Japanese flower arrangement with me as though I was any luncheon guest, elevating me to a state of triumphant, honoured ignorance instead of knowledgeable boredom that the old ropes of grown-ups with children induce. For lunch we always had roast chicken and meringues – which my grandmother probably considered my favourite meal.

Afterwards, I was made to lie on the floor with my head on one of the coloured cushions that my grandfather called after any of the students he examined in music whose names were exotic or silly enough. I can now only remember a small, hard, dark purple one called Gertrude Peppercorn. I was given a bull's eye or a piece of chocolate, and a book was read aloud. After a while, I was allowed to sit up and 'play' with some of the curious and interesting objects that were scattered about the room. This usually meant staring at things — not allowed to touch — while my grandmother told me about them. I had no resentment about this, content simply to gaze — at a complete set of Japanese dolls' furniture lacquered in red and black; at a strand of Mozart's hair, fine and golden like an angel's, which was tied with a piece of pale blue silk and framed in a pinch-beck locket; at a thin, stiff wooden doll that had belonged to my grandfather and was called Mr Hampshire, whose painted face, sad and discreet, stared back at me with an expression a thousand years old.

When, by mutual consent, it was time for my visit to finish, I didn't race back down the street, but walked slowly, crammed with important, tragic thoughts.

'Well,' they said, when I got home, 'was it fun, and what did you have for luncheon?'

They were, in comparison to my grandmother, talking down to me; 'Roast chicken and meringues' was too frivolous a reply, and I searched for the most stern and sophisticated substitute. 'Cold beef,' I said, and many Sundays after they had ceased to believe me, I stuck stubbornly to this formula.

Some time that year, we moved from Bedford Gardens to a larger house in Lansdowne Road, Holland Park. Nanny Wilshire had left and was replaced by a much younger nurse called Violet Dunn. She must have been in her twenties, was enormously fat, and wore navy blue dresses that I think she must have made herself. Robin and I called her Felix. She was very quiet and never got into rages like Nanny Wilshire — even her displeasure was calm. She played card games with us and helped us with painting. I suspect that she was very sensitive about her appearance, which I think

6

now was down to some glandular disorder, since she ate very little and was very active. In the new house we slept in a large bedroom with her and I remember her dressing in the mornings with her back turned to us and enveloped in a very large dressing gown from which she emerged immaculate in her close-fitting navy blue with white Peter Pan collar.

My mother taught me to read, but I was always slightly afraid of her when she taught me things, and didn't learn until I was six and a half. I wanted to read, and used to take one of the fairy books off its shelf, and sit in a chair turning pages at what I thought were suitable intervals. Robin, however, could read when he was five, and when he turned six he wrote a book called *Percy Rainsbull Edwards, the Adventures of a Pig.* This, I thought, was my chance to prove my superior grasp of life. He was so young that he had to make up his own story; I'd actually write a real book, which meant taking one from the bookshelf and copying it. Percy's life was a dangerous one, and my brother wrote it in a state of abominable fear, while I ploughed away at transcribing the first chapters of *Happy Families* in block capitals into an exercise book. There was a mixture of boredom and complacency about my task, but in the end, boredom won and I abandoned it. Robin, trembling with uncertainty, reached a happy conclusion to Percy's life – back in a field with his mother – after a journey to Africa, with a suitcase marked PRE, where he was nearly eaten by a 'snack'. He illustrated the adventures with many pencil drawings and my mother – who could bind books – bound it in soft crimson suede. I realized then that he had beaten me again, that his book engendered far more interest than mine.

Before we moved – and afterwards – we used sometimes to be taken to Airlie Gardens at the top of Campden Hill. At the end of this short road were wooden gates that opened on to a courtyard on the left of which was a large rambling house. This belonged to a cousin of my mother's – a bachelor known as Uncle Mont. We hardly ever went into the house in which Uncle Mont never seemed to be, but we were given the freedom of the enormous and wonderful garden – probably about two acres – which was filled with interesting things. For instance, there were beds all round the house that were filled with cockleshells. There was a terrace on the south side that had squares of aromatic plants interspersed with the paving. At one end was a perfectly round pond tiled with azure; at the other a veranda with black and white tiled walls and a Chinese gooseberry and a vine smothering its roof. There were flights of steps made of shaven grass – very soft and charming. They led to a long pergola with roses, and lawns studded with interesting trees. There was a winding path round the edge of this domain and at intervals there were sunken barrels that collected rainwater. Once I fell into one – head first, and had to be hauled out and taken, black with mud, white with terror, into the house where I was bathed by my nurse and the housekeeper. Apart from that single misfortune, the place was magic to me at all times of the year. There were gardeners; the only one I remember was called Dick, but for some time I thought he was Uncle Mont, and it was only when I called him 'darling Uncle Mont' (for having such a lovely garden) that they put me right. He had been Uncle Mont's batman in the war and was badly wounded, they said. A batman. Did he protect Uncle Mont from bats? Had they wounded him? Were bats dangerous? I never asked: I'd reached an age where I hated people's patronizing and laughing response to a serious question. I did ask why we never saw Uncle Mont and my mother said he had a lot of work to do as he was Governor of the Bank of England. This was another hazard of being my age: often, serious answers made things even more mysterious.

My grandfather was a composer. (He was called 'Mo' because he had a beard and was thought to look like Moses.) I don't think I realized this until I was nearly seven when I wrote a poem that seemed to me the most beautiful words I'd heard in my life. In those days I was constantly having sore throats, and one day, lying fevered with my throat like a burning cart track, they brought me an exquisitely written sheet of music. 'Your grandfather has made a song of your poem.' At seven, I couldn't read music, and my grandfather sang in a squeaky, out-of-tune voice, so somebody else had to sing it. 'Lovely,' I whispered hoarsely.

'Very nice words,' they said, 'about a lovebird coming out of a wood. Why did you think of a lovebird?' I wanted a blue bird flying out of a dark wood, that was why. 'But lovebirds are *green*,' they said. I argued weakly, but the song was ruined for me. I could now see that green bird flying obstinately out of the dark wood – green on green, and the feeling of colour lost. I never wrote another poem.

I was steeped in Andrew Lang fairy books, and the problem of living half by fairy formulae and half by the strict justice demanded between cousins and siblings occupied me for some years. It was a long time before I understood the justice in fairy tales and still longer before I perceived the fairy tales in elements of justice.

One day, my grandfather took me to tea with Henry Ford, the illustrator of fairy books, in his studio. I loved his pictures and admired him deeply. The studio seemed dark and dirty: it was autumn, and the smell was so overwhelming I felt the chairs and tables and curtains were covered with wet paint – even the bread and butter had possibly been varnished. There were small cherry cakes for tea. The cherries kept falling off and bouncing on the floor, and Henry Ford pounced on them like a dirty bird and popped them into his mouth.

My grandfather asked what he was painting. He was painting thirteen princesses being turned into swans, he said, in a practical voice – here – and he pulled the easel round for us to see. He was painting exactly that. I counted the princesses and my heart swelled with pride to be having cherry cakes with somebody who had such magical powers, but I was most carefully polite to him in case his powers extended beyond painting.

Soon after we moved to Lansdowne Road I began to have morning lessons in the dining room with half a dozen other children. A kindly lady called Miss Kettle taught us. She had a gentle voice, eyes like some nervous nocturnal bird and cheeks like a rubber doll. My fellow pupils fascinated me.

One girl called Rosemary told us that her family kept a python at home. 'Of course, she's an only child,' people said of her. This utterly confused me: for some time I toyed with the idea of her mother having given birth to a python by mistake, and went to tea, not so much to see the python as to gaze at its mother.

I was by then so steeped in fairy tales that this seemed perfectly possible – indeed, looking at the terms under which I lived, it's astonishing to me that I was so calm about them. For instance, the maxim of most fairy tales – that beauty was invariably allied to goodness – caused me only passing regret. I wasn't one, therefore there was small chance of my becoming the other. My brother Robin, on the other hand, with his platinum blond hair, brown velvet eyes, and a voice as charming as it was deep and commanding, seemed all set for goodness on a large scale. I remember one winter afternoon when we were discussing what we should most like to be, and I, assuming an expression of what I hoped was irrevocable goodness, said I should like to be kind and brave. My brother looked at me, evidently didn't like what he saw, and gazed dreamily up at the ceiling. 'I should like to be rich and pretty,' he said.

You would, I thought, angrily retreating from my hypocrisy, but what would be the good of *my* saying that?

Robin and I had by now accumulated a number of imaginary people: some were fairies, but all of them were more or less magic – that is, unaccountable and powerful. It's difficult to say how much we believed in them, but we each 'owned' different people, and thus developed a kind of oblique balance of power. Here again, my brother had the whip hand. He owned the most frightening creature called Ciggi who lived largely in his garden, a piece of cement out of which grew a drainpipe and a Michaelmas daisy. Ciggi was capable of the most terrible rages and nothing ever *pleased* him: he rumbled with disapproval at everything we –

particularly I – did, with frequent eruptions of threatening wrath. Robin eventually married him off to someone called Rose, who had golden hair and a nervous giggle, but this didn't improve his temper and hardly a week passed without my brother announcing that 'Ciggi is very, *very* angry.'

Robin himself was capable of Ciggi-like rages when we quarrelled. I remember one awful afternoon when he followed me round a square garden trying to kill me with a huge piece of crazy paving. His intentions were so bad that they were counterproductive – the paving was too heavy for him to throw it far and I was easily able to evade him.

Robin was a success with all ladies – particularly old ones. He knew exactly what to say to them and it was clear that they thought him delightful. When we both started to learn the piano, it was Robin who had the ear and could play before he could read. I suppose now I must have been jealous of him although I don't remember *feeling* that. I was very well aware that he was the favourite – with our first nanny, with the Yorkshire cook who adored him, but above all with our mother. All I can remember feeling about this is a sense of inferiority. I was thin, with thick brown lamentably straight hair and a sallow complexion; my brother was clearly more lovable. His being musical was also much in his favour: both my parents, above any other art, revered music and I had no discernible talent for it.

When Robin was five and a half, he joined the classes with Miss Kettle. Our days were very ordered. Breakfast with our parents in the dining room. After lessons, we had lunch with our mother and Felix. Then, if we weren't going to the Swedish gym in Linden Gardens, or having a piano lesson, we went for long walks that lasted until teatime, which we had in the nursery with Felix. Sometimes our mother would appear, would join us in a game of Old Maid or *vingt-et-un*. She would stay, perhaps, for half an hour and then disappear, to use the telephone – kept in a bleak little study, which was never used for any other purpose – or to change for dinner. We would see her later in one of her evening dresses when she came to say good night to us; by then, we'd have been bathed and given our suppertime apple.

Usually our father would also come and say good night – glamorous in dinner jacket, sometimes even more dazzling in white tie with his medals pinned to the breast of his tailcoat. How little I knew of their lives! Not only were they parents, as opposed to people, but also I saw comparatively little of them. The occasions when I spent time with my father always seemed especially festive and unusual – like a birthday. Sometimes he took me out by myself. I remember vividly a winter afternoon when it was the nurse's day out, my mother had a cold and he drove me to Kensington Gardens. There was snow – it had snowed off and on for several days and the Round Pond had ice on it. We walked until it was dusk and the park was almost empty of people. I found an enormous snowball higher than myself. It was a dirty white from much handling, and in the dusk gave off facets of an unearthly blue. As I was staring up at it, wondering how it had been made, my father, who'd joined me, said in a quiet almost conspiratorial voice, 'Anyone looking?'

I looked round the snowball and could see only the distant backs of people trudging home.

'No.'

My father suddenly drew the handle of his walking stick upwards and unsheathed a long, narrow sword with which he cut a large cake-shaped slice out of the snowball. Then he took out his silk handkerchief, wiped the blade and returned it to its sheath. 'Don't tell anyone,' he said, and I haven't – until now.

2

It's time to say something about my parents and there has to be an element of hindsight in any sketch I make of them. My memory of how I saw them when I was a young child is too scrappy, confined to fleeting sensations and pictures – probably from old photograph albums.

After a fairly inadequate education my father left school when the First World War was declared. His brother, a year older, enlisted with the Coldstream Guards and my father naturally tried to do the same, but they wouldn't take him because he was seventeen. So he went to the Machine Gun Corps, lied about his age and was accepted. Both brothers went to France in 1914 with their own horses, but they didn't meet for fourteen months until, on a lane near Ypres, their horses neighed to each other before they came into sight. Both brothers survived the war.

My father was a major before he was twenty-one. He got a Military Cross and bar, and was recommended for a Victoria Cross – I think the bar was given instead. When I asked him what he had done to get his medals, he said one was for peeing on a machine-gun to keep it cool so that it would go on firing. The only other information he gave me about his war was when I asked who the people in yellowing baggy uniforms *were* – the photograph that stood always on his dressing-table. They were his friends, he said. Where were they now? They were all dead. There was a pause and then he added, 'All dead, except me.' He never talked about his time in France. He had spent weeks in gas-ridden trenches, and his lungs never recovered from that, but otherwise he was physically unharmed. I think now that in other ways he had been badly damaged. The schoolboy who went to France and did his best there for four years returned to England as if he was a schoolboy embarking on the holidays.

As I never heard him talk about his war experiences – I never heard any grown-ups talk about the war – it was years before I understood the great conspiracy of silence that must have tortured so many young men when they came home on leave during the nightmare. How much worse this must have made it for them, and how, to survive, did they deal with it? In my father's case I think he dealt with it simply by not growing up. He was a boy when he went out, and he came back crammed with awful knowledge that was never revealed or digested.

He remained a boy – a dashing, glamorous boy – determined to make the best of the holidays, determined that they should go on for ever. He had a job to go to in the family timber firm of which his father was chairman. He knew nothing whatever about business, but he loved meeting people; he loved buying and selling wood; he loved shooting, skiing, sailing and playing games – golf, tennis, squash, billiards, chess, bridge. Contract bridge was all the rage after the war. He loved dancing and parties of any kind, and he loved women, who fell for him like rows of shingled ninepins. I hardly ever heard any women talk about him without mentioning how good-looking he was and how charming. His charm was real, because it was largely unconscious. He was over six feet tall, had bright blue eyes, a small military moustache, and wavy brown hair that he plastered flat with hair oil. He dressed very well: his suits – many and varied – were always beautifully cut; with an enormous silk handkerchief in the breast pocket. I always enjoyed watching the grace with which he took off his hat to any lady he met in the street.

He loved music, played the violin, though seldom in my child-hood, and music made him cry or at least brought tears to his eyes;

Tchaikovsky was a great favourite. Men liked him; women were sometimes dangerously keen on him. He was definitely not intellectual, practically never read a book; like Uncle Matthew in *The Pursuit of Love*, he had read one or two and they were so frightfully good that he didn't need to look further.

He was one of the most gregarious people I have ever known, totally uncritical of any company he kept, and he behaved, at the slightest encouragement, as though it was his birthday. These mythical, frequently recurring birthdays were at first a mystery to me – they seemed to happen about once a month without him getting much older. 'It's my birthday,' he would tell the wine waiter when he ordered champagne, or the shop assistant when he bought five pounds of chocolates to take home.

He was physically very brave and morally a coward, although naturally I'd no idea of this until much later. His younger brother, my uncle John, told me towards the end of his life that after the war my father had nearly become engaged to a girl called Cicely. Both families were against the marriage, so it didn't take place. My father married my mother on the rebound, on 12 May 1921.

My mother was the second of four children by my Somervell grandparents. Her older sister, Antonia, was always considered a beauty and married in her early twenties. They had twin brothers. Antonia was admired for her beauty and her gentle disposition; the twins were admired for being twins and boys, and my mother came a poor last with *her* mother, at least. She was very small, with a tremendous head of hair – as a young girl she could sit on it – heavy eyebrows, brown eyes, an aquiline nose, and high cheekbones. She was, one of my twin uncles told me, the intellectual of the family: she read a great deal, and when she was sixteen decided that she wanted to be a ballet dancer. Her father must have supported her in this, as my grandmother wouldn't have considered any career necessary or desirable for a woman.

Somehow, my mother got into Enrico Ciccetti's class, the teacher whom all ballet dancers revered. Visiting ballerinas from the Ballets Russes would come for classes with him. I have a picture – a drawing of all the people in the class with her: they include Ninette de Valois, Mimi Rambert, Lydia Kyasht and Lopokova. From this class she was picked up by Diaghilev to join his company in the *corps de ballet*. Her first rehearsals were in Paris, conducted chiefly in Russian of which she knew hardly a word, and she had three days to learn her parts in three full-length ballets. This was after Nijinsky's tragic departure, when Massine was principal male dancer. My mother taught him to read music.

She spent just over a year with the Ballets Russes, after Paris, when they were in Monte Carlo and then Rome. Then she encountered my father and wanted to marry him. This was only possible, my paternal grandfather said, if she gave up dancing. My mother's family was pretty hard up. She wasn't conventionally good-looking, and in 1920 the wholesale slaughter of thousands of men meant that many women had either lost their husbands or fiancés, or had little hope of finding either.

My mother was clearly bowled over by my father's glamour and easy charm. I think he was probably the first man she fell in love with, although what precisely that meant for her is hard to say. She certainly wanted to marry him – according to my uncle John – and that happened. She gave up dancing and took to middle-class married life with more money than she'd ever had before, servants, a house to keep, but nothing else to do.

My mother wasn't gregarious. She loved her family, but had few close friends outside it. From her demeanour and attitude to it, it was clear that she never enjoyed sex. What did she and my father have in common? They both had a sense of humour – could laugh at the same things and make jokes together. They enjoyed sailing and skiing together. I really can't think of anything else. A year after marriage she had a daughter – who was either stillborn or died soon after birth. In my grandmother's prayer book against the date of her birth or death there is a cross, marked in ink, and 'I have no name.' This wasn't so: she was called Jane – the name my mother had used for dancing: she had been called Jane Forrestier, it being *de rigueur* for women dancers to have French-sounding names.

I was born a year later on 26 March 1923 and I was also named Jane although this time there was the prefix Elizabeth. Two and a half years later, she had my brother Robin, and Colin, the youngest, was born nine years later.

Outwardly my parents' lives were full of social incident. They had a fairly large circle of friends with whom they went to the theatre, to concerts, to the 'flicks', as the cinema was called, to dinner with each other in their various houses, and to restaurants often to dine and dance. Sometimes they went away for shooting weekends and every year they skied for two weeks in Switzerland, and went sailing in Cornwall. Robin didn't mind them going away, but I was miserable for weeks before they left: used to cry in bed about it. I'd not have minded my father going away, which he sometimes did anyway, on business, but I couldn't bear the idea that my mother wasn't in the house, was nowhere, out of sight, unreachable. In those days the telephone wasn't used as a means of keeping in touch, so there was silence for the two weeks, which always seemed interminable to me.

Christmas Day of my sixth or seventh year had been a haze of excitement. There was feasting and everybody was smiling. There were wonderful presents that were deliciously divided between things I'd always wanted and things I'd never even heard of, the best being a little toy pony with real pony fur, and a cart for him to draw, and a stable for him to sleep in. Suddenly, after tea, a stroke of doom – a ripple of departure in the room, an acceleration of bonhomie and then the blinding moment when I realized that both my parents were going away, that minute, to a place called Switzerland for a holiday. They'd kissed me and had gone. I was left sitting on the nursery floor surrounded by a sea of presents and undulating waves of tissue paper. In vain did various aunts and uncles point out their generosity to me. The gorgeous presents became valueless as the front door distantly slammed. They couldn't compensate for the interminable time and unknown distance of two weeks in Switzerland, because I suddenly knew that they had nothing to do with each other. After the nursery formula of 'You can have a sweet after tea if you're good,' this was a discovery. Presents couldn't always be equated with feelings or behaviour and were sometimes entirely unrelated. I remember looking at the toys and finding that I'd exchange any one or the whole lot of them for my mother's immediate return.

I can't now think how my mother managed to get through the days with the hiatus between breakfast and the time when she had to dress for the evening. Sometimes a friend came to lunch or she went shopping. She went riding before breakfast in Rotten Row. There was a loom in one of the attics on the top floor, but I never saw her use it.

She had many, some unusual, accomplishments, most of which she seemed to have relinquished by the time I became aware of her. She could bind books, weave, spin; she was a most accomplished needlewoman – she made christening robes and little white muslin frocks for Robin with a great deal of drawn thread work and fine white cotton embroidery. She could play the piano and recorder, and later learned to play the zither – a tortuously difficult and unrewarding instrument. She could use gold leaf and designed beautiful elaborate capital letters for a book of Shakespeare's sonnets that she'd made and bound for her mother when she was about twenty. She became one of the two women in London allowed to school the Life Guards' horses at their riding school. At one point she tried to teach me the rudiments of ballet. I remember agonizing mornings with me holding on to the bath rail while she hit my bare legs with her riding crop in an endeavour to get me to place my feet properly in the positions. I was clumsy, terrified of displeasing her, and acutely aware that I was doing so; I became paralysed with stupidity and fear.

When I was about seven, something happened that impressed me very deeply. We were walking with our mother one spring evening along a narrow pavement on one side of which was an enormously high wall that enclosed Campden Hill reservoir. At intervals there were gas lamps, which were lit each evening by a man with a mysterious long pole. The street was empty, except for a shabby little man about half-way down it. He was leaning with his back to the wall. As we approached, he took a few uncertain steps away from us, put his hand to his head and pitched forward straight into the road. My mother told us to stay where we were, and went up to the man. We watched him speechlessly; he was sitting now in the kerb – rubbing his head with his hands. He was a pale old man with dirty white hair. My mother helped him to his feet and then gave him some money: his trousers were round on his legs and he had crabbed, nervous hands that he kept putting in and out of his pockets. Eventually, he trembled off down the road and disappeared in the soft grey evening.

What was the matter with him? Was he very ill? He was just very weak from being so hungry, my mother said. She had given him half a crown and he would buy some food and then he would be all right, she added, and I suddenly saw her looking at me and didn't believe her. The idea of somebody fainting with hunger was as new as it was horrible: I had no idea how many meals could be bought with half a crown, but when the old man had eaten them what would he do then? He might faint again when there was nobody to give him anything. Why had we not given the old man more or, better still, taken him home where there were meals for ever? I don't remember a satisfactory answer to my questions, and the argument – then presented – that there were other old men or people in the same predicament simply widened the horror that this first impingement of the world outside my life exposed.

I don't remember having any serious friends before we moved to Lansdowne Road. There were children's tea parties – usually near Christmas – but I dreaded them: the milk tasted different and I was frightened of pulling crackers. A nanny stood behind each child's chair – like a footman – and they talked to one another while the children ate silently, or wept because they weren't enjoying themselves. The first friend I do remember having was a charismatic girl, several years older than I, called Nicola. She told me that she could do magic, and one day, when we were walking to Kensington Gardens, she told me that she'd lost her doll. 'But I can get it back any time I like.' How could she do that? She stopped, selected a stone, and stamped on it. 'There! Now the doll will come back.' The next day there she was with the doll. I was most humbly impressed, knowing I could never do anything like that.

We went to stay with my paternal grandparents in Sussex, but although I subsequently got to know and love the house and the country that surrounded it, early memories are faint and hazy. I remember the beautifully kept lawns, the scent of lavender hedges, the exciting and wonderful aroma of the stable – four loose-boxes with the names of the occupants on the wall of each box. I remember being lifted up to stroke the satin-furry noses of the horses, whose mobile lips would move to reveal what looked like large yellow false teeth. The greenhouses built against the back of the stable walls, full of tomatoes and nectarines and grapes, smelt overpoweringly sweet, and my grandmother would pick the smallest ripe tomatoes for me to eat.

She gave me a little piece of garden and bought me a rose to put in it, but this gesture had a catch: I was to drink a glass of hot milk every evening in return because, she said, I was too thin. I loathed hot milk, indeed any milk in a glass – milk had to be in china – and water in a cup tasted quite wrong too. I struggled with the hot milk for several nights before I said she would have to take her garden back because I couldn't bear the milk with its perpetually recurring skin. I don't remember the outcome of this, except I can clearly hear her saying, 'At least you spoke the truth. You must always do that. There is no such thing as a white lie.'

This grandmother was one of seven sisters born to William Barlow, a crystallographer of some note. I was always told that there were few men in Europe versed enough in his subject for him to talk with. He was a member of the Royal Society, and his gardener once entered a competition in the local pub for whose boss was the definitive gentleman; he won on the grounds that he had been with my great-grandfather for thirty years and never saw him do a stroke of work. My great-grandmother was tiny, and reminded me of a rag doll. One couldn't imagine that she had a body: she was simply a face with her hair smoothed back into a bun, clothes underneath and black shoes peeping out at the bottom of her grey and black attire. The only story I remember about her was that when she was eighty-nine she picked up *The Times* one day, went carefully through the deaths column, then threw it aside in a rage: 'Not a soul that I know.'

It's clear that their daughter, my grandmother, Florence – invariably called the Witch because she had such an unwitchlike nature – was the beauty of the family. My earliest memories of her are clear and easy, because she didn't seem to age. She wore the same sort of skirt with cardigans of the same shades, black shoes and pale stockings and a gold wrist-watch in whose band was tucked a fine lawn handkerchief. She had a high white forehead, good cheekbones, and eyes that were charming because they looked at you with such direct and simple honesty. She was without vanity or pretension of any kind; she loved music and jokes and would literally cry with laughter. She played the piano remarkably well: used to accompany my aunt's violinist friend and play duets with Myra Hess who was a great friend of the family.

She also loved gardening, her rock garden and her roses being special pleasures. She kept the house with Victorian thriftiness: food was always seriously plain. Boiled mutton and semolina 'shape' were usual, and she wouldn't allow me to have both butter and marmalade on breakfast toast. Toast was indeed a luxury to her. It was taken at teatime when she boiled the kettle on a spirit lamp and made the tea herself. I don't remember her ever leaving the various houses and gardens in which she lived, except in the country when she was sometimes driven to Battle where she'd visit the butcher and Till's, the wonderful ironmongery and garden-implement shop. Otherwise, I think she was content with her marriage, her three sons and one daughter.

Sometimes, on the surface, my paternal grandparents seemed rather ill-matched. He was a man of enormous energy who enjoyed whatever he did, loved good wine and food, his clubs, his riding, his family and almost everyone else. She was domestically and musically inclined – I don't think music meant much to him. However, there was a feeling of stability and success about their marriage. There were moments of strain when he would come down from London and announce that the Rajah of 'Somewhere or other', the Governor General of Western Australia, and a very nice man he had met in the train were coming for the weekend. 'Really, Alec!' And she'd get up from the table and send for house-maids and the cook, but she was only serenely cross.

Alexander Howard, this grandfather – called the Brig because he had never been in the army – was devoted to his family, but as a young child I was terrified of him. Although he was known for his instant rapport with people, he felt with children that the impersonation of some wild animal at maximum volume was the most genial approach. He would emerge slowly from his study, roaring or growling, and accompany either noise with gestures of such ferocious goodwill that I screamed with terror and, when old enough, fled from him. I was his eldest grandchild, and sub-sequently he had many opportunities to temper his approach, but it took me years to recover from it.

In all his houses that I can remember, he always had a study where he must have spent a good deal of time, but where I imagined he lived or even, possibly, was kept. These rooms, in London or the country, had an identical composite smell and appearance that seemed perfectly suited to his savage and danger-ous disposition. As he bought, sold, grew, wrote about wood, they were usually panelled and furnished with a heavy profusion of bookcases and overwhelmingly rigid clocks that I naturally assumed were named after him. A carpet of violent irreconcilable red and blue covered the floors. Sporting prints of hares, foxes and stags, pursued by packs of healthy men and fierce hounds into a kind of moonlit *extremis*, regimented the walls. There were several glass cases of stuffed salmon and pike, whose faces were congealed into expressions of such murderous malevolence that I once examined them carefully to be sure that they couldn't escape. There were dozens of smaller clocks that fidgeted insistently behind the taller ones. There were pots of scarlet geraniums in full unwinking flower, and boxes and jars of cigars, these two scents so confusing in my mind that for years afterwards I expected one to smell of the other. There were weighty decanters filled with whisky and port. Quantities of wood samples were always strewn over his desk – of every colour from the palest skin, to the darkest animal fur; they were striped, whorled and figured – parched and breathless – the grain gaping for nourishment like the dry palm of a hand, or seasoned and slippery, like a blood horse's neck. There were small chests of shallow drawers with ivory knobs: if pulled, they sprang open with fiendish alacrity to reveal dozens of dead beetles pinned to white blotting paper.

My grandfather was then, and was for many years, invariably accompanied by a sleek mongrel of hideous aspect. This dog was mostly black with some ill chosen splashes of white and was both shrewd and cowardly, with a sickly smile and a strong personality. He was a careerist and a snob, wholly lacking in self-respect – in fact, he was a kind of fifth columnist in the household. His name was Simon, but he would answer with hysterical sentiment to Si.

I can remember only two other alarming facts that confirmed my view of Grandfather. The first was that he wore an eyeglass slung on to a black-corded silk chain, and tucked into one of his beautiful waistcoat pockets. For some mysterious reason I confused it with an eye, and felt that when he pulled the chain an eye would emerge from his pocket. The second was his gargantuan vocal range when snoring. It sounded like a steamroller heaving itself over a humped bridge – a steadily increasing effort to the top of the hump, and then a surge of uncontrollable freedom down the other side. The effect, even from the end of a long passage on a summer afternoon, was unnerving.

Then, one hot Sunday morning, I was taken to Rotten Row to see the Brig ride. The riders pranced, jolted, streamed up and down their strip of tanbark separated from an enormous ambling summer-dress crowd by iron posts and railing. He appeared, riding his favourite mare, a bright chestnut called Marigold. When he saw us, he stopped, and then, suddenly, I was hoisted in front of him on to the horse. The senses of fear and privilege were so violent that, frightened though I was, I turned speechlessly to him. His face was very close above me. He wore a pale grey bowler hat, below which his eyes gleamed with the most keen and reassuring kindness. He had a clipped moustache that was almost white and a beautiful dark satin stock with a pear pin in it, which rose out of his lemon waistcoat like a dolphin with a misplaced eye. He had put me in front of him on his horse: he wasn't frightening any more. I looked down once at the crowd, then concentrated on clutching Marigold's slippery shoulders.

In 1929, when I was six, the Brig bought a house for his sons, their wives and families to use for holidays. It was three and a half miles from his house, Home Place, near Staplecross, stood on the top of a hill and was called the Beacon because beacon fires had been lit on the site since the arrival of William the Conqueror. The house was originally Gothic Victorian with wings of an older house attached. My grandfather, who adored building projects, resuscitated it with the help of a local builder. The result wasn't distinguished: the Gothic windows were replaced with something more modern; the house was covered with roughcast painted white. It had eight bedrooms, two bathrooms and various other loos, a hall, a dining room – both panelled by the Brig – a drawing room, a billiard room and a fiendishly cold little room called the gun room where the only telephone was kept. As the house was on top of a hill, there was almost always a wind, and no water except from various wells that tended to run dry in summer, and even when they didn't brought forth reluctant brown water that tasted odd, and caused concern to my mother and aunts. The lack of water was a positive advantage to us: we much preferred sea bathing and having a bucket of water chucked over us occasionally on the lawn in the evenings. My grandfather enjoyed the drought: he adored water divining, sinking artesian wells and organizing the pumping of water from a neighbouring desolate pond in which Mr York's – a local farmer – fiancée was supposed to have drowned herself.

He was a good grandfather in other ways, lining us all up – there were ten of us in the end – and giving us each half a crown at Christmas. Better still, he gave us what we called the Very, Very Old Car, an immense square vehicle, one of the earliest of its species, which he put in a field where it rotted in noble decline. Thistles grew round it up to its roof; mice nested in its upholstery and bits of its angular body fell gradually away. We took turns to drive it as long as its steering wheel remained. It smelt of warm prayer books and was a great joy.

3

When I was nearly nine, in 1932, I stopped having lessons with Miss Kettle and went to the Francis Holland School in Graham Street near Sloane Square, a long ride in a 46 bus from Notting Hill Gate. The school – I think there were about four hundred pupils – seemed to me enormous and smelt of floor polish, cottage pie and gym shoes. I don't remember being particularly afraid of going to school, and indeed my first week passed off smoothly. Miss Kettle had done a good job on my primary education – in some ways, it turned out, too good, because after the first week I was moved up a form, where everybody was a year older than I, and my troubles began.

I was self-conscious, with a desperate love for my mother that I felt was unrequited and the family thought was morbid. I believed in fairies, and was stupid enough to let this be known. My grandfather examined the school once a year in music and although I kept quiet about that, the headmistress didn't, and constantly referred to my musical connections and capacity – non-existent – and the form's hostility was provided with yet more fuel.

What makes bullies, and how do they select their victims? At the time I'd no idea about this. I was too anxious to please and had considerable experience of failing. I was an unsuccessful toady. This can ignite any bully, and I certainly did that. The form, run by three ringleaders, organized themselves into a team for making my life miserable. There were fourteen of them, and they left nothing to chance. They hid my books or spilled ink over them. They locked me in the lavatory so that I was late for prayers or lessons. They

26

scattered salt all over my lunch so that I couldn't eat it. In the ten-minute morning break they often linked arms and ran up against me in pairs. They periodically twisted my right wrist so that writing was difficult and painful, and apart from these practical torments, they gibed and sneered at me. The practical assaults meant, among other things, that I accumulated a large number of black marks and became very unpopular with the staff. I was nine; the oldest girls in the school were eighteen. I spent seven hours on five days each week at school for thirty-seven weeks of the year, and since one moved up the school as a form, this situation showed every sign of continuing for a further nine years.

The work was hard. After the seven hours at school there was a long bus ride and walk home where I had half an hour's violin and half an hour's piano practice, plus at least an hour of homework before bedtime.

It didn't occur to me that I could escape – either the teasing, as it was called, or indeed the school. I dreaded every day, but endured it all in a spiritless manner; neither sinking to public sneaking – which I'd been taught at home was out of the question – nor rising to any kind of effective resistance. Once, goaded beyond fear, I went for them; got through three of them before a huge Canadian girl, two years older than I, twisted my arms behind my back and kneed me in the stomach.

Once, the headmistress came into our form room and said, 'It has come to my notice that you are bullying one of your form mates and I should like you to stand up and name them.'

There was a short silence and then someone got up and said, 'Jane Howard.'

For one blissful moment I thought I was going to be rescued, but no.

'Oh.' She looked put out. 'That wasn't the person I had in mind.' We had had, two weeks earlier, a new addition to the form: a pale rather fat girl who smelt. Almost as soon as she arrived, she, too, had become a target, and I do remember my shameful relief when this meant that they paid less attention to me. I didn't take part in the bullying, but I didn't defend her. The headmistress gave us all a talking-to about our behaviour, a warning that if it continued punishments would ensue, and marched out of the room. The form didn't bully Eleanor again, but redoubled their assaults on me.

My only escape was in illness, and, being prone to chronic sore throats and frequently going without lunch, this wasn't difficult to achieve. It was decreed I was to have a whole summer term off and stay in Sussex at the Beacon with Felix.

We went there in June, and I'd never seen the country in that month before. We arrived in the early evening, in windless sunlight, and out of my bedroom window I could see one of our large meadows at the end of which were silhouetted two graceful pines. I didn't want tea: I wanted to be in the meadow immediately and rushed out to the middle of the green and golden field. It was full of flowers and delicate grasses: ox-eye daisies, toadflax, poppies, little purple orchids and some taller pale mauve ones, buttercups, ladies' smock, meadowsweet, Queen Anne's lace, bugle, cow parsley, clover, both red and white, little daisies with crimson tips to their white petals and purple vetch tangled with the grasses. I lay down in it; the whole sensation of being in this richly embroidered place, with the minute buzzing and ticking and whirring of its many insect inhabitants, gave me intense feelings of pleasure, of happiness, of perhaps the first joy in my life. I can shut my eyes now, nearly seventy years later, and go back to it. It was then that I began to love the country.

All that summer term I luxuriated in my freedom and spent the mornings up apple trees in the orchard reading E. Nesbit and Captain Marryat and L. R. M. Ballantyne – I had a great wish to be shipwrecked. Often I'd stop, simply to think of the hot classroom full of enemies, now so far away and I where they could never find me. The house was empty except for Felix and me. She took me for walks in the afternoons, but they weren't like London walks and I enjoyed them.

A couple that lived in a cottage above the stables kept the house. Mr Woodage was the gardener and Mrs Woodage the cook. She had a lemon-yellow complexion, which contrasted fiercely with her pitch-black hair. She wasn't a good cook, even by British standards of food in those days. The family called her puddings 'Mrs Woodage's Revenge'. She produced grey meat, potatoes boiled until they had a battered, furry appearance, and cabbage until it was almost colourless. But in June there were strawberries, followed by raspberries and luscious dessert gooseberries. Milk arrived in the evenings, steaming in a pail from Mr York's farm. I didn't mind drinking cold milk from a mug, and steadily became less scrawny and pinker. There was a yellow satinwood piano in the drawing room and, free from tuition or having to practise overseen by my mother, I could spend hours sight-reading easier pieces by Mozart and Haydn without criticism.

But in September, I was sent back to school. I dreaded it, of course, but the alternative – only idly suggested as a kind of threat for any subversive behaviour – was a boarding-school and that filled me with such icy terror I felt anything would be better. I'd also decided on a possible way to lessen my troubles. There were, of course, a number of things that weren't allowed at school and consequently quite often the more daring pupils would break a rule or two to show that they weren't intimidated. I'd do as many of these things as came my way, and thus earn a reputation for daring. And so . . . I can't remember all of them, but a good example was climbing up an outside staircase at one end of the playground in order to pick the leaves from the mulberry tree that leaned against it at the top. Silkworms were in fashion. One was always caught: it was simply a matter of how many leaves you could pick and stuff into your capacious navy blue knickers before a mistress called you down. I always came down with a few leaves in my hand that were promptly confiscated, but the others were shared out in the changing room, and briefly – but only too briefly – I was accepted.

There were two other compensations that winter. The school was to perform Gluck's *Orpheus* and, as in those days I could sing quite well, I had the good luck to be included in the chorus. I enjoyed the rehearsals very much, and they sometimes got me off games, which was a great relief. I loathed netball, so singing and listening to Orpheus and Eurydice was a marvellous alternative.

The other plus was that I actually made a school friend. She was called Tony Imrie and came from Cape Town. Unfortunately she was two years older than I, and therefore a form ahead, so I could only see her in breaks or at lunch. She saw that I was bullied, and remonstrated with one of the bullies who left me alone after that. She used to come to tea with me at home. I loved her; I don't think I had a passion for her, I simply felt comfortable in her company as well as proud of having a friend.

Towards the end of that winter term the blow fell. She was going back to South Africa. For good? For good.

We didn't talk much about it. I knew, somehow, that it was far sadder for me than it was for her. She was going home, and although she was too kind to say so, I sensed that she was looking forward to it. 'I'll miss you,' she said, when she came to tea for the last time. 'I'll write to you,' she said, as we parted.

She did write once, sending me a photograph of herself sitting on a beach. I wrote back. That was the end of it.

Two other things happened while I was at school. In the spring term my grandfather came to examine those pupils who played an instrument. Part of the test was sight-reading and I came second. 'Favouritism!' howled my form, but in fact I think Grandfather would have erred on the stern side when it came to judging me in public. The headmistress adored him, and alluded to me in her speech to him in the assembly hall, which didn't help matters.

The other thing was far more serious. One morning when we were in the hall for prayers, she said she had a very sad announcement to make. Margaret Jennings had died the previous weekend. She'd fallen out of a window on to a stone terrace. The headmistress wanted the whole school to pray for Margaret and her poor parents. Margaret Jennings was in a form lower than mine, and therefore I didn't know her well, but her death, the first I'd ever confronted, impressed and shocked me for months. I kept imagining her leaning out of her bedroom window – perhaps to smell the garden below her, or to see something that seemed too far away – and then the awful moment when she must have known that she'd leaned too far, was falling, couldn't stop herself. How long could she have felt that before she hit the stone? And was she then instantly dead? While writing this I have realized for the first time how many events occurred, people I knew, and feelings I had in these years that I kept to myself. There was no one to whom I could talk about things that touched me most nearly.

After the winter term, I was ill again, and it was decreed I should still attend school, but do no homework. I staggered through one more term, after which I learned I was to leave. The relief was enormous, but I'd sunk to such a state of fear and stupidity that my only accomplishment was a shaky literacy. I could read and write, but otherwise I felt a complete failure, was afraid of people my own age and, above all, distrusted myself. I didn't seem able either to do or to be anything that engendered affection.

Robin had gone to a prep school and I missed him desperately and refused to sleep in the nursery where we'd both been. Felix had left the previous summer. For some reason, my mother had told her not to tell me she was going, not even to say goodbye. I thought at first she was having her day off and the discovery that she had gone – that I'd never see her again – made me feel more frightened of life than ever. I didn't know what was going to happen; I desperately wanted to tell someone about the awfulness of school, to dispel some of it by telling Robin. Pinewood, his school, seemed to me perfect and I longed to join him there, but in spite of wearing grey shorts all the holidays I completely failed to change sex as I'd hoped I would.

4

Weeks of summer and the country lay before me. I always felt sick in the car going down, but once we arrived, I was like a dog let off its lead. The freedom! There was a pony to ride, and bicycles – all the cousins had one. To begin with I could only dismount by running into a hedge, a practice much disliked by the gardener. There was an old apple orchard with trees to climb; there were nutwoods – little shaded gnome-like trees that in the autumn were full of Kentish cobs. There were two walled gardens – walls were also much climbed. There was the Very Very Old Car – Robin was particularly addicted to driving it, making engine noises and sounding the imaginary horn. In the house there were two dining rooms, the hall for children and the real one for grown-ups. If there weren't too many of us, we were allowed to eat with them. And here I come to the household of cousins and their parents.

My father had two brothers, the one older than him who'd preceded him in going to war whose real name was Alexander but who was invariably called Geof, and John, much younger, who was a painter and taught at Oundle School. He was usually called Jerry and sometimes Jibe, and we all admired his capacity to imitate people and his general funniness.

Geof's wife, Aunt Helen, was an American of striking beauty. She had a fine, pale complexion, very fine, curly dark hair, but the most attractive feature was her eyes: they were sea blue and looked at you with a wonderful frankness. She was an intellectual, she read widely, she was volatile, and she had . . . not wit exactly but a dry sense of irony that could be entertaining, even to a child. My uncle Geof adored her, and she had two traits that were much approved of by the Howards: she was extremely family-minded – joined the club, as it were, with ease – and she had a rigorous talent for self-deprecation that was deeply approved of by my grandmother and my aunt Ruth, my father's sister who never married and lived with her parents all their lives. Indeed, it seemed to me, Aunt Helen was adored by the whole family.

You were *never* good-looking or, worse, clever, or actually good at anything; you could admire others, and if they were present, they'd instantly deny, discount and throw off praise. When any of us children innocently announced some minor triumph, we were firmly put down. It has occurred to me that the difficulty I have had all my life in hearing or taking in anything nice that is said to me stems from this family tradition. Modesty was uniform: you must at all costs not get *above yourself*.

Aunt Helen had one obsession that didn't go down well. She was an early follower of the Hay diet, and the family considered food simply as good plain fuel presented at regular intervals – the less said about it the better. To want outlandish things like orange juice or salads, or a baked potato at teatime was regarded as both faddish and foolish. Food at the Beacon consisted of eggs and bacon and Force or grapenuts for breakfast followed by bread and butter and marmalade. Lunch was usually a roast of some kind with boiled potatoes and greens, and dinner for the adults much the same. We were given a substantial tea, and supper hardly existed. Salads meant a few lettuce leaves, cut-up tomato and cucumber, with slices of cooked beetroot lying on top and bleeding unattractively on to the rest. Cheese was Cheddar. Puddings were rice, steamed sponges or jelly. There was delicious fruit in season: strawberries, raspberries, gooseberries, the currants of all three colours, plums, apples, pears and a black grape grown in the greenhouse that bore heavily every year. The grown-ups drank gin, whisky and wine. We drank water, with orange squash for birthdays.

Talking about food was considered to be what Aunt Ruth called 'unnecessary'.

Uncle John's wife, Kathleen – Aunt Kate – was Anglo-Irish, and even when I was quite young it was clear to me that neither my mother nor Aunt Helen liked her. I think that they tried to be nice to her, but neither of them seemed to realize that it's no good being nice *to* someone and nasty *about* them: the insincerity rings true to the unfortunate subject.

These intimations I had of adult relationships were occasional; for the most part of those years of Easter, summer and Christmas holidays I was absorbed in life with a steadily increasing number of cousins.

The Beacon wouldn't hold all these cousins, their parents and nurses at once, so we took turns to occupy it. This meant that occasionally my mother took us to stay with various relations of hers, Balfours, Collets and Normans, in their far grander houses: to Dawick in Scotland near Peebles owned by cousins Freddie and Gertrude Balfour. I have dim recollections of the house – a huge nineteenth-century pile approached by a long drive whose verges were flooded with daffodils. Cousin Freddie bought his daffodils by the ton, they said. This impressed me deeply.

The gardens were beautiful; Cousin Freddie was a keen botanist and gardener. There was a pheasantry with pens of exotic varieties – the Lady Amherst and the Golden Reeves I remember – and brilliant little jungle fowl ran wild over the walks and lawns. There was a rectangular lake with a battered boat in which Robin and I spent a great deal of time quarrelling about who should row. Back for meals in the house we graduated from rage and sulks to neutrality and eventually to our ordinary comfortable relationship.

At one end of the immense garden was a glen that ascended to a small mountain. One afternoon I decided to climb the mountain by myself. I set off feeling calm and adventurous, but when I was little more than a third of the way up through the heather and tufted grass I suddenly became exceedingly frightened, menaced by some terrible unknown, unseen force. The fear became panic: I fled back down the mountain into the steep glen, hurtling down past its mossy rocks and banks of wild garlic and ferns. I was sobbing with terror as I ran, but when the edge of the garden came into view, I felt safe and stopped and sat on a large boulder to recover. I couldn't go back to the house crying because they'd ask me why and I'd no idea. It's very distant now but for years afterwards I'd stumble, in memory, upon that first moment of unaccountable fear and it would all flood back – the crying, the urgent need for flight.

Cousin Gertrude was a lady of great dignity. Children were as distinct a species as might be the shooting dogs or servants. I remember that when she spoke to us it was with a distant – though kindly – sense of duty, rather like royalty singling out one of the troops under inspection. She would ask us questions so general as to be idiotic: we didn't wish to tell her anything and she didn't wish to hear it, but we did and she did.

Cousin Freddie was jovially altogether out of our orbit, reciting the Latin names for flowers, which simply meant that we didn't know what on earth he was talking about. My mother admired Cousin Gertrude very much. She was, my mother said, a wonderful organizer, always answered letters by return of post and knew where everything was. She had short, iron-grey hair, a fine complexion, and wore horn-rimmed spectacles that, naturally, she never lost. The house ran like clockwork.

She was Uncle Mont's sister, I discovered much later, and their mother, Cousin Susie, lived in a large dark red house on Campden Hill with a wilting companion. Once, when her horses were lame, she was said to have resorted to a motor taxicab. When she reached her destination and was handed out, she asked, 'How much?' The cabbie said one and nine pence. 'No, no – I mean for the *cab*. I should like to buy it.' To me, this was on a par with daffodils by the ton.

Years later, when I had my daughter, she came to pay me a formal call after my 'lying in'. She must have been nearly ninety by then.

We also went occasionally for holidays with another cousin in Scotland. She was French, a widow – I think she'd been married to yet another Balfour, and we always called her Cousin Yolande. She lived near Montrose, first in a tall dark grey house called Duninald, and later, when her son married, in a much cosier little house on a sunny bank and further from the town. I remember once going to Montrose by boat from the Thames and paying, I think, my first visit to the cinema where *The Informer* was being shown. It seemed extremely menacing and foggy to me, but the grown-ups said it was very good. One summer one of Cousin Yolande's nieces from Paris was there. She was called Henriette and was very pretty with abundant, carelessly dressed hair and lustrous brown eyes. Her clothes seemed to me the height of glamour; she was seventeen and I particularly remember her in a long white organdie dress for a ball, with a brilliant green sash round her tiny waist. I remember thinking that if she'd been English, the sash would have been a soppy pale pink or blue. We shared a bedroom. She had beautiful manners and was nice to me although I was at least six years younger, but her English was minimal and my French non-existent, so intimacy was doubly restricted.

Cousin Yolande was both gay and cosy; she wasn't unlike a very large tabby kitten. She took us to castles where there were Highland cattle and ceilings with fragmentary murals, and marvellous raspberries for tea. In one, I remember being shown Bonnie Prince Charlies's wig.

Once our mother took Robin and me climbing in Westmorland – the county her father came from and where a good many Somervells still lived, in Kendal and thereabouts. We climbed every day, beginning with the Lion and the Lamb, and Silver Howe, and graduating to Scafell Pike and eventually Helvellyn. Our mother made us climb for half an hour, rest for ten minutes and then go on. We used to get tired, but she said we'd get our second wind if we kept trying. I'd no idea what this meant, until I was on Striding Edge on Helvellyn and suddenly I felt I could walk for miles and would never get tired. It was a wonderful feeling: a great rush of new energy and the sense of lightness and triumph. Robin and I used to collect unfortunate beetles from our walks, put them in matchboxes and attempt to race them in the evening.

I remember the enormous pleasure, once, of taking off nearly all of our clothes and trying to come down a mountain in a ghyll. The ice-cold water, the small sudden falls, the beautiful little crystal pools and the sound of it hurrying on as effortless and continuous as a cat's purr enchanted me. Sometimes we'd come upon a water-fall too steep for us, and we had to walk down beside it, our feet so paralysed with cold that we didn't feel the sharp shale or scratchy plants. Eventually we were made to stop, put on our jerseys and eat Kendal Mint Cake – hard white peppermint sugar fudge that my mother said our cousin Howard Somervell had taken with him up Everest with his friend Mallory.

I think my mother enjoyed all these holidays away from Sussex: she certainly liked visiting relations, and the mountain-climbing expeditions suited her active nature, which seemed to find too little outlet in London or Sussex. But the long walks were also designed for our benefit and I remember being happier and more at ease with her on those occasions.

In the evenings she played cards with us. Once we went to visit my grandfather's two sisters, Aunts Annie and Amy: they were called Tannie and Tamie and emerged from their cottage to greet us, two tiny grey Victorian dolls who spoke in little mewing whispers and smiled so much that their eyes became thin crescents. Their faces, when I was told to kiss them, were as soft as snow.

When I was ten, my mother told me that she was going to have a baby. A sister? I passionately wanted a sister. But she said no one could know whether it would be; it might as easily be a brother. Great preparations had to be made for its arrival. The roof of the attic floor of our house in London was raised to make a large, airy nursery, and I helped my mother to paint it – a rather livid light green. I got more and more excited about this baby's arrival, and made my mother promise I should be the first to see it.

Alas for the treachery of grown-ups. One sunny day in March, on my eleventh birthday, my mother told me I'd been invited to spend the day with my paternal grandparents whose house was in Regent's Park. I loved my aunt Ruth, who lived there, particularly, and was deposited at 15 Chester Terrace by my father on his way to work; it turned out that I was also to stay the night. The next morning after breakfast the telephone rang, and my aunt announced that I had a brother.

I was appalled. How could I get home in time to be the first to see him? They'd take me home in the afternoon, they said. I remember storming down the stairs to the front door and only just being prevented from opening it. My aunt caught me, whereupon I burst into such racking sobs of frustration and despair that she took me home then and there in a taxi. I rushed upstairs to my mother's bedroom where she was lying with a basket beside her. In it was a tiny baby, his face the colour of a pale tomato, his wispy damp hair growing in all directions. I loved him on sight. What was his name? He was to be called Colin.

My Somervell grandfather, Mo, had been the youngest in a family of nine. His parents hadn't been able to afford music lessons for their younger children, so he listened to an older brother's lessons, afterwards practising on his own. He subsequently became responsible for any standard of musicianship in teachers throughout the country: before him, anybody could teach any kind of music with little or no knowledge or capacity. He taught me about key signatures, so that from having been a torturing mystery, they were suddenly as easy to understand as words on a page.

As I grew older, my grandfather changed: he was still very old, but he was otherwise less misty as a person, and life with him became more definite and interesting. At the same time, a streak of conspiracy crept in between us against my grandmother. The underlying difficulty was that she had a great sense of occasion with little opportunity to exercise it and he, in a mild and innocent manner, had a great sense of opportunity for which there was almost no occasion. A granddaughter increased his range: we went to the zoo, where we both ate ice cream 'in a vulgar manner, in public' and to Kew, where after proper consideration of the flora, we rushed to the fair by Kew Bridge and had double rides on the merry-go-round. I shall always remember him on a piebald pony that had a painted rollicking sneer on its face, upright, being borne on the crest of each rich, tinny wave of music that pulsed from the centre of the machine, his face set with pleasure.

On the way back in the 27 bus he would tell me jokes that seemed the last word in wit, his voice squeaky with impending dénouement, tears pouring down his face when he laughed – which was even more than I did. When we got back from these excursions to tea with Grandmother in her chair, we'd always had a lovely time, but we selected the more sedate pleasures to relate to her, our vulgar giggles and undignified behaviour remaining a tacit secret.

Only once did he let me down. 'Come up to my study, little dear,' he said one day, and then on the stairs, 'I have something for you.' His study was dark, bleak and stuffy. There was a desk, a piano, and a huge picture of Brahms who, from the way in which all spoke of him, I confused for many years with God. His stature was abjectly diminished when my grandparents moved house, when he was described as 'Bearded Gent in Beaded Frame' by the removal men.

Here my grandfather wrote his music, spending long hours in mysterious silence, while downstairs my grandmother, with a rubber-tipped stick and painful, pointed shoes, creaked about in an exaggerated and mournful *pianissimo*. She treated his composition as a mild but chronic illness; his attacks of music could be gauged like a disease – his violin concerto went on for so many weeks that it was rather like whooping cough.

On this occasion, with a grin that meant some private treat, he said, 'Do you like liquorice?' Oh, yes, and I could see that it was something one wouldn't eat in the drawing room. I was thinking of delicious striped sweets, but he pulled a great stick, like a piece of park railing, out of his drawer and chipped two pieces off the end of it with his penknife. 'Pop it in.' It was violently bitter, and tasted of all the medicine I'd ever had in my life. 'It's *real* liquorice,' he said, with pride. I thanked him, endured it solemnly for about five minutes and finally hid it in my handkerchief. Afterwards, when he offered me more, I managed to refuse without his knowing how poisonous it had seemed: he was so extremely gentle, deprecating in his approach, that I couldn't bear to hurt his feelings. Thus when he gave me a stuffed lion called Marco, a present I felt far too young for me, I was meekly enthusiastic, until I found that he owned one himself – called Jeremy – and was ashamedly devoted to it. Out of sheer devotion to him, I accepted the presence of both lions.

In spite of digressions, I am still not much older than eleven. The summer after leaving Francis Holland School, there were long restorative holidays. As they grew from being boring little babies into children who could play games – mostly invented by ourselves – my cousins became more interesting to me. There was a grass tennis court, and we all started playing as soon as they were large enough to hold a racquet. Eventually my father and uncles had a squash court built. Children were allowed to use it whenever the grown-ups didn't want to play. We played, however hot it was, until we dropped.

Our parents sometimes took turns to look after us while others went on holiday, and I particularly remember one Christmas when my parents were left with all ten of us. This really meant my mother was *in* sole *loco parentis*, as my father could only join her at weekends. One Friday evening he arrived with a barrel of oysters and some champagne and announced that he was taking her to the cinema in Hastings before this feast. While they were away, the house caught fire: the heavy oak beams over the fireplace in the billiard room began to smoulder, sending quantities of smoke up the chimney into the bedroom above it, in which slept two small cousins and their nurse. When the nurse went to retire, she found the room filled with smoke. The alarm was raised; we were all got out of the house and sat, bundled in blankets, on the lawn. The Fire Brigade arrived and, eventually, the fire was vanquished, and we were sent back to our beds. There was a delicious smell of smouldering wood in the house and people gave us hot drinks; we enjoyed it all hugely.

About then my parents returned. After the firemen had been refreshed with tips and tea, my father, determined to continue the treat he had arranged for my mother, opened the champagne. After a glass, my mother began to open the oysters. Almost at once, her hand slipped and she drove the oyster knife into the cleft between her first finger and thumb, and the telephone rang. It was an uncle and aunt in Switzerland wanting to know if all was well. My father assured them heartily that, indeed, all was well, and they accepted this. He said afterwards that he couldn't bear to spoil their holiday. In fact, if the nurse had stayed up any later, two of my cousins would have died from the smoke.

The next morning we surveyed the billiard room – inches deep in ashy water and many of the complete sets of bound *Punch* were damaged.

Christmas holidays were full of games, beginning with Monopoly at about six thirty in the morning. We played in our freezing bedrooms, blue with cold. There was, of course, no heating in the house other than the reluctant fires on the ground floor. Between tea and supper we played a fearful game called Torchlight Ogres. This involved turning off all the lights, except in the drawing room where the parents lurked – it maddened the servants who were trying to lay dinner or put babies to bed and I don't know why we were allowed to get away with it. There was an ancient gramophone, the kind you wound up, and we had about six records that we played again and again. 'The Teddy Bears' Picnic', 'The Grasshoppers' Dance', 'The Gold and Silver Waltz' were three that I especially remember, and later, Noël Coward singing 'Don't Put Your Daughter On The Stage Mrs Worthington'. We played rummy, and pelmanism, and Adverbs and Head, Body and Legs, and charades, and as we grew older, I produced plays, bits of Shakespeare, and once a play devised by everyone for the benefit of the Howard grandparents. Uncle John played his father, who sat with tears of laughter, enjoying being taken off. There were trips to Hastings to spend our Christmas book tokens – it was when I began collecting Dickens, but I was also extremely keen on ponies and riding and bought books about horses. We went for long, freezing bicycle rides in the steep lanes surrounding us. When we were too young to rebel, we were forced into dreary walks with nurses – on *roads* in our *wellingtons*.

5

I was eleven and a half when my mother decided I should be educated at home. To this end, she procured the services of Miss Cobham, who'd been her governess, and who, she admitted, had seemed old to her then.

The point about Miss Cobham was that age couldn't wither her: she was one of the ugliest women I have ever seen in my life – large, fat and almost blind, but infinitely gentle. She had sparse greasy hair screwed into a tight bun, small grey eyes armoured by steel-rimmed spectacles, and a varying number of soft pale chins that meandered into her clothes, which she wore on the Chinese principle: layers and layers of loose – and, in her case, indiscriminate – garments, which were increased or discarded according to climate. She wore thick, lazy stockings and sensible shoes, and in spite of her bulk, she trotted everywhere – lightly, in a zigzag fashion. But she was a woman who seemed to have accepted her appearance: she ignored it – she behaved as though it didn't exist – and this comforting dignity left one's mind clear for her gifts and advantages that were at least as remarkable as her appearance.

She was a woman of good intellect, encyclopedic knowledge, an active, almost buoyant intelligence, and a quality of appreciation I have never met in anyone else. As a teacher she was endlessly patient, and with some subjects too gentle to push me into the disciplined concentration that they required of me. I spent five years with her. Lessons began at ten thirty a.m., and Miss Cobham always arrived on the dot at twenty-five minutes past. It was my duty to let her in, and a further duty to kiss her. I'd hold my breath as she bent down for me to brush her soft, many-folded face with my lips. She smelt of damp, dirty clothes – of weary mushrooms, of antique sweat. Somehow I knew that this greeting was important to her so it had become a daily hurdle to be got over somehow. In the middle of the morning she drank a large glass of hot water. She taught me until half past one and on Fridays she stayed for luncheon.

Apart from the three Rs, we read aloud the whole of Shakespeare together, at my request, and she allowed me to write, as English composition, an interminable book about a horse, and my first play, a domestic comedy. Miss Cobham was such an encouraging audience that I often wrote her poems and stories as a kind of extra treat outside my homework. She tried to teach me English grammar and algebra for much longer than anybody else would have done, but the former I have only ever understood by ear, and the latter in no circumstances whatever. She refused to teach me French, although she would read French history aloud to me, translating extempore into English, and it was a long time before I realized she was doing that. She didn't teach me music, drawing or needlework, which were left to a number of interesting people to attempt.

I had a series of French governesses; the first was a widow who had been married to a Frenchman. She was always dressed entirely in silvery grey, had a complexion congested with self-pity, and reeked of the violet cachous on which I imagined she lived. I could do what I liked with her by asking her about her past which she took far too seriously to tell me in French, but after a while my lack of progress oppressed us both. By the time I seemed to know as much about her husband as she did, our relationship came to an end. She was succeeded by a hardy little Frenchwoman – like an evergreen shrub, always the same and always dull. We went for biting winter walks in Kensington Gardens, and from her I got the impression that French conversation consisted entirely of banalities. She only came to life when we crossed a road, when she would shriek, '*Attention!*' like a parrot. This made not the slightest difference, and I crossed roads alone with an air of dignified British incomprehension. Either my continual danger or infuriating immunity from it depressed her and she left.

The third governess was a terrifying creature – like a brunette frog – with a fiendish energy and devotion to her task, and it was quite difficult not to learn any French from her, but by then I'd had a good deal of practice and succeeded. She had a voice like a cheese-grater and, what seemed to me, a wholly misplaced sense of fun, and a childish passion for coloured chalks that I quickly found could be used to deflect her.

Why, I now wonder, had I set my face against learning French? I think it was because I associated it with the dullest conversation – cliché upon cliché. The idea that there were *interesting* books written in French that I might have learned to read was never suggested and seems not to have occurred to me. If it had, I should have had the necessary incentive, but learning how to pass the bread and butter or make boring remarks about the weather didn't encourage me. There was also not the slightest chance – I then felt – of my ever being taken to France or anywhere else abroad, come to that. For these reasons, learning French seemed both difficult and pointless.

Drawing, or art, as it was optimistically called, I learned from a sad, bronchial young man who lived in a basement, invited me to get on with expressing myself, and waited with apathetic incredulity while I tried. Very occasionally he painted a picture himself: they were usually rather angry overstatements of very simple objects – a kind of painting equivalent of 'I told you so'. Afternoons with him were peaceful, and as neither of us embarked upon them with any expectations other than his earning a little money and my using up a decent quantity of materials, we were both unmoved by my lack of talent.

I was taught to ride by a flinty little Irish earl, with despairing blue eyes and a hacking cough, who was always late for lessons.

After some time he acquired a German mistress, a tough, enigmatic blonde, who rode with us and quarrelled with him in a manner I labelled grown-up – since nobody said what they meant, but one knew what they meant by the way they said it. This made him later than ever for lessons; to make up for that, they sometimes gave me tea at his mews stables, and cup cakes have seemed slightly raffish to me ever since.

Then I learned needlework – mostly embroidery – with Great-aunt May. She was fat, arthritic and, of course, phenomenally old, with short, straggling white hair and joyous blue eyes. She lived with a Siamese cat, and a bony, witchlike woman called Frances, who managed to have unsatisfactory relations with this world and the next, and who cooked for her. Her room was always boiling hot, but she didn't observe it, and wore gigantic blue cardigans she knitted herself – but she was a beautiful needlewoman. She taught me how to frame a piece of silk and transfer the design by pricking with pins and painting through the holes on the silk with a tiny brush; to do gold and silver thread work; to make simple kinds of lace and much else. She scorned ready-made designs, and drew whatever she needed – birds, animals, flowers, angels, even dragons – as she or I required them. Lovely roving decorations or patterns came out of her fingers as easily and naturally as the design for a web by a spider. I went on two afternoons a week for several years. Sometimes she read to me: Toad, Rat and Mole and a very old book about a brownie – a Victorian fairy – but usually she talked a great deal. Her mind seemed regularly to sweep a broad circle, but I never discovered its centre. She was always making something, and whenever she rose – with difficulty – from her chair, she left a nest of little balls of wool or silk, which I came to believe she must have laid, like a chicken. At intervals Frances swept into the room in an indiscriminate frenzy about the spirits and the milkman, both of whom had been rude to her. My great-aunt preserved a Victorian indifference to any aspect of her elderly servant's social life, and although I felt vaguely that the next world was in the basement and didn't much like to go there, her indifference saved me from acute anxiety.

During all these years I was taught music, which consisted chiefly of my struggling with the piano, first with my mother and then with the music mistress at my horrible day school. Miss Luker was a tall, willowy creature, whose movements had an incongruous grace that suggested she was under water: she swayed and undulated over me in her jersey suits, reeking of the stout she drank for her health at lunchtime and bathed in perspiration at my incompetence. I had a respect for her rages, feeling that they were honestly founded, and that without them I should not progress even the little that I did. The lessons usually began with effusive greetings: she adored my musical Somervell grandfather and felt that – however deeply hidden – the same talent must reside in me. However, my playing generated in her paroxysms of horror and impatience and, trying again and again, her rage would mount until, in an avalanche of furious despair, she would lose her temper and spit. I never questioned her methods: I felt that she really cared about teaching me, and also that – unlike in the rest of my dealings with the school – I merited her fury. I wasn't good at the piano, and I wanted to be. Long after I'd left the school I continued with her, and our relationship staggered on, top-heavy with her temper and my incapacity, but founded, none the less, upon a mutually honest desire to succeed.

I think I spent about a year alone with Miss Cobham before the appearance of fellow pupils. This began one morning when I came downstairs to hear my mother on the telephone saying, 'That will be splendid, then. They can leap along together.' Somehow, from the tone of her voice, I could tell that she was talking about me, but 'leap along?', '*they*?' – it all sounded more embarrassing even than it was mysterious.

'What were you talking about?'

'A neighbour up the road has a daughter your age and she

would like her to join the classes with Miss Cobham. Won't that be nice?'

I wasn't sure that it would. All my terror of people my own age who weren't my cousins repossessed me and I didn't reply. Over the ensuing weekend, I tried to come to terms with the idea: she would only be one, after all. Miss Cobham would always be present; there wasn't much that one girl could do to me. And we were certainly not going to stop reading Shakespeare, whatever this girl thought about it. Nobody had asked me if I wanted to do lessons with other people, and nobody asked me what I felt about it. In between my Saturday ride in the Row before breakfast – my best treat of the week – my visits to the nursery to play with Colin, my long morning of reading in the battered old leather armchair by the dining-room window, my nervy hours of piano practice, I struggled with the way I could be ambushed by decisions and events over which I had not the slightest control. And then, out of the blue, I wondered how *she*, the new girl, was feeling about it. Probably not good. It was far worse for her: I was in my own house and she had that, plus Miss Cobham and me, to contend with. It was up to me to be nice to her unless or until she was horrible to me, whereupon I'd stop at once.

I need not have worried about Carol joining the class. In no time it was as though she'd always been there. She loved our Shakespeare reading and got on at once with Miss Cobham. I know now that she and I had met when we were about seven or eight, but I don't remember that. We were both about twelve when she joined the class, and she became my best friend. We spent as much time together as possible, rang each other up every day, went to tea with each other, and spent hours in Ladbroke Square to which she had a key. She lived two blocks away from me, so that frequent meeting was easy.

Her family always seemed to me rather glamorous. Her father was head of advertising in England for Shell, and was the first person to use painters to produce posters: Carol would talk about

Barnett Friedman and Ted McKnight Kauffer and other painters she knew. Her mother was small, dark and very attractive; always beautifully dressed as though she was just going to a party. I particularly remember her lying on a sofa in a mysteriously dusky drawing room, wearing a black dress with an enormous dark red velvet sash, with one lamp illuminating her novel. She wore the newest scents; Tweed was a favourite. Some of this grooming had brushed off on Carol, who was always immaculately dressed and learned early the trick of making quite ordinary clothes look special. She taught me to wash my hair with egg yolks, and we made face cream of the whites. She also had a dachshund called Vernon and, not being allowed a dog, I envied her. Like me, she had a much younger brother in the care of a large kindly nurse, but Carol didn't live a nursery life: she had her own room on a floor above where tea on a tray was sent to us. The Beddington family were very kind to me. When Colin, aged about two and a half, got pneumonia (long before any antibiotics) and was exceedingly ill for weeks, they had me to stay until he was out of danger.

It was with Carol I began acting pieces that I'd either written or learned by heart or improvised, and she was a wonderfully appreciative audience. It was with her that I learned I could make people laugh, and this gave me a streak of hitherto unknown confidence. Sometimes she'd say: 'Oh, Jane, don't be so silly!' We called each other 'my dear', I think because we thought that this was what grown-ups did. She was less than a year older than I, but those months gave her the lien on authority. I admired her appearance. She had a beautiful complexion, small but very lively brown eyes, and fine silky hair that curled naturally. I was pasty and my hair was lamentably straight and that was absolutely not the thing to have in those days. Together, we discussed Shakespeare, Austen, Dickens and other books available to us, the arts generally and particularly the theatre, which neither of us had really experienced. The theatre was for special treats.

At this point, another girl joined our class. Penelope Fletcher was the daughter of a doctor who lived and worked in Malaysia. She had spent her early years there and Kuala Lumpur was frequently mentioned. She, too, wanted to be an actress and together we put on a performance of duologues with Carol producing us. Penelope had seen Ruth Draper, famous then for her one-woman shows, and introduced me to the idea of improvising sketches that we played to each other, and subsequently to grown-ups, who seemed to like them. We put on one serious production of Shakespeare and Austen, which was enacted in our dining room. Penelope played Juliet in the balcony scene, Lady Catherine de Burgh to my Elizabeth, and the Nurse to my Juliet. It was a time of the most hectic excitement: some kind friend of my mother's gave me a bunch of mimosa – the first time I'd ever seen it or smelt its unique scent, and even now the sight of it reminds me of that first heady evening.

My piano teacher, Miss Luker, either because she thought my playing had improved or possibly because her patience was becoming exhausted, took me to play to Harold Craxton, a professor at the Royal Academy of Music. He was a first-class musician, and one of the best teachers in the country, and for this she has my lasting gratitude for I became his pupil.

6

Mr Craxton taught me for half an hour a week, and during that time he gave me his unremitting and acute attention, endless patience, and the deep confidence that he really loved what he was doing. He taught me something about how to learn; how to take the trouble and go on taking it; and above all, how to listen to what I was doing. Although I never emerged as a serious pianist, his lessons have been useful to me in learning to write.

This was how one of his sons, John, came to join us at lessons with Miss Cobham. John was going to be, and became, a painter. He had my unspoken respect for having been to eight schools and having been expelled from the last one for biting Matron. According to him, she had scraped his chicken-pox spots with a knife. Miss Cobham managed all of us with ease, and in spite of being deluged with plays, drawings and all kinds of writing, she contrived to slip in some history (dates), geography (exports), arithmetic (we didn't get beyond fractions), plus a smattering of Latin and Greek – all this between the streams of poetry we all liked to read or learn by heart, and the flood of our own contributions.

The Craxtons' home, Acombe Lodge, was a most exciting discovery. It was a large, semi-detached house in St John's Wood adjacent to Lord's cricket ground, the sort of house that had rooms opening out from one another, often rather dark in spite of the french windows in most of the ground-floor rooms. The only part of it that seemed consistently furnished was Harold's studio at the back, which had two concert grand pianos, shelves for music and busts of composers. A large jar contained something like pampas grass. There was a feeling of professional order about it – quite unlike the rest of the house, which was entrenched in disarray.

Harold and Essie had had six children – five boys and eventually the girl they wanted. The struggle to feed and educate them must have been immense: Harold worked very long hours, and Essie had the whole house to manage with little, if any, help. As well as their own children they frequently took in talented and impoverished students. The rooms were furnished with the barest essentials – gaunt beds, upright pianos, weatherbeaten armchairs, and thin spiritless strips of carpet. On the landings were chamber-pots in which the innumerable socks soaked before Essie eventually washed them. In the kitchen and the passage outside it stood trolleys on which lay unconsumed remnants of past meals: a piece of apple and blackberry pie, some junket, half a shepherd's pie, and snacks so debilitated by time that they were unrecognizable. Meals weren't regular, indeed nothing except the music lessons adhered to anything so dull as a timetable. I don't think Essie ever knew how many people there would be for lunch or supper: she simply toiled incessantly to feed and look after anyone who came to the house.

It was a revelation to me, who had until then experienced nothing but a bourgeois state of punctuality and hygiene, and I fell at once irrevocably in love with the house and its family. They seemed to embody all the glamour of Bohemian disorder, and I longed to live as they did. To begin with, my visits were confined to my weekly lessons, but after John joined Miss Cobham's class, I used to go there to see him. He had a small room on the first floor at the studio end of the house, which was usually dark and adorned with all kinds of objects he had picked up in markets. I remember a small table covered with a piece of orange velvet as a kind of altar cloth for the most beautiful ivory Buddha, who sat on it, holy and valuable. When I asked where he had got the Buddha from, he told me that some people in Richmond had said he could have it if he promised to *carry* it home. It was, among much else, extremely heavy, and I was duly impressed. John had a very sharp eye. He found a Reynolds and a Blake in junk shops. He used to take me early in the morning to the Caledonian market where we bought Elizabethan manuscripts, Turkish knives and slippers, pieces of Chinese embroidery, incense and second-hand books with our pocket money.

One Christmas, the Craxton family put on a production of *Ali Baba and the Forty Thieves*. John did all the scenery, which was enchanting and remained in the dining room for weeks; the household revolved round the play. John and I spent those weeks dressed in turbans, long silk robes, pointed slippers and elaborate beards that involved a good deal of spirit gum. We only divested ourselves of these for concerts as both sets of parents drew the line at taking malignant, turbaned Turks to the Queen's Hall. Whenever I turned up Essie was welcoming and behaved as though she expected me. I was pressed to stay for meals – simply adding to her vast extended family, that included various pupils of Harold's: Denis Matthews, Noel Mewton-Wood, Ross Pratt and Nina Milkina.

I have said Essie toiled to feed and house this motley crew, but although this must have been true, she never gave the impression that she was either overworked or put-upon. When younger, she must have been a staggering beauty: she had wonderful eyes – very large and round and blue – a milk-and-roses complexion, dark wavy hair and a wide, friendly mouth. She also had one of the most open, affectionate and accepting natures I have ever known. She thought ill of nobody and treated anyone who came her way with serene equality. She'd been a promising musician when she met Harold, but love and marriage, lack of money and, as she once told my mother, any knowledge of birth control had put paid to her career. I don't think she minded: she adored Harold, who in turn loved her deeply. They were *happy* and, like pollen, some of this rubbed off on anyone who came in contact with them.

Harold was an excellent all-round musician. At one time, he had been one of the best accompanists, and had played with such distinguished musicians as Jacques Thibaud, Joseph Szigeti and Pablo Casals; he also edited Beethoven's piano sonatas with Donald Tovey. In appearance he bore a marked resemblance to Holbein's drawings of Erasmus: intelligence, wit and a certain fastidiousness were apparent at first glance. He was the first person I knew who *entertained* with a piano: one of his party turns was improvising and parodying any composer to the theme of 'Three Blind Mice'. He also had an endless fund of musical stories.

When I first came to know the family, they had an ancient car in a Heath Robinson state of amateur repair with an ingenious method for tying the front door shut with a piece of string. Much later, they acquired an extremely old Rolls Royce and Harold said people might infer that he had gone up in the world, but it was the Rolls that had come down.

It's odd how selective memory constricts past experience. I have thought, for years, that this part of my childhood was fairly isolated, relationships confined to Carol, Penelope and John – and cousins. However, I did have several meaningful relationships, with both children and adults. Christabel Russell came to dinner parties at home around this time. She was the personification of glamour – always beautifully dressed, with a perfect figure and hair immaculately set in the little flat ram's horn curls that were the fashion then. She spoke with a 1930s drawl, and her face was in keeping. She wasn't beautiful, but each feature was groomed to maximum effect: eyebrows plucked to perfect arches, dark blue mascara and eye shadow, and scarlet lips set in a smooth powdered expanse. She looked and spoke like a Noël Coward heroine, but there was far more to her than that. She was unlike anyone I'd ever met before. She treated me not as a child but as an equal; she wanted to know what I thought and listened when I told her. When I noticed that she accorded animals the same charming consideration I was even more attracted to her. On top of that, she was very funny. Her attitude to everything wasn't quite like anyone else's, and infinitely more interesting. Very gladly did I join the ranks of people who would do – and were often persuaded to do – anything for her.

Shortly after I first knew her she became Lady Ampthill, and by then I'd heard her story. Her divorce had been a *cause célèbre* as her husband's family was challenging her son's paternity. Her husband, who had brought the case against her, claimed that the child couldn't be his as she'd never allowed the marriage to be consummated. She, while accepting this, insisted that she'd never had sexual relations with another man. These salient matters of fact were unknown to me at the time – I knew nothing about sex and was without any curiosity. I was simply told that Chris had won her case, which had gone to the House of Lords. That this had made her the most notorious woman in London didn't impinge; she was simply one of my parents' most fascinating friends who became, over the years, almost a surrogate mother to me – often having me to stay when my parents were away. When I was fourteen she told me I should not frown or wrinkle my forehead, 'or you will have deep and completely unnecessary lines'. I looked at her glamorous, smooth face: her large grey eyes, fringed with midnight blue mascara, that looked back at me with a penetrating intelligence that belied the drawl and makeup.

She was a brilliant horsewoman – the Master of a hunt in her seventies. I remember her telling me that every time I pulled on the reins I was hardening my pony's mouth. 'Talk to your horse, and use your knees,' she said. Her appearance conformed to the fashion and good grooming of her time, but inside that was a formidable free spirit; she was utterly without fear, didn't give a damn about what anyone thought of her, remained herself in all circumstances and with everyone. She enjoyed herself and everybody enjoyed being with her – a real and unusual life-enhancer.

I never remember her to be without suitors, admirers, but her life with them remained a mystery.

There was a Somervell cousin of my mother's called Leonard of whom she was very fond. He married – late in life – an old friend of the family and I remember thinking sadly that there went my last chance of ever being a bridesmaid.

From about eleven to fourteen I led a quiet, contented life: lessons in London, with Carol, Penelope and John as friends. My worst deprivation was not being allowed to keep animals: no pony, no dog, no cat was the rule. I responded to this by digging up fifty-six earthworms, which I kept in a large orange box filled with carefully selected soil. There wasn't anything to be done with these creatures beyond digging them up every now and then to count them and the practice soon palled. I graduated to goldfish, and a catfish that bullied them; but these, too, were unsatisfactory pets, taking absolutely no notice of me except when I fed them. There was a shop in Notting Hill Gate that contained a delectable display of domestic pets, and I persuaded my mother that a tortoise would cause no trouble and bought one for a shilling. I called him Peter and got him to feed on a mixture of chopped-up dandelions and plum cake – apart from his usual boring lettuce. He did seem to know me in a grudging sort of way, and would extend his scaly head to be scratched and eat from my hand. But he was silent except for the tiny pneumatic hiss he gave when he withdrew his head from some startlement. Then came budgerigars – green ones (the cheapest) and my pocket money had to be saved not only for the birds but the cage in which they were to live. For a short while I managed to keep a white mouse, but he never liked me and I couldn't like him enough. He smelt of damp breadcrumbs and had a weary, furtive air that didn't promote intimacy. Carol – lucky creature – had Vernon, but try as I might, my parents wouldn't let me have a dog.

In the country, I somehow obtained a pair of white rabbits: one could at least stroke their sumptuous white fur and admire their ruby eyes, but most of my time with them was spent cleaning out their hutch. The next holiday I went to Sussex to find thirteen rabbits in the hutch. There were clearly too many of them, but it was surprising how many people didn't want a single white rabbit. 'It would be nice for you in your office,' I said to my father, but he smiled uneasily and said, not really. None of the cousins seemed interested. 'If there was a flower show or something, people could win them.' The gardener said that meant people would have to buy tickets and he would rather have a pig. When I returned in the Christmas holidays there were no rabbits. 'Your grandfather had them put down,' someone said. I displayed a token amount of grief, but actually I was relieved.

There was a pony at the Beacon, procured by my grandfather for all of the cousins to ride. He was called Joey and was a very small bay of about twelve hands. He had the disposition of a wicked old man: he bit, he kicked and he threw all of us, and I felt sure he delighted in the numbers of us that he could terrify or discomfort. Nobody could stay on him except the groom's son, a hard-bitten little boy, who at ten already looked like a jockey. Joey was sold, and Peggy took his place. She was also a bay – of Dartmoor extraction, pretty and fairly good-tempered. Her companion in the field was an ex-police horse called Angela and they were most devoted. In London, before breakfast, I rode a horse hired from a livery stable. The Row was at its best then, uncrowded but for the early morning regulars.

I used occasionally to ride with a distant cousin, who mostly lived in Westmorland. Ann Somervell was far older than me – eighteen or thereabouts – a tall, gaunt, pale girl whose passion was flat racing. We talked about horses a bit, but were otherwise silent. One morning, when we'd dismounted and parted, I to catch my bus back to Holland Park and she in the opposite direction, I had a sudden fear that something awful was going to happen to her, and began to run in the direction I thought she'd taken, but I missed her. A week later, I was told that she'd been killed in a race. For some time afterwards I was haunted by the idea that if I'd succeeded in finding her that morning, she wouldn't have been killed.

Premonitions bring with them a sense of powerlessness and guilt – what can be the point of even half knowing something about which one seems able to do nothing? At some level I felt responsible for Ann's death, a thought too awful for me to tell anyone.

7

In the early 1930s my Somervell grandparents moved from Bedford Gardens, to a small Gothic villa in St John's Wood. It was much lighter, and had a larger drawing room with more space for the piano. There were three bedrooms on the first floor – one for Grannia, one for Mo's study and a tiny third room in which he slept. On the top floor were two small attics in which grand-children used to stay and one was papered like the sky, with clouds. Each time we stayed we were given a paper seagull to stick wherever we pleased on the sky. Often I used go to spend the day with them, allowed by then to travel on buses on my own.

I was growing older, but my grandfather seemed to be getting smaller and even gentler. I have fleeting recollections of him stand-ing with Victorian dignity on concert platforms after performances of his work with various conductors and singers, who towered and slouched beside his small figure. His voice was still furry and some-times squeaky, but there seemed to be less of it. One Easter holidays when I was thirteen, I was going to stay in Westmorland, and went to say goodbye to him.

He was in bed. 'He is just rather tired,' they said. He was sitting up wearing pyjamas, widely striped in blue and white, like breakfast cups. On the bed was a tray covered with his ties, which he was sorting and neatly rolling into separate coils. For the first time I felt oddly constrained with him and, for want of anything better to say, asked him what he was doing with them.

'I like to leave everything tidy.'

'Why? Are you going away?'

He looked at me for a moment, and he wasn't my ancient beloved grandfather, but simply somebody who was tired and very sad and I didn't know which had come first. I kissed him, and the sweetbriar smell was there for the last time.

We came back from our holiday because he was dying. The doors of his study and tiny bedroom were left open and people came to play to him: Ernest Lush, because he was so good at sight-reading, and several times a very beautiful young girl with high cheekbones, enormous eyes and a Russian accent who played Brahms and Chopin. I used to sit on the stairs and listen to her. This was Nina Milkina, who later became a great friend.

These long days went by, my grandmother creaking slowly about, leaning on her rubber-tipped stick, the servants in the kitchen speaking in hushed voices while they prepared trays of food for the family who came and went.

He died as gently as he had lived; slipped out unassumingly, as softly as a candle, and left us in the dark.

He was the first person to die whom I'd known well and loved and I mourn him still. I knew that for my mother it was a terrible loss. He was the parent who'd truly loved her and, given her reclusive and isolated nature, she must have felt utter grief. But neither her feelings about him nor mine were ever exchanged. She talked to me of it only in dramatic clichés, which I hated and was unable to respond to. They took his ashes back to Grasmere where he had been born, but I was only told this after they'd done it.

It took some years for me to recognize that I would not get from my mother what I wanted – the kind of uncritical affection that transcends everyday mishaps, arguments or wrong-doing on my part. Now, I think that she made efforts to love me, but she couldn't do anything without criticism, and I suspect she experienced it herself from *her* mother. I felt constantly on trial: her approval had to be earned and I wasn't much good at earning it. A niece told me recently that my mother had once told her that she didn't really like little girls – 'Of course I don't mean you, Claire,' she had added. From my earliest years, I was a disappointment to her. My shortcomings were magnified by her disapproval; my anxiety about doing the wrong thing accelerated the likelihood.

The only times that were enjoyably *Angst*-free at home were when she read aloud to me while I was sewing. She was a very good reader; as Dr Manette in *A Tale of Two Cities* is asked his name I can still hear her replying, in a ghostly, faraway voice, 'One hundred and five North Tower.' But I never felt I could confide in her – since any confidence would be a kind of exposure that could only count against me. I could never tell her how horrible my day at school had been, or how afraid I was when she made me ride bareback and jump fences with folded arms, or how I was terrified of putting my head under water, or how frightfully sick I felt in cars, or how embarrassed and ugly I felt when she made me go to parties in bottle-green silk with bronze stockings and kid shoes to match. There was an ethos then that parents didn't openly admire or extol their children's behaviour and talent, and my mother certainly subscribed to that.

There were other, more serious fears I dared not tell her, or indeed anyone. The worst one was the possibility of another war. Ever since I'd seen the photograph on my father's dressing-table and had been told that all his friends had been killed, I'd become steadily more and more terrified by the prospect of war. Nothing that people said about this was in the least reassuring. Miss Cobham described the Great War as the war to end all wars. But almost at once, war broke out all over the world – in China, in Spain, in Abyssinia. My father had a book called *Vainglory* in his bookcase, an anthology of his war, and reading it confirmed my worst fears. In the next war we'd all be bombed or gassed to death. Even if anyone survived, the world would be a dreadful place. My being taken to see the film *The War of the Worlds* exacerbated this horror. The combination of H. G. Wells and Tchaikovsky's Fifth Symphony made a deep, unbearable impression on me, and for years afterwards I couldn't hear that music without tears. Sometimes it seemed extraordinary to me that people laughed and joked, had parties, carried on their ordinary lives as though there was nothing to worry about.

But by then I'd begun to notice that grown-ups never *did* talk about anything that distressed or frightened them, or if they did, it was never in front of children like myself. Even when my small brother, Colin, contracted pneumonia and was in serious danger of dying, my parents attempted to conceal the truth from me. It was eleven days before his temperature dropped, and I was told afterwards that few babies survived so many days of high fever. I adored Colin, and if I'd known how near he came to dying I'd have been prostrated – mad with grief.

The other anxiety that haunted me for many years, although it decreased as I got older, was that I might be sent to boarding-school. My father sometimes threatened this, generally when he felt I was leading a life of lazy intellectual isolation. He thought that everyone was better off being active in the open air in groups. It was all very well for him, I used to think: after his war, leaving his home and family, and seeing all his friends killed, a boarding-school would be nothing to him, but to me it was a temporary equivalent of Hell. It was a recurring threat, which was probably not serious, but it seemed real enough at the time and induced violent home-sickness at the prospect of going anywhere by myself.

On the animal-owning front, I eventually achieved not my wildest dream, a dog, but a cat. My aunt Ruth said one day that she would like to take me out to choose a birthday present. We'd spend the afternoon looking for what I should like to have. One of our first calls was to the pet department of Selfridges, and there was a full-grown tabby cat with a good deal of white fur and a twisted tail. He cost ten shillings and I wanted him quite desperately. My aunt said she wasn't sure that my parents would agree to a cat, and we must look elsewhere. Two or three hours later, I'd found nothing I wanted and my aunt gave in. We carried the cat home in a carrier-bag with his desperate white paws scrabbling at the handles to get out. I called him Bill and adored him. He was accident-prone: got run over several times and I carried him to the vet, but he always recovered even though he had used one of his lives when his tail got broken. He was also given to fishing my goldfish out of their tank, and I'd find them writhing feebly in his basket. He had beautiful eyes and at least pretended to be fond of me although, being a practical cat, he preferred the cook.

During these lesson years with Miss Cobham, an aspiration and an activity preoccupied me one way or another almost every day of my life. I wanted to become an actress when I grew up. It had started when I began to read Shakespeare. Penelope and I continued to invent monologues and enact them to Carol, but we both agreed that what we really wanted was to play parts in complete plays in real theatres. I wanted to play Shakespeare, but soon realized that all the best parts were written for men. This was initially daunting. However, I conceived the idea of playing Hamlet, never mind my sex – Sarah Bernhardt had done just that. The way seemed open. The yearning endured for the best part of ten years and was only quelled by marriage and the war – both far into the future.

My primary activity never left me. It began when I was eight and, despairing of getting enough books to read, I began to write one. It was an interminable tale about a horse – influenced by *Black Beauty* – and I wrote it off and on for six years until it bored even me to a full stop. But I wrote other things too: short stories, cautionary tales about wicked children and the heartless consequences they provoked, some poetry and eventually plays. The only short story I can remember was written when I was about nine. It was a tale of the birth of Christ written from the harassed innkeeper's point of view. Grannia was so impressed by the story, largely because of its religious content, that she read it aloud to her wretched servants on a Sunday afternoon when they must have been longing to clear luncheon and put their feet up.

When I was fourteen I wrote my first play, a domestic comedy on the lines of *George and Margaret*, although I'd never seen any plays of the kind. My play was called, with a certain sense of proportion, *Our Little Life*, and Miss Cobham and I laughed at it like anything. All the stage directions were written in Shakespeare's terms because at the time I had read no other plays. I also wrote a Jacobean melodrama, which involved a good deal of fighting with fire irons – and ringing doorbells all round Ladbroke Square trying to find a girl who would play the soppy heroine.

But through all this I never had the slightest intention of becoming a writer: acting was my aim. To be allowed to go to acting school was my dream, and one of my chief grudges about life was how seldom I was ever allowed to go to the theatre. Once at Christmas and once for my birthday treat I was taken to the theatre. *Peter Pan* terrified me. I used to lie in bed gazing at Felix's dressing-gown, hung on a hook on the back of the door, as it turned in my imagination into Captain Hook with his hook raised menacingly. After *Peter Pan* came a children's play called *Where the Rainbow Ends*. It contained a wicked dragon king – wickedness was easily discernible in the theatre since the subject was invariably bathed in bright green light. Then there was an Indian fairy story called *The Golden Toy*. It was the first time I saw Peggy Ashcroft, who played the princess. I still remember the moment when the lovers are made to swear that they will part for ever, because of the way she said, 'I swear: for both of us.' Subsequently I saw the famous 1936 production of *Romeo and Juliet* with Laurence Olivier and John Gielgud alternating the parts of Romeo and Mercutio, Peggy Ashcroft as Juliet, and Edith Evans as the Nurse. Carol and I were mad about Gielgud: we'd both been taken to his *Hamlet* as well as the Romeo. She actually met him, or perhaps her father did – anyway, pangs of hopeless jealousy assailed me. I was allowed to see several other Shakespeare plays, but nothing else.

The same strictures applied to the cinema. The films that my mother deemed suitable seem to me now very strange choices:

The War of the Worlds, for instance, full of destruction and terror, and, even more odd, only the beginning of *The Private Life of Henry VIII* – the part where Anne Boleyn is executed, which I found frightening and awful. The rest of it was reputed to be too 'full of sex' for a young girl.

It must appear extraordinary to people now, but at fourteen and for some time after I knew nothing whatever of sex. This was partly the result of not going to school and partly a sheer lack of interest in the subject. I was extremely interested in love, and anything from Jane Eyre's vicissitudes with Mr Rochester to Viola's unrequited passion for Orsino both gripped and touched me. But I saw it all as romantic passion.

Carol was of fastidious disposition: in all our endless chats, and teas and walks and earnest discussions about life and art, neither of us mentioned sex. When I was fourteen I began to menstruate and, having no idea what was happening, I thought I was bleeding to death. I staggered into the drawing room where my mother was having tea with someone high up in the Red Cross and asked her to come out of the room to speak to me. When I told her, she simply gave me some pieces of towelling, a belt and two safety-pins and said that this was an unfortunate thing that happened to girls – they became 'unwell' every month, but one didn't talk about it. Her evident disgust with the subject – and with me for having raised it – was so clear that we never said anything more. I did ask Carol, as she was slightly older, whether it had happened to her, and she said yes, years ago. The only other piece of information I gleaned from her was that she used bought sanitary towels and her mother provided them for the servants as well as themselves. I envied this as I battled with the rags that had to be stuffed into a special bag and sent to the laundry every month. My mother told me also that I must not swim or ride during these times, but the headaches and appalling stomach cramps were never touched upon and I used to dread them. My mother made it plain that everything to do with bodies was disgusting and the less said about it the better. If my mother labelled someone as having a lot (meaning too much) of SA (sex appeal), it was done with a kind of facetious distaste. And, as I knew by now that Grannia couldn't be seen either going to or coming from the lavatory, I realized, even then, that it ran in the family.

From my earliest years I had been assured of my father's love. He always seemed pleased to see me, to spend time with me, to laugh at my jokes. He took me to Hampstead Heath and Richmond Park. Sometimes we'd drive to Sussex together, and I'd sing him all the songs I knew and he would just drive and listen, and when I glanced at him there was always a small smile beneath his moustache. He called me Jinny and the name stuck for years, in spite of my mother insisting that it should be Jenny. On these drives, he would stop at Tonbridge at a handmade-chocolate shop, and he would buy five or six pounds of truffles, and coffee and violet creams – he never did that sort of thing by halves.

On my mother's Red Cross evenings, I'd dine in state with him – he had always given me wine from the age of four when I was, in his view, old enough, and he would tell me the provenance and vintage of the claret, burgundy and port that we drank and would subsequently test my memory. After dinner he would play his gramophone, which had a huge horn and required thorn needles. He once started the Pathétique Symphony and I wept. He stopped at once, and he asked me what was the matter. I answered that it was too sad. 'He was a sad *bloke*,' he said, 'but he wrote wonderful stuff.' When I was about fourteen, he took me to the theatre to see a musical piece called *The Two Bouquets*. I remember that the very young George Cole was in it, and that the setting was Edwardian with parasols and pretty dresses, but nothing else. Afterwards we went across the road to the Ivy restaurant, where we had a wonderfully grown-up supper. 'I expect one day I shall come and see you acting in a theatre,' he said, 'if I'm not too old.'

'If you are, I'll wheel you about in the mornings, toothless and dribbling in a bath chair.' His laughs made the waiters glance at him smilingly: I noticed how they always liked and served him well. Going out with him I noticed that everyone liked him. He would park his car right outside the restaurant, and the commissionaire would touch his hat and say, 'Very good, sir,' when asked to look after it. The programme girl would give him a dazzling smile and the head waiter would offer him his choice of table. He looked glamorous and wonderful in his dinner jacket, and he treated me as a treasured grown-up. I loved him. He would introduce me as his eldest unmarried daughter. 'But, Dad, you haven't *got* any other daughter!'

'Nor I have. It slipped my mind.'

He bought me a wonderful crimson velvet cloak lined with crimson satin that touched the ground for my fourteenth birthday: the most beautiful thing I'd ever possessed.

My father loved sailing, and he acquired a small 30-foot yawl called *Wych*. He kept her on the Hamble river with a crewman called Godden. Godden looked after the boat, and went in her with my father and mother, his chief duties being to prepare the meals and look after the small engine whenever the wind failed. I never liked it. The process of cruising to A, then to B, then back again seemed pointless and unenjoyable. We never really *went* anywhere.

My dislike of the whole business culminated one awful weekend when my father had taken me sailing on my own. We set out for Cowes in the morning. There was a slow, heavy swell and I felt queasy. At lunchtime, Godden presented us with tinned grapefruit, whose surface was decorated with an iridescent spot of engine oil. Tinned crab followed. Godden, always cheerful and chatty, emerged from the galley to say, 'Do you ever get 'ot, sir?' My father agreed that he did. 'When I get 'ot, I get so *salty*. I can scrape the salt from under my arms with a knife.' When he had gone my father shrugged and smiled, but I couldn't finish the crab.

Eventually we moored. This was only Saturday, I thought. There was a whole Sunday to be endured. I became more and more silent, until my father asked me what was the matter, whereupon I broke down. 'I don't like sailing,' I wept, 'I *hate* it.'

My father was aghast, but he rose to the occasion. He put his arms round me, and said we could go ashore; we'd have a lovely time in Cowes and he would take me out to tea. He did. But first he took me on a buying spree. He bought me an autograph book, and a pen and a lovely shiny exercise book to write in and other things that I can't now remember. We had tea and I cheered up. He was extraordinarily kind and gentle and didn't make me feel anything was my fault. With him I never felt plain or clumsy or intellectually not up to the mark: he was simply affectionate, easy, undemanding company. Until, without warning, he ceased to be any of those things.

It's difficult to write about early shock without hindsight but I have, until now, tried to avoid any older, more experienced conclusions. Here I have to fail. At some time during my fifteenth year, my father stopped treating me as a child. I can't remember the exact circumstances of his first assault. We must have been alone, and it was evening. Anyway, one moment he was remarking on how fast I was growing up and the next minute I was caught in his arms, one hand hurting my breast, and stifled by what I afterwards learned was a French kiss. There was a timeless struggle, until I managed to break free and fled. This recurred several times until I learned never to be alone with him. Nothing was ever said about it. I snubbed his attempts at ordinary affection, which incurred my mother's displeasure. I felt so frightened and betrayed by him that any endearment increased my fear: sometimes I simply hated him. I also felt too ashamed of what had happened to tell anyone about it. This state persisted until I was married.

I didn't realize then the damage that had been caused. Long before I began to reconcile myself to that, I understood that he loved me as a father – that his was a very sexual nature – that *he* had suffered shocks when not much older than I was then, and that as a consequence he had never, in some senses, grown up. He loved me, and when I ceased to be a little girl he simply added another dimension to his love. This was irresponsible and selfish, but it wasn't wicked. So at the time the signals I received from my parents were that sex, or anything to do with the body, was disgusting and that sex in any explicit form was horrible. This was to influence the next thirty years of my life.

8

My fifteenth year was the last I spent with Miss Cobham. Carol's
mother had decided that her daughter should leave and spend two
terms at a domestic science school, and it was my idea that I should
accompany her. The main reason for this was my appalling homesickness when removed from either home. I'd reached the point
where I could just about manage to spend a weekend with the
Beddingtons in their cottage near Princes Risborough, but even
that was something of an ordeal.

It wasn't going to be possible to be an actress if I couldn't leave
home, so somehow this weakness had to be conquered. My terror
of a possible war had been inflamed and then dissolved by the
Munich crisis in the autumn of 1938, and homesickness seemed to
be the next hurdle.

We went in the summer term of 1939 when I'd just turned
sixteen. At least it wasn't an ordinary school. I didn't have to wear
uniform. And I was going with Carol. Everyone is familiar with the
miserable sensation of a dreaded future sliding slowly towards them
– an event that looms inexorably nearer, larger and blacker until it
blots out any sense of proportion, until there is almost a relief at its
actual presence. By the time I reached the school, driven there by
my father's chauffeur and trying to weep silently in the back of the
car, I'd temporarily exhausted all feeling and lived the first few days
with a kind of watery curiosity about the place. There were about
forty girls, mostly older than I; they wore makeup and smart clothes
and seemed to me indescribably glamorous. The school was at Seer

Green, near Beaconsfield, and as the course was only two terms, at least half of the pupils were as new as myself. But it didn't feel like that, and I soon realized that as they had all spent half their lives at boarding-schools they knew the ropes.

We were taught by the simple method of everybody practising in turn every branch of domestic science. There was no theory: we ate what we cooked, wore what we laundered, did all our own housework and cleaning. Twin sisters, the Misses Laidler, ran the school and the members of staff were mostly related to each other and very good at their work. The girls were a disappointment to me as I found them unconscionably dull. I'd been used to the company of people very much older than myself, or of a few friends whose interests were much the same as my own. I was sixteen, had violent ambitions and was narrow-minded. Faced with people whose interests and opinions I was totally unable to discover or understand, I became a prig about them. Leaving aside any discussion of the reasons for life, the future of the theatre, or the comparative merits or pleasures of art, I couldn't even have a good conversation about submarines or snakes.

What was there left to talk about? They discussed their schools, and the variations of routine there; their personal appearance – hair, makeup and clothes – and, most frivolous and unseemly of all, *men*, from Ivor Novello to a friend of their brother's at school. Their futures, I used to ask desperately: what were they going to *do*? Visions of my own packed professional life – to begin the moment I was seventeen – would float impatiently before me. Some were going abroad, and some were staying at home, but to my dismay nearly all of them ended by saying, 'And then I shall come out.'

At some point during term in 1939, Gielgud produced and played *Hamlet* at the Lyceum Theatre, this time to commemorate jointly Henry Irving and the closing of his theatre. I went to the headmistress and intimated that this was a piece of theatrical history that absolutely required my attendance. She heaped fuel on to my little cultural torch and took me and a large party of anybody who wanted to go, asking me to give a résumé of the play before we went. I did this with mingled feelings of self-importance and incredulity that so many people should be ignorant of and indifferent to such a play.

Although I must in many ways have been intolerable, what with prostrating bouts of homesickness alternating with intellectual priggishness, the staff liked me, and the girls regarded me with amiable tolerance as brainy and eccentric. In fact, the easy time I had at that school is as much a mystery to me as the hard time I had at the other. I shared a room with Carol, and our natural, equable relationship continued: we discussed a great deal with passionate ignorance and laughed at each other when this became apparent.

Carol and I believed in God. I think that she influenced me here. For about two years before we went to Seer Green, we'd both been going to church. I can't remember our going together, partly, I suppose, because she usually went away with her parents at weekends. I used to go to the eleven o'clock service at St John's church in Ladbroke Grove. I went by myself: my mother never commented. I sat at the back of the church, and I never talked with the vicar. For Carol, her faith seemed a joyous business; for me it was fraught with anxiety. At the Seer Green school Miss Laidler asked everyone whether they wished to attend church in Beaconsfield on Sundays, and I elected to go. The Anglican service was very High Church, with incense, and the priest who officiated was interested in his parishioners. I began to feel more fervent and went regularly.

Something else happened that first term, which had far-reaching consequences for me. We were allowed two weekends at home, and the first time I returned, there was a girl, not much older than me, who my mother explained was living with us. She came from a large family in Westmorland and knew my Somervell relations, so when she came to London to study at the Royal College of Music, it was suggested that she should lodge with my family. Her name was Dosia (pronounced Doshia) Cropper. She told me later that my mother had said I might feel jealous and put out to find her living there, but this was not so. I loved her at once, and after sixty years we are still great friends. She was funny, full of life, and altogether charismatic; everybody who knew her felt the better for it. She also played the piano extremely well, and I had a healthy respect for good pianists. Not beautiful, she was intensely attractive, and she had a dashing personality that I very much wished I had myself.

Musical life at home was rich and Harold Craxton's pupils were often there. They used to come to supper, then play in turns, and it was electrifying. It was hard to go back to school on Sunday evenings, but this slowly got easier. That first term I learned how to turn out a room, goffer a surplice, make pastry, bread, pies, tarts and soufflés, how to order appropriate cuts of meat from the butcher, lay a table properly and interview a servant – beginning with 'What is your religion?'

Then came the summer holidays before the war. By now, there were so many of us that we overflowed into other housing provided by my grandfather – a barn that he had converted into a house, a small unconverted cottage with an outside privy, and a pair of cottages that he renovated for himself, my grandmother and Aunt Ruth. People came and stayed: I particularly remember Harold and Essie Craxton because I'd developed a romantic passion for Harold, and his visits were a highlight. I loved him in a devoted and adoring way; just to be in a room with him was rapture. I painstakingly knitted him a sleeveless blue pullover that he loyally wore on these occasions. Harold made me play *The Arrival of the Queen of Sheba* with him; he wrote some exercises and one was dedicated to me – what more could I ask? I was perfectly content with this amount of attention and affection, wanted nothing more.

I'd reached that amorphous age when I was neither child nor adult. I stopped playing children's games, stopped reading in apple trees and building tree-houses, and only climbed one special tree when I wanted to get away from everyone. I played countless games of squash with my cousin Dana, and tennis with uncles and aunts and older cousins. We went to the beach to bathe and to Camber to collect bottle glass. We went blackberrying, and in the early mornings collected mushrooms that grew plentifully in our field and Mr York's. I read. I worried about my straight hair; spent hours scrunching up strands of it in lead curlers that were hard and knobbly to sleep on. I experimented with Tangee lipstick, which looked bright orange but on your mouth became bright pink. I'd been promoted to dining with the grown-ups and bought a housecoat of aquamarine furnishing-brocade with long sleeves and a large collar that I changed into every evening. I now had an allowance of forty-two pounds a year with which to buy my clothes, hair ribbons and anything else I needed. I was growing at a great rate, was thin and gawky and still clumsy – someone in the family had nicknamed me Bump, which I hated. My brother Colin had always called me Dee-dee when he was a baby, but changed this to Deeds, as he didn't wish to sound babyish.

The political situation darkened throughout August as it had the previous summer, but I no longer had the dread that I'd experienced then. After all, Mr Chamberlain had gone to see Hitler and resolved everything, and so, in as much as I thought about it at all, I assumed the same thing would happen again. News was nothing like so ubiquitous then: we were, perhaps, unusual in that we didn't possess a wireless. I'm sure my parents took a newspaper, but it was strictly for them. So news was confined to the occasional guarded remark made at the dinner table. However, by the end of August it was clear that the possibility of war had escalated to likelihood. My grand-father decreed that my aunt Ruth's Babies' Hotel – a charity she ran that housed unwanted babies and trained student nurses to become nannies – should be evacuated to the estate. The Barn was to house the babies, and the student nurses were to sleep in the squash court. All this was rather exciting. A wireless was procured.

I remember Chamberlain's announcement, made at eleven o'clock on the morning of 3 September, because at the end of it and in the silence that followed my grandfather got to his feet and kissed all three of his sons, which I don't think had ever happened before. He then decreed that we were all – and this included small people with wooden spades – to set about digging ourselves an air-raid shelter. About half an hour later, the first air-raid warning sounded, and then I felt awful fear: my visions of bombers flattening London in one terrible raid returned. My cat, Bill, was in London, and I knew that cats weren't going to be issued with gas masks. Minutes later, the all-clear sounded, but that was only temporarily reassuring. Then there was a lull, which continued, from the civilian point of view, for many months.

I went back to Seer Green, but Carol didn't come with me: her parents wanted her to qualify for some war work. The family returned to London. My father volunteered to join the Navy, and when they turned him down, the Air Force; he was given the job of protecting Hendon aerodrome. My uncle John joined the Army. Geof was left with the Brig to run the family firm: timber was in great demand and the continuance of the firm was regarded as essential to the war effort. Shelters were dug in the parks in London, and built all over the city. Gas masks were issued: they came in cardboard boxes with a strap to hang them over your shoulder, and we were enjoined never to be without them. A huge Expeditionary Force was sent to France, and everybody said the Germans would never penetrate or get past the Maginot Line. Children were evacuated from cities, and some were sent to America. My aunt Helen went with her three younger children on a boat to New York, took them to relatives and then discovered that if she was to return to England she must take the next ship. She had to leave without saying goodbye to her children with whom she'd hoped to spend a week settling them in.

At Seer Green, school continued as before. I did an extra term to help get over homesickness. Rationing didn't start until December, so that was the last term when we were still being taught to deal with recipes that began, 'Take a dozen eggs and two pints of cream'.

I'd become more religious. Miss Laidler, with whom I went to church every Sunday, suggested I might like to meet a woman called Jessie and wheel her to church. Jessie had been a housemaid whose employer had put her into a damp bed whereupon she contracted rheumatoid arthritis so badly that she couldn't walk. I first met her in the small house where she lived with her family. She was sitting in her chair, with her poor twisted, useless fingers lying on the plaid rug that was wrapped about her knees. She was very pale, and had fuzzy brown hair and beautiful glowing eyes. Religion was her life.

I used to take her to church every Sunday. I knew I could never match her faith and goodness, but I desperately wanted to be a better person. Father Dix had volunteered to be an Army chaplain, and his brother, Father Gregory, a Dominican monk, had taken his place. I learned it was possible to go to Confession, and went. Even my sins, and I tried extremely hard to be honest about them, seemed trivial and I felt they were probably a waste of Father Gregory's time, but I struggled on, painting myself as black as I could. Jessie talked a great deal about Jesus Christ and the glorious life that would come to her after death, and I could believe it for her, but not for myself. I was too selfish: my desire to be an actress hadn't waned and I couldn't renounce it in favour of some more worthy, less selfish pursuit.

During that winter the war seemed so distant that to me my future was an entirely personal matter, and the idea of becoming a saint, or at least a nun, was far beyond my nature: both professions seemed to involve giving up everything I knew of ordinary life. Life at school was nothing more than an interim step: I knew that beyond it lay dazzling possibilities as yet unknown, but all the more alluring for that. I'd gradually overcome my homesickness and no longer lay tearfully on my bed, and had almost stopped breaking pudding basins from a distracted longing for home. By the time

I finished at acting school I'd be able to go anywhere without a qualm.

But, meanwhile, the question of goodness preoccupied me. I didn't have Jessie's faith which seemed to transcend her cramped and, to me, indescribably dreary life. All I could do for her was to take her to church each Sunday and stay and talk to her until Miss Laidler came to fetch me. She'd once been to stay in London, at a Christian hostel run, she said, by a wonderful lady of almost saintly stature. This short visit was the highlight of her life and she never tired of talking about it.

This was the first time the classic controversy of injustice and God's power to change it struck me. I prayed for her recovery every night, but it made no difference. I couldn't – like so many others before and after me – equate His mercy with His apparent indifference to Jessie's fate, and the arguments against this notion were too sophisticated for my honest belief in them.

Looking back, I am astonished at how undisturbed I was by my colossal ignorance about almost everything. It's laughable to realize now that the only point on which I was utterly sanguine was my future as an actress. I was going to be famous: I'd play any Shakespearean part I pleased – it would all come to me, although I'd no idea how.

In London Dosia had left the Royal College of Music to return home and help her mother with the evacuees who'd descended upon them. I missed her, but we wrote to each other. Christmas was spent at the Beacon. I spent the mornings at the Barn, learning how to bath and feed the babies there. My favourite was an eight-month-old Indian, an imperious little girl called Mira. I adored her. There was also a very small – he can't have been more than a few weeks old – baby boy called Billy. I loved him too, largely because everyone kept saying how ugly he was. He was, indeed, a strange sight, bright yellow, with a careworn, wizened face and a shock of long spiky dark hair that looked like a silly wig. I'd cuddle him and privately lie to him about how lovely he was to cheer him up and was sometimes rewarded by a ghastly, fleeting little smile followed by a look of shock – as though he'd surprised himself by being pleased about anything.

In the spring term at school – I'd stayed on, because I'd been such a slow learner – there was an outbreak of measles. Those of us who succumbed, and I was one, were moved to a smaller house where we were nursed. We lay in dark rooms feeling awful, and all our letters to home were baked in an oven to prevent further infection. The worst thing was being forbidden to read.

Food rationing had begun, but hadn't yet achieved the full rigour that was to come. Sometime the previous autumn Myra Hess had written to my father, of whom she was extremely fond, asking him teasingly for some 'anti-Semitic' wood for the platform for the lunchtime National Gallery concerts that she was to organize. In the holidays, I used to go to some of them: Nina Milkina performed, and Denis Matthews, and the Griller String Quartet, and Myra herself, sometimes with Irene Scharrer, playing two pianos. It was at one of these concerts that my mother met Kathleen Kennet whom she'd known, though not well, since the First World War when she'd danced in Kathleen's studio. Kathleen was accompanied by her second son, Wayland, who was nearly the same age as I. 'You must send Jane to Fritton in the Easter holidays to come and play with Wayland.' I remember that Wayland and I looked at each other warily: the idea that we 'played' was below our sixteen-year-old dignity, and would we like each other? Horrified at the thought of staying with people whom I didn't know, I hoped that this notion would die a natural death, but it didn't. My mother got a letter from Lady Kennet a few days later confirming the invitation and my mother said I must go. I consented with the proviso that my brother Robin should accompany me: this was agreed by all, and there was no way out.

I left Seer Green at the end of the spring term. I'd made no contemporary friends there, but had become fond of some of the staff and felt bad about leaving Jessie, although Miss Laidler promised that someone else would take over wheeling her to church.

I was chiefly preoccupied with my impending audition with the London Mask Theatre School, which was run by John Fernald: J. B. Priestley, Ronald Jeans and Michael MacOwan were also directors. If I was accepted as a student, my parents had agreed I might go. The school was a studio in Ebury Street and also had some use of the Westminster Theatre, where several of Priestley's plays were performed.

There were a number of us waiting to audition, but I don't remember feeling in the least nervous. We had been told to prepare two pieces, one of which should be a speech from Shakespeare. The auditions took place in a small room off the main studio where Fernald and someone I no longer remember sat behind a large desk.

My name was checked and I plunged in. I did Juliet's 'The clock struck nine when I did send my nurse . . .' speech, followed by an improvisation of a genteel lady conducting a children's dancing class.

I was accepted. I was tremendously excited at the prospect of starting on my career at last, but I don't remember that I was surprised. My confidence in this area was as extreme – even arrogant – as it was lacking in almost every other context. I knew I could act, and I knew I could make people laugh.

Otherwise, I was a mass of anxiety. My appearance dismayed me. I'd grown so much and so quickly and it had been much remarked upon that I walked about with hunched shoulders and my head stuck forward. I had long, stick-like arms, and what my mother described as 'English legs': knees like root vegetables and no ankles to speak of. My hair was straight – not fashionable then – and 'perms' simply made it frizzy. I had a low forehead with a widow's peak – off centre, of course – and my nose was far too large for the rest of my face. I remember looking in the glass with the sombre thought that I was far too plain for anyone to want to marry me, so it was a good thing I had a career – or was going to have one. I was also beginning to realize how uneducated I was. I wasn't even much good at games or sport of any kind. I was still clumsy and, having thought I had overcome homesickness, was assailed by fears of the coming visit to Norfolk with the Kennets.

Before I went there, my father took my mother, Robin and me for two weeks on the Norfolk Broads. All I can remember about that was that I invented a character called Violet who kept worrying about people falling into the water, and that my St Swithin's prayer book fell irretrievably into the bilges.

My parents dropped us at Fritton Hythe, which the Kennets had leased for the duration of the war. It was a long, low bungalow looking on to Fritton Lake and surrounded by woods. It was carpeted in colours of fuchsia and gentian blue and consisted of one long passage with rooms off it, all except the kitchen and one bedroom facing the lake. We were taken to the drawing room at the far end where the family were about to have tea. Lady Kennet sat on a sofa by the fireplace embroidering with wool, and Wayland was playing the piano. By the window a stocky man in a roll-necked jersey was painting at an easel. K, as I soon discovered the family called her, introduced us: 'Jane and Robin Howard, you've met Wayland, and here is my older son, Peter, who is on sick leave. And here is Bill,' as he came into the room. Lord Kennet was white-haired and balding and his right arm was missing. I just managed to hold out my left hand to shake his. He was K's second husband. Tea appeared with chocolate cake: conversation rioted – jokes, literary allusions, teasing, political figures and artists referred to by their Christian names. Robin and I weren't left out – indeed we were skilfully drawn in; it was somehow made implicit that this was also our life. This was achieved through charm: the whole family were charming collectively, and it took a few days to sort out the variety of it peculiar to each one. As we felt more at ease Robin and I were able, in our different ways, to join in. We were encouraged to sing for our supper, and were appreciated for our slightest efforts to do so. We played duets with Wayland, and I did some of my sketches. K loved the young: she adored her sons, and her relationship with Bill held none of the dark, disparate undertones I'd experienced at home.

We spent about ten days at Fritton. On Sunday, I wanted to go to church – clearly not the practice of the Kennet family, but neither was it a practice of my family. I was told that there was a church at the far end of the lake and that Robin and I could sail there in one of the little Norwegian prams that they kept for lake sailing. This we did, and quarrelled on the way back as people so often do in boats.

The second day we were there, Peter asked if he might draw me. I was entranced. Draw me? Half of me wanted to say, 'Why on earth *me?*' and the other half was too nervous of his possible second thoughts. To sit for a painter was better even than being asked to turn pages of music for a pianist: it was being a kind of associate member of the arts, and I could think of nothing more desirable than that.

Peter arranged a chair for me, sat down on a low stool in front of me, and with his paper pinned to a board began his pencil drawing.

I sat like a statue and thought about him. By now I'd learned a little: he'd volunteered for the Navy the moment war had been declared, and after some training had been sent to a destroyer as lieutenant. He was on sick leave for several weeks after a severe attack of jaundice.

'*So* lovely! You've moved!'

I settled back into the position that made my neck ache.

'That's it. Just stay that way. So *lovely!*'

There was a further silence during which he worked very intently, and I collected what else I knew about him. I knew, of course, that he was the son of Captain Scott, who had died heroically on his way back from the South Pole, and that he looked very like his father. I knew that he was unaccountably devoted to wild geese and had been living in a lighthouse – that was romantic – on the Wash. I knew that, as a painter, he concentrated on wildfowl because I'd seen prints of them in people's houses. I'd picked up that he was an expert sailor of 14-foot dinghies and had twice won something called the Prince of Wales Cup. He was also, according to K, an incredible skater, and had been asked to enter international competitions in that field. He seemed successful in everything he did, and was famous in more than one field. He was, to me, quite old at thirty-one years, which increased his glamour.

The drawing was finished and the family gathered to have a look at it. It was good, they all said, but Peter said he could do better, and I felt it looked distressingly like an idealized version of me.

In fact, as the days went by, I became – temporarily – an idealized version of myself. Whatever we all did – walks in the woods, sailing on the lake, silly word games at meals and charades after dinner – it took place in the sunny climate of mutual admiration. For one who'd been brought up with the puritan ethic that *nobody* could be publicly acknowledged to be good at anything, this atmosphere of confidence and triumph was intoxicating. It was also, to some degree, infectious. There was something invincible about the family that provoked both excitement and comfort.

Bill had been a war hero, a cabinet minister who'd got five hundred thousand people out of slums; he was a poet, an ornithologist, and one of the most noble and completely civilized men I'd ever met. K was a sculptor of renown, trained by Rodin. For a long time she'd been the widow of Captain Scott and half London had been in love with her: George Bernard Shaw and J. M. Barrie both read their plays to her. Explorers, prime ministers, artists of all kinds had flocked to her. I don't think she was ever beautiful but she loved men, to whom she was the most wonderful, unpredictable company, and she knew exactly how to preserve adoration until it ripened to friendship.

Her two sons were the apples of her eye. Wayland was to be a great composer, or failing that, prime minister (these asseverations were presented light-heartedly, but somehow gained in gravity from that), and Peter – Peter was a paragon. I think she loved him more than anyone else in the world because he was her firstborn, because he was fatherless and, no doubt, because he'd provided the anchor, the reason for making the most of life immediately after and in spite of the grief of widowhood.

Peter certainly hadn't let her down. His paintings were well known and sold. He'd become a considerable naturalist, as his father had wanted. And now he was embarked upon a career in the Navy. K was passionately interested in everything that Peter did, said and thought. The family, of course, were all used to this, but I wasn't. In this atmosphere I felt surer of myself – except at a dance where Peter turned out to be a wonderful ballroom dancer and I stumbled and stuttered around the room in his arms, with all my family retorts of clumsiness ringing in my ears. 'You've just got to relax, darling Jenny.' Afterwards I watched, with sad and hopeless envy, as he and the daughter of the house danced beautifully. I'd never be like that. Still, I came into my own with the charades.

Ultimately, I was dazzled by the attention of this older, glamorous man. Until then, my relations with the opposite sex had been sketchy and unsatisfactory. At my nursery school a little boy called Richard, with a hot face and bitten nails, had brought me a bunch of daffodils and two goldfish. 'You can have them if you'll marry me.'

I badly wanted the goldfish. 'All right,' I said. Afterwards my conscience assailed me. Would I *have* to marry him? Could I give the goldfish back? The daffodils had died. Someone explained that at that stage of my life such a promise couldn't be binding. So I got up enough courage to tell him I didn't want to marry him.

His face went redder. '*I* don't want to,' he said, 'I simply *don't*.'

A second cousin, older than I, who'd just begun his naval career, went riding with me and later sent me a brooch with a pearl crown and a note saying, 'Je t'aime.' His mother asked me to stay, but I wouldn't go. And finally, the son of my mother's friend Angela Thirkell, the novelist, wrote me impassioned letters for about eight years. In each, he proposed all kinds of ways of meeting, but I generally managed to elude him. He was four years older than I, and I was frightened of him.

Peter was different. During that visit, he set out to charm me – he liked flirting – and I *was* charmed, dazzled by such continuous and flattering attention. Robin, although two years younger, was far more sophisticated in these matters than I, and told me, much later, that he used to stand outside my bedroom window at Fritton for part of each night in case Peter turned up – a cold and frustrating exercise since nothing of the sort happened.

Back in London, the Mask Theatre term started. Not only did I have thrilling days of drama school, but every evening for the last week of his leave Peter came to fetch me, drove me home so I could change, and then took me out – to the theatre, to dinner, to dance. My mother told me later that K had rung her and warned her not to let him break my heart. 'He has broken many hearts,' she had added. He took me to the current fashionable review, *New Faces*, and afterwards backstage to meet Judy Campbell who was starring in it, and sang 'A Nightingale Sang In Berkeley Square' in her beguiling, husky voice. He'd known her since she was sixteen, he said. I'd never been backstage in my life, and was fascinated by the dressing room, with its mirror surrounded by lightbulbs, its vases of flowers, its screen hung with clothes from the show. Judy was sitting at her dressing table cleaning her face with wads of cotton wool dipped in a large tube of Trex. She rose to her feet with a cry of delight at the sight of Peter. 'Can't kiss you, darling, as you see.' She was tall, with black hair, and when Peter introduced me as a student training to be an actress, she turned to me with enthusiastic kindness. Her eyes, which were widely set, were brown. She was very short-sighted, and they glowed at me with a kind of misty radiance. I still know Judy, and our paths were to cross at intervals over the ensuing years. She became a great star; Noël

Coward was reputed to want her to replace Gertrude Lawrence, but a happy marriage and children took precedence. She combines an indomitable spirit with an entirely sweet nature. Like the best actresses, she found no need to act when she wasn't acting. However, at that first meeting, she simply seemed kind and incredibly glamorous.

Peter asked her to dine with us. Ah, no! What a pity, she was already bespoke. She went behind the screen and emerged seconds later in a dress the colour of her eyes. We left her painting her beautiful wide lips.

That week was full of new experiences, impressions, and feelings all so compressed that there was no time for reflection, if indeed I had been capable of anything so serious. I was giddy from such a headlong, intoxicating sequence. One evening, Peter drove me to the Serpentine and we sat in the dark; he talked a little of going back to his ship, then he kissed me, and I felt nothing but a kind of gratitude.

Before he went, he took me to Ackerman's gallery where he showed his pictures and gave me a black and white drawing of a nightingale – one of the originals from his stepfather's book *A Bird in the Bush*. This thrilled me – an original drawing! The first picture I had ever possessed.

After he'd gone, head a little turned, heart untouched, I resumed my drama studies with single-minded fervour. At last, I felt, my real life was beginning. I possessed boundless energy and, as a bore, I must have reached a peak that mercifully few people attain. Fortunately, many of the other students were so inclined and we discussed plays, performances, techniques and inspiration and read Stanislawsky like the Bible. We were taught by a mixed bunch: actors with melodious voices, cynical expressions, and a wholly understandable lack of conviction about the whole business; stingy, bleached women, who seemed emotionally bankrupt but who continued to go through a reflex of feelings for our benefit, and a few tense specialists who felt that if we could be got to emulate a chicken picking up grains of corn it must make some difference to our movements. We also began to rehearse the end–of–term plays we were to perform. I really don't think we learned much, but we enjoyed ourselves enormously, and it must have been a great help to our families to be relieved of our egocentric theatrical shop for six hours a day.

9

Suddenly the war escalated as France fell and the British Expeditionary Force was stranded at Dunkirk. The director of our school disappeared for several days, and on his return we were surprised to hear that he'd been part of the extraordinary effort to collect the men from the beaches. My family shut the London house and moved to Sussex, but perversely, like my fellow students, I stuck to the drama of my own making, and travelled six hours every day in order to spend six hours at school.

The war hung over our heads, but we hardly referred to it. Glass fell reluctantly from the roof of the school studio, and was kicked aside by earnest, sandalled feet. A train I was in was briefly machine-gunned by a German fighter plane, but we new students were rehearsing our first play and were more concerned about whether we'd be allowed to perform it in the Westminster Theatre.

We were selfish, preoccupied and, I think now, we simply didn't understand what was going on, as we never considered it long enough to find out. Behind it all was the feeling that we'd be dragged into it eventually so we had a kind of greedy desperation to get every drop out of every second of the time we had left to pursue our own ends. The play that had been chosen for us was Barrie's *Dear Brutus*, a piece that had been very successful in the 1930s when Faith Celli had enchanted audiences in her role as Margaret, the child that the hero does not have. I was cast as Alice Dearth, his childless, rather bitter wife. I had to play someone nearly twice my age, and for this reason decided I must have a red wig. I think I was awful in it – both the play and the wig – but the excitement of playing in a real theatre was tremendous. However, that term was the end of the school: it closed in the autumn as the blitzes on London began.

I spent the summer in Sussex, where the Battle of Britain was fought over our heads – literally. It became common practice for the family to rush to crashed German planes to prevent the local farmers attacking the aircrew who'd survived. Feeling was running very high. I remember a bomber, belching black smoke, scraping the trees at each side of our lawn; Colin and Bill, our cousin, both six years old, eyed it dispassionately. One of them said, 'Junkers eighty-eight.'

'Eighty-nine,' the other responded.

They didn't mention its state or the enormous explosion when it crashed in a neighbouring field. The weather was cloudless; sometimes one could count up to sixteen parachutes descending after the zooming noises of engines banking steeply or diving upon their adversary. In the early evening bombers would start their steady drone above us.

My grandfather had decreed that our house, covered in white roughcast, must be camouflaged. Various paints were procured and we all set to; the colours chosen or available were sky blue, salmon pink and tinned-pea green. The result was staggering, and we must, thenceforward, have provided a most comforting landmark for the bombers as they made their way to London.

I spent much of the summer writing my second play. It was about a woman faced with the choice of continuing her career as a dancer, or marrying a man she loved. The first act presented this dilemma, the second showed what would happen to her if she stuck to her career, and the third what would happen if she opted for marriage. It was called *Outrageous Fortune*. Each act was divided into two scenes and I wrote at prodigious speed – a scene in two days. I still used exercise books with lines in those days and read it to my aunt Roona, the wife of one of my mother's twin uncles.

She'd been an actress and kindly said she thought it was jolly good.

In the autumn that the Mask Theatre school had closed, two of its staff decided to start a student repertory company in Devon. Eileen Thorndike, sister of Sybil, and Herbert — Bertie — Scott, a Northern Irish singer who now specialized in voice training, offered 'scholarships' to some of the students, and I was one. With difficulty, I persuaded my mother to let me join the company. I think they had to pay a small fee for my keep, but nothing for tuition, although there were some paying students as well. There was a small theatre in Bideford, North Devon, and Eileen found an abandoned house at Instow, three miles outside, in which most of us were lodged. It was a rambling Edwardian house that looked out on to the estuary with the isle of Lundy visible in good weather.

I was allotted a large bedroom with two other girls, Phoebe and Barbara. The other large bedroom contained Eileen and her three daughters, Phil, Elisabeth and Donny, aged respectively sixteen, fourteen and twelve. On the same landing were three smaller rooms, two occupied by two more female students, and the other by a sad — we all thought rather old, though she can't have been much above forty — Romanian actress called Tansy, who'd just ended a disastrous affair with an English director and had come to get away from it all. Apparently she'd been a leading comedy actress in her own country and there was a huge photograph of Queen Marie of Romania, corseted to a shape resembling a large cigar, on her dressing-table.

There were two other single rooms, which were occupied by two of the male students, Paul Scofield and Seth Holt. On the ground floor a room had been appropriated by a Canadian actress who claimed to be twenty-five, although we all thought she was far older. She must have been a paying student, as her room contained a coal fire and was altogether better furnished than any other. We ate — when we ate — in the large, old-fashioned kitchen: a stone floor, long pine table and a range. Every morning, we had to catch the bus into Bideford and walk to the theatre, which was freezing cold, smelt faintly of leaking gas and had dressing rooms like concrete cells. In one of these, Bertie Scott conducted his voice-training lessons. We were joined at the theatre by four or five other students who lived in a house nearer Bideford owned by an old lady who presided over it and provided meals for the inmates. We, at Instow, had the impression that these students lived in far greater comfort, but we infinitely preferred the ramshackle freedom.

Eileen Thorndike must once have been a very pretty woman, but three children, widowhood and constantly uncertain finances had worn her down. She had short, grey-white hair, a weather-beaten face and blue eyes that blazed with random enthusiasm. It was she who cast us and conducted rehearsals. We broke for lunch, which we provided for ourselves. Every evening when we got home, Phil cooked dinner. The menu never changed: roast lamb, boiled potatoes and boiled cabbage. We were always hungry, and there was never a scrap left.

Our first production consisted of scenes from *Macbeth*, *The Taming of the Shrew* and *Richard of Bordeaux*. As there were twice as many girls as boys the girls' parts were double-cast, which meant we performed our roles half the times that the boys did theirs. My first parts were Katharine in *The Shrew* and Anne in *Richard of Bordeaux*. Paul and Seth were Petruchio and Richard.

Bertie Scott gave us all individual tuition. He'd been trained as a singer by Harry Plunkett Green 'whom I expect you have never heard of'. I had: he'd been a great friend of my grandfather. I'd even heard his light, pleasant voice in my grandfather's drawing room. This sent my shares up hugely with Bertie. His lessons were some-times maddening; try as I might, I couldn't do what he wanted, and on the very few occasions when I partially succeeded, it took me a long time to understand why. He constantly made me put my hand on his diaphragm, which expanded – rock hard – to gargan-tuan proportions as he drew in an enormous breath, then held it before deflating it in slow motion. But he taught me how to 'follow through' after finishing a line or a speech, which meant a kind of split-second freezing, an immobility that lent credence to what had been said. He also showed me how to use the lower register of my voice without strain. Breathing properly, he repeated endlessly, was the essence of being heard and, more than that, understood. However, as I learned these things, all my original amateur ease with acting, of which I'd been so confident, deserted me. Rehearsals with Eileen and the others partially restored it.

The Spartan character of our life drew us together. We were permanently hungry; breakfast was almost non-existent as neither the milk nor the bread arrived in time for it. We were also cold and, with the exception of the Canadian, Honorine, desperately short of money. I remember lunches in the teashop where we split a fried egg in half and counted the chips before sharing them so that lunch cost sixpence each rather than a shilling. We used to tout for lifts from Instow to the theatre, and I worked out that lying in the middle of the road pretty well guaranteed one.

Near Christmas, a local lady-of-the-manor appeared and said she'd written a pantomime she thought we should do. It was based on *The Rose and the Ring* and was written in rhyming couplets of such banality that we used to pre-empt each other's lines with a question mark in order to put each other on the spot. Something like 'Which she had left beneath the spreading oak?' so that the other person was forced into agreement: 'Well, yes.'

Schools sometimes came to our performances, and sometimes we took plays to neighbouring theatres at Lynton and Ilfracombe. We did a new play every three weeks: *Hay Fever, Berkeley Square, Night Must Fall* – Paul scored a tremendous hit in this – *Ladies in Retirement, Goodness How Sad* and *Granite*.

Peter wrote to me at irregular intervals and I wrote back, each of us filling the pages with accounts of our doings. Several of the girls had men they wrote to, but it was all very innocent. Honorine dubbed us a bunch of bloody virgins or lesbians – we were unsure what the latter were – and she told us at length about her many affairs. We didn't like her: she had exceedingly long nails that she painted a bright white, and her clothes always made the rest of us feel shabby. She also belted on about what a great actress she was going to be, but while, naturally, we all thought that that was our future too, we didn't go on about it.

After *Richard of Bordeaux* I got to know Seth. He was probably the most sophisticated member of the company; he was blond and was a wonderful raconteur with a soft, pedantic voice. When he began to show an interest in me, I was flattered. He seemed widely read, and took to lying on my bed beside me, alternately reading poems aloud, and making – very mild – love to me. I have to say here that we resorted to our beds because of the extreme cold. There was no heating in the house except Honorine's luxurious coal fire, to which we had virtually no access, and the range in the kitchen whose temperature was in no way consistent. It was cosy to lie with Seth under the slippery eiderdown having my breast stroked while he read me pieces from *A Farewell to Arms* and the poems of Louis MacNeice, W. H. Auden and Dylan Thomas. Both experiences were new to me, and I felt a kind of respectful affection for him. I knew little about him – none of us ever made more than a passing reference to our lives elsewhere, our families or anything that we'd done before the Mask Theatre. I knew that he had a sister called Joan, married to a film director working at Ealing, but that was about all. He never asked me anything about myself; we were content to live, entirely untrammelled, in the present. I didn't even know Seth's age, although I realized that he was older.

When winter was at its height, or depth, of bitter cold, the entire company at Instow became infested with nits. This, it transpired, came about because the charlady's child had them and used to sit close to Donny, Eileen's youngest daughter, while she was reading. Eileen didn't notice, and we brought the situation to her attention. I think by then that we were all infected, even poor Tansy, who reacted in horror. Nit combs were bought from the chemist in Bideford, but he soon ran out of them and we had to share.

We were also prescribed some evil-smelling shampoo that we had to use every few days. With one bathroom and very limited hot water, and the fact that nearly all the girls had long hair and no means other than threadbare bath towels for drying it, life became more austere even than usual. We all got colds, sore throats and bronchitis.

Rehearsals and performances ploughed steadily on through this, though, as Eileen maintained a blithe indifference to ailments, or what she called 'drawbacks', of any kind. But I think – with the exception of Tansy – that we were all absorbed and happy and didn't notice or care much about anything else. Tansy, a refugee left high and dry without her love or the practice of her profession, must have been intensely lonely. She used to spend hours walking backwards over the sands of the estuary because she said it was good for the body. Her obsession with hygiene had limitless scope in the cold and steadily dirtier house.

At some point during this winter, Peter wrote that he was getting some leave: could I join him at Fritton? I wasn't in a play and was allowed to go. As soon as it was known that I was going – and to see the man who'd been writing to me – Honorine became interested. She said it was high time I stopped being a fucking virgin, and to this end made me borrow two of her nightdresses, one cyclamen-coloured and the other black, both diaphanous. I thought they were horrible and would look silly on me, but I was too weak to refuse, so they were packed and remained unworn.

After two long cold train journeys, I was met at Great Yarmouth by Comber, the family chauffeur, and in no time was sitting around a civilized dining-table with silver, glass, white napkins and three courses. At once I was under the spell of the family – the feeling that everyone was the best at everything they did, that even I was funnier and cleverer and prettier than anyone had ever thought me at home and, last but by no means least, Peter's charm and attentions. I began to feel that I must be in love with him as he said he was with me. We went for winter walks and he kissed me – I enjoyed the idea of it more than the practice. It did seem a kind of landmark towards being in love, although what that would be like I'd no idea. He took me wildfowling very early one freezing morning and I couldn't see the point.

I realize now that, although I had a certain precocity, I was lamentably young for my age at a time when girls were, in any case, far less clued-up than they are now. Sex was still a mystery, something of which I had only a wary, dawning curiosity. But like the young at any age, I wished to seem older than I felt so I responded to Pete's attention and kisses with what I hoped was appropriate ardour. I was secretly amazed that someone so old and glamorous should notice me – more than amazed, fascinated, and I *wanted* to be in love with him. The attitude of the family reinforced this. K often told me how attractive Pete was, and that numerous hearts had been broken on his account. Also K was kind to me, even affectionate, apart from disapproving of my smoking and drinking wine. When the leave came to an end, Pete went back to the rigours of his destroyer and the North Atlantic and I returned to Instow. Honorine immediately asked me whether I'd lost my virginity, and was disgusted when I admitted I hadn't.

I also returned to find difficulties with Seth, who intimated that stroking me and reading poetry were no longer what he had in mind. One evening when Phoebe, Barbara and, indeed, everyone was out, he came to my room and flung himself on my bed, and talked of how stubborn I was, how unfeeling. 'You know, of course, I can make you do whatever I want?'

'No, you couldn't,' I said, but I was beginning to feel frightened. I tried to get up, but he pinned me down with one hand round my neck; with the other – he was smoking – he suddenly pressed the lighted stub on the back of my hand, saying 'You're afraid of me, aren't you?'

Some moments are so short that any attempt at description distorts their duration. I saw his pale green eyes fixed with an enquiring malice on my face. I knew that he was waiting for me to scream or cry, and I was determined to do neither. I jerked my hand towards him and he removed the stub. A split second sufficed for his challenge and my response. I tried again to shift him, or at least to get into a less vulnerable position, but he was very much stronger, and he was angry. He tried once more with the cigarette, just under my left breast – the mark remained for years afterwards – and now the pain was too much for me. He threw it away, but before I could feel relief he put his other hand round my neck and began – slowly – to tighten his grip. I remember thinking that he was going to kill me, and this sharpened my mind. I stared at him – willing myself to look calm – and, when he loosened his grip slightly, I managed to say, 'Don't do that, it's silly.'

Just then there were sounds of the company returning. He heard them, and his attention faltered – just enough for me to make a sudden lunge to escape. I ran out down the passage and into someone else's room, where I hid. I stayed there for what seemed like hours waiting to hear him leave my room and walk down the passage to the stairs. I heard him in the passage, calling my name very quietly, and when he reached the door of the room where I hid he began to turn the handle. Then there were other people in the passage – I heard them talking; they spoke to him and he answered – quite normally. The occupants of the room came in and turned on the light. I put my finger to my lips, and they shut up at once. One came up to me. 'What's up?'

'Are Phoebe and Barbara back?' They didn't know. 'Please go and see.' They did. They were. 'Will you come with me?'

One did. 'What's *up*?'

'It was Seth. I think he's mad. He tried to kill me.' They took this for the dramatic language then current in the house.

Phoebe and Barbara were undressing. They were already pretty sick of Seth turning up and reading to me, and they said, 'He won't come any more.' I crept into bed, teeth chattering from cold, my heart still thudding. The burns had really started to hurt and I felt sick. I also felt completely out of my depth. Frightful things could happen suddenly, and I could neither predict nor understand them.

After that, I had a sort of breakdown. Perhaps it was just flu, I really don't know. I lay in bed for at least two weeks with a fever that alternately burned and soaked me, and had awful nightmares of being powerless in menacing situations that each time threatened to engulf me. Days and nights went by. Honorine took up with Seth. I felt nothing but a kind of watery relief. Sometimes Phil brought me a cup of tea; otherwise nobody seemed to take much notice of me.

Eventually, one evening, Eileen paid me a visit. 'Time you got up,' she said. 'You're supposed to be an actress. You can't lie there for ever. There is a part for you in the next play.'

I got up. When I was dressed, I realized I was famished. Going down to the kitchen was an ordeal: I dreaded meeting Seth. But one of the unspoken edicts of the house was that we were all tremendously sophisticated. I decided that the most sophisticated thing to do would be to greet him as though nothing had happened. Perhaps, after all, nothing very much *had* happened. But as I sat down at the long kitchen table, I knew that it had because Honorine, sitting next to Seth, shot me a triumphantly malicious glance. It soon transpired that he was sleeping with her in her room; I felt safer.

Life in that enclosed world continued; nothing impinged that happened outside it. Nobody ever talked about the war: Eileen set the tone here. She was a member of the Peace Pledge Union and if she mentioned the war it was with vague distaste. My only contact with it was the letters from Pete, full of guns and terrible weather and naval life. I used to rush through them looking for the affectionate bits about his feelings for me before reading them fully and replying. My family hardly ever wrote, and when my mother did, occasionally, her letters were imbued with disapproval. Many of the company's parents came down to see their offspring when they were playing a lead, but mine didn't.

My father came once, stayed the night in the local pub and gave me dinner there. He charmed Eileen and the girls thought he was marvellous. He came when it was a rehearsal week, so he didn't watch a play, but I was glad to see him. He asked me if I was happy, and I said I was. For once, I didn't feel uneasy with him and he gave me news of home. Robin had left Rugby and was working on the runway for an aerodrome, which seemed pretty dreary to me, but my father said it was good experience for him. Colin was at the Beacon. Grannia had been moved out of London to a local nursing-home: she wasn't quite herself. His visit came and went like a flash.

John Christie, of Glyndebourne fame, had a house near us and used to ask us, two at a time, to dinner with him. All I can remember was his kindly interest in each of us, and the serious dinner with glasses of wine. It was meant to be a treat, and it was. The meal was particularly welcome: for weeks there had been a potato famine, which curtailed our evening meal, and we were hungrier than ever.

At one point, Eileen thought she might produce my play, *Our Little Life*, the domestic comedy I'd written when I was fourteen, which was exciting for me, but she changed her mind and it came to nothing. Instead, she gave me the lead in *Granite*, by Clemence Dane, a melodrama in four acts set on Lundy. It was my great chance, a huge part and the heroine not off the stage for more than ten minutes. I was no good in it. My only achievement in this play was that it had a song with no music. I'd write that, I said, and Bertie, in deference to my grandfather, allowed me to do so.

We took it to Ilfracombe, and after a matinée Paul Scofield and I were invited to have tea in the local hotel with Radclyffe Hall and Lady Troubridge. By now I knew − theoretically, at least − about lesbians, so I very much looked forward to meeting some. Radclyffe Hall wore a severely tailored coat and skirt with shirt and tie, shingled black hair and pearl stud earrings. Lady Troubridge wore the same outfit, except that her shirt was a blouse with a large droopy silk bow at the neck. 'Don't let Radclyffe Hall make a pass at you,' my fellow actors had said, and I went determined not to invite any such thing. I needn't have worried. They both had eyes only for Paul, and I was left contentedly to the scones and strawberry jam.

Our most successful production was a triple bill of Coward's *Tonight at Eight Thirty* plays – *Fumed Oak*, *Red Peppers* and *Still Life*. Paul was brilliant in all three plays, Joan Heal was his fellow red pepper and taught him some tap dancing for the music hall act of the fading and quarrelsome stars, and I played Laura opposite Paul in *Still Life*, later made into the film *Brief Encounter* with Celia Johnson and Trevor Howard.

Joan Heal became ill; as with my illness, nobody took much notice. I remember lying in the garden with Mavis, Joan's bedmate, and asking idly how Joan was. 'She doesn't seem to get much better,' Mavis said. A warning bell rang in my mind, and I knew suddenly I must do something about her.

She was lying in bed, very restless with a high fever. There was, of course, no such a thing as a thermometer in the house, but touching her burning forehead was enough to know that. She said she was terribly thirsty, but her throat hurt too much to swallow. I said I'd go to Eileen and she would get a doctor. But here I met with unexpected and total resistance. Nonsense, there was no need for that. She probably had a mild attack of flu. If she stayed in bed for a few days and kept warm she would pick up in no time. I looked after Joan for the next few days; changing her sheets – I remembered how much I'd wanted someone to do that for me – giving her aspirin, and trying to encourage her to drink. She got worse. Her throat, when I looked at it, was covered with a yellow crust. I went again to Eileen, who sulkily agreed to ring a doctor. He came, a shadowy old man, a locum who surveyed her from afar, and prescribed aspirin and hot drinks. I bought a thermometer in Bideford. Joan's temperature was veering between 103° and 104°F. I told Eileen I didn't think the doctor was much good and that Joan's parents should be told how ill she was. Eileen blew up: 'You really must learn not to interfere in other people's lives'. She was rattled and very angry with me for confronting her. Was she going to telephone Joan's parents? She would do so when and if she saw fit.

I got their telephone number from Joan and went to the local pub to call. They came at once, another doctor was called, Joan proved to have diphtheria and was moved to a fever hospital. There the poor girl remained in isolation for weeks. We were all tested for being a carrier, and Mavis turned out to be the culprit. None of us caught the disease, but Eileen never forgave me.

Some months later, Joan's parents wrote to me, saying that she was home and recovering slowly, and thanking me for probably saving her life. By then, at Instow, it was almost open warfare between Eileen and me.

Shortly after this, Eileen decided to split with Bertie and take some of the company to Cambridge where she proposed starting a company. I wasn't asked to go with her and returned home.

I didn't get a very good reception. I later discovered that my mother considered that my time at Instow had had a very bad effect on my character. This was probably true: we had pursued our own ends, oblivious to the war; we thought it sophisticated to say 'fuck', whether appropriate or not; we didn't get up in the mornings unless we were going to rehearse. At home there was no rehearsal. I was indolent, selfish, insular and frivolous. My mother told me I ought to join one of the services, but all I wanted was to get another acting job. I was eighteen, with all the jagged inconsistencies of a late developer. The arts seemed to me the only thing that really mattered. I was bored by the endless talk about rationing, the preoccupation with the nightly news. I continued doggedly to learn speeches from plays and practise them, once driving my arm through a window, which enraged my mother, who didn't seem to understand that this was simply a proof that my gesture had arisen from sincere work. I must have irritated her intensely but one of the chief marks of adolescents is that apart from a capacity for being hurt, they have little or no idea of their effect upon people.

When I wasn't writing, or acting, or reading, I went for long rambles by myself, collecting blackberries and trugs full of the horse mushrooms that grew so plentifully in the fields round us. I wrote long letters to Peter, and to Dosia, who was nursing in a hospital in the Midlands. Her first letter from there spoke of her first morning and being ordered to make a round of an enormous ward of soldiers to ask them if their bowels had opened that day. Their responses turned her crimson, but she said she managed.

The pressure to join up continued from my parents. Behind my selfishness about this was the real fear of being sent to an institution that might be much like a boarding-school, only worse, and the return of the paralysing homesickness, which I had by no means conquered. In hindsight, it's odd to me that neither my parents nor I ever thought of my becoming a nurse, something I think I should have been able to achieve.

Then an RAF friend of my father's got married and he and his wife spent their honeymoon at the Beacon with us. His bride, Lesley Waring, had been an actress. Lesley was glamorous, charming and funny, and I loved her on sight. It was through her that I got an offer to join the winter company of the Shakespeare Memorial Theatre at Stratford-upon-Avon, which was run by Balliol Holloway, an actor whom I'd seen in many Shakespeare plays and revered. Lesley's ancient father lived in Stratford with a housekeeper. He'd been a pioneer in the theatre: the first man to stage Ibsen in England. I was due to go to Stratford in September, but some time in August, Peter got a few days' leave, and came down to Sussex for two nights.

By now our correspondence had become more intimate. Pete told me more about himself – how he'd had a long affair with a beautiful girl but didn't want to marry her, about his friends, John Winter and Michael Bratby, with whom he used to go sailing and wildfowling before the war, about his lighthouse on the Wash where he painted and collected. He reiterated that he thought he was in love with me but that, of course, I was far too young. When young, one doesn't take kindly to being reminded of it; the general ambition is to be mature – utterly grown-up and treated as an equal.

On the afternoon he arrived, we went for a long walk and eventually rested against some haycocks in a meadow and had a long talk about this. He kissed me and said he wanted to go to bed with me, but that my age made this dangerous. I assured him that it wasn't. I had no idea what was entailed and wasn't prepared to tell him, as it would surely relegate me to the ranks of the humiliatingly young. It was clear to me that I *ought* to know. I basked in his admiration and approval and I didn't want to lose his interest, which so charmed me. Eventually, it was agreed I should come to his bedroom that night.

Pete had been given my parents' bedroom, and I had a little room at the extreme opposite end of the house. I can't remember now where my mother was sleeping – other family and friends were staying – but I do remember how every floorboard creaked, and how the danger of discovery added excitement to the adventure.

I returned to my own room in the early hours of the morning, and lay awake for some time. What had happened was surprising, but Pete had been very affectionate and gentle. It hadn't hurt very much and he'd repeatedly told me how lovely I was and how much he enjoyed it. Somehow I'd thought I'd enjoy it too, but nothing was said about that. This, I concluded was because women – and surely now I was one – did it for love, and if you loved somebody, you must want to please them.

After a repetition of that night, Pete left; or, rather, we took him in my mother's car to Lympne – a small aerodrome where he was to be picked up by a Stirling bomber to go on a night raid over Germany. I knew this was a dangerous mission, but when I asked him if he'd been ordered to go he said, no, he'd volunteered because he was interested in camouflage and also wanted to experience a bombing raid.

The airfield was so small that the commanding officer said he doubted whether such a large aircraft would be able to land. I found myself praying that it couldn't. But, of course, it did, its nose pressed against the hedge at the end of the runway. Pete gave me a quick kiss and disappeared into it. We watched it make a circuit out to sea and fly east. It was then I realized that Peter might be killed, if not on this raid then in his ship. People were being killed all the time.

We sat in the drawing room that evening listening to the news, which included the raid over Germany, and, for the first time, I felt love and fear congealing. Recent unconsidered thoughts and images came to me – of the possibility that the Battle of Britain might have been lost; of the naval chaplain who, although rescued, insisted his place was with the crew trapped below or in gun turrets and was returned to his sinking ship; and most of all, of Jean Gilbert who'd been staying with us when I first returned home. 'Jean's husband has been killed,' my mother said. She was silent all day and wept every night, as her poor swollen face, with its haunted, red-rimmed eyes, made plain. These things happened – had been happening now for months and months – and I'd been heartlessly unaware of and indifferent to them.

No longer. That night I prayed desperately for Pete's safety. I must love him or surely I'd not feel this aching anxiety? He had become my lover – something I'd never thought would happen to me – so it followed that I was now in love. When he rang the next day to say that he was back and on his way to his ship, and he loved me, I told him I felt the same.

My family liked him – to some extent, I think, they were dazzled by his charm. Only my younger brother, Colin, of whom he'd drawn a fierce little portrait, didn't seem to feel the same, but of course, I thought, from my eleven years' seniority, he was only a child.

I0

In September 1940 I went to Stratford. It was a beautiful golden autumn. I took a taxi from the station to my digs, as I'd been told to bring any decent clothes I possessed for a modern play. My digs were in a small terraced house in Mansell Street owned by an old stagehand, who lived there with his daughter, Dot. I had a small room on the first floor, which was almost entirely filled by a large iron double bedstead. My rent was thirty shillings a week; my salary was six pounds a performance week, and three pounds on rehearsal weeks. The first play was Shaw's *The Doctor's Dilemma*, with Margaretta Scott playing the lead. The other cast members were all incredibly old as a result of the war: the average age of the company was seventy. I had the small part of Minnie Tinwell, who turns out to be the real Mrs Dubedat. Early rehearsals took place on the terrace overlooking the river.

Balliol Holloway was directing. I was excited and nervous and wasn't much good as Minnie, but he was very kind to me. The first evening he took me back to his lodgings where his wife gave me a splendid tea with potted-meat sandwiches and rock cakes. Food, I quickly became aware, was a real problem. Dot provided me with breakfast, bread and marge and tea, and dinner – usually something like stuffed sheep's heart with gravy and cabbage and potatoes – at six o'clock before the performance. Aside from that, I had to fend for myself.

In those days Stratford didn't provide much in the way of eating-places. There were one or two hotels, where the meals were quite

103

out of my reach, and one teashop, where very small but delicious doughnuts cost four pence each – a ruinous sum. I couldn't buy food in shops, as Dot had my ration book. I subsisted on cups of tea and Players' Weights, the cheapest cigarettes available.

The first Friday night that I returned to my digs I was met at the door by Dot's father, brawling drunk. 'What do you think you're doing?' he said, and when I said I lived there, he yelled, 'Damn thee black, thou cream-faced loon,' and slammed the door in my face. It was a fine but chilly night. I wandered the streets disconsolately; the theatre would be closed, and I'd nowhere else to go. I was also rather frightened: Stratford was full of lonely Czech soldiers who were reputed to collect women in pairs and rape them.

Eventually, in sheer desperation, I returned to Mansell Street, hoping that Dot's father would have retired for the night. He had. Dot met me apologetically. 'It's only on Fridays,' she said. 'Just be quiet on the stairs.' Thereafter, on Fridays, I waited outside until Dot gave me the signal. On rehearsal days I used to spend the evening sitting in bed, wrapped in the slippery eiderdown, writing another play, and letters to Pete.

Margaretta, or Peggy, Scott was astonishingly kind to me. She invited me to her dressing room, and when I told her I was writing a play asked to see it. I said I'd have to read it to her, since my writing wasn't legible enough for other people. She was a good listener, and made helpful comments. Sadly, she left when *The Doctor's Dilemma* finished, and I missed her very much.

Pete came to see me – suddenly. He took me to dinner in a hotel, and asked if he could come back to my digs for the night. He was very upset about something, but he said he didn't want to talk about it at dinner. By the time we got back to Mansell Street the house was dark, and as it wasn't a Friday, it seemed worth the risk. I thought, though, that I'd better ask Dot and she was very nice about it. 'After all, there is a war on,' was all she said.

In bed, in the dark, Pete, after some persuasion, told me what was the matter. Someone he'd loved for a long time, he said, had decided to get married, and although he'd no right to, he felt utterly bereft. 'I simply had to tell you,' he said. I remembered the beautiful girl with whom he'd had an affair but didn't marry. Once when I was at Fritton, a very lovely girl had come to lunch, and she and Pete had gone for a long walk together; when she returned I thought she'd been crying. 'Poor little girl,' K had said to me, 'another broken heart.' I hadn't liked the way she said it – more like a triumph for Peter than misery for the girl. It must be the same one. Wasn't it rather a good thing that she'd found someone else so she could stop being unhappy about Peter?

It wasn't a girl, it was a man, he told me. He had loved him more, probably, than anyone else in his life, and now it was at an end. He talked and talked about it – poured out all his misery and conflict. He could see that this was the best thing for *him* in every way; it was just that he couldn't bear to think about the loss. He couldn't help feeling angry as well as miserable about it; he had to tell someone, and he felt I'd understand. 'And you do understand, don't you? You're so wise, so grown up for your age.'

I said I did: and in one sense this was true. I could understand what loving someone and being rejected for another might be like. I'd never seen Pete so unhappy – or unhappy at all, for that matter – and all I wanted to do was try to comfort him. He wept. He made love to me and said afterwards how glad he was that he'd told me and he'd known I'd understand. We got up very early in the morning and I walked to the station with him. 'Darling little Jenny,' he said, as he kissed me from the train window, 'I do love you, you know.' I walked back to my digs, light-headed from lack of sleep. I didn't feel little at all. I felt older and *needed*.

The next play was a truly frightful piece called *His Excellency the Governor*. I was to play the *ingénue* with whom the much older Governor falls in love. All I remember of it is freezing in my backless chiffon evening dress, being steadily upstaged by cunning, more experienced actors, and being described by Balliol as 'thin as a toast rack'. We were performing it because it had been one of *his* youthful successes; the actress who subsequently became his wife had played my part.

The only nice thing that happened was that Wayland turned up unexpectedly to pay me a visit. I was terribly pleased to see him. He arrived during a matinée, and could only stay a few hours. I put him in the dressing room I shared. It was pointed out to me at once that we weren't allowed men in our dressing rooms during performances. He was only there for a couple of hours, I explained, and there was nowhere else for him to go. I could only talk to him when I was off-stage and during the interval. It was lovely to see him and I felt very sad when he went.

Some of the older actors often offered to take me home after evening performances but, after being groped by two of them, I gave this up for the alternative hazard of the Czech officers who sat outside the stage door. After Peggy left I'd no friends in the company. I was feeling less and less sure of my ability to act, and the lack of food and the cold induced a kind of chronic fatigue. I got sore throats and felt generally rotten.

Shortly after Peter had stayed, Dot told me I'd have to leave. She didn't give any reason, but I suspected that her father had found out that he had stayed the night. When I told the tall blonde, Sheila, who shared a dressing room with me, she told me she'd found digs with a twin-bedded room, which was too expensive for her alone. I went to the tall Georgian house and was interviewed by a forbidding woman who turned out to be Lesley Waring's father's housekeeper. The rent was three pounds a week for the room and breakfast only, and I didn't see how I could afford it, but it seemed the only place to go.

The third play was by Maria Marten, *The Murder in the Red Barn*, and I was cast in a tiny part. Sheila was playing the lead. I'd hardly been in the new digs a week before I fell ill – a fever and another sore throat. I went to the local panel doctor who, without looking at me, reached for a bottle of brown liquid that he gave me to take. It did no good. I was too ill to go to rehearsals. Sheila was full of her part, and took very little notice of me. I think I should have starved had not kind Dot, who'd discovered where I'd gone, turned up with a covered plate of good old sheep's heart and cabbage. As soon as I could stand, I staggered into the theatre, to be told I was fired for not turning up for rehearsals. I didn't much care. I'd made no friends, hadn't had a decent part and had certainly not done much with those I'd been given. I was eighteen and a half and didn't seem to have achieved anything. All I had was a new idea for a play, the construction of which was defeating me. All I could do was go back to Sussex.

I I

I can't remember how I met Ronnie Jeans, probably through his son Michael, who'd been at Instow. But I met him with his secretary, Ray Gregerson. Ronnie had been a famous revue writer, for Charles Cochran, and André Charlot. He also wrote plays, and somebody suggested I should send him one of mine. I sent him *Outrageous Fortune*. He asked me to go and see him. He must then have been in his fifties, but he seemed very old to me. He had a quiet voice, a humorous face and he seemed kind and interested. I found myself telling him about the new idea I had, which was that different actors should play the different aspects of the major character. The idea fascinated him, and when I said I found it difficult to know how to treat it, he suggested that we collaborate.

I instantly agreed; there was a great deal of mutual enthusiasm. I asked him what he thought of the play I'd sent. He said it was good in parts, but the construction was fatally flawed, one couldn't go back on one's tracks in the second and third acts, as I'd done. This was a dreadful disappointment, and I didn't feel he was right. It crossed my mind that he might be dismissing the play because he wanted me to concentrate on the new idea. Anyway, that was what we did – for weeks and months. Ronnie had a flat in Hallam Street where I worked with him. Then we'd part, and write the scenes we had allotted to each other. He also had a house at Walberswick in Suffolk, where his wife Marjorie, who wrote novels and was 'into' Ouspensky, spent some of her time. However, the Craxtons found me a room in a block of flats near them – Acomb Lodge had been bombed and they'd been forced to move. I lived with a sad Jewish spinster, who loved music and what she called 'the little daintinesses of life'.

The play, called *Triple Harness*, was written and rewritten, but never seemed right. Ronnie took me to lunches in posh restaurants where I met theatre luminaries. I particularly remember a lunch with J. B. Priestley when Ronnie, enthusing about our play, told him the entire plot. About two years later Priestley wrote a play that contained my idea.

That winter I got a small part in a radio play and I remember John Laurie saying, 'This is such a bloody awful play I am going to play it without my teeth,' whereupon he removed them and they sat glaring at us on his reading desk. The rest of the cast smiled kindly, but I felt too new to dare to join them.

A great many new things had happened to me, but I felt it important never to look or sound surprised and thereby avoid people remarking on my youth. I was hell bent on maturity, and the appearance of it seemed the first step. Ronnie – I called him Jay – was extremely kind to me; treated me absolutely as an equal, seemed interested in my opinions and constantly told me how good I was at playwriting. I remember telling him that I'd not put Esquire on envelopes in my letters to him, as I thought it was silly; that men should be allowed to have long hair, and wear gold earrings – like Shakespeare. I always sat on the floor during our work sessions, and my clothes, such as they were, were awful. I had very few, in any case, since clothes coupons had come in while I was still growing. I remember a leaf-green woollen dress, bought at C&A for three pounds, which I wore to restaurants with him. Otherwise I had two pairs of trousers, some Aertex shirts and a sleeveless pullover, knitted by my nine-year-old brother in rainbow-coloured wool that arbitrarily changed violent shades every few inches. I also had a whitish coat, my only one. I bit my nails, and still wore the good old Tangee lipstick.

Sometimes I went back to Sussex for weekends. My mother had a studied lack of interest in the all-important play, but otherwise she didn't obstruct me. She didn't like my association with Jay. I think eventually I arranged for them to meet, and his age seemed to reassure her.

I told Jay about Pete, and he simply said, 'Well, you have all the time in the world.' Pete had been transferred to the Coastal Forces to command a motor torpedo boat. He now got more frequent though shorter leaves, and I joined him at Fritton several times that winter. Once I went straight from Walberswick to Fritton to find Bill alone, as K was in London and Pete had not yet arrived. I felt rather nervous of an evening alone with Bill, but need not have worried: he was a gracious and warm man.

Shortly after that Christmas, my parents insisted I should make some attempt to join the Wrens. *Triple Harness* had failed to get a producer: at one point an impresario called George Black had seemed interested, but then he died. It was finally clear to me that I had to join the war, so I went to a recruiting centre. Up until now nobody had ever attempted to test me or the methods by which I'd been educated. The following interview cut new ground from under my feet.

The lady who examined me was a Wren officer who sat at a desk in Westminster while an unsteady stream of English girlhood queued to pass her fire. In a few short minutes she'd discovered I hadn't matriculated, or even passed my School Certificate; I'd hardly been to school, had no languages and couldn't even type. On being asked what I *had* done, I mentioned the theatre and play-writing. The first she regarded with suspicion, and the second she dismissed as an occupation. As there were dozens of candidates behind me all looking as though they'd passed School Certificate, she announced that the only vacancies in the service were for cooks and stewards and that she didn't think I'd be suitable. I opened my mouth to say I could cook, but her watertight attention was thankfully on the next girl. My terror of community life boiled in my throat and I left. It seemed too much for the Wrens to accept me at such great mutual sacrifice.

I went back to the country and told my family that the Wrens didn't want me, and it was decided that I should be of no use for anything until I'd learned to type. It seemed extraordinary and sad that, after years of education, I couldn't do the only thing I was any good at, and that to do anything else required further training.

The next morning I went to get some shoes repaired. The cobbler worked at the end of the village in a little hut. He was a kindly, tragic-looking man and very good at his job. He was deaf and dumb, but could read and write, and he had a slate on which one wrote one's requirements. He would then examine the shoes and give a written estimate of time and cost. Our smiles that morning were stretched to embrace the whole greeting, and I wrote my needs — new soles and heels — on his slate.

He turned my shoes absently in his hands — he wasn't really looking at them — seized the slate suddenly, wrote furiously upon it, and pushed it into my hands. It read 'You lovely girl like princess me like marry you.' Then there was a pause and '?'. I looked up, his face was lit with intention. He pushed the pencil into my hand and rubbed the slate clean carefully for my reply. I wrote, 'You very kind. Can't marry anybody must learn typing for war.' He read it, and his face changed slowly like the sun going in. He shrugged his shoulders very gently, and wrote, 'Tuesday. 12/6 don't get bombed.'

'Thank you, I will try not to get bombed.'

He smiled with great sadness and underneath my writing put 'Goodbye Goodbye' and I stroked the words on his slate to say it back.

Walking home, it was clear how very little I knew and how little I understood of anything I'd thought I knew. Even learning to type wouldn't help me with his feelings, which meant that either education, as I'd thought of it, wasn't education at all, or it was merely a preliminary, at its best, for something that was going to last for the rest of my life.

The best thing about learning to type was that Dosia was also coming to London for the same purpose. We enrolled together for Pitman's intensive course conducted in a gaunt house near Lancaster Gate in Bayswater Road. Dosia had found us a flat in Warrington Crescent, Maida Vale. It belonged to a musician and consisted of one large room, with a bed, a grand piano and a table and chairs, a tiny kitchen, an equally small bathroom, and a sort of cupboard in the entrance hall, with no door, in which I slept. We called it Mon Debris and loved it. We gave dinner parties there – frozen cod, stewed rhubarb and nothing to drink. We invented a butler called Chortle, who was always away or ill when wanted, and who made expensive demands on us, leaving imperious little notes. We were light-hearted and full of silly jokes that we thought deeply amusing. I remember Dosia telling everyone at a party at the Admiralty that I was a famous Swedish pianist but unfortunately had no English.

She had a huge capacity for making friends. Soon we were going to parties, having parties, going to the cinema, eating out at a small Cypriot restaurant, all with people Dosia hardly knew and I not at all. Our parents paid our modest rent and my allowance was upped a little in acknowledgement that I was at last doing what was expected of me. Every weekday morning we toiled off to Pitman's where we sat for an hour typing very slowly from cards propped up on our typewriters to hide the keyboard, and military music forced us to keep a plodding time. Then we had an hour of grammalogues – an early version of shorthand and much harder work – and every now and then an hour of double-entry bookkeeping, which I never mastered. I enlivened the time there by getting Jay to send me telephone messages as Lord Marlinspike, which were pinned to a baize board to be read during lunch hour. There were three more hours in the afternoon before we were free to enjoy ourselves.

Sometimes my father took us to the Gargoyle Club, off Dean Street, and we had a proper restaurant meal and danced. We went high in the building in a tiny claustrophobic lift and emerged into a bar whose walls were covered with drawings by Matisse. The walls of the restaurant and dance floor were lined with little squares of mirror glass, which made it much larger and more glamorous. David Tennant, married to Hermione Baddeley – the very funny actress who used to do revue with Hermione Gingold – owned it. The club was frequented by the literati; I remember Dylan Thomas and Philip Toynbee usually rather, or very, drunk. I can't imagine what we wore; I do remember that we'd both bought little crêpe dresses in 'Marina blue' from C&A for three pounds, and we used to draw stocking seams on our legs.

We also went often to the Players' Club in Covent Garden, where Victorian music-hall songs were performed and Leonard Sachs was the spontaneously witty compère. Occasionally, we slipped out for a National Gallery concert if Denis Matthews or Nina Milkina or any of our other friends were playing. In the interval we'd go down to the basement where we'd buy cheese and sultana sandwiches, served as often as not by Joyce Grenfell. When she had qualified, Dosia was going to be secretary to the Bishop of Willesden, and I? I'd no idea what lay in store for me, the typing pool at the Admiralty had been suggested by someone.

We had hardly been at Pitman's for a week before we both noticed that there was one student utterly unlike the others. She was far older than any of us, very tall, with iron-grey hair that fell carelessly across the side of her high forehead. She had the most ravishing smile, became a beauty on the instant. She had a kind of seductive liveliness, an inward amusement at anything we said. She carried her remarkable appearance with an assurance that fascinated both of us. She was Austrian, she told us, a refugee now living in England. She was, or had been, married to a Dutch doctor and had spent much of her married life in Malaysia. She had three children who were here too: Matthius was training to be a doctor, Brigitte was married and lived in Cambridge, and Tony was at Gordonstoun School. She knew Kurt Hahn who'd started a similar school in Germany. She was a painter, and she wrote. Her name was Marie Paneth. She used to enjoy amazing and shocking us with her stories, and when she'd finish we'd cry, 'Oh, *no*, Marie! Surely not!' and she'd laugh and say, 'Oh, *yerse*! That is how it was.' We felt excited and proud to know anyone so unusual and exotic.

When Pete rang to say that he was coming to London for a night as he had to go to the Admiralty, we decided to give one of our dinner parties for him. Two of Dosia's friends called Kit and Freddie, who worked in the Admiralty, were asked and they brought a quiet girl called Philippa. We used our entire meat ration in a shepherd's pie, and Dosia made a pudding, a kind of whip, from Carnation Milk. We even managed to buy some drink. We had a very jolly party – played charades, rang people up at random in a competition to see how long they could be kept on the telephone, and explained that Chortle had gone to a nursing-home as he was afraid he might be ill. When the others had gone and we'd cleared up the room enough for Dosia to go to bed, Pete and I crammed into my small bed in the cupboard and he told me that in a month he was going to get three weeks' leave. 'So I thought this might be the best time for us to be married.' I can remember saying, 'Do you *want* to marry me?' and his replying, 'Darling, I wouldn't be asking you if I didn't.'

I was stunned, flattered, dazzled. I'd not thought about marriage at all, except to conclude, years before, that nobody would ever want to marry me. I hadn't thought about it much then, and I didn't now. 'Unless you feel that you're too young' he said.

That did it. 'I shall be nineteen in a month,' I said. 'Of course I'd love to marry you.'

In the morning we told Dosia. Pete rang his mother, and we both spoke to mine in Sussex. Everybody seemed pleased, and Pete left for Portsmouth, where it was arranged that he would spend an evening with my father.

Two days later, the telephone rang, and thinking that it would be one of our jokey friends I yelled, 'Yes?' into the telephone, doing my best imitation of a char.

'This is *The Times*,' a measured voice said. 'Is it true that you're to marry Peter Scott, the son of the famous explorer?'

Later that morning, as I walked to the bus to go for the last time to Pitman's – my mother insisted there was so little time that I must come home at once to prepare for the wedding – I felt suddenly uneasy. Something inside me said, 'Do you really want to do this?' but I stifled it. Of course I wanted to do it. I was unbelievably lucky to be marrying a brave and famous man. I'd be Mrs Peter Scott, safe from all the things I'd pushed so far down I need no longer acknowledge them, safe from my mother's disapproval, and safe from joining the Wrens. We'd have our own house, and I'd cook and give parties for Pete when he came home on leave and one day the war would be over and I'd be married to a painter and he wouldn't talk about guns any longer, and I'd encourage him to paint and draw people more than birds.

So it went. During the next few weeks there was hardly a moment to think about anything but the wedding, which was to take place in London at a church in Lancaster Gate – it wasn't practical for people to travel to Sussex. My mother concerned herself with my clothes and took me to Curzon Street, where Chris Ampthill designed and made my wedding dress of off-ration white lace, a soft turquoise dress and short-sleeved jacket to match, and two pinafore dresses, one of blue linen and the other of a pretty flecked tweed. Underclothes had to be made of parachute silk and curtain netting. I think people must have kindly given me clothes coupons even for this. Shortly before the wedding Pete gave me thirty pounds to buy an evening dress, which I did; it was of pale grey satin damask with grey roses and had a tiny waist and enormous skirt – the nicest dress I have ever had.

Bill Kennet thought that it would be patriotic to have a dry wedding but my father – white to the lips at such a thought, my mother said – refused. There were to be four hundred people at the reception, which would take place at Claridges Hotel.

At some point I went down to Fritton and Pete was there, and everyone made much of me. Bill gave me a gold wristwatch, my first watch, and K gave Pete a turquoise and diamond ring for him to give me to mark our engagement. I remember feeling rather sad that he'd not chosen it himself.

The only person who was appalled at my impending marriage was Jay. He wrote me bitter letters telling me I was far too young, was throwing away a promising career, and was letting him down. I wrote saying I didn't see why it should make any difference to our relationship, but he replied that it would, and it did. He didn't come to the wedding, but sent a Revelation suitcase with my new initials on it.

Dosia reluctantly agreed to be my bridesmaid. I didn't know until years afterwards how much she hated being dressed in furnishing material. My uncle Hubert, one of my mother's twin brothers, who'd become a clergyman, was to marry us, and his daughter Frances was the other bridesmaid. Wedding presents were pretty scarce at that time. I do remember receiving a crate from an admiral that proved to be full of glass so shattered that it was impossible to tell what it had been in its original state. 'Thank you so much for all that lovely glass,' I wrote as tactfully as I could.

The wedding took place on 28 April 1942. I spent the night before in a dingy hotel near the church with my mother. There was a good deal of tension. When she asked whether I knew about the 'difficult' side of marriage, I said coldly that of course I did – there was no need to talk about it. She subsided with relief.

The next morning, when I was dressed, she went on to the church with Colin. My father came to fetch me. He looked very glamorous in morning dress, and brought a half-bottle of champagne with him. 'Good for the nerves,' he said. He opened it, and we each had a glass. 'Here's to you, darling,' he said, and gave my shoulder a little squeeze. He seemed shy suddenly – something I'd never seen. Before we left, he picked up my hand and kissed it, 'You look lovely, darling,' and I knew that whatever I looked like he would have said that: affection bloomed.

The only thing I'd arranged for the wedding was the music. My friend Geraint Jones – a wonderful organist and later a conductor – let me choose what he was to play. I didn't want Wagner, but chose Bach's organ sonata in E flat, a lovely welcoming piece. K had brought a bouquet of rather spiky white flowers from Fritton, which was very kind of her but disappointed me. James Lees–Milne and Wayland were two of the ushers, Barbara and Phoebe – both in the Wrens – came and so did much of my family. Everything I'd read about in novels happened. Pete put the ring on my finger, and pushed back my veil. I signed my new name for the first time, then walked down the aisle – a sea of faces on either side. It was all as shadowy, as glassy as a dream.

Outside photographs were taken by friends and newspapers. I thought I looked like a new potato in white lace and said so when I saw *The Times* the next day.

The reception went on for a long time. I stood for ages with Pete, my parents, K and Bill, receiving congratulations from people most of whom I didn't know. There were a great many naval officers, and various luminaries who were part of the Kennet world – Joyce Grenfell, who had written saying that she would gladly come and dance in a pew, Malcolm Sargent, an old friend of the family, and mysteriously Gillie Potter, a famous radio comic and music hall star, who made an impromptu speech. Eventually, speeches over, toasts drunk, I was whisked away to a bedroom with a very grand marble bathroom to change.

We were driven down in the Kennets' car by Comber to the Lacket, Bill's cottage in Lockeridge near Marlborough. It had been let to T. E. Lawrence's mother, but had been made available for the first part of our honeymoon.

A kind village lady received us. She'd made us a dinner of roast chicken, and there was a bottle of white wine. I shivered in one of the two pretty chiffon nightdresses that my father had given me for birthdays past. I knelt to say my prayers, Pete, studiously tactful, ignoring me, and after 'Our Father' and prayers for my parents and brothers, I prayed I might be a good wife.

PART TWO

I

It's odd how little I can remember of that week. It was a beautiful fresh green spring. We hired ponies and went for a long ride over gentle hills that had harebells and cowslips, and Pete knew every bird. We talked about our future; Pete said his lighthouse wouldn't be big enough for a family, and we'd have to find somewhere else. In London, I said, I didn't want to live in the country away from the theatre. Well, anywhere I liked, he replied.

He was full of admiration for how I looked, and for almost anything I said, and I basked in his indulgence. 'We're going to be so happy, you can't imagine,' he said – often. He told me about keeping dozens of crayfish in the bath with mud, and how splendid his mother had always been about these ventures. I told him how, as we went home on a bus after my mother had taken me to a film about his father, she'd pointed to Leinster Corner and said that was where Captain Scott's widow now lived. I'd wept copiously throughout the film and burst into tears again and asked if we couldn't see her to tell her how sorry we were? He talked about his ship, and his ambition to have a good war, and I tried to be interested in the differences between a Rolls-Royce engine and an Oelikon gun.

Sex remained very much as it had been at the beginning, except from my point of view it no longer hurt. He told me repeatedly how much he enjoyed it, and what a wonderful girl I was. I played up to being wonderful, to being what I thought was expected of me. This was marriage, and I was now grown-up.

121

But in intimacy, I now see, we didn't progress. He'd make a pre-emptive remark such as 'I'm just a sentimental old thing' or 'I'm just a painter with a vulgar facility', and I'd defend him against himself. He never said, 'Actually I have to have courage. I have to live up to my father, and sometimes I'm afraid I won't be able to manage it.' I never realized what a serious and informed naturalist he was. He never realized I'd no idea about my own sexuality and that my continuing ignorance of it might prove a danger to us both. As he was so much older, I assumed that he knew a great deal that he didn't.

Whenever he talked about his war, I relived the terrifying thought that he might be killed. It became something I couldn't bear to think about, and yet couldn't ever dismiss. This was common, of course, for thousands of people married to anyone in the front line of the war. I quickly learned that in Coastal Forces, it was the officer and the coxswain who were most liable to be killed, just as the rear gunner in a bomber was deemed most vulnerable. This was the emotional shadow cast over those few, otherwise carefree days; the domestic shadow others lived under was unknown to us both.

We spent the rest of Pete's leave at Fritton, where everything was very jolly. Wayland was home from Cambridge, and we played duets and charades, and K was pleased that Pete seemed so happy, and everybody was affectionate and kind to me. I felt one of the family.

Pete had been told that he was to command a new kind of Coastal Forces vessel – a steam gunboat, now being built at Cowes. Six were to be constructed, and Pete was to command the flotilla. To Cowes we went and were installed in the Gloster Hotel. Except the one night before my marriage, I'd never stayed in a hotel, and I was disconcerted when Pete leaped out of bed at seven a.m. to get to his ship by eight. 'How do I have lunch?' I asked.

'Darling, just go downstairs and ask for it. May be back for dinner.' And he was gone.

There was an enormous amount of shipping in Cowes Roads, and thousands of troops were billeted on the island. I was the only wife staying in the hotel, and when I went out I was undone by the host of whistles, catcalls and ribald asides. I crept back to the hotel. The lounge had ancient copies of the *Field* and *Country Life*, and it didn't take long to read them. At precisely one o'clock every day, a single German aeroplane came over, and every ship in the area blasted off at it. Pieces of glass would drip slowly from the entrance hall and the noise was deafening. There was lobster for lunch, however, which was cheering until I found that there was lobster every day – and in the evening as well. I felt lonely and homesick. Pete sometimes came back for dinner, sometimes not. After dinner, when he was in, he drew me, a series of ink drawings.

After a few days, he said a boat was coming to pick him up at five p.m., and if he didn't come back within three days, I was to go home to Sussex. This was the preparation for the Dieppe raid, although I didn't know it then. I can remember the icy fear when I said, 'Three days?' I knew that if he didn't come back it meant he'd been killed.

He came back that evening: the raid had been postponed because of the weather.

Somehow, Pete came across a whole lot of hawk moth cater-pillars. These he kept inside a muslin sleeve on poplar branches. It was part of my job to find and supply the branches. I enjoyed this; it was something to do.

At some point, Pete's boat was finished, and K came to Cowes to launch her, but I went down with flu and couldn't be at the ceremony. I thought I'd have liked to launch Pete's boat, but felt I wasn't grand enough, and I'd not been asked.

While his boat was doing her trials, we moved from the hotel to the home of Uffa Fox, the well-known sailor and boat designer, who'd built the 14-footers with which Pete had twice won the Prince of Wales Cup. Uffa was a dark, hirsute, eccentric man of great friendliness. 'You can stay as long as you like,' he said. 'Glad to meet Mrs Pete.' His house had one unusual feature: it had no roof because of the bombing so the top floor was out of commission, 'But go anywhere else you like,' he said.

While we lived there, I used to cook Pete and Uffa breakfast – Uffa had a supply of eggs and bacon. I also got a job at the local Mission for Seamen: I was to strip and remake the bunks in which they slept. The sheets were grey with use, and smelt of engine oil and sweat; they often contained empty beer bottles and the odd evil-smelling sock. I felt queasy, but at least I was doing something useful.

I shopped for food to cook for Uffa and Pete, but one day in the greengrocer's, without the slightest warning, I fainted and came to with my head half in a sack of potatoes. Somebody kindly took me home; it was a few minutes before I remembered where I lived. When I told Pete about it, he smiled and said, 'You know what this means, don't you?' I didn't. 'It means our son is on the way. Oh, darling, I'm so pleased. Mummy will be *delighted*.' He rang her that night.

I didn't faint any more, but I felt very sick in the mornings, and the breakfast fry-up was too much for me. I couldn't face the seamen's bunks either. Pete, who spent more and more time at sea, suggested that perhaps I should go home to Sussex for a bit. 'Have a nice quiet time,' he said. 'You need looking after.' The homesickness I'd been trying to ignore reasserted itself and was overwhelming. 'Don't cry, darling, it'll only be for a few weeks until I know where the flotilla will be based.

'You can take the hawk moths with you,' he added. 'They're going to need more and more food before they pupate.'

And so two days later, he put me on the little train that went from Cowes to Ryde to catch the ferry. There was unforeseen trouble in the train. The caterpillars, very active now, escaped from their muslin sleeve and were soon rollicking all over the furry upholstery, which provided them with excellent camouflage. The sleeve was in a shoebox that fortunately still had its lid wedged underneath it, and I spent a frantic twenty minutes trying to locate and recapture the creatures. There had been about ninety of them, and I only managed to collect about half before the train drew into the station. The others were left to their fate. On the ferry, I spent most of the time trying to punch holes in the shoebox lid so that they could breathe, but my only weapon for this was a kirbigrip. Pete, I thought desperately, would have collected all of them or, better still, would have noticed earlier that they'd found a tear in the sleeve.

At home, the Beacon now, everything was just the same: the shabby old sofa in the drawing room, the old satinwood piano, the ancient gramophone in its laurelwood box, and the stark cold bathrooms whose taps frequently emitted rusty water. I remembered the dark gunroom – cold even in summer – where the telephone was kept, the noisy pump that provided electricity, and the children's bedrooms, bare and stark as dormitories. I was now promoted to a little room of my own at the end of a long passage. For the first time since I'd lived there, I wanted to make this room my own, with all of my own things in it. Our London house had been shut down, more or less cleared out by my mother, and I asked her for the things I'd kept in my room. She'd got rid of most of it, she said, and put the furniture in store. 'My books?' I said. 'My Delft china candlesticks? My gymkhana cups? My treasured theatre programmes? My dressing-up box?' They'd all gone, except for some of the books and eventually the candlesticks. The feeling that all, or nearly all, of my childhood had been stripped away without any consultation kindled an urgent need in me that still lasts now, to make the places that I live in wholly mine.

In other ways my mother was much mellowed towards me. She adored Peter, and took to the hawk moths with enthusiasm.

My father had given me no money when I married, and my dress allowance had also stopped. I'd no money, and hadn't really noticed, but K sent me a hundred pounds out of the blue: she said she thought all women should have some money of their own. She must, I think, also have talked to Pete about it, as he then suggested an allowance of fifteen pounds a month. This was far too much,

I thought, I really wouldn't need it, but he insisted. He was always generous. I bought material to have two smocks made by a lady in the village: clothes for pregnant women simply didn't exist in those days, and we must all have looked hideous. I also bought yards of white Viyella that my mother cut out and taught me to smock in white embroidery cotton. This was for Falcon, as the baby was invariably called, after his grandfather, Captain Scott, who'd been called Con. She, like everyone, was delighted I was having a baby. I hid my fear of and anxiety about motherhood and the guilt that I didn't have the maternal feelings that were expected of me.

Shortly after I returned home, the Dieppe raid took place. As the distant rumbling of gunfire began one fine morning and continued all day, there was no doubt that something was happening. I knew that Peter would be in the battle whatever it was, and sat anxiously on the front lawn facing the coast – the sea was nine miles distant. I was skinning two rabbits and pegging their fur on to two boards to make a pair of gloves for Colin and to take my mind off the danger Pete was in.

Pete went on the raid as part of the naval back-up. It was the first attempt by the Allies to land in France, and it failed with a terrible loss of life – notably among the Canadian forces. Pete came back to Sussex for a couple of days and said the flotilla was to be based at Weymouth for further trials, and I should come to Weymouth and live in the hotel there.

The hotel was large and grand, and Pete stressed how lucky we were that he could afford to have me there; most naval officers had to do without their wives. However, he was out all day, and I was back to hotel life, bored and lonely. I went for walks in the town, and bought books to read as my chief occupation. I felt lazy and tired, and there were hours and hours to get through until he'd come back for dinner, and even that didn't happen sometimes, as there were night exercises. Then one day he came back with an officer called Alan Lennox-Boyd, who was very jolly and charming. Pete said the naval joke was that Alan had been assigned to motor torpedo boats, called MTBs, because he'd a tendency to run into other ships and they thought that the smaller boat he had the better. He often turned up at the hotel and was very nice to me. He was married with three little boys. Pete had told him I was pregnant, and he once asked me how many children I wanted. I said six, because I thought it would be so nice for them. I didn't add that I had wanted to get used to being married before I started a family. This was something I'd tried to discuss with Pete, but he'd laughed and said I'd love the baby when it arrived. I knew also that K was very keen on having a grandson -the pressure for me to get on with it had begun on our first visit to Fritton after our marriage. Pete told me in Cowes that K had advised him to put a pillow under my knees after intercourse to increase the likelihood of pregnancy and this he repeatedly and tenderly did.

We stayed at Weymouth for six weeks, and then the flotilla was moved again, this time to Newhaven. I was sent home, while Pete found a small house to rent in nearby Seaford. I was accompanied to Seaford by my cousin, Audrey Tuck, whose mother was very keen on her joining me – I suspect she hoped that Audrey would find some nice young officer to marry. It was lovely for me as it meant I had agreeable company.

The house was small and dark and heavily over-furnished with pieces of furniture too big for the rooms. It had a large, unkempt garden. The whole place had a desolate air, but it was my first house and I was excited at the prospect of settling down. The address was 3 West Downs Road, and one morning the road was heavily spattered with worms. I spent ages picking them up and putting them where they would not be run over. Audrey, who thought this rather silly, stood by kindly and watched me. We cooked meals for Pete when he could come to us, and sometimes he brought a fellow officer, but they were always married.

One evening, when we'd been there about six weeks, Pete came back and said the flotilla was being moved again – the next day, but he had to go back to his ship immediately after dinner. I burst into tears, which upset and, I think, annoyed him. 'It seems too much that we can never stay anywhere,' I sobbed.

'Pull yourself together, darling, make the best of it.'

In the end he couldn't even stay to dinner, as they sent a car for his immediate return. This was just as well, as it turned out. Audrey and I finished up the contents of the larder for supper, which included some rather old ham. We were up all night being sick, and in the end my mother came and fetched us home because we were too ill to manage trains.

In September when Pete had leave, we went to Fritton for a week. K was very keen on my swimming in the lake, because she said it was good for the baby. I felt shy about it, because I'd begun to bulge, but the cool feeling of weightlessness was wonderful, and everyone was so pleased about the bulge that I soon got used to it. She decided that after the war she would present me at Court, and that I'd look very well in the dress she'd worn for the purpose, which turned out to be a peacock-coloured brocade, rectangular in shape. I felt I looked horrible in it – and finally she conceded that it didn't look right on me. 'I made it myself,' she said. 'It was quite unlike any other dress there.' I explained I'd already refused to be presented and didn't see the point of it, but she said it was different now. I think that this was an attempt on her part at affection, since she told me that she'd only known two women well, Isadora Duncan and Tamara Karsavina, 'And now there is you – my son's wife.' I remember feeling that it was unlikely I could live up to the two famous dancers.

By now I'd got to know K more clearly. She was of medium height, with an unremarkable body, rather sturdy and shapeless. She had 'bad' legs and her hands were like a man's – strong and well shaped. Her most beautiful and striking feature was her large head with her hair cut very short, shingled at the back, which accentuated its shape. She had a fine complexion, with a large, well-shaped nose, and beautiful eyes of a blue between gentian and cornflower that looked at everything with a penetrating intelligence. If the family made jokes that seemed too silly, or that she didn't understand, she would laugh with some discomfort and say, 'Silly ass.'

She told me fascinating stories. When she was in Paris, studying with Rodin and living in a small room on the Left Bank, someone came and told her that an English poet had died in a neighbouring hotel, and would she come and help to sort out his books. This she did, and was given one for her pains. The poet was Oscar Wilde. She'd been a great friend of T. E. Lawrence, and once let me have breakfast dressed in his Arabian headgear.

Wayland was very like her, with exactly the same shaped head and blue eyes. She told me that she'd had proposals of marriage from both Bill and Lawrence at the same time, and that she'd gone abroad to make up her mind. For weeks, she said, the newspapers speculated that she was going to marry J. M. Barrie, but there was no truth in that story. She loved dancers, and beautiful bodies. When I knew her she'd begun to have heart trouble, and wasn't sculpting any more; she spent much of her time on a sofa doing wool embroidery that she devised freehand.

She had an inexhaustible interest in everything that Pete was doing and he delighted her by telling her every single detail. From these conversations I learned more about his job in the Navy. I discovered that the merit of the new steam gunboats was silence; you could hear the engines of an MTB long before it was hull up on the horizon. The disadvantage was that its steel plating was so thin that a single well-placed bullet could put it out of action.

It was during this time that Derek Leaf, a commander of an MTB operating from Yarmouth, was killed. He had come to lunch at Fritton only a week before. K invited his widow to the next lunch she gave. The girl sat silently throughout the meal, looking stunned, as though she hardly knew where she was, even though a little mechanism in her involuntarily produced acceptable responses to Bill when he talked gently to her. I wanted to cry. When she'd gone, K said, 'She was always a pretty girl, but really she looked quite lovely in her grief.' A jar.

2

When Pete's leave came to an end in the autumn of 1941, I journeyed to London with him where we parted, he to his boat and I to Sussex, where I spent the rest of the winter. It was decided that it was no good my continuing to follow Pete from port to port: much better if somewhere was found in London.

That winter was very cold, or perhaps it was simply the Beacon that was so cold. Grannia, doubtfully in her right mind, was now in a nursing-home near there and we visited her when petrol allowed. She lay in bed, fat and restless, but her face was still beautiful and her complaints continuous. Colin was at Summerfields, a prep school fairly near. A few people came to stay, and my father occasionally turned up at weekends. But much of the time it was simply my mother and me. She'd acquired five hens called Flossie, Ruby, Queenie, Beryl and Connie – because my mother disliked those names and didn't care much for hens. They were to provide me with a few extra eggs. As I was pregnant, I got an extra pint of milk a week and priority eggs – that is to say, any left over after the rationed ones had been claimed. I got four of those during the nine months. During that winter, my teeth went to pieces, and I had to pay endless visits to Tunbridge Wells for fifteen fillings – or 'stoppings', as they were called. My mother also took me to London to see our family doctor, who'd brought Colin into the world. I'd begun to feel sick again, and he said I had a mild liver complaint, but that nothing could be done about it until I'd had the baby. It was on this occasion that I went to Harrods to buy a bear for Falcon, as I felt that no one should start life without one. While I was there, it occurred to me that he would also need a suitcase, and I chose a very handsome leather one. 'What initials, Madam?' they asked. I thought quickly. Although it was generally assumed I'd have a son, there was always the chance I might not, and in conversations with Peter on the subject, I'd said if it was a daughter, I wanted to call her Nicola, which seemed to me a beautiful name. I'd recently read Rosamond Lehmann's *The Weather in the Streets* in which there is a very beautiful girl called Nicola Maude. 'You've chosen Falcon, so I think I should be allowed to choose the girl's name,' I'd said to Pete, who agreed.

So, 'F. or N. Scott,' I said.

'I beg your pardon, Madam?'

'Here, I'll write it down for you.' I did, and he went away with a the-customer-is-always-right look. I'd chosen a charming toffee-coloured bear with a reliable expression. The next thing was his name. Colin immediately said it must be Roper, after his best friend at school, so Roper he was and remains to this day, in spite of Colin coming home for the holidays soon after and saying that Roper was now his best enemy.

I was simply longing for the baby to arrive – for it all to be over, was how I thought of it. My back ached, I often felt sick, and I looked awful in my gathered skirt and clumsy smocks.

My mother and Aunt Antonia decided that, as their parents' house was empty, it might suit Pete and me to have it at a very low rent of two pounds a week. It was 105 Clifton Hill, St John's Wood, a small, detached Gothic villa with a large drawing room, a small dining room leading off it, two large bedrooms and one small on the first landing together with a bathroom, and two little attics on the top floor. There was also a cavernous basement and a small, square back garden.

My mother came up with me about four weeks before the baby was due. The house still contained much of my grandparents' furniture, but the décor was drab and dirty and much in need of repair. The baby and nurse were to have the sunny bedroom that looked on to the garden, and I set about painting it white. My mother – this sort of thing brought out the best in her – helped me. I struggled up and down ladders imbued with a kind of feverish nest-building energy. We managed to get the nursery and the drawing room painted before I gave up, feeling too sick to do anything.

My mother had procured someone from Sussex to come as cook, and there was a daily woman called Mrs Jessop who came to clean. It was still a stage in the war when it was taken for granted that there would be servants – not so many of them, nor necessarily such good ones, but none the less the work would be done by people paid to do it.

Three weeks before the baby was due, Pete came up for some leave. My mother, who had been going to Sussex the following day, went out for the evening. After we'd had dinner, he said an early night would probably be a good thing. I'd begun to dread what was now routine on these occasions. 'I'm too fat,' I said.

'Nonsense, darling. I love you however enormous you are.'

I gave up after that. My mother had said two things to me that had impressed themselves deeper than I knew at the time. The first was 'Never refuse your husband – whatever you feel,' and the second, which I was to remember in the near future, 'People of our sort never make any fuss or noise when they are having a baby.'

Pete went to the Admiralty, and my mother went out for the day after an early breakfast. I stayed in bed. Still, I was going to have quite a nice day. I was going to *Gone With the Wind* with Dosia in the afternoon, which she had off from the Bishop.

We met at the cinema and sat through the long, hugely enjoyable film, and Dosia came back for supper. It was arranged that she would lodge with us, and my heart rose at the prospect.

I felt very achy, tired and sick again, and told Pete I really didn't feel well. I was having small, clutching cramps at irregular intervals, but they didn't hurt, and I thought that it was just fatigue, with which I'd become very familiar. Pete said, Never mind, I still love you, and did.

The next morning, my mother said a music publisher was coming to lunch as she wished to discuss the possible printing of some of my grandfather's unpublished manuscripts. He came, and we had lunch, and now I seemed to be getting pains about every half-hour – not bad, but sharpish and disturbing. I waited until the publisher had gone before telling my mother. She was going to Sussex that afternoon, and advised me to stay in bed until Pete came back.

That night, the pains began in earnest. This time they hurt rather, and they seemed to come about every fifteen minutes. Pete rang the nursing-home where I was to have the baby. It was eleven at night, and they told him that it was doubtless a false alarm since the baby wasn't due for three weeks but that he'd better bring me in. He drove me to the nursing-home, a gaunt stucco building about seven storeys high just off Kensington High Street, delivered me to the nurse on duty and left. I wanted to ask him to stay, but he was gone before I could get up the courage.

The nurse took me up innumerable stairs to the top of the house. 'We weren't expecting you, so this will have to do.' It was a small room. She told me to get undressed and I crept into the freezing bed. She had a look at me, and said it was probably just hysteria, she'd give me something to help me sleep and I'd doubtless be going home in the morning. I swallowed the pill, and she left. I lay rigidly in the dark, and the pill took over and I fell asleep.

Some time later I woke because the pains were so bad. They seemed to have got much worse and lasted longer. And then I realized that the bed was wet and sticky. When I turned on the light to look, it seemed to be full of blood. The baby has died, I thought; I was really frightened now. I rang the bell by the bed, rang it several times, but nobody came. Eventually I staggered on to the landing and shouted for someone to come, and eventually they did.

It was the same nurse, clearly displeased with me. 'You'll wake everyone up, shouting like that. Let's have a look . . . You're having the baby all right – of course it's not dead, that's just the show.'

I'd no idea what she meant by this, and was too cowed to ask. What courage I had was fully occupied with the extraordinary surges of pain. 'I'll have to shave you next,' and then, 'I'll get someone.' Shave me? It was then I realized I knew absolutely nothing about what was going to happen. I'd read a bit about childbirth in novels, of course, and a review of one where the writer had said how bored he was with the cliché of women straining at bedposts. Wayland and I had once had a conversation when we tried to define the cliché, and decided that it was when one recognized its truth by experience. Here I was, recognizing one of them. Then I stopped thinking.

The nurse came back with a bowl of water and shaving equipment.

'Pull up your nightie, then.'

I lay, unable to see what she was doing below the vast mound of my belly, and when she hurt me – a petty little pain – she said the razor blade was blunt and it couldn't be helped. She went, and was replaced by a sour-looking elderly nurse, who'd clearly been woken up to sit with me since she yawned a lot and then placed herself in a chair in a corner of the room furthest from the bed and read a paper.

An air raid began, the usual droning and anti-aircraft guns popping away and distant explosions. The only good thing about the pains was that having reached a crescendo, when I felt my backbone was being split in two, they slowly receded and there was a period of calm. After what seemed like hours, I asked her how long this was going to go on. Without looking up from her paper, she said, 'I'm sick of people asking that question.' Hours passed. I reached the point where I almost wished a bomb would drop on me and put an end to everything. At last, when I could see the thin line of light at the edge of the blackout curtains, and the pains were

With my father (c.1933). His charm was real, because it was unconscious.

My mother, a dancer in the
corps de ballet (c.1917) of
Diagehlev's Ballets Russes.

Enrico Ciccetti's class; the teacher whom all ballet dancers revered. Visiting ballerinas from the Ballets Russes would come for classes with him. This drawing shows members of the class including Ninette de Valois (Edris), Mimi Rambert, Lydia Kyasht and Lopokova. My mother was called Jane.

With my brother, Robin, and Si, my grandfather's monstrous mongrel (c.1929).

At Lansdowne Road, aged about eight (c.1931). I was steeped in Andrew Laing fairy-tale books, and the problem of living half by fairy formulae and half by the strict justice demanded between cousins and siblings occupied me for some years.

My father loved sailing (c.1930). He was one of the most gregarious people I have ever known, and behaved, at the slightest encouragement, as though it was his birthday.

My father's mother, Florence Howard, with the reprehensible Si.
She was invariably called the Witch because she had such an
unwitch-like nature.

My father's father, Alexander Howard, almost always called the Brig,
because he had never been in the army.

The Beacon, our family's holiday home in Sussex (c.1927). It stood on the top of a hill and was called the Beacon because beacon fires had been lit on the site since the arrival of William the Conqueror.

Home Place, my father's parent's house, 3½ miles from the Beacon.

My mother with Colin, shortly after his birth (c.1932).
His face was the colour of a pale tomato and his wispy
damp hair grew in all directions. I loved him on sight.

Edith Somervell, my mother's musical mother.
She was called Grannia by the family.

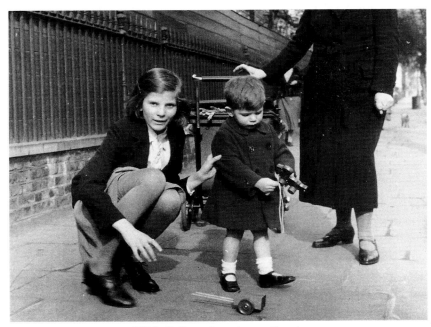

With Colin at Lansdowne Road.

A very small selection of family at the Beacon, Robin is two in front of me
and Colin is in the first pram. Colin's nanny is in the white hat.

Peter Scott and Lady Kennet, his mother, known as K.

Peter, my first husband (1942).

After my wedding with Peter Scott (1942).

My portrait in *Country Life* (1942) at the time of my marriage to Peter Scott.

Above: With Peter and K
(c.1943).

Wayland, Pete's brother,
drawn by Pete (1940).

Pen drawing of me by Pete
at Cowes (1942).

The naval production of *The Importance of Being Earnest* at Anglesea (1942).
Bored with life as a naval wife I suggested that perhaps I might produce the play.

Number 8 Edwards Square. The house, built for refugees from the French Revolution, was pretty.

With Robert Aickman at
Covent Garden.

At the publication of my
first novel (1950).

On the *Ailsa Crag* with Robert Aickman and Anthea and James Sutherland.
I grew to love canals and narrowboats for their secretive beauty and the way
they slipped though large industrial towns and into country.

Cecil Day-Lewis (c.1936).

so awful that I couldn't help gasping, someone brought in a black rubber mask that they put over my mouth. They said it would make it better. It didn't have the slightest effect. I said it didn't seem to be working and they took it off. 'It's broken again.' I asked when the doctor was coming and they said he was on his way.

Jock Ledingham had been our family doctor for years and was famous for his skill in delivering babies. I'd seen him only a month before when he'd said the baby was the wrong way round and had gently manipulated my tummy with his hands and put the baby back into the right position. When he finally arrived, I was so glad to see a familiar face and someone I could trust that my eyes filled with tears of relief. 'I'm so *thirsty.*' I'd been thirsty for hours. He put a glass to my lips and as quickly removed it and said when the next pain came I was to push. This happened three or four times with increasing agony, and just as I was going to protest that I couldn't do it again, he put a pad over my face and I was out.

When I came to it was to see smiling faces above me – the nurses and Jock – all looking very pleased. 'You've had a lovely little daughter,' someone said.

'Where is she?'

'She's being washed and dressed.' It was ten a.m. on 2 February 1943, and Pete came into the room carrying a white bundle that he put into my arms. I looked at the tiny crumpled pink face, frowning with sleep – this mysterious, completely unknown person – and then at the faces above me, which seemed full of expectation that I'd be radiant, joyful. But all I felt was an immense, over-whelming fatigue. Pete said how lovely she was, and I agreed. Then they took her away. If *they* had all gone away, I thought, I might get to know her, have her to myself, but even during that thought I fell asleep. The sleeping pill, the first I'd ever had, had battled all night against the pains and now came into its own.

They kept waking me up and pouring cups of tea and water down me 'to bring the milk in'. It came in all right, but poor Nicola, premature and probably as tired and sleepy as I, didn't want to drink it. Countless times they put her to my breast, and pinched her to wake her up, and she turned her head away and cried. My breasts became agonizing, they produced a pump, but that, like the rubber mask, proved to have something wrong with it. On the day that Nicola was born Jock had been called up to the forces, and his wife, Una, also a doctor, had taken over his practice. On the second day after Nicola's birth I screamed if anyone touched my breasts, then couldn't stop crying. When Pete, on one of his visits, said he had three more days' leave and was going to Fritton, I cried more than ever. 'You really must pull yourself together, darling,' he said, and I recognized the irritation I'd provoked when I had cried on leaving Seaford. 'K is sending a hundred snowdrops and a hundred pounds for Nicola,' he said, before he left.

I was in the nursing-home for a further week. I never saw Nicola except when she was screaming. They'd bring her in a quarter of an hour before feeding time and leave her in her basket howling out of my reach 'to encourage the milk'. There was no problem about the milk, I had enough for two babies, but when I suggested that perhaps I might feed one of the other babies in the nursing-home whose mothers had no milk, they looked shocked and said it wouldn't do. My father sent me some flowers, which made me cry because I wished that Pete had done that instead of simply going away and leaving me. When, after ten days there, I was allowed to go home to bed – you were meant to stay in bed for three weeks then – it was with a monthly nurse. We soon discovered why poor Nicola had been screaming so much: her bottom was raw, as her nappies hadn't been changed anything like often enough.

It was a great relief to be home, but the monthly nurse wasn't much better than the nurses in the home had been. She, too, adopted the practice of keeping Nicola in the nursery until she started to cry with hunger, then placing her out of my reach to howl for ten minutes before her feed. When she'd drunk enough, she fell asleep. For the first month of her life I had no time with her that wasn't fraught with this four-hourly trauma. I became afraid of her. I'd not wanted her enough and was no good as a mother.

An extraordinary letter I got from the wife of one of my father's friends reinforced this feeling. It was long, and began by congratulating me on having the greatest joy known to women. 'Now, at last you will understand that everything we have to go through in marriage with a man is recompensed by this great joy – the only reason for marriage.'

Eventually, the monthly nurse left. She'd not enjoyed her time with me, frequently making it clear that she was used to grander establishments where there was a proper staff. The only good thing she did for me was to introduce me to Tampax. She'd also been impressed by ancient Cousin Susy's visit, in a very large old car with a chauffeur and a companion.

My aunt Ruth had procured a young nurse for Nicola, who'd been trained at her Babies' Hotel. Rose was nineteen – the same age as I was. She was pretty and very serious about her job. It was she who taught me how to change nappies and bath Nicola. We were shy with one another, but I was grateful for her expertise. Also she didn't bring Nicola in to cry before feeds. On her days out I had some time alone with Nicola when she was awake. We could look at each other and I could talk to her. I felt very tentative about this, afraid I'd do the wrong thing, which, of course, sometimes happened. Usually she would regard me with her slaty blue eyes in a wondering, appraising manner, but the first time she smiled I was so excited that I kissed her, whereupon she squirmed away from me with an expression of distaste. She doesn't love me, I thought. How could she? I wasn't good as a mother; I didn't seem to have the feelings that were expected, and while I could conceal this from other people, I couldn't deceive her. Alone with her I'd say things like 'I do *like* you, and I do want us to be friends.' But I felt guilty about her, as I'd never felt about anything else in my life.

3

When Nicola was about two months old, we went to Fritton. We went by train, which in those days took four hours. Once before I'd travelled with Bill from Liverpool Street where he was met by the station master in his top hat and we were conducted to a splendid empty carriage, but this time we had no such advantage, were crammed into a compartment crowded with servicemen. About three hours into the journey it became clear to me that Nicola was hungry and I needed to feed her, so I did. Everybody in the compartment behaved perfectly about this; a few tactful smiles and otherwise they took no notice.

K was overjoyed to see the baby. The whole family loved babies, and Nicola bore a marked resemblance to Pete, with a slightly turned-up nose and a little dimple in her chin. I remember Wayland asking me how I felt and saying that, according to the wedding service, I was supposed to be like a fruitful vine, and look at me, one little grape. Thereafter, he always called her 'the Grape'. But when I innocently let out that I'd fed Nicola on the train, I could see that K wasn't pleased. There was a lunch for a lot of old admirals (as I called them – they can't *all* have been admirals), but they were certainly, in my terms, old. After we had eaten, K suggested that I should bring Nicola into the drawing room to feed her, she was sure that nobody would mind. The thought of a lot of old men eyeing my breasts filled me with nausea, and I escaped to my bedroom. Why was it all right for the admirals to watch me – lecherous old sods – and not all right to feed Nicola in the train

138

when she needed it and there was nowhere else to go? These rifts were beginning to appear between my mother-in-law and myself. She also made it obliquely clear that as I'd not had a son I should return to the charge as soon as possible. The thought appalled me. It was lovely to go about in my normal clothes again, not to feel ill, cumbersome and unwieldy, but I felt guilty.

Wayland had a friend – a fellow Stoic, an old boy from Stowe School – staying with him. Charles Newton was an exuberant eccentric: his mother was French, a widow, and he used to ring her up pretending to be Proust. He was in the Army and very light-hearted about it. He would do imaginary charges down the lawn ending in an exaggerated fall when he would shout, 'Death of Charles!' He cheered me up as I had bouts of intense depression about motherhood. 'What's it like, having a baby?' he asked me one day.

'I don't know, I haven't been doing it long enough,' I answered, and he looked at me carefully and dropped the subject.

K didn't think much of my capacity in that direction. I think she was keen enough on babies to detect my failure in this respect. It would have been so far from her deepest convictions I don't think she would have been able to understand it. It was 'unnatural', as indeed I felt too. To be unnatural is like a sin, judged wrong by other people and, worse, by oneself. I see now that Nicola and I had the worst possible start in life, and that most of what happened to me wouldn't happen now, but this is hindsight, which, by its nature, is no good at the time. I can say now, and could have said for many years, that I love my daughter as much as I love anyone in the world, but the bad start led to much unhappiness for both of us, and I, being the elder, must accept the blame.

I think now that things might have been different if there had been anyone who I could have trusted enough to talk to about all of this, but there wasn't, or at least I could think of no one. I was certain that any confidence I made about my lack of maternal feeling would simply be treated as unnatural or mad, and I couldn't face either indictment.

Something happened when I was at Fritton that further undermined me. I had gone for a walk in the woods with K. She was talking about Peter, and then she suddenly said, 'I suppose you've realized now that Pete only married you to have a son.' I said, no, I hadn't, but my heart began to pound. She looked me straight in the eye and then said, 'If you ever make Pete unhappy I shall want to stab you. I should enjoy doing it.' The woods around us were chequered with flickering sunlight and I suddenly thought of the Iroquois in Conan Doyle's book *The Huguenots*, their terrible savagery and courage, and the same sense of chill recurred. Then she put her arm in mine and said, in a quite different voice, 'Oh, Jenny, you're very *young*. Let's go *home*.' And we went.

Two other incidents occurred during the first two years of my marriage. I can't place them exactly in time, but they were both illustrative of the mutual distrust that was building between us.

One was when I was lying in bed with Pete, who'd gone to sleep. The bedroom door opened noiselessly and, silhouetted against the light in the passage, I saw K standing motionless. I waited to see whether she would speak, but after a few moments she retired, and the door was shut again. I remember I actually felt frightened of her, and lay awake for a long time afterwards wondering whether she would come back and what would happen if she did.

The second was when I came in to breakfast late; everyone else had had theirs. Pete was away at the time, and on my plate was a letter from him. It was addressed to me and it had been opened – quite carelessly, no steaming of the gum from the envelope, but torn, and I knew at once that K had opened it and presumably had read the contents. The envelope was addressed to me; it was *my* letter. This time I didn't feel afraid, I felt furiously angry, but I was too craven to confront her. Instead I told Pete the next time I saw him. His reaction was far from reassuring: she always liked his letters, he said; when he was away, she always opened them, and he didn't mind. He couldn't, or wouldn't, see any distinction between a private letter in his hand addressed to me and any other letter that people might write to him. His handwriting, I must say here, was beautiful, absolutely clear and distinctive. 'Couldn't you tell her not to do that?' He answered easily that he was sure she wouldn't do it again and so far as I know, she never did.

It was a great relief to return to Clifton Hill. Dosia was installed and she attracted friends like a magnet. Geraint Jones and his first wife Margaret came to stay. They had a daughter of about the same age as Nicola. Rose was on holiday, so Margaret and I struggled with the business of getting through our babies' day. This was far more arduous than it is now.

To begin with we had dozens of nappies to rinse, soak, rinse, boil and dry. This had to be done every day, as in spite of two dozen Turkish towels and two dozen Harrington squares there was always the danger of running out of clean dry ones. At three months my milk began to give out, and I began weaning Nic. For some reason I was dead set against giving her tinned or powdered baby food, as I felt that fresh cow's milk would be far more healthy. This had to be diluted, sugar added and the feeds made up. When a feed was needed the bottle was reheated in a pan, then the milk tested on the back of the hand for the right temperature. Then there was the ceremony of the morning bath. This happened in the nursery, in a tub that was filled with jugs of warm water from the bathroom. Nic enjoyed her bath, but hated having her hair washed.

In the afternoons, Margaret and I wheeled our babies round the streets – we were too far from a park. Margaret was a frenetic, intellectual girl, no more handy than I with all the paraphernalia, and when, by seven thirty, we got Isobel and Nic fed and to bed, and could turn our weary attention to knocking up some sort of supper, Margaret would look at me and say, 'What have we *done* today?'

'Nothing, except get them both a day older.'

Rose eventually left to get married when Nic was a few months older, and my mother found a nanny from Sedlescombe, a neighbouring village in Sussex. Bombing raids had started again that autumn, and I'd taken Nic down to Sussex, because every time I took her out in her pram in London an air-raid warning went off.

I was very much on my dignity meeting Nanny Buss for the first time; she wasn't young like Rose, but had been a nanny for years. However, my dignity was punctured before I'd said a word to her by Colin bursting into the room and saying, 'I say, Jinny, I suppose you know that Nanny is at least twice your age.' Nanny Buss was gentle and kind and pretended not to notice. She was a wonderful nanny, very untidy but everything was kept spotlessly clean, and she adored Nic from the moment she saw her until she died many years later. I returned to Clifton Hill with a light heart.

Inmates there had proliferated. Apart from Dosia, there was my cousin Audrey, who had a job in London and went home at week-ends, and Denis Pipe-Wolferston, a friend of Wayland. Wayland and he had met when they were both ordinary seamen, and Wayland had made some disparaging remark in Greek about the man drilling them, to which Denis had instantly replied in kind. Denis had some job in the Admiralty. Apart from the four of us, many people came to stay – some quite regularly. Roland Oliver, another Stoic and Cambridge friend of Wayland, came almost every weekend. He worked at Bletchley and never mentioned the nature of his work. He was appalled by my ignorance, and was the first person to make me a reading list that I remember began with the Miracle plays and ended with *Middlemarch*. There was Peter Tranchell, another Cambridge friend. He turned up one afternoon – I'd never seen him before – and said, 'Is Wayland here?' I said no, he wasn't, but that he did come sometimes. 'All right, I'll wait.' And he did – for days.

He was a composer, and sat in my grandmother's huge chair enveloped in a mothy fur coat – the house was always cold – writing music. He introduced me to the works of the novelist Ronald Firbank, and the Russian/Armenian composer Aram Khachaturian. He was very funny and had a faintly devilish appearance. We called him Mephi, and he used to write me long, nonsensical letters in his large, sprawling hand. Sometimes the paper would be scorched and he would put 'pardon my enthusiasm' in the margin.

My grandfather's grand piano was still in the drawing room, and was much played, by Dosia, by Wayland, by Mephi, by me, and sometimes by Denis Matthews when he came on leave. He was having a wearing time. By then, the RAF had accumulated a remarkable orchestra of musicians. The Griller String Quartet were among them but as they were all aircraftmen, they had to be conducted by an officer, who turned out to have been a conductor for a band at the end of a pier, and knew nothing very much about classical music. 'What do you *do*?' we asked Denis.

'If I am playing a concerto, they follow me, otherwise they take no notice.' Denis, who looked like some charming nocturnal creature with ginger hair, large, myopic brown eyes and a surprisingly delicate little mouth, was always white, but now had dark circles under his eyes. He was playing all over the country, he said, on ghastly pianos with no time to practice.

Then there was Wyndham Goodden – again introduced by Wayland. He knew the Kennet family and he also worked in the Admiralty. He'd married an intensely pretty American girl, an heiress with the looks of Grace Kelly. They had two children, but then the marriage came unstuck. Pete did a very good drawing of Catherine, as Wyndham called her – her real name was Judy, but this didn't suit Wyndham's intensely romantic disposition. He wrote poetry, sonnets mostly. I still have two that he wrote for me, and he wrote a very good poem that illustrated François Couperin's beautiful piece for recorder, 'The Nightingale In Love' – we were all mad about Couperin. Among many others, he also introduced me to Mozart's concerto K499 on gramophone records, which became and remained my favourite Mozart concerto.

Audrey and I had become air-raid wardens. This consisted of wearing an immensely hairy dark blue trouser suit and a tin hat, counting people into their shelters when there was a raid, going to lectures about what to do in air raids, and drinking bright brown tea in a basement flat in Abbey Road. I do remember one lecture that took place somewhere near Oxford Street. We must have observed, the lecturer said, that the tops of all pillar boxes had been painted a pale green. This was because a new gas might shortly be dropped by enemy aircraft on the city, and we'd know when this happened because the paint would change colour at once – to blue, I think it was. This went on for a long time, but eventually reached the stage when the lecturer asked if there were any questions. What were we to do, I asked, when we saw that the paint had changed colour? He looked shocked. There was nothing we could *do* about it, he replied, nothing whatever. Our gas masks wouldn't be a blind bit of use to us *then*.

Only once did Audrey and I have to deal with what was called an incident. It was during the time of the V1, the pilotless aircraft that buzzed away overhead, then ominously ceased to make any noise as its engine gave out and it fell. This happened one night when Audrey and I were at home. When the buzzing noise stopped, there was a menacingly short silence and then an enormous crash. We weren't on duty that night, but the explosion was so near that we put on our tin hats and went out. It was soon clear that the V1 had come down in Mortimer Crescent, about a hundred yards from our house. Wardens and firemen were already on the scene, and the shocked inhabitants of the partially wrecked house were being helped out of it. I was assigned an old lady in her nightdress and slippers. We were in the hall and I had her by the arm, making what I hoped were comforting noises, when she suddenly eluded me and started to hare up the stairs that we'd been told weren't safe. 'My son's photo!' she cried.

There was nothing for it but to follow her. I caught her on the first landing and almost dragged her down, cursing under my breath with fear. She was bleeding from her shoulder, and we took her back to our house, bandaged her up and used up our sugar ration on cups of sweet tea.

The staircase collapsed and the house was boarded up for demolition at a later date.

Ever since I'd left the domestic-science school, Seer Green, I'd remained in touch with Jessie. In her letters back to me – she could just manage to write in a cramped spidery hand – she nearly always referred to her amazing visit to the Christian hostel in Ealing. Now that I had a house, I thought, why should I not arrange for her to come to me? She would have to sleep in the dining room and that would mean shifting whoever was sleeping there to the drawing room, but there was a basin and a loo on the ground floor. I told the others what I wanted to do and everyone was agreeable. I rang up Miss Laidler to ask her how I could transport Jessie, who clearly couldn't go by train. She said she would arrange that part of it.

I wrote to Jessie, who demurred, saying she would be too much trouble. Of course not, I wrote back, I should love to look after her. A date was arranged, she was to come for a fortnight. I got very excited at the prospect, arranged the room, put flowers in it, and a comfortable chair for her visitors. I knew that all the household would spend time with her, and there were double doors that opened from what would be her room to the drawing room, so that she could hear music and not feel cut off from us. I decided I'd make a wonderful nurse; she should have everything she wanted. There was also, I have to admit, a certain feeling of complacency about it all – here I was, at last doing something useful and good.

She came in summer, a beautiful day. The driver picked her up out of the back seat of the car and carried her to the bed in the dining room and I brought in the rest of her luggage, which included, among other things, a bedpan wrapped in brown paper. She will tell me what to do with it, I thought, with faint misgivings. When the driver had gone I looked at her lying awkwardly on the narrow bed. She was just the same; the dry frizzy hair round her pale face, her lovely eyes glowing with excitement, her useless feet in rather pointed shoes with single straps turned towards each other, her twisted hands emerging from the cuffs of her usual brown overcoat like gnarled little roots. I kissed her and said how glad I was to see her at last.

'It's so good of you, Jane, to have me. I do hope I shan't be a nuisance,' she said.

'Of *course* you won't,' I replied.

I asked her whether she would like some tea, and she said she would like to get out of her coat first. That proved extremely difficult. The divan, on casters, slid away from the wall, as I battled with the coat. 'No, no, you must get one of my arms out first,' she said. I know I hurt her getting that wretched coat off, and by the time I'd succeeded, the pillows had slid from the back of the bed to the floor and she was perforce lying on her back. I got some piles of music and wedged them against the bottom of the bed, having retrieved the pillows. 'I'll need more of them,' she said. We had no spare pillows. Owing to the number of people sleeping in the house, we were down to one each. I rushed upstairs and got my pillow and Dosia's – she often slept with me in the double bed called the Hump. When Jessie was more or less propped up I again offered tea. But when I came back with it she said she was afraid she was cold and I remembered the hot little room in which I'd always seen her. I got the eiderdown off my bed, covered her with it, and poured out the tea. 'It's not hot enough,' she said. 'The one thing I do like is really hot tea.' I got some more. I thought this was fussy. I had absolutely no idea how important things like that could be for someone as helpless as she. It was my first lesson.

Nursing her – something I'd imagined myself doing with romantic smugness – proved awful. The first time she wanted a bedpan she had to issue me with a series of querulous instructions on how to hoist her on to it. 'I have to take laxatives, not to get constipated,' she said. The smell made me retch, and I realized as I removed the bedpan that I'd have to clean her up. I hadn't had the foresight to provide the means to do it. Another mission over the house to find a bowl in which I could put warm water, bring paper and a towel. During this she lay with majestic dignity – she was used to it: it happened to her every day.

By then some of the others had come back from work, and I introduced her to them. This was a great success, and my spirits rose. 'It's wonderful, Jane, to meet all these people you've told me about.' Everyone was very nice to her and she loved the company. But then, after supper, I had to undress her and get her into a flannel nightgown, clean her top teeth which were false and had to be taken out and soaked in Milton for the night, and another bedpan had to be brought. Then, poor thing, because she couldn't turn over or move in bed, I had to settle her in what she felt would be the most comfortable position. I put one of my grandmother's cowbells between her hands, in case she wanted me in the night, and left my bedroom door open so I'd hear it. That first night I hardly slept for fear I should miss her ringing.

During the next week I learned a little better how to nurse her, but my revulsion increased. I like to think I concealed from her the degree of it, but I probably failed there too. She was both intelligent and sensitive, but except for wanting the boiling tea, she'd learned a kind of saintly patience. I had become unable to eat, and I remember going out into the back garden and pouring out to Wayland how dreadful I felt about my inadequacy and how disgustingly smug I'd been at the outset about the whole enterprise. It seemed to me, I wept, that I was peculiarly selfish and unfeeling, did he not think so? 'No, I think it's just tired and sensitive,' he said, with a look of affection that went to my heart.

I'd asked Jessie when a doctor had last looked at her. She couldn't remember, so I went to my doctor, still Jock Ledingham's wife, Una, at her practice, which was in their home in Ladbroke Square.

Una listened to me kindly, and then asked if anyone was nursing her. 'Only me.' There was an awkward pause, and then I added, hardly audible, 'And I'm afraid I'm very bad at it.' Lack of food and sleep made me start crying again.

'I'm going to make you a tomato sandwich,' she said. 'All my family can manage a tomato sandwich whatever they are feeling like.' She did, and I ate it, and felt much better.

'I'll come and see your Jessie,' she said, 'and if there is anything I think can be done for her, I'll put her in the Royal Free for a week.' So in the end Jessie only stayed with me for a week, and then went to the Royal Free Hospital, where I visited her every day until she went home. She seemed happy there, and said they were very kind to her, and she thought that they'd helped her. She was affectionate and grateful and kept thanking me for arranging it. But then, and for years afterwards, I felt that it had all been a great failure of love on my part. I had arrogant ideas well above my station in this regard; and when it came to the point, I was too selfish and frivolous to put others' misfortune and pain above my own squeamishness. I had grandiose ideas of myself that bore no resemblance to my actual nature. However, this insight didn't restrain me from wanting things for myself – to have a good time, be admired, and gain affection.

4

During the summer of 1943, I fell in love with Wayland. I hardly noticed it was happening, but he, who now had a job at the Admiralty, came more and more often to the house. All the kinds of conversations I'd never been able to have with Pete, I could have with him. He fitted into the household like the most important bird in the nest, whereas when Pete came on leave the atmosphere was always strained and awkward, Pete gallantly trying to keep up with our silly jokes and behaviour.

To begin with I wasn't very much alone with Wayland. We would all go for a picnic on Hampstead Heath, visit friends of Dosia's who lived in the Vale of Health, walk home through the dusty shabby streets singing invented pieces of Handel oratoria with words we made up. We went to the Arts Theatre, and to cinemas and to cheap little restaurants. We picked up American soldiers in the Underground and brought them home for supper. Dosia and I had a game that consisted of her collecting bishops and I collecting admirals. As she still worked for a bishop, she met others, and I met admirals through the Kennets. There were points for how senior they were. We played a lot of silly games like that.

People were falling more seriously in love. Denis Pipe-Wolferston became engaged to a friend of Dosia's called Penelope Gough. She was a lovely girl, but a surgeon had screwed up one side of her face, so it was particularly good when Denis said he loved her. Audrey was going out with a mysterious man called John Rideout, a Chinese scholar who taught at London University.

'I say, Jane, I used to think you were rather soppy about Peter, but I do now see what it's all about.'

And, most important of all, Dosia met Barry. Barry Craig had been a friend of my uncle John at the Slade. I'd first met him when I was very young at Home Place when he was married and had a serious little girl called Ming. His wife had left him for someone else, and he was on his own. He was a good deal older than Dosia, a good painter both of portraits and landscapes, and he had the same kind of funniness as my uncle John. He and Dosia hit it off at once.

So, love was in the air. Gradually Wayland and I began to see each other alone. I'd bicycle down to the Admiralty at lunchtime, we'd eat sandwiches in St James's Park, and I'd toil back to St John's Wood, sometimes strap-hanging on the backs of lorries in Edgware Road. He came to stay at weekends. The first time he kissed me I discovered what physical desire meant. Our feelings for each other were – nearly always – counterbalanced by guilt. We always knew it was an impossible situation, that it could only end sadly and badly, but I was his first love as in a sense he was mine. If the others in the house noticed any of this they remained tactfully silent. That summer, Wayland used to rent a boat on the Thames just outside London, and we'd sometimes go for a weekend, taking Colin as unwitting chaperone. We also occasionally spent nights in my bed, the Hump, which in the end led to sex. We were both so overcome by guilt, then and subsequently, that in my case, I have no distinct memory of it. Wayland has since told me that *he* remembers it.

We decided eventually that we *had* to tell Pete about this. I don't know what we thought would happen but it was as least as terrible as we could have imagined.

The next time Pete came on leave, Wayland came to lunch, and afterwards, in the drawing room, we told him. He was at first incredulous, then appalled, and then very angry. He talked at Wayland about me, until Wayland said, 'You're saying all these things about her as though she doesn't exist.' Our only defence was that we couldn't help it, but that only added fuel to the flames. Pete treated us as though we were unspeakably disloyal children; he was breezy as well as furious. We should be ashamed of ourselves, and it must all stop at once. The scene went on for hours, until Pete said he was going out to dinner and that Wayland must leave the house with him. They went, and I cried myself into a stupor. I couldn't imagine what would happen next, except I knew it would be awful.

It was. Pete came back in the evening. He'd dined with K and I knew at once that he would have told her all about it. His ship was going to be based at Holyhead in Anglesey and I was to accompany him there by train the next day. I wasn't to attempt to telephone or write to Wayland ever again, and he'd been told the same. By now Pete had resorted to a kind of sulky self-pity. How could I do that to him, how could I be so wickedly disloyal? I didn't know, and said so. There were more tears and he said he simply couldn't understand it. I must know that he loved me, and it was pretty difficult to fight a war with that sort of thing going on behind his back. I said again and again that I knew it had been wrong and that I was very sorry. But sleepless in the dark, I thought he didn't love me as I knew Wayland did.

The Station Hotel at Holyhead was an immense Victorian pile of dark red brick, carpeted corridors and dreary bedrooms. There had barely been time to pack, let alone say goodbye to all my friends in the house. Dosia assured me that they'd look after everything, and Audrey said how nice it would be for me to have more time with Peter.

It wasn't nice, at all. I was back to lonely hotel life with the added anguish of missing Wayland every single waking moment of the empty days. It rained nearly all the time. There were no other wives in the hotel and Pete was out all day. When he came back he was still very angry. He bedded me doggedly every single night, which I found more and more unbearable. I remember once bursting into tears after one of the joyless occasions, and saying that he was digging his own grave. In the daytime, I went for solitary

151

walks. I longed more than anything to write to Wayland, but at least I kept to that promise.

Holyhead was a port for the ferries going to and from Ireland, and the hotel had been built to accommodate the travellers. The ferries continued but now the harbour was full of naval shipping, mostly Coastal Forces who were training for the eventual invasion. The town was a steep, grey little place and most of its inhabitants were bilingual in Welsh and English. There were no amenities, except for pubs; there wasn't even a decent bookshop. To begin with I walked into the town and on to the small mountain behind it, had lunch on my own with a book, and spent the afternoon lying on my bed sleeping. Sometimes in the evenings Pete would take me to fellow officers' boats, where we'd drink gin and they'd talk about naval matters. Then we'd climb up the slippery weed-encrusted iron ladders from the boat and go back to the hotel where we'd have dinner and grey coffee in the cavernous lounge before going to bed. Days passed in this manner.

Occasionally, there were letters: from my mother telling me about Nicola, about Robin starting to train as a Spitfire pilot and being sent to Arizona, and one saying that Grannia had died in the nursing-home. I remember writing to her about that, and getting the most affectionate reply from her I'd ever had. I'd tried in my letter to write a sort of portrait of my grandmother, recounting all the good things I could remember about her: her beauty – even when she was old; her lovely voice when she read aloud to me; the way in which she could arrange one branch of cherry blossom in a jar and make it look completely perfect; her little bell ringing every day at the same time to summon the wild birds to be fed; the encouraging letter she'd written to me about my first story . . . Writing; I'd not written anything for a long time, but now all I wanted to do was write to Wayland.

During those days – perhaps it was a week or two – I felt paralysed, as though I was caught in some web of despair where the slightest movement would either unravel it, hurtling me into some abyss even more awful, or tighten its hold on me until I should be literally suffocated by despair. There seemed to be no way out. At some point, some self-preserving instinct intervened: I had to do something, take the risk and make some move, however small. This wasn't brave: somewhere, in the back of my mind, I was afraid of going mad. I discovered that a band of women – it may have been the WI – were making camouflage nets in the town. I asked if I could join them and was accepted.

The work was very dull. Huge nets were let down on rollers from some bar in the ceiling on to which we had to tie strands of green and khaki pieces of cloth, at random intervals. The work was in the mornings only, and I did it for some weeks. Even this activity was an improvement. Outside I felt more sanguine, but inside I was hardening. I knew now that I didn't love Pete in the way that I should, and rationalized this by blaming him for his present treatment of me.

Then something else happened – out of the blue – that had a profound effect on me. Pete came back one evening to say that someone he'd known slightly before the war who was the agent for some neighbouring large estate had a young wife who'd just given birth. She was ill: he had to go away on business for a night, and didn't want to leave her alone with a sickly baby. Would I go? An hour later the husband came to fetch me in his battered little car, and we drove through the rain for what seemed like miles. We stopped at the beginning of a drive where there was a small lodge. He took me upstairs to the bedroom and introduced us. She was called Myfanwy. The midwife would be coming first thing in the morning, he told her, and your mother is coming later in the day. This is Jane Scott who is going to spend the night with you. Then he went.

The room was lit by just one small lamp, but I could see that Myfanwy was ill. She was very pretty with dark hair and enormous glittering eyes and she was throwing herself about the bed. Her nightdress was half off one shoulder and exposed her breasts –

blue-veined and very swollen. 'He won't take anything from me,' she said. 'He will die,' and her eyes overflowed.

'Where is he?' She drew back the sheets. A tiny, heavily swathed baby was lying against her. 'I'm trying to keep him warm,' she said, 'but he will die if he won't take the milk.' He will die from not being able to breathe, I thought. I said I'd get her something to help her sleep and that I'd look after the baby for the night. There was a tiny bathroom at the head of the stairs, and to the right of it was a small second bedroom that I could see had been prepared as a nursery. It had a cot and a small single bed in it. All I could find in the bathroom was some aspirin. I got a glass of water and made her swallow them, saying with all the calm authority I could muster that this would make all the difference. 'You *will* look after him? You will not sleep and leave him to himself?' She had a pretty Welsh accent. I promised that I wouldn't, picked up the baby and laid him on a chair while I tidied her bed. She seemed relieved by my promise, and turned painfully on to her side – I knew how that hurt – to settle for sleep. 'I am so *tired*,' she said.

I took the baby into the next room. It was icy cold. The only thing to do was to get into bed and keep him in my arms. He was the smallest baby I'd ever seen. After I'd got into bed, I realized that the only way I could keep him warm was directly against my skin. I pulled off my jersey and the shirt underneath it – in those days I didn't wear a bra – unwrapped him from his shawl and unbuttoned the little jacket that he wore underneath it. I held as much of his body as I could against mine, and covered the rest of us with the shawl. He had a pinched little face, very white, but he wasn't asleep. His eyes roved over my face unseeingly. His tiny hands were clenched and he seemed too weak to move them. Perhaps he *is* going to die, I thought, and then I thought that I must not even think this. 'You're going to be all right,' I said, and other things of this kind. At one point his eyes stopped roving, and he seemed to look at me, which made me feel a great love for him, and I told him this. He made a little mewling sound, and then, very slowly, his eyes

shut and he fell asleep. But *I* must not, I thought; at that point I'd
no idea how difficult this would be. As his face slowly became the
palest pink and I could feel that our warmth was becoming mutual,
I started to feel more relaxed and the temptation to sleep began.

It was a very long night. Twice, he woke and made small petu-
lant sounds, turning his head this way and that, and I knew that he
was thirsty. This meant getting out of bed, fetching water from
the bathroom and heating it in the kettle that was fortunately in the
small room. There must also have been a bottle with a teat, because
I remember that, back in bed, I squirted a little of the water on the
back of my hand to test the temperature as I'd been taught at the
Babies' Hotel, then squirted a little of it into his mouth. His face
contorted to an expression of astonishment and distaste, and then,
with his eyes on my face, he accepted a little more. At least the cold
of getting up had woken me for a while. Twice more this happened,
and in between I held him closely, *willing* him not to die. Whenever
he was awake, we stared at each other. He was majestic in his frailty.

It was still dark when I heard the midwife's car stop outside.
I got up and quickly pulled on my clothes as she came bustling up
the stairs. Myfanwy had slept. The midwife went down again to
make her some tea, she sat up in bed and I gave her the baby. 'He
is all right?'

'He's fine.'

'I must thank you for keeping him for me,' she said, very sweetly.

I cycled back to Holyhead on a borrowed bicycle. It was barely
light, and raining. I'd been aching from staying in the same position
for so long, but now I felt as though some great weight had been
lifted from my heart. Love, which I still thought of as the most
important thing in the world, hadn't deserted me. I was good for
some part of it at least.

By the time I got back to the hotel I was soaked and famished.
I went straight into the dining room, where the rather prissy wife
of one of the officers was breakfasting with her husband. She'd
already been staying a few days, and I knew that she disapproved of

me. '*You* look as though you've had a night on the tiles,' she called across the dining room.

'Yes, I have,' I answered, not caring what she thought. I ate an enormous breakfast, went upstairs and fell into bed.

When I woke, several hours later, it was with the memory of the tiny trustful face that I'd probably never see again. The thought occurred to me that I'd never had that sort of time with Nicola, but it all seemed too late now. Whenever I saw her it was Nanny whom she loved, and quite rightly. I'd never been good with her. Guilt, that dreary and lethargic sensation, rolled down with the easy familiarity of a blind.

After that, I got ill, with one of my frequent sore throats, and Pete said it would be better if he slept aboard his ship until I was better.

When I recovered, I found that the camouflage netting had come to an end, and looked about for something else to do. The Port Amenities Liaison Officer – the Palo, he was called – was a nice man, and when I suggested that perhaps I might produce a play with the Navy, he agreed at once, and dubbed me Assistant Palo. Honorary, of course. There was a convent in Holyhead, and the nuns were prepared to let us have the hall for the performances. It was agreed that *The Importance of Being Earnest* should be the piece, and I sent to Messrs Samuel French for copies. Jack Lambert, a friend of Pete's, was the perfect Jack Worthing. I found a pretty, very young Wren to be Cecily, and two others who were prepared to take on Lady Bracknell and Miss Prism. The chance of acting was too much for me and I decided to play Gwendoline. An Algernon was suggested to me whom I didn't know. His name was Philip Lee. He was blond, with large grey eyes, a slightly crooked nose and a delicately curling mouth. He was charming, and read the part beautifully; I took to him at once. Rehearsals were difficult because of the cast having to go to sea without warning, and the Wrens having similarly pressing duties, but we managed all right, until two days before the performance when Jack's boat was sent to Lowestoft. We found another Jack, who gallantly did his best, but he barely had time to learn the part. The play went off quite well, and everybody seemed pleased. Pete, particularly, was pleased that it had been a success, and was most encouraging about it.

Things had eased a little between us. For some time I had been writing a story — longish, based upon my encounter with Seth. It was rather a highly coloured and intense affair, but it was my first attempt at writing prose for a long time and I was anxious for an opinion. Pete suggested showing it to Jack who, he said, knew about that sort of thing, but after he'd read it, he simply remarked that he was getting rather tired of the streams of consciousness that had become so fashionable. I didn't know then what he meant, but I was dashed. I asked Pete, rather hesitantly, whether he would send it to Wayland. To my surprise, he said he would. He got a letter back about it, but all I can remember is 'What a hectic, subtle mind she has.' However, that was better than Jack's reaction. I didn't make any attempt to publish it: it had simply been an enjoyable occupation. The letter to Pete from Wayland had disturbed me: I wanted it to have been to me, but I knew that would have been against the rules.

I still thought sometimes about the summer, and the carefree life at Clifton Hill, with all the talk and jokes and music, but then Wayland came into the picture — the times on the river — and I'd learned to stop thinking about that because I couldn't bear any more of the sick, raw unhappiness that lay in wait. It wasn't possible to love Wayland; forbidden, hopeless. He'd probably found some-one else by now; someone it would be all right for him to love. But I didn't want to think much about that either. The whole thing had been wrong and irresponsible, I'd put it all away.

That was all very well, but it didn't make me love Pete the more.

And so, I suppose, with dull predictability, I began to fall in love with someone else — with Philip who amused, entertained and flattered me with his attention. It wasn't easy for us to be alone together, but he took to turning up at the hotel to have tea with me, or a drink at the bar, and we'd carry the drinks into the enormous lounge where we could sit in a quiet corner. He had a slight drawl, was rather a Wildean character. He told me that before the war he'd got a scholarship to Cambridge. 'I don't come from your sort of background at all,' he said. He asked me about my marriage, and I said things weren't going well. He'd perceived that. 'The first two things I noticed about you was that you didn't wear a bra, and that you weren't happy.' I didn't want to tell him more about being unhappy, and he didn't press me.

Then, one wintry afternoon, he turned up, said he had the afternoon off and proposed that we should go for a walk. We went high up the small mountain where there was snow in the crevasses between the rocks, and we lay in it and he made love to me. And so I became in love. I honestly don't know now how much, or indeed whether this was at all true: I certainly wanted it to be. I loved his gentleness and his wit; it was balm to be wanted, approved of, to have someone to talk to about books and ideas. And, of course, the very secrecy that had to be preserved made it exciting. The time on the mountain – although it was never repeated – had been thrillingly romantic. Pete didn't seem to notice anything, but the temperature between us had lowered to a kind of affability – wary on my part, breezy on his. I found it much easier now to play my part.

Holyhead came to an end. The boats were all going south in preparation for the invasion. I went back to London and Clifton Hill.

I got back to find the house teeming with romance. Audrey was going to marry John Rideout, Denis was going to marry Penelope Gough, Dosia's sister Nancy had fallen in love with one of the Craxtons, Anthony, and, best of all, Dosia and Barry were all set for marriage. I was a witness at their wedding; that morning, the three of us sat in our dressing-gowns eating burnt toast and discussing the gloomy alternatives of birth control. Eventually Barry said we'd better be off to the registry office. When we came back to Clifton

Hill, Barry said, 'Now, where were we? Plenty of time to discuss it now.' He had a studio in Kinnerton Street in Knightsbridge where they went to live, and I used sometimes to stay with them there. I told them about Philip, and they met and liked him.

It was through Philip that we all got to know Anne Richmond. He had often talked to me about her, said she had become his friend at Cambridge, but when I asked if he'd been in love with her he said no. She was madly in love with someone called Pete Piper, who'd been taken prisoner by the Japanese. She wrote to him all the time, but hardly ever had any news. He took me to her room in Percy Street, near where she worked in the Ministry of Information. She was a tall, red-haired beauty, with a soft voice in which she made unexpectedly ironical and funny remarks.

One winter afternoon, on the top of the 53 bus in Abbey Road, I met a man who was sitting with an actor I vaguely recognized. The man I knew turned out to be Jack Watling. His companion changed seats to be nearer to me and asked if I was an actress. The theatre still smouldered in my mind, so I said that I was, or had been. He said he'd like to take me to see someone who was looking for a girl to play a part in a new play. We made arrangements and he took me. The playwright was Terence Rattigan, who at that time lived in Albany, just off Piccadilly. Mr Neuman – I think that was his name – introduced me as not only an actress but a writer. I'd told him about the fragmentary novel I was working on. I was given a script and asked to read two scenes. The play turned out to be *While the Sun Shines* and the part I read was a good-time girl, so well played subsequently by Brenda Bruce. It was clear that I was hopelessly unsuitable, but Rattigan was courteous about it. He asked me what I was writing. A novel. Title? I was going to call it *The Deep Blue Sea*. 'That's a very good title,' he said, '*Very* good.' That was that. When I did finish the novel I called it *The Beautiful Visit*, but I like to think I gave Rattigan his title for that excellent play.

By then, in 1943, I'd got a job. Wyndham Goodden had

introduced me to Norman Collins, the novelist, who had a high-up administrative position in the BBC. He employed me as a continuity announcer. I had to work four floors underground in what had been the Peter Robinson department store in Oxford Street. As the most junior of the announcers, I had to work the night shift. I was to trail someone who already knew the job. This turned out to be a girl of about my age, very beautiful, with black hair, dark eyes and a very white skin. She was dressed in a flowered silk dress, and was extremely friendly and helpful. Her name was Jill Balcon and she'd trained to be an actress. She had a good sense of humour, and we got on at once, but in no time I was on my own – with only two junior programme engineers on the other side of a glass panel.

The job consisted of reading news bulletins every hour, announcing live concerts, selecting and playing gramophone records but, above all, never allowing more than fifteen seconds of 'dead air' in case the Germans used the airwaves. This doesn't sound arduous, but it was, because quite often we had to stop live concerts in mid-phrase for air raids, and substitute a record very quickly. Every single detail of every recording broadcast had to be laboriously logged, and if the news bulletin arrived thirty seconds before it was to be put out, it had to be read without rehearsal of often difficult and unknown place names.

There was a break sometime during the night when you could go to the canteen and have a dried-egg omelette and coffee. Through Jill, I met Noël Iliffe who was producing a programme called *Chapter & Verse*, and I used to read the poetry for him sometimes. He was a man with a gentle, pedantic voice, who was devoted to the theatre and had met his wife, Simona Pakenham, when they were both at the Abbey Theatre in Dublin.

At the end of the shift I used to walk across the road to the Underground where the platform would be full of sleeping bodies lying on newspapers and wrapped in blankets and overcoats. Every three or four minutes a train would rumble into the station, with its preceding rush of brown air, but the bodies were used to this and didn't move. As the weeks went by I saw that they each had their particular place staked out. Many of the women slept in curlers, some had Thermos flasks beside them; the men slept in their boots or shoes and women in bedroom slippers.

I'd leave the train at St John's Wood and walk, in the blackout, home to Clifton Hill where, soon after, my housemates would be getting up, hurrying each other about the bathroom, eating slightly burnt toast and drinking tea. The discomforts, looking back on them, were considerable: there was no way of heating the house except for the gas fire in the nursery and a coal fire – when we could get coal – in the drawing room, and food was pretty awful. 'There's nothing to eat in this house but cork mats,' Wyndham remarked one day, morosely biting into one. The cook I'd started life with there had soon given notice – she couldn't get used to our ways, she said. We didn't mind. She used to riddle the range furiously at night, which we called 'Mrs Upton taking off her stays'. We lived on music, and jokes, and falling a little in love – but not too much – with one another.

It was a carefree, light-hearted life and I felt happier than I had for months.

Anne Richmond came to Clifton Hill and everyone loved her, but some time during that summer, her anguish about Pete Piper became so strong that she decided to join the FANY, the First Aid Nursing Yeomanry, and go to India, feeling it would be that much nearer to her Pete. On the night before she left we played Ravel's choreographic piece 'La Valse' on the gramophone and she got up suddenly and danced – by herself – for the entire piece. Marie Paneth was there that night; she said how beautiful Anne was and we were all very moved.

Leaves became rarer, but Philip managed to get up to London from time to time and Barry lent me his studio for our meetings. I wrote copious letters to Philip, and he replied, but in more guarded terms. He had been put in charge of a frigate that was to be the headquarters from which naval operations were to be conducted.

This was a dangerous job: Philip already had a DSC and had proved himself. He told me rather wryly that Pete had assigned him.

I remember particularly a night in June when he rang to say he was coming up for the evening and would I meet him at Waterloo. We met in the blackout at the station and got a cab to Knightsbridge. It wasn't until we were safely in the studio that I saw how haggard he looked. 'I've been up for three nights,' he said. 'I had to stop a train to get here.'

'How do you mean?'

'I had to get them to make a train stop at a station it doesn't usually stop at, or I wouldn't be here at all. I said I was an admiral. And now to bed.'

He left very early in the morning and the next day was D-Day – 6 June 1944.

The next few weeks were nerve-racking. Occasionally Pete rang, and once came up for a night. He was tired but exhilarated. The weather had been bad, which had made the landings much harder for the wretched troops in the assault craft – most of them were seasick crossing the Channel. I couldn't imagine anything more awful than having to wade ashore, sick and laden with weighty equipment under heavy fire. On the other hand, the bad weather and the stretches of coast chosen had been an element of surprise. Philip was doing a marvellous job, he added casually.

I went on writing to Philip. I thought now that he'd taken all that trouble to get to London that night because he knew that the invasion was starting and that he might be killed. Occasionally, he rang up. It was 'madly war', he said – a phrase coined earlier by some officers and which later entered the language. He thought he might get some leave in a few weeks' time, wasn't sure when. Then, perhaps we might go away together? We might indeed. This was something to look forward to.

I'd been twenty-one in March; had celebrated my birthday, wanly, in a pub with Barry and Dosia. I thought I was old now, but I wasn't; neither old nor mature – that longed-for goal.

One hot evening in July, I checked into my continuity studio to find a new girl just preparing to leave the shift. 'Oh, by the way, you know Philip Lee, don't you?' Yes, I did. 'Isn't he charming? He's just come to collect my flatmate Elena and they're off for a heavenly holiday in Westmorland. Isn't she the lucky one?'

I noticed that she looked rather hard at me when she said this and I was careful to look back expressionlessly.

Then she went. I was reeling, almost faint with shock, but I wasn't alone: on the other side of the glass window were the two junior programme engineers cheerfully waving good evening to me. The news bulletin was brought in, and in twenty seconds I'd have to read it.

Somehow, I got through the night, logging programmes, select-ing records to play for the following evening, reading bulletin after bulletin. In the break, I went to the lavatory to cry, but found that I couldn't even do that. I took refuge, dramatic refuge in giving an impeccable performance in front of the JPEs.

Leaving the train at St John's Wood, I was alone at last. It was beginning to be light, but there was no one about, and I walked home streaming.

I thought he would write to me, but he didn't. That was the end of it. I didn't see him again for years, until we met at a party. He was drunk.

I find it difficult to know now *how* unhappy this made me. I suspect that I dramatized it, tried to make it more than it could ever have been – simply a wartime affair of which there were so many at the time. I don't think Pete ever knew about it. If he did, he was silent on the subject, and continued to be the same to me as he'd been for months now: affable, sometimes sentimental. Like many who have very little interest in people, sentiment was often his substitute for anything significant (I'd begun to recognize that he wasn't really interested in people).

The pressure for me to have another child continued. Even when I went to Sussex to visit Nicola, Nanny would say, with nauseating coyness, how much Nicola would like a little brother.

5

I knew that, with all the marriages, Clifton Hill was going to break up and I had to think about an alternative. Love, which still seemed to me the most important thing in the world, had eluded me; I seemed incapable of sustaining, inspiring or receiving it. This reinforced all my secret feelings of being worthless. The war, despite successful invasions, stretched interminably before us – indeed, after the Japanese assault on Pearl Harbor, it had seemed simply to proliferate.

And so I went to Fritton as I was told to do.

Pete was sometimes sleeping on his ship, sometimes at home. There was a new ordeal for me now. K received me blandly with no hint of trouble while Peter was in the house, but the moment that he was gone she began to cross-examine me about Holyhead. It was clear she knew something, and that she was very angry. Eventually, she mentioned Philip and asked me what I'd thought of him. I said I liked him and that he'd been a very good Algernon in the play. 'Oh, Jenny! What a little *liar* you are!' She said she knew all about it, that I need not think that she was so stupid. On our return, at our first meal, Pete had asked her whether she'd seen Jack Lambert when he'd been stationed at Lowestoft. Several times, she'd said, and how nice it had been, and I realized that he'd betrayed me – no doubt under close questioning, but none the less he had. She asked me whether I'd had an affair with Philip, and I answered, would it matter what I said since she thought I was a liar?

This sort of thing went on for days; she couldn't leave it alone.

We were on our own all day as Bill was in London. She followed me around the house, from the dining room to the drawing room, even to my bedroom, to which I'd attempt to escape. In the evenings when Pete came back she was sunny and interested in everything he'd done that day, and blandly courteous to me.

I found some ways to escape her. I'd go to the woodshed and chop firewood. 'Where have you been all the morning?' she would say at lunch. And 'You're not to be trusted, are you?' One afternoon, I asked the gardener if I could help clear the herbaceous border, and he said he'd no objection. This was soothing work, and I was interested enough in it to feel distracted from her disapprobation. But she discovered what I was doing, and followed me, and stood on the gravel path telling me what a worthless, shallow little creature I was. 'I know that,' I said desperately one day. 'Why do you go on about it?' But she couldn't stop. She told me what a bad mother I was, and I said I knew that too. She brought up my youth – maybe as an attempt at reconciliation – but by then I'd become savage and retorted that I wasn't *so* young, had *never* been as young as she thought. There is nothing more awful than feeling that you have nothing to lose.

There was no escape from Fritton. I couldn't drive, and in any case there was no petrol. Eventually I told Pete that K didn't like me, and I was finding the days alone with her very difficult. He must have said something to her, because after that she maintained a guarded truce. It occurred to me that what she'd wanted was a full-blooded confession on my part, with my saying how dreadfully badly I'd behaved and begging for forgiveness, but this I couldn't or wouldn't do. I think a great deal of her anger was about Wayland, but she couldn't bring herself to mention that. I think it was during this visit that Pete did an oil portrait of me. I have a small photograph of it, but the painting has gone. It was a terrible six weeks and I left to go and see Nicola.

Clifton Hill came to an end. Pete was expecting to get command of a destroyer and to be sent east to fight the Japanese.

We were to look for another house in London. There was an enormous choice at that time because so many had been deserted during the bombing, but I was entirely inexperienced in looking. I'd been brought up in Kensington and didn't look much beyond it. The choice eventually boiled down to a house on Campden Hill Square, but it cost six thousand pounds and was in need of much repair, or a smaller house in Edwardes Square for eight thousand that had nothing much wrong with it. We opted for no. 8 Edwardes Square. Dosia and Barry had moved to Bedford Gardens, which was comfortingly near.

The idea of leaving Peter had crossed – or, rather, skidded – more than once across my mind, but it was a thought so terrifying I was unable to confront it for long. I told myself that life would be different and better when he wasn't away all the time, that in a house of our own we could make some sort of life, which up until now hadn't been possible. Nicola and Nanny would be able to live with us, since there would no longer be any fear of bombs.

The house, built for refugees from the French Revolution, was pretty. It had a long narrow dining room, a beautiful drawing room on the first floor and a large bedroom at the top. But the back had been built on to in a nasty modern manner, with mean proportions and ugly windows. Two hideous bathrooms had also been installed, in black and a strident dark pink. However, there was enough room and we didn't have much money. I bought a William Morris wallpaper of tiger lilies for the bedroom, painted the drawing-room walls white and bought lengths of red and cream damask cotton, which I cut in strips and machined together to make stripes. I bought a large oval gilt-framed mirror in Portobello Road for thirty shillings, and Harold Craxton found me a beautiful old Blüthner concert grand. Otherwise the house was furnished with what Pete had had in his lighthouse, plus bits that the family gave or lent us. Nicola had a day nursery on the first floor and a night nursery in which she slept with Nanny at the top.

Before we moved in, we stayed at Leinster Corner, the Kennets'

London home. This wasn't as awful as Fritton because Bill was there, and sometimes Wayland. Enough time had passed for us to meet as friends. K had assumed her former, affectionate, slightly patronizing behaviour towards me and I was grateful for the truce. She also knew that Wayland had had affairs with several girls, so there was no tension between us.

It was during this time that I got a job, briefly, at Ealing Studios, run by Jill's father Michael Balcon. I had an interview with him, which was conducted at cross-purposes: I discovered that although I thought I was being seen for an acting job, he thought I wanted a scriptwriting one. However, he let me be an extra in a film they were making with Frances Day and Tommy Trinder. It was a farcical Roman epic, and I was to be one of the many slave girls. This entailed getting up at about five a.m. every day and catching the tube to Ealing, where my hair was washed and pinned up in rollers. Then I went to Makeup to apply dark pancake foundation, huge false eyelashes and a large fictitious crimson mouth. We were dressed in yellow satin bras and tiny yellow satin skirts, edged with gold fringe. This done, we waited. The first day we waited in vain. Eventually, we got on to the set, which had a large bath filled with milky liquid – meant to be ass's milk – in which Frances Day was made to immerse herself. In a dark corner one day I came upon Tommy Trinder, clad in a very short toga. He was doing a little dance, lifting his toga and muttering, 'Now you see it, now you don't.'

E. M. Forster used to come to dinner at Leinster Corner. He was an old friend of Bill, who, I was told, had got him to write *A Passage to India*. He was a small man, with a soft moustache and an enigmatic smile – I thought he looked like an H. G. Wells character. He liked to be amused. He was curious to know what happened in a film studio. I regaled him with tales of Tommy Trinder, of the deck-chairs with people's names on them, and the huge dark coils of cable that lay all over the floor like writhing anacondas.

One day Bernard Shaw came to tea. It was a cold spring day, and he'd walked across the park. He took off his muffler and laid it on a spare chair. During tea he told the story of his wife's death. He made it a riveting drama, without any hint of what it might – or might not – have made him feel. He was devoted to K and wrote many letters to her. A postcard I particularly remember simply said, 'The nearest I've come to homosexuality is with you.' He said a great deal of his time nowadays was spent arranging what was to happen after his death.

I was still constantly plagued by sore throats, and when, after a particularly bad attack, I went to see a doctor, I was told it was high time my tonsils came out. They were removed on VE Day, and I remember sitting in a chair in the theatre at University College Hospital, with two men bending over me, being given some anaesthetic, and feeling the most blinding pain just before I passed out. I came to to the sound of people singing and cheering in the streets below, and the distant thuds and bangs of fireworks. I felt pretty ill for some days, and could hardly speak. 'It's always worse when you're older,' they said.

During my stay there, a nurse came in and said I had visitors – they were only in London for the day, and particularly wanted to see me, if only for a few minutes. They turned out to be Myfanwy and her husband. They'd brought me a bunch of very yellow daffodils. Conversation was rather stilted – we were shy with one another – until Myfanwy said suddenly, 'We've come to thank you for what you did. We're both so grateful.' I asked how their baby was, and she said he was fine; her mam was looking after him while they were away. 'She's never been to London before,' her husband said. He was very much older than his wife. They didn't stay long. 'We mustn't tire you,' one said. I felt extraordinarily grateful to them.

When I was out of hospital, still feeling very weak and with no energy, it was decided that I should have a fortnight's holiday in the Isles of Scilly, and that Marie Paneth would come with me. She was writing a book about a children's project in Paddington, and I'd begun a longish short story that was turning into a novel. So off we went by train and then two boats to St Mary's and thence to St Martin's. It was my first real holiday for years and the island was a revelation to me. It felt wonderfully foreign, had no roads and consisted of three settlements called Lower, Middle and Upper Town. We lodged with a Mrs Bond – there were 105 people on the island, I later discovered, all called Bond. We had a bedroom each and slept in feather beds, and there was a little parlour where we ate and wrote. They grew flowers and tomatoes on the island and its fields were striped with brilliant gladioli that looked wonderful against the background of gorse and heather and grey rocks. The sea creamed round the rocky shores and the air smelt of salt and honey.

We went for walks, collecting shells and wild flowers, and when we came back to have baths, we found that Mrs Bond had arranged the shells in beautiful patterns in the fireplace, and put the flowers in water on our table. We wrote, and read to each other in the evenings. I wrote at a tremendous rate in those days; Marie was far slower, but her book was awfully good, I thought. She thought my heroine was rather snobbish. I'd begun to realize that Marie was very left wing and I'd always lived in Conservative circles.

I told her that my marriage was very difficult and I didn't know what to do, and she was sympathetic about that. She was very much into psychology, had known the Freud family, and attributed many of my quite light-hearted observations to some murky ill-feeling and bad motive. Then, one day, I said, 'Marie, why do you always think I mean something else that's nastier than what I do mean?' She stopped after that.

She told me that her marriage had come to an end some time ago, and that she'd had a lover, the love of her life, who was now a famous psychiatrist working in New York. He was married, but they'd lost touch since the beginning of the war.

One day we took a boat to visit another island, St Agnes, and while we were moored there, a calf was loaded on board. As we set off, a cow plunged into the sea and began swimming after us. The boat increased speed, and the cow was left further and further behind until we lost sight of her, but she didn't stop swimming. I couldn't bear it, because I couldn't stop the boat and return the calf to its mother. 'It's what happens, Janie, it's life,' Marie said. I felt that she knew about life, and I didn't.

One evening, when we were having supper, Mrs Bond came in and said someone had come to say that there was a telephone call for me. There was only one telephone on the island, in a box at the end of the village. I ran all the way because I was afraid that something awful had happened to Nicola.

It was Pete. 'I have a bit of a problem,' he began. He'd been invited to stand for Parliament at the coming election, a fairly safe seat in Wembley, but he also had the chance of commanding a destroyer in the war against Japan. Which should he do? Which did he *want* to do? Well, he rather liked the idea of being an MP, and it would mean he could stay at home. On the other hand he'd wanted this command for a long time and would be promoted from lieutenant commander to commander, which was given to few in the RNVR. Mummy thought he should stand for Parliament, he added. On the whole, he thought that perhaps he should, but he wanted to know what I thought. I said I thought he should opt for Parliament – I felt it was what he wanted me to say. 'I expect you're right.' He said it with evident relief. 'Only it will mean, darling, I'm afraid, that you will have to cut your holiday short, because I shall need you to come and make speeches with me, or at least shake hands with people – that sort of thing.' So back we went.

I knew nothing whatever about politics, party or otherwise. I don't think Pete did either, but he was a war hero, a natural leader, and very good at making speeches and subsequently skating over thin ice if he was asked awkward questions.

The three weeks leading up to the election were a nightmare to me. We campaigned from morning till night. I got used to having to have four teas with the wives of Wembley worthies, to answering the same questions again and again, to trying desperately – and sometimes failing – to remember people I'd met before, the previous week. A Liberal and a Labour man were standing against him, but everyone we met thought Pete would easily get in. K got some big guns down to speak for him, including my cousin Donald Somervell, who was Home Secretary at the time.

The day came, the vote and then the count. Pete lost by 225 votes out of a poll of around twenty-five thousand. He was a good loser and was the first to congratulate the Labour Member. So that was that, and we were back to the destroyer.

But he didn't get that, because two atomic bombs were dropped on Japan and the war finally ended. At the time I and many other people had little or no idea of the dreadful implications of those bombs. There was simply a sense of enormous relief that it was all over. London was shabby, people were exhausted by the years of small daily privations: what to eat, how to keep warm, and the threadbare exhaustion from hard work and sleepless nights. And the grief of losing sons, husbands and lovers was terrible. Relief at the prospect of peace and a government that was to implement the welfare state was predominant.

However, the knowledge that Pete wasn't going away and that I had to face up to a chronically married life induced feelings in me that were ambivalent and, some of them, unworthy.

We now had a household that consisted of ourselves, Nanny and Nicola, Mrs Mackie, the cook, and a series of secretaries – they didn't live in – who came to help Pete with the enormous and varied correspondence. It was my job to order meals. Mrs Mackie was a rotten cook, but all that Mrs Lines, the domestic agency from which I obtained her, could provide. I also had to arrange dinner parties and keep the peace between Nanny and Mrs Mackie, who didn't like each other. Pete went out quite a lot, and I'd go to see my friends.

One morning, Malcolm Sargent's secretary rang up and said Sir

Malcolm wondered whether I'd dine with him that evening. He was one of Nicola's godfathers and was very friendly with K. I said, yes, I would. He took me to an obscure little restaurant where the food was extremely good – 'Entirely black market,' he said. Conversation was innocuous. He talked of my grandfather's choral works – Malcolm was wonderful with choirs – and of the Kennets. 'How do you get on with Lady K?' he asked. I was carefully, diplomatically enthusiastic, saying how much she loved Nicola and how kind she'd been.

When his chauffeur drove us back to Edwardes Square, I asked whether he'd like a drink. He said yes, and told his chauffeur to return in half an hour. I left him in the drawing room and went down to get the whisky and soda he'd opted for. When I returned it was to find him without his trousers. I told him that anything like that was out of the question, fighting down panic with the reassuring knowledge that I wasn't alone in the house. Unabashed, he put on his trousers again. He did hope I hadn't misunderstood him, he said, as he left. I wondered what he meant.

He was incorrigible. Some time later, Pete said we must have him to dinner. It was to be a party of about eight, black tie, of course – everyone changed in those days. When he arrived, he said he would so much like to see his dear little goddaughter. She was asleep, I said. 'Take Malcolm to see her,' Pete said. 'She looks very sweet, even asleep.' There was nothing for it. I took him upstairs to her cot. He gave her a cursory look, then seized me, tearing one of my shoulder straps. I escaped down the passage to the nursery where Nanny was sewing. I said I had somehow torn the strap and could she mend it quickly, which she did. After that, I took care never to see Malcolm again, except in company.

Pete was painting, mostly wildfowl, but he was also drawing some people and I encouraged him to make a book of his drawings, which he eventually did.

In November he had his first post-war show at Ackerman's. I was helping to hang it, and as it was cold, I was wearing two pairs of trousers. I was up a small ladder when it became apparent to me that Queen Mary was at the bottom looking up, and that K was indicating I should descend at once to give her a bunch of flowers. It's quite difficult to get off a ladder in two pairs of trousers and curtsy, particularly with any grace. Queen Mary, looking at me with some distaste, said, 'Is this a *boy*?'

Also in 1945 Pete and I took Dosia to the nursing-home to have her first baby. Barry and she didn't have a car, so Pete drove and I sat with her, already in labour, in the back seat. She'd chosen to have the baby in Blackheath – a long drive at the best of times – but that night there was fog, and the whole thing became a nightmare. Pete was very good and steady, but said afterwards he'd been terrified of losing his way. I rubbed Dosia's back when she gasped with pain and prayed that she wouldn't have the baby in the car because I'd no idea what to do if she did. We got her there, and Adam was born.

Some time in the spring, my parents rang and said they wanted to come and see me – that morning. Was Colin all right? I asked. It wasn't Colin.

They came and stood agitatedly in the drawing room and my mother said, in tones of high tragedy, that Robin had married a girl in Arizona – without getting his CO's consent. She pulled a letter out of her bag and gave it to me. It was disingenuous, written, I could see, with a view to winning my parents round. Hope, Robin said, was twenty-one years old, a marvellous girl, great fun, with a deep nature. She liked to sit quietly in churches from time to time. I could see that he was fairly worried about what sort of reception he would get. He was to be demobbed and was returning in July. Hope would follow later when she could get a place on a boat. It was startling news – Robin was twenty – but I certainly didn't see it as the disaster that clearly my parents did. It seemed rather exciting. I also realized from this visit that I'd been promoted to a grown-up, and said cautiously that she was probably very nice, and wasn't it lovely that he was coming home? I'd lost touch with

Robin and had little or no idea of what his life, training as a Spitfire pilot, had been. Now he would go straight into the family firm as my father had done, and with an American wife, like my uncle.

Eventually, my parents left, and I recalled later that there had been an air of unease – particularly with my father – that went beyond what they'd come to tell me.

During that year I persisted with my novel, often writing it at night: that gave me the twofold advantage of peace and quiet and not having to go to bed with Peter. We had had some fairly acrimonious rows about my dislike of bed, but they gradually died down, and I suspected that he'd found someone else. He was looking for somewhere to keep wildfowl, and spent some time on these searches. I didn't accompany him.

Gavin Maxwell used to come and see us in the winter. 'He comes to London then to litigate,' Pete said. Gavin was a tense, volatile creature, with beautiful manners and huge amounts of energy that he seemed unable to place to his advantage. He'd had a brave war, which ended in training Polish paratroopers in Scotland. They would come back after a drop, having been caught, imprisoned and sometimes tortured – with no fingernails, for instance – and simply say, 'Train us better this time.' He took up shark fishing after the war which, he thought, would be a good commercial enterprise, but Gavin and commerce never blended well. Pete said he was very unhappy about an affair, and would keep him talking in the evenings until the last Underground train had left – 'Or he might kill himself.' I didn't see him for years after, by which time he had taken up with otters.

6

One day my father, whom I saw occasionally – more often than my mother who was still in Sussex – asked me to lunch at his club and told me that he was deeply in love with a lady called Ursula Beddard. He'd been in love with her for ages, he said, and the situation had become so serious that he thought he would have to leave my mother to live with Ursula. I'd met her as she had come to parties at home in Lansdowne Road before the war. I felt very sympathetic – I've always felt sympathy for lovers. He would so like me to know her, he said. She was living in a rented cottage in Hampshire and he would like me to go down and spend a night with her there. 'I so want you two to get to know each other,' he said, 'and I think it would be much better if I wasn't there the first time you meet.' So I went.

She had three sons; the two eldest were at school and the youngest upstairs asleep. She was very welcoming and charming, told me how much she adored my father, and how worried she was about my mother's reaction if she was left. By the time we'd had several drinks and dinner, which she'd cooked, I was confiding in her – something I'd not have dreamed of doing with my mother – and told her how miserable my marriage was. Afterwards, my father said she'd simply *loved* me and how glad he was that his two favourite women had got on so well. She was very good-looking with hyacinth eyes, dark hair and a habitual expression of slightly noble sincerity. She knew about unhappy marriages, she said, as hers had been one for a long time.

After the meeting, my father confided in me a great deal more. He couldn't decide whether he should tell my mother that he was leaving her while she was still living in Sussex, or whether he should find a house for her in London first. He took me out to lunch to ask me what I thought. I felt he should find a house for her that he knew she liked before breaking the news. I couldn't believe that she knew nothing about his affair – or, indeed, affairs of many years – but he seemed sure that she didn't. I also had little idea about how she would feel, except that whatever she knew or didn't know, it would come as a great shock. Better, I thought, for her at least to have a home, rather than find one by herself. I still don't know if this was right, but my father, who really wanted his mind made up for him, decided it was. So my parents began to house-hunt in these dishonest circumstances. They settled for a small one-storeyed house in St John's Wood, Clifton Hill, the same road that I'd lived in during the war. It faced north and south, so one side of it was always dark. It had three bedrooms and a sunny garden at the back. My mother thought it was perfect, and my father was guiltily agreeable to anything she wanted.

I now come to Robert Aickman. I've not wanted to write about Robert, I suspect because I am uncomfortable about my behaviour with him. However, that is not a good reason for leaving him out – indeed I can't, since he exercised a strong influence on me for several years.

He came into my life almost imperceptibly; I'd first met him before I was married, when he came to lunch with Ronnie Jeans one day, bringing his wife Ray, who was Ronnie's secretary. I didn't like him very much: he seemed rather supercilious, and I thought he despised Ronnie. Then, long after, when I was at Clifton Hill, he wrote out of the blue, asking if he might come to tea with me. I kept an open house, and could think of no good reason for refusing him – in those days I didn't think about such things. He came and talked about the theatre, about which he seemed to know a great deal, but I found him heavy going. Later, he asked me to go to a play with him. He turned up from time to time; nobody in the house took to him much, but he was quietly persistent. I used to put him off a lot, but I never stopped him coming. I think at that time I felt mildly sorry for him.

He was unprepossessing: he had thick horn-rimmed spectacles through which his small brown eyes looked out with an almost cynical intelligence, thick brown hair scraped back from his forehead and held firmly in place with a good deal of Brylcreem. He had a large, but not insensitive mouth, and a pale, almost colourless complexion. He had beautiful hands, and a voice whose tone implied, with some irony, that he thought little of anything apart from the arts. He was devoted to all of them, seemed to have read everything, gone to every play, opera, film and concert, looked at pictures and had an encyclopedic knowledge of England. There was nothing usual about him, neither his appearance nor his demeanour. His conversation was wide-ranging, and imbued with his knowledge and opinions. I discovered gradually that he was the only child of an architect; that his parents had taken virtually no notice of him from an early age. He was reading *The Times* when he was four and preparing his own meals. They lived in a small house in Stanmore, a suburb of London, and he got a scholarship to a school in Highgate. Fairly early on in his life, his mother left, and he continued to live at home with his father. It was an extremely lonely and unhappy childhood. His father died and he inherited some money – I never knew how much but it enabled him to live modestly, spending it on his many interests. He was a pacifist, one of the few to go through a tribunal and be released from any work connected with the war.

He asked me to lunch with Ray at their flat. They lived on the top two floors of 11 Gower Street, the house where Jonathan Cape and Wren Howard had begun their publishing concern.

The flat had a bathroom on the mezzanine, and an office, lined with books, with a desk and typewriter and two easy chairs in front of the gas fire and a door that led to their bedroom. On the next floor there were two little attic bedrooms, and a small, charming dining room that led to a tiny kitchen. Ray was a tall, large-boned woman, with a face reminiscent of a du Maurier drawing, but enlivened by remarkable eyes, blue and shining with intelligence. She had a high, rather childish-sounding voice, and she clearly adored Robert. Conversation was easier in her presence, and we all got on very well. Robert told me that she, too, was an only child, and that her mother had committed suicide.

Thereafter I saw them at irregular intervals. I didn't invite them to Edwardes Square, as Robert said he hated parties and Ray was conditioned to dislike what Robert disliked. But often I saw Robert alone, and he wrote constantly to me. Ray said how good I was for him, as he was very depressed.

I can't remember exactly when he exclaimed that he was in love with me and had loved me from the first moment that he saw me. 'You're the most beautiful woman I've ever seen, let alone met in my life.' This was water off a duck's back: I'd never cared much for my appearance, and took this compliment to be something people always said in these circumstances. But the fact that he loved me was a hook. I was flattered to be so important to such an unusual and intriguing man. I had – how clearly I see it now – a great hunger to be loved, to *be* in love. I was well aware my education had been sketchy: here was someone who apparently knew everything and wanted to teach me. Also, I was anxious about my novel; Robert and Ray ran a small literary agency and were professionally informed. Robert read my novel and, after much encouragement, went through some of it with me, giving me my first lesson on the pluperfect tense. He wrote himself, he said, mostly reviews and articles for the literary magazine *Nineteenth Century*. I think at the time he'd had very little published.

Once, I spent a weekend with them, and I realized how continuously and completely Ray looked after him. The weekend was strenuous: a rich fare of cinema, a concert, a picture gallery and a train taken to somewhere in Buckinghamshire where we went for a marathon walk, finishing at a place where we could all have tea. He wouldn't go to bed until about one a.m., and at midnight had an extra meal, of yoghurt, bread and butter. I went home exhausted on Sunday evening.

Gradually, I got to know more about them. Ray said they'd only married to stop her being called up. They'd been living together and one morning Robert said he'd been reading the paper and had decided to marry her. Neither of them wanted nor even liked children. So, as we became more intimate, I admitted my lack of maternal feeling and how awful I felt about it. Their response was shockingly different from any I'd encountered before. Why should I like children? None of their friends had them: they made civilized life impossible. Ray called them wombats. 'Not that I'm against wombats,' she said, 'but I wouldn't want to live with one.' There was a great deal of this: it was an insidious influence I am ashamed to have succumbed to.

But the main tenor of all our conversation – what everything came back to – was that everything had declined. Before the beginning of the century, life had held more promise. The arts, architecture, hotels, food, clothes, furniture, the governance of the country – everything you could think of – had been better. Robert was particularly incensed by the closure of the tram system. This was later to lead to his interest in canals and the subsequent foundation of the Inland Waterways Association. There had been nothing, since those unspecified and halcyon days, but a steady diminution in all standards. We were approaching the end of a civilization.

I asked Robert if he'd told Ray that he thought he was in love with me. Of course he had, and she didn't mind at all. Theirs was a marriage of convenience. They were very fond of each other, and Ray only wanted him to be happy. This, like so many things that Robert told me, was only half true. By now they both knew my marriage was in trouble and were sympathetic. It was a relief to have people to whom I could talk about it.

One day, I was having tea with Ray and I said, 'Robert seems to be in love with me.'

She said she knew that. 'As long as you don't want to marry him,' she added. I said, truthfully, that I didn't want to marry anyone ever again in my life.

I now have to describe another incident that occurred sometime in the spring. It had started when I was in the Isles of Scilly with Marie. She'd said then that if I ever felt the need to sort myself out, she knew a man who could help me. I told Peter I wanted to do this, and he agreed.

Oswald Schwarz was a psychiatrist of Freudian persuasion. He lived in a small ground-floor flat very near Leinster Corner. I began to see him twice a week. He was small, and seemed extremely old, was almost bald, with spectacles and dark violet smudges under his eyes. My visits consisted mostly of my telling him things and him encouraging me to continue. He seemed to be on my side, and I became increasingly anxious to tell him everything and gain his good opinion. After a time, he asked if he could come to the house and meet Peter, who was perfectly sanguine about this, so it happened.

Afterwards, he said he could see I was in a very difficult situation. I thought he must know everything, and turned him, I suppose, into a father figure. One day he said to me, 'Do you know Cecil Day-Lewis?' I didn't. 'He is making poor Rosamond Lehmann dreadfully unhappy. He is a wicked man.' I knew of Rosamond Lehmann, of course, but had never met her. He sighed, and returned to the matter in hand.

Then, because I was going to be away for some weeks, I told him I'd not be able to come for a while. He asked me to change my hour from three p.m. to five p.m.. I agreed. When I arrived, I saw that there was a plate of cakes and a small bottle of wine on the table between us. 'For a little celebration,' he said, 'as you're going away.' At the end of the session, he lunged off his chair suddenly, knelt before me and enclosed me in a vice-like grip. 'I love and adore you and want you,' he said, and made a further lunge to kiss me. A shock. For a split second I was paralysed. Then I pushed him with both hands so hard that he fell back.

I rushed out of the flat, leaving my overcoat and bag in the waiting room. I ran up the street to the park, looking back, terrified that he would follow me, where I realized I hadn't the money to get home. I hailed a taxi and sat in it, shaking. I felt frightened and betrayed; nothing was safe, nothing could be trusted. I recalled, fleetingly, the first bad time with my father, and pushed it down where it usually stayed, airless and subdued by deliberate lack of attention. Thereafter in my life, whenever real intimacy or trust seemed to loom, I withdrew to avoid any possible ambush. At home, I got Nanny to pay for the taxi. 'You look upset, Mummy, would you like a cup of tea in the nursery with us?' I said I had a headache and was going to lie down.

That was the end of that. 'Oh, darling, you never stick to anything,' Pete said, when I told him I didn't want to go back to Dr Schwarz. The next day a young man delivered my coat and bag. I never saw or heard of Dr Schwarz again.

At some point, Robert and I became lovers. I never found him physically attractive, but in all other ways I was, under his spell. He became my mentor; he taught me things that I was eager to learn. He made verbal love to me, which I enjoyed. He flattered me, telling me how good and wonderful I was, and this sank into me like water into dry sand. I confided in my father about this affair, and he, immersed in his own, was understanding.

And then, in 1946, when I was nearly twenty-three, it was decided that Peter and I were to go to New York, where Peter would have a show of his paintings and we would also do some broadcasting. When I broke this news to Robert, the balloon went up. How could I leave him? And to go to America, the place that *he* had always wanted to go to. How could I be so callous as to make him so unhappy in this particular way? I did point out that I was still married, that I could think of no valid excuse for *not* going. There were endless scenes about it: he wouldn't be able to survive without me; I might never come back and this would ruin his life. Ray, though she was far more reasonable – realistic – about this, took it all at Robert's level of drama. The date drew nearer; eventually, it was agreed I should stay at Gower Street the night before we sailed, and my father would drive me down to South-ampton. I don't know how I swung this with Pete: I suspect that he knew what was going on, and chose not to talk about it. Any-way, that was what happened. Pete went down the night before with our luggage and his paintings, and I spent a tear-torn night at Gower Street, from which my father collected me very early in the morning.

7

We sailed in the *Aquitania*, with four hundred GI brides. It was the roughest crossing, the captain said – we sat at his table – that he'd known for twenty years. Thirty-foot waves assaulted the ship, and almost all the passengers were seasick. I lay on my bunk a good deal of the time, reading Charlotte Brontë's *Shirley*, and managed not to be sick. Pete, who was illustrating Paul Gallico's *The Snow Goose*, searched the ship for a suitable model for Fritha, but with the general prostration and the fact that the brides were unexpectedly a series of 'no oil paintings', he had to fall back on me. I stood for hours, holding a pillow, which he turned into the wounded snow goose. The crossing was so bad that we stopped at Halifax where we stayed the night in a boarding-house; our bedroom had the curious feature of an enormous creeper growing up one wall. There we had the choice of continuing by ship, or flying south over Canada to New York, and Pete opted for the latter, as the ship was going to be late.

I'd never flown before, and the small planes were unpressurized, which hurt my ears throughout the flight. We stopped at Monckton where we had lunch in a hotel and then proceeded in another plane to New York. The view of Canada – frozen lakes and endless evergreen forests for hour after hour – reminded me of Sibelius.

We arrived in New York in the early evening, and the moment we got to our hotel, photographers rang to say they wanted to take our pictures because of the party we were going to that night. We struggled into our evening clothes and went through the session, then took a cab to Park Avenue where there was to be a large dinner party. In the lift – or elevator, as I learned to call it – was a small grey-haired man with his wife. 'Are you going to this party?' he asked as we ascended. Yes. 'What do you do, then?' he asked. Light-headed with fatigue and the strangeness of everything, I said I was writing a novel. 'I should like to see it,' he replied.

'If I'd said I build bridges in South America, would you pop down to look at them?'

'No,' he said, 'I am a publisher.' He turned out to be Robert Haas, the vice president of Random House.

Everyone at the party seemed so *old*. I sat next to a handsome saturnine man, and when it was my turn to talk to him I said, 'This is all rather like *H. M. Pulham Esquire*.'

'I am John Marquand,' he replied. The Pulitzer Prize winner's gently satirical society novel had been published in 1941 to great acclaim. I was too cowed to think of anything else to say to him.

The first thing that had struck me when we got off the plane in New York was the lights. The whole city seemed ablaze, and although the blackout had ceased in England, there were no huge buildings lit up at every window. There was also the food. The first dinner party was full of rich food, and I assumed this was because it was a grand occasion – the Pulitzers gave it – but *all* the food was like that. Our first morning we had breakfast in our room and I ordered a boiled egg – a treat for me. Two eggs arrived, with muffins, toast, masses of butter, and cream for the coffee. My liver couldn't stand up to this: at the end of a week, I felt sick, and could hardly eat anything.

A glamorous life ensued. There were a great many parties, where everyone drank very dry martinis for hours before settling down to enormous steaks, baked potatoes dripping with sour cream and, to top it all, most of the men accompanied it with a large glass of milk. Pete's show was hung and opened, and a lot of rather grand people came. He sold a good many of the pictures, and also got commissions to draw portraits.

People were very kind and made a great fuss of me. One of Robert Haas's daughters took me shopping. This was another heady revelation. After years of clothes rationing and utility garments, the sight of racks and racks of lovely things was intoxicating. I had my twenty-third birthday party on the sixty-seventh floor of Radio City in a club. A great many people came and gave me wonderful presents. I was getting used to being the youngest person everywhere.

But there was a nagging fly in the ointment. Robert was so miserable about my being in New York that I felt it was disloyal to enjoy myself too much. How misplaced loyalties can be! He wrote me long, despairing letters almost every day and, of course, I wrote back, but he wouldn't really have known if I *had* abandoned myself to the excitement and pleasure of being in a foreign country. On the other hand, there was no doubt that I was being disloyal to Peter. I was unhappy a lot of the time and, worse, felt I *ought* to be so. Sexual life with him had been over for some time, at my request. It is hard to say whether he minded or not. Pride was involved and he minded in that kind of way. From time to time he made half-hearted scenes, but he was proud, too, that I was – from his point of view – 'a success'.

He was extremely generous with money, and let me buy anything I wanted. The only thing that couldn't be procured, which I wanted most, was entry to a Toscanini concert or, at least, a rehearsal. Impossible, everyone said.

Pete was asked to draw a portrait of Walter Pidgeon, the actor, then at the height of his fame. He took me with him to the hotel where Mr Pidgeon lived, since he'd found that if I read to sitters they were more inclined to sit still. Pidgeon turned out to fidget if he was read to. He wanted to be told stories, preferably funny and risqué ones, about the war and London. I did my best, but soon ran out. I searched my mind for anything that might amuse him and recited a fairly dirty limerick that had been current during the Blitz. The session ended, but during it Pete had mentioned that he was going to Chicago the next morning, catching an eight a.m. plane to fulfil another commission. 'Are you going too?' Walter asked me. I wasn't.

The next morning, at precisely eight a.m., the telephone rang. 'Mrs Scott? I have someone on the line for you.' It was Walter. 'Just give me your room number and I'll be up,' he said.

There was a slight pause while I thought what to do. Even if I didn't tell him, he might still find out – did the door lock? Then, in tones of shocked severity, I said, 'I can't think what you mean. Of course you can't come up.'

There was another silence and then he said, 'You must forgive me. A terrible mistake.' I said nothing. 'What can I do to show you how sorry I am?' A wonderful thought occurred to me. I said coldly, as though granting a favour, 'You can get me a seat for a Toscanini rehearsal.' He did. This was one of the most ruthless exploits of my life, but it was worth it. I also heard Jascha Heifetz, who was a disappointment.

Robert Haas and his family became my friends. He asked for my manuscript and gave it to the chief editor of Random House, a man called Robert Linscott, who took me out to lunch and said he would be very interested to see the novel when it was finished. Linscott was a very attractive man in his fifties; we became friends, and remained so for years. We indulged in mild, but regulated flirtation, something quite new to me, and very pleasant. Someone else suggested I should send the novel to Scribners, where Maxwell Perkins read it, and said much the same as Linscott.

I was generally spoiled, but I think the most delicious treat was that the people at Scribners took me to Brentano's bookshop and told me to look round and make a pile of any books I would like. I remember Mo, my grandfather, saying that when he was sent to Germany as a young student, where concerts and opera abounded, he felt like a dog being let out into a field full of rabbits; that was how I felt in Brentano's. I collected all kinds of books about opera for Robert, poetry, stories by Ambrose Bierce and works by William Faulkner and F. Scott Fitzgerald, and other novels or classics I didn't possess. I thought I was meant to select a single volume from this list, but, no, I could have the lot. They'd crate them to go back in the ship with us; riches. I went shopping for clothes, shoes and stockings – nylons, almost unheard of in England.

I made a list of all the people I wanted to give things to and bought them presents. I bought two years' worth of pretty frocks for Nicola, and shirts and ties for Pete. The exchange rate at the time was five dollars to the pound. I knew nothing about money, the dollars felt like tiddlywinks and I used them like a greedy child. After years of lacking pretty or new things the temptations were continuous and completely frivolous, and I succumbed to them. I didn't buy anything extremely expensive, but it all mounted up. Bill Kennet had once said he liked Tabasco – unobtainable during the war – and I bought him a crate. My father had long finished his Havana cigars, and I bought him a box of fifty.

There was something else I bought regularly. Men on the street corners displayed trays of tiny turtles, their shells painted in bright glossy green or yellow, which they sold. Pete said they'd die, as their shells would let in no air. So I bought them, cleaned their shells with nail-varnish remover, washed them in soapy water, and then put them in the bath in our hotel. They cost about ten cents each, and as the days went by it took longer and longer to transport them to the basin, have a bath and then put them back again. Pete entirely approved of this, although he did point out that the more of them I bought, the more the men on the street corner would find it worth procuring new stock.

Robert's letters kept coming, and although I wrote back faithfully, selecting what to tell him, and saying quite truthfully that I loved and missed him, it was sometimes a relief when we were asked away for weekends, where there could be no letters. We stayed with Arthur Harlow, the owner of Pete's gallery, and his wife in their vast gloomy house up the Hudson River. We stayed with the Lloyd-Smiths, a very rich family with two daughters, Ginny, recently married, and Clara, very attractive and *soignée*. She was the first girl I saw wearing blue jeans, a man's shirt, and polished idlers on her bare feet. She looked wonderful.

I was, however, haunted throughout the trip by chronic backache and a slight, but continuous feeling of nausea. Pete said I should see a doctor, and as my cousin Nemone Balfour, now living in New York, was married to one, I went to him. He was Russian and had a very successful practice. He told me to lay off butter and cream and not to overdo it. Then he said, 'Eleanor Roosevelt, a great friend of mine, has recently lost her husband and I have to write a letter of condolence. Would you read it, and see if you think it's the right sort of letter?' I did, but found little to say. However, he thanked me and refused to be paid for my visit.

Marie Paneth had asked me to look up her old lover, Heinz Hartman, now living in New York, and tell him about her. This I did. He practised in an apartment on Park Avenue. When I rang, the over-protective secretary told me to make an appointment. I said it was a personal matter and I particularly wished to speak to him. He came on the line, sounding very guarded. 'It's about Marie Paneth,' I said. His voice changed completely. He was extremely glad to have news of Marie, whom, clearly, he loved. He asked for her address, thanked me again and again for being in touch and that was that.

Pete and I did some broadcasts; he was very good at it, and I had to talk about London during the Blitz. Afterwards, someone involved in the programme came to me and said, 'We had our small privations too, you know. It was often quite difficult to get cream.'

Sometime during those weeks I managed to lose the sixty pages of my novel. I was frantic and Bob Linscott took a lot of trouble looking for them, but to no avail. I had a dim recollection of having put the manuscript down in the ladies' loo at a restaurant, but this was later, after we got back to England. There was nothing for it but to rewrite it.

One of Pete's pre-war friends was a French zoologist called Jean Delacourt. He now ran the Bronx zoo, to which we went. During our visit it was arranged that we'd take back some snakes, various

188

kinds of turtle, and some alligators for English zoos. When the day came for our return – we were sailing in the *Queen Mary* – the crates of creatures duly arrived at the dockside. When the porters saw huge crates marked 'Alligators', they refused to move them into the ship. Pete went to the other two crates, rubbed out their labels, and put 'Fragile. Cabin only'. So, our cabin contained sixteen snakes, and sixty turtles, including my rescued ones. We let the turtles out, and I became used to Pete saying, in the restaurant, 'My wife would like two lettuces and a small saucer of raw minced beef in the cabin.' When he said we must let the snakes out of their sacks to give them a drink, things became trickier.

'Won't they bite and escape?'

'They're not poisonous, so their bites won't matter, and we'll put them in the bath for their drink.' This we did and none bit us, but one garter snake escaped. I saw its head sticking out of the overflow pipe of the bath, and when we tried to catch it, it withdrew completely. 'It may turn up in Lord Halifax's bathroom,' Pete said gloomily. The Halifaxes, next door, came to tea in the cabin to see the turtles. They were friends of the Kennets, and Pete knew them slightly. The snakes weren't mentioned. One morning, as I was washing my hands, I found the little snake tied in an elegant reef knot round the hot tap. I got Pete, and he retrieved her. He and I collaborated about animals more than we did about any-thing else. It's sad to me now to think that this, the most serious and interesting part of his life and nature, was so overwhelmed by war and guns. It struck me again what a great naturalist he was – not simply someone who was interested in wildfowl but an all-rounder, although his greatest passion was always wildfowl.

We left New York with much else besides the reptiles. I'd no idea of it then, but I'd spent nearly all of the money that Pete had earned from his exhibition. He was uninterested in money, but I still think of this with shame. If he'd ever told me to stop spending, I would have, but he never did. I don't think he had much more idea of money than I. He'd always earned it easily, and his wants were simple.

Conflict and confusion had been growing steadily in me for months. My marriage was hopeless, but I could see no way out. Guilt about my failure with Pete, and my complex feelings about Nicola blocked me. A chief feature of guilt is paralysis; on one hand I felt I should be able to love Pete and have a family with him – I hated the idea of Nic being an only child – on the other, I couldn't bring myself to do something that felt wrong. Without trying to excuse myself, I think now that, as some people eat or drink when they are unhappy, I'd resorted to buying things in an attempt to compensate for failure, unhappiness and the misery of blaming myself. Pete was a gifted and interesting man; he was never wittingly unkind to me, but he didn't understand that my youth presented him with responsibilities as well as advantages. I could never really talk to him seriously about anything – he wasn't interested in me, really, or in anyone else, in that way.

As so many men do, he wanted me to settle down to marriage and a family, so that he could pursue matters that did interest him. He was thirty-six, had always known what he wanted to do, and had been successful all his life: he was full of optimism, confidence and energy. I was twenty-three, precocious in some ways, but essentially immature, even for my age, and I'd succeeded in nothing. I wasn't fulfilled in any way, had very little confidence. We had reached a point, had perhaps been trapped there for years, when it didn't seem possible to talk about these things. The only time when there had been honest and real communication between us had been the night he spent with me in Stratford. But when I thought of leaving Pete, panic assailed me. I had no money, no training except in acting which I'd more or less given up as a possible career. I had nowhere to go. My novel, half finished, might never be published, and even if it was, I knew enough from Robert and Ray to understand it wouldn't provide me with a living. *And* there was Nicola. How could I earn my living and keep her? I realized that at least some of these difficulties had to be solved.

8

We were met at Southampton by K, Nicola and Nanny, and Marie Paneth. But before that we had to get through Customs. Pete managed the crates of turtles and snakes with an easy charm and they weren't unpacked. But my copious luggage was looked at. 'Do you always travel, Madam, with twelve dozen pairs of stockings?' the Customs man asked after he'd opened the drawer of my cabin trunk.

'Always,' I said, trying to look that sort of person.

He shrugged, but he let me through.

And there was Nicola wearing her winter coat and white socks, with her silky honey-coloured hair tied at the side with a blue velvet ribbon. I'd always thought her the most beautiful child, and in these few weeks she seemed to have grown. I lifted her up to kiss her, but she'd never liked me doing that, and wriggled to be put down.

K was clearly delighted to see Pete. When we reached the car with her chauffeur, she said there wouldn't be room for everyone, and that she would drive with Pete to London; the rest of us were to go by train. I didn't mind this because it meant I could ring Robert and tell him I was back, but Marie was incensed on my behalf.

Robert was clearly relieved to hear from me. 'When can I see you?' I didn't know, but I'd ring him as soon as it was possible.' 'Make it soon, my dearest love; I ache for you. I can't endure life without you. Ray sends her love,' he added.

In the train I managed to tell Marie I'd seen her friend in New York and that he'd asked for her address. We all went back to Edwardes Square and had tea. Pete dined with his family that evening; I received a half-hearted invitation, but said I was tired. I bathed Nicola and she told me about a person she'd invented, a Mr Leafie, who wore winter combinations and lived in the dirty-clothes basket in the bathroom. 'Quite often his wives die and we have a funeral tea.' He was clearly a rather frightening character, rather like Robin's Ciggi. I once asked her how he was, and she laughed nervously and said, 'Oh, he's full of beans. He's been eating beans all day at the office.' That evening, Nanny had another go at me about Nicola having a little brother.

Some time later, when Pete was on one of his hunts for a suitable place to keep wildfowl, I spent my first weekend with Robert in his father's house at Stanmore. Ray had provided a couple of lamb chops and some bread, and we set forth by train on the Friday evening.

The house was half-way up a hill from the station, a detached, rather dark place with small rooms and a neglected garden. Indeed, the whole house had a Miss Havisham-like air. It was thick with dust and very cold. All the curtains were drawn and the kitchen was full of dirty crocks that had long waited to be washed up. There were two gas fires, one in the sitting room and one in the large bedroom. There was spinach in the garden, Robert said, I had only to pick it, and we had supper of the chops, enormous amounts of mashed potato and the spinach. Afterwards, Robert played me very old records of Rosa Ponselle and Giuseppe Martinelli singing the main arias from *Aida* – all new to me. I was entranced.

It's difficult to describe what extraordinarily good company Robert could be; I was dazzled by how much he knew and how greatly he cared about Verdi, for instance, whose music I'd never heard. He was full of esoteric pieces of information: he introduced me to Wyndham Lewis, to Norman Douglas, to opera, to ballet, to the earliest films, and all this was interspersed with such repeated, romantic asseverations of love, for my beauty, my wonderful character, my general *goodness*, that he scored a double, as it were, to my head and my heart. It was a wonderful respite from what I felt about myself.

He could also be very funny, the more so because it was unexpected. He had a great sense of irony, always aptly employed. He'd always been unhappy, didn't fit in with modern life. He couldn't get on with men much, but he'd always loved women, who, he said, were far the superior species. He was full of sympathy for what he called my most wretched situation. Marriage, he said, was an impossible institution and he deplored it. He was interested in psychic phenomena, knew Harry Price, the famous psychical researcher, and had once spent a night at Borley Rectory, the most haunted house in England. He read aloud to me Matthew Arnold's *Dover Beach*, and Russell's *History of Western Philosophy*.

He concealed from me his neurotic fears. Then it was all romance and the amazing chance that he'd found me and how wonderful our life would be together. The privations of the house, which I got to know well − the dust, the lack of any hot water except from the kettle, the dreary light, the cracked gramophone − were nothing to me. To be with someone so tender, so admiring, so knowledgeable was more than I felt I could ever have hoped for. I loved him, and wanted to do anything that would make him happier. During that summer I lived an uneasy, unresolved life, three-quarters of it at Edwardes Square, and the rest with Robert.

Peter had found the place where he wanted to have his wildfowl, at Slimbridge on the Severn marshes. When he first went there, there was only a small cottage, and we stayed at an inn nearby. It was a bare and virtually treeless place except for a small clump in which there was an old duck decoy. The only time I went there I was ill, and the prospect didn't hearten me. I'd not learned to appreciate wild geese; I'd not then become interested in gardening, and it was miles from anywhere. I remember that we went to Berkeley Castle, where Rob Berkeley lived; it was his land that Pete was to lease. At that point, Pete didn't talk about living there, but I could see that he had it in mind.

During the winter of 1946 – soon, I think, after Christmas, K became ill. Since I'd known her, she'd always had heart trouble, but this was different: it turned out to be leukaemia. I went, with Peter, to see her at St Mary's where she lay in a small room. I don't think she can have wanted to see me much, she knew that our marriage was breaking up, but she was very gentle and dignified, and as one thing I knew for certain about her was her love and intense enjoyment of life, I could recognize the enormous courage she was using to deal with her death. I also knew that her passionate love for Pete, and desire that everything should always be perfect for him, meant that she must be desperately unhappy at having to leave him. I felt I'd let her down in almost every way: I'd not made Pete happy, I'd failed to have a son, I'd been unfaithful, a spendthrift and a bad mother. I think it was the first time I could see all of this from her point of view – possibly because she'd always seemed so powerful to me, and now was nothing of the kind. I remember asking Pete whether he thought that there was anything I could do for her. He said she would like me to read to her, which I did on subsequent occasions. I never knew whether she actually *wanted* me to do that – probably not – but she thought that Pete wanted me to, and that was enough. She died within a few months, in July, and Bill, Pete and Wayland scattered her ashes.

I left Pete and Edwardes Square in August. I can't now remember an exact moment when this decision was taken, any more than I can remember what preparations I made for it. I must have done some flat-hunting – I think Robert helped me. London was full of run-down or even derelict properties. After wild ideas, such as Tower Bridge itself or Floral Street in Covent Garden (on Shelley's principle of living in a street with a name he liked), I found a maisonette in Blandford Street off Baker Street above a grocery and poultry shop. It was eighteenth century, had one medium and one small room on each floor and a plaque outside it that said, 'Michael Faraday, Man of Science, was Apprenticed Here'. The rent was one hundred and fifty pounds a year and clearly I'd have to share it. At some point during my marriage, my father had settled some family shares for me that brought in just over a hundred pounds a year. Even I, pretty unclear about what life actually cost, could see that there was going to be a gap. I'd have to get some sort of job, and soon.

Blandford Street was in a poor state: I had to pay for some plumbing, a boiler, a very small bath that would just fit into the narrow slip room that contained a lavatory and basin. The walls were like sleepy pears – bulging, soft and crumbly. Whoever had lived there before me had left illiterate notes pinned to them: 'Hole house roting' or 'Look out for seeling'. I had to buy materials to plaster and paint the rooms, and it's interesting, looking back on it, to remember who lent me the money for this.

Earlier that year, in the spring I think it was, Pete had needed a new secretary. Wayland said he thought he knew the right person. He brought her round, and we all went out to dinner. I remember a very pretty girl, about my age, in a black velvet dress. Her name was Elizabeth Adams; Pete engaged her at once, and she was there when I left, in a taxi with two suitcases and ten pounds. I'd asked my father if I could stay with him and Ursula until my flat was habitable – he'd taken a large house in West Hampstead, and he'd said yes. It was Liz who rang half an hour after I'd arrived there, to see if I was all right. It was she who later lent me three hundred pounds to get the flat going, unsolicited, to pay back when and if I liked. It's lovely and consoling to have, among so many others of that time, a memory that engenders pure gratitude.

I didn't get a very good reception at Ranulf Road. It quickly became clear to me that Ursula didn't want me to be there, and this was made plain by all kinds of small, subtle manoeuvres. I was put into a room that was really somebody else's, which meant there was nowhere to put away clothes. The house was quite large, with a housekeeper on the top floor. It was also clear that I was expected to be in for as few meals as possible. This was simple during the daytime, as I spent most of it painting my flat, but evenings – when I didn't spend them with Robert – were sometimes tricky. I couldn't afford to eat out, and sometimes resorted to a bun in my bedroom. My father was unaware of this and, indeed, when they were in, I did eat with them, but he never asked me how I was managing for money, and I was determined not to broach the subject. In front of my father, Ursula was blandly amiable, but I left the house to sleep in my flat long before it was really habitable. I remember my first night there, a bare bulb in the ceiling, wooden floors full of malignant nails, the odour of decay that seeped through the wet paint smell and the unpleasant feeling that everything was dirty except my bedclothes. Above all, I felt alone, and the only thing I was sure of was that I wanted to write.

For the next few months and the beginning of winter, I struggled to equip the house with necessities. I bought a job lot of second-hand gas fires and a second-hand cooker called the New Suburbia. I painted the house in furiously bright colours – brilliant yellow up the stairs, which I carpeted with coconut matting. The smell of decay receded, but odours from the North Brothers' shop – the plucked and singed birds in the basement – came into their own. As Christmas approached, the odour of bacon and burned feathers and the uneasy smell of what was being taken out of the birds rose steadily up the stairs. Food was still rationed, even bread, and it was an exceptionally cold winter. I asked Jill Balcon if she would like to share the flat with me – two rooms each and a shared kitchen and dining room on the top floor – but the squalor was too much for her.

I was rescued from doom by Robert and Ray, who'd found a young painter called Joanna Dowling, whose work we all admired, and she came to live on the first floor. Robert offered me a part-time job typing for his Inland Waterways Association, which brought in two pounds ten shillings a week. Once, having dinner with him in a small local restaurant, somebody sent a card to my table asking whether I'd like to model clothes for *Vogue*. This was a tremendous bonus. I got three guineas a day – the first of which was with Norman Parkinson, or Parks, as he came to be known. The other new girl, Wenda Rogerson, was a beauty who became Parks's wife. Occasionally, I was asked to read some poetry for radio. I lived from hand to mouth. The most extravagant purchase I made was a small walnut davenport desk I bought second-hand at Heals for thirty pounds. I wrote four books at that desk – by hand, in those days – and I have it still.

Sometimes Robert came to stay with me; sometimes we went at the weekend to Stanmore. Divorce proceedings began. I'd explained to Pete, and subsequently to his lawyers, that I didn't want any money from him, but it became clear that the lawyers didn't believe me – thought, for some reason, that I was holding out in the hope of getting more. I got so upset by this that I went to see Bill Kennet about it. He received me with great kindness, but when I told him what I'd come about he seemed very put out. 'Is that *all* you came for?' And I realized that he must have thought I'd changed my mind and wanted to go back to Pete. I never saw him again. I felt sad about that.

I had known that the most difficult aspect of my leaving Pete was what would happen with Nicola. I'd been going to see her every week at Edwardes Square, and poor Nanny couldn't understand why she and Nic couldn't come and live with me. I knew that Pete would pay her wages, but I couldn't begin to have bought them food or provided any reasonable space or comfort for them. I realize now I could have negotiated with Peter about this, but at the time it didn't seem right. Looking back, this seems ill judged and certainly selfish, but I couldn't handle nursery life with what my own had become. When Edwardes Square came to an end, Nanny and Nicola went to live with a friend who had a child of the same age, and I went there every week, miserably aware of how unsatisfactory this was and guilty. Besides the material difficulties, there were emotions I was too frightened and ashamed to confront. I was afraid I should never have had Nicola and that I didn't love her enough. I was selfishly determined to be a writer at any cost, to put it first, and I knew that I had to do it alone.

Looking back, it seems strange to me that I knew nobody with whom I could have discussed this impartially. Robert and Ray, the IWA and their friends formed my chief society. None of them had children and I see now it was clearly against Robert's interests to have me with other responsibilities than himself. He wanted, as I slowly came to see, all my maternal feelings to be centred on him. Ray poured love and attention into him, but that wasn't enough: he wanted me to do the same. Over the next year or so, Ray and I formed a close friendship largely because of this and our mutual work for the IWA. Robert and Tom Rolt, who had founded the organization with Robert, were a brilliant combination and managed between them what remained of England's waterways. At the time, immediately after the railways were nationalized, canals were considered redundant, useless for either trade or pleasure. In the past the railway companies had bought hundreds of them, then neglected them to the point where they could apply for an Act of Abandonment. Of the four thousand miles of navigable canals at the beginning of the century, only two thousand remained. In 1947, the railway companies owned 35 per cent of them. They were surprised when we told them this.

Robert dictated a huge quantity of letters with facts and statistics and persuasive reasoning without faltering or changing his mind. He could also speak fluently and well without notes. He was good at collecting influential people to back the IWA, including MPs of all parties whom he persuaded to ask pertinent questions in the House of Commons. He ran the IWA on a shoestring with the utmost assurance. Inside himself, he had an insatiable need for attention and a virtuosity in the ways of getting it. He was deeply depressed, in danger of going mad, he said, and in some way this was true but, as so much with him, not entirely true. He'd learned to manipulate people close to him so that they'd always feel protective and anxious and fall in with what he wanted. He was paranoid about not being liked or understood or appreciated enough. He was endlessly demanding and, in short, such an exhausting person to live with that Ray and I were thankful to share him.

One of the most exhausting aspects of all this was that life was chronically *serious*. We weren't supposed to be either light-hearted or happy about anything much – with the exception of per-formances in the theatre, cinema, concert hall or opera house. These were all things that Robert did enjoy, indeed they were his refuge from what he called the despairing reality of life. He ran his small literary agency to augment his private income, and there Ray was his helpmeet. He also liked walking, was indefatigable and had detailed maps of most of England from which he planned mara-thon walks. Later he went on canal trips with the Rolts. On the evenings when he didn't go out, he would read to Ray or me until well after midnight, when he would require his last meal. Ray had early taken to giving him breakfast in bed, but she had to get up – as did I – to start the day and I remember often having to type his letters hardly able to keep my eyes open.

He didn't like me to have friends outside his circle, but I introduced him to one or two people of whom he approved, James and Anthea Sutherland, friends of Wayland, and Jill Balcon, for instance, but generally he sulked or was jealous of any life I had outside his orbit. However, with the IWA work which grew quickly in volume, my own writing, and any extra jobs that came my way, I didn't have much time. What I had I spent with Nicola, and visits to my embittered mother in her dark little house.

My relations with her were at an all-time low. My father had made the appalling error of telling her I'd thought she would prefer him to find her a house before he left her, and she was under-standably very angry at what she felt was my betrayal. Before I'd left Peter and when I told her I was going to do this, she asked why, and I'd said I wanted to be a writer and couldn't do it married to him. Her retort had been, 'What on earth makes you think that anyone would ever publish anything that *you* wrote?' This had profoundly depressed me, and drove another wedge between us. At the time I felt it wasn't love for my father that had driven her to her endless recriminations but pride, and I was too young to recognize the painful validity of pride.

She lived with Great-aunt May, to whom she was uniformly kind, and my younger brother Colin, who I think bore the brunt of her shock and rage. She adored him, but she preyed on his feelings and his sense of pity and responsibility to a damaging degree. She was determined that he should have nothing to do with Ursula, which suited Ursula as she didn't want my father's attention diverted from her own children. But it made an irrecoverable rift between Colin and our father. By now he was at Radley where he was very unhappy. It was some years before I realized what a hard time he was having; in those days I hardly ever saw him alone and we shared no confidences. I moved into Blandford Street in the autumn of 1947, and spent the next three years trying to come to terms with my new life.

9

I was chronically short of money, as was my flatmate Joanna, who was trying to get work as an illustrator. Food seemed to go on being rationed for ever: we lived on coffee and toast, kippers and unnamed frozen fish and cheap cuts of what meat we were allowed. I remember going to dinner one evening at my father's house, being given two martinis and passing out because I hadn't eaten anything that day. Hating the idea that they'd think me drunk, I told them this, whereupon Ursula remarked that I should live on cheap food. I'd thought that her hostility to me was largely based on her own insecurity, but she had now married my father, and I had to recognize that she simply didn't like me. My father frequently said we were his two favourite women, which made the situation worse. I came to approach her with caution. Now, I'd probably confront her, have it out somehow, but then I didn't feel up to a scene.

Joanna and I lived fairly separate lives, but we got on well with each other. She had a predilection for French counts with whom she spent many tense and often tear-stained evenings. There seemed to be a lot of love about that was either unrequited or hopeless, and we discussed the difficulties of life and our relationships with amiable despair. Although I'd no money, I still possessed a set of fairly decent clothes, but Robert didn't like most of them. He wanted me to wear straight black skirts and shirts with ties. I'd cut my hair very short because it was easier to keep, and found a wonderful Swiss hairdresser in St James's Street who cut it every three weeks for three shillings. I also came upon a Polish dress-maker, Mrs Grodzicka, who made me skirts that fitted beautifully for three guineas.

On days when I didn't go to the IWA office in Gower Street, I struggled on with my novel. It took a long time to write, largely, I think, because I didn't know how to end it, but eventually it reached a rather improbable conclusion. I paid somebody to type it and Robert and Ray sent it to Jonathan Cape. They were in two minds about whether it should go to Cape or Macmillan, but the editor they knew at the latter was away, so it went to Cape. It was accepted three weeks later, to my surprise and joy, and I was invited to lunch with Mr Cape at a flat he had round the corner from his publishing house in Bedford Square. It was a rather dark and dingy mansion flat; he was standing in front of an oak fireplace in the dining room when I met him. 'I've made rather a strong martini,' he said, 'very good for ladies who are menstruating.' This wasn't a very cheering start, but I reflected that he had my future in his hands, so I smiled and pretended he'd said something entirely different.

Lunch was served by an Irish lady, dressed like a poppy, but at least she was intermittently there. As we ate he said the book would benefit from some cutting. I said I didn't want to do this, and he said, 'Well, I will publish it as it stands, and you will learn that way.' As soon as lunch was over, he became amorous and mildly blackmailing. 'Of course, I could change my mind,' he said, as he pursued me round the table. Fortunately it had sharp corners that I was more agile at negotiating than he. In the end he gave up gracefully, the waters closed over the incident, and it was never repeated. I got fifty pounds in advance of royalties.

I began to feel rich and professional. I wrote a couple of pieces for *Vogue* for Siriol Hugh Jones, their enchanting features editor who became a friend. Siriol – who died when she was still quite young, of cancer – was one of those life-enhancing people: immensely funny, clever, warm and more gifted than her job allowed her to be. She could write well about anything, but there was always something perceptibly vulnerable about her which perhaps got in the way of her finding her true métier. I remember her coming to dinner one evening – I'd progressed to giving occasional dinner parties – with a handsome young actor and saying, 'This is Derek Hart: I am in love with him.' Derek became a well-known TV presenter on the *Tonight* show. She married him and they had a daughter, but the marriage went wrong. She became ill, and was valiant and funny about it – '*Birdseed* instead of my breast! Isn't that an extraordinary thing to think of?' It's odd: I didn't know her very well, but I still miss her and remember her with great affection.

My friend Phoebe Noël Smith who'd been at Instow and with whom I'd shared a room brought her uncle Mathew Smith to dinner. He looked not unlike a friendly, enquiring prawn, with glasses so thick that you could hardly see his eyes. One winter, Phoebe said he had suggested to take her and me to Brighton for the weekend, as he wanted to get away from things. 'Things' turned out to be various ladies, but although Phoebe and I had a good time poking about in the secondhand bookshops and staying in a luxurious hotel, Uncle Matthew, as we all called him, was distinctly uneasy throughout. When we left the hotel, he was constantly looking behind him in case any of the ladies had discovered his hideout and were pursuing him. He painted Barbara, the third occupant of the Instow ménage, a great deal: her beauty was both calm and voluptuous and suited him well. Uncle Matthew admired my dining-room décor (the only person who did) with its intense pink walls and scarlet woodwork. He was a very modest man – seemed to fit in with any company – and although by then he must have been fairly old, he didn't seem to be any age at all.

But most of my life in terms of energy and time was spent in dealing with the IWA and Robert. I'd been promoted to being a member of the council and it didn't take long to discover that this all-parties association had spawned its own internal politics. Tom

Rolt, like Robert, was a man of many gifts. He'd been an engineer, had a passion for railways and canals; it was his book *Narrow Boat* that had drawn Robert's attention to inland waterways. They had things in common, such as an intense dislike of modern technology and mass-produced artefacts, and nostalgia for the – carefully selected – past. They both loved and explored England; Tom lived on his boat *Cressy* with his then wife, Angela. They also shared tastes in literature – notably ghost stories. Tom wrote a collection entitled *Sleep No More* that impressed Robert, who also began writing ghost stories and encouraged me to do the same. They were a powerful combination when it came to running the IWA, which I think would never have achieved its eventual influence without either of them. But inevitably they began to grate against one another, and council meetings became tense with unspoken criticism. Robert also started a flirtation with Angela that didn't go down well with anyone.

However, the eventual break was several years off, and during that time we all, together and severally, made trips on various canals throughout the country. The most notable was in a small hired boat called *Ailsa Craig*, in which we explored the northern canals with the Sutherlands and the Rolts. The lock dimensions were unsuited to the narrow boat, but for six weeks we journeyed in it and its engine never failed to fail us. Somehow, between them, James Sutherland and Tom Rolt kept it going. I learned to work locks, cook suppers on a primus with steamers, and to steer. The high point of our journey was the navigation of the Huddersfield Narrow Canal, which ran across the Pennines from Ashton to Huddersfield. It had seventy-four locks in its nineteen miles, all of them in bad repair, and at its summit a tunnel, Standedge, that was three and a half miles long with adits to the main railway line, which meant it frequently filled with dense black smoke. We got stuck in it, and had to remove our rubbing strakes, which gave us an extra three-quarters of an inch leeway. It was an adventure, and we were the last people to go through the tunnel.

I grew to love canals and narrow boats: their secretive beauty, the way they slipped though large industrial towns and into country at a speed so leisurely – less than four miles an hour – that you could notice where you were. I loved the ingenious simplicity of the engineering: the locks that took you up or down and the occasional staircases that rose or fell dramatically in the landscape. The tunnels dripped silently, sometimes with a towpath in them, sometimes not, and aqueducts bridged wide valleys. There was the amazing swing bridge in an iron trough at the junction of the Bridgewater and Manchester Ship Canals and the wonderful hydraulic mechanism that lifted boats bodily from the river Weaver up to the Welsh section of the Shropshire Union Canal. Thereabouts we went through a tunnel that had an inn at the end of it. In the inn there was a large portrait of a cow that had swum right through the tunnel, they said, and had been given a pint of brandy to restore her. This event was spoken of as though it had occurred the previous week; in fact it had happened before the First World War.

The boat trips taught me a lot about the country that I might never have known. Robert and I slept in a tent that had to be pitched every night in pouring rain – it seemed always to rain. But boats can bring out the worst in people. Robert, who was never handy in an ordinary domestic way, expected everything to be done for him. The only thing he wanted to do in a boat was to steer it and, in the beginning at least, he was very bad at it. This made him cross, and he quarrelled with me, and argued with Tom, and was an uneasy member of the crew. All the same, that whole trip in the north was a wonderful adventure to me, and I remember thinking, *Why* does he have to spoil something so exciting and enjoyable with black moods and scenes? Why can't we just *be* in it without all this drama and tension? It was much the same feeling I'd had as a young adult, when I knew that my parents weren't getting on, a bit like being shot at by snipers when you were on a picnic.

I kept no journal or even a diary, and I am aware as I write this that although I have assembled the main events of these three years the order of them is shaky. Looking back, I can see that my feelings about Robert were slowly, undramatically changing. In fact, our threesome was on the move: Ray had taken a lover about whom Robert knew nothing. She and I still confided in each other and there was affection and trust between us, but in different ways our lives were beginning not to revolve around Robert.

During that time I'd learned much; I'd written more and had begun to earn money from it, and I was earning more from the increased IWA work. In fact, the money situation, though far from secure, wasn't so worrying. However, I hadn't been happy and was inwardly rebelling against Robert's despairing ideas about life. I was also managing to have some life apart from him, initially made easy when he took Ray on country trips, but gradually not dependent upon that.

James and Anthea Sutherland had moved from London to a village outside Doncaster where James had a job. They very kindly let me take Nicola to their home when Nanny had her holiday. I did this for two summers and she and I had some good times together. I began teaching her to read from a wonderful Victorian book called *Reading Without Tears* and she made great progress. She loved, as all children do, being read aloud to: 'Reege to me,' she would say, the moment things looked like getting dull. There was also a cat that she called Plucifer, who entranced her. She'd inherited her father's love of animals, and her favourite afternoon treat was to be taken to the zoo, to which we went many times.

Once we went to the smaller mammals' house, which contained pottos, kinkajou and tree pandas. It was presided over by a very old keeper, who took one look at Nicola and then invited her to go through the house with him. He took animals out of the cages for her to handle and stroke. At the end of the tour, when I thanked him, he said, 'It's nothing but a pleasure. I used to do just the same for her father when he was her age. I'd have known her anywhere.'

Indeed, as far back as I can remember, she'd always had the right touch and confidence with any creature.

There was one awful moment when, with Peter, we were taken behind the scenes in the reptile house. Nicola put her hand into a tank that contained a horned viper, coiled to strike. Pete saw this and said very quietly, 'Take your hand out of there, darling, *very* gently,' and she did. I broke into a cold sweat with fear, but no fuss was made. Pete simply told her never to put her hand into any of the tanks.

She longed more than anything to have a dog, and Pete gave her a white Pekinese who combined extreme beauty with a cheerful disposition. He'd been called Butterfly of Mulberry, but she called him Bushy and he was a great joy to her.

Robert couldn't very well object to the time I spent with Nicola, but he made difficulties about other people, and I took to concealing from him any time I spent with friends. The fact that I'd written a book that was to be published also caused resentment. Robert had ambitions to write, but so far he'd only written critical pieces for the *Nineteenth Century*. He was writing ghost stories, but no magazines were accepting them. He also wrote a play, a Ruritanian romance, but nothing came of that either. Wanting to help him with this, I suggested we could both write enough ghost stories to make a book that Cape could publish. We wrote three stories each, and Cape, though reluctant, agreed to do it. The volume was to be called *We Are For the Dark*, and at that point, the stories weren't individually attributed. I thought that this would ease the situation, but it didn't really.

I hadn't left my marriage *for* Robert; I would have left anyway. I'd never wanted to marry him, if, indeed, that had been possible, but I felt guilty that he'd become more of an emotional responsibility than anything else.

IO

At the beginning of 1950, when I was nearly twenty-six, Dosia and Barry asked me to a New Year party. I wore a beautiful dress that Peter had given me and my only grand piece of jewellery, an opal and diamond necklace with earrings to match.

Dosia and Barry had moved from Bedford Gardens to a studio flat in Carlton Hill, a few yards away from our St John's Wood wartime home. The studio was large, the perfect place for a big party; everybody had dressed up and it was full of friends whom I'd not seen for ages, including Anne Richmond, now married to her Pete who had survived years in a Japanese war camp. Also there were Marie Paneth and one of her sons, and Dosia's youngest sister, Ruth, who arrived late with a young man called Kenneth Tynan, both looking as though they'd arrived late for a very good reason. But there were also a number of people I didn't know, among them a dark, glamorous man who asked me to dance with him. He wasn't very good at it, which was reassuring, because I wasn't either. The party went on until one or two a.m., and somebody must have given me a lift home, but I don't remember who.

The next morning I was woken by Joanna who said that a man with a big black poodle wanted to see whether I was as beautiful by day as by night. 'Tell him certainly not,' I said, grumpy and hung-over over. She came back and said he'd invited me to dine with him that evening: he'd left his address and would I come at about eight p.m.? His name was Michael Behrens, she added: he'd told her to say this in case I'd forgotten. I'd known he was called Michael, but really nothing else. I rang Dosia and asked her about him. She said he worked in the City, was married to a very nice person called Felicity and had three sons. 'If he asked you to dinner, I should go, Jane, no harm in that.' But in one quite serious sense there was.

I went, assuming that I was going to have dinner, with Felicity, in their house in Hanover Terrace. When I got there, and before I rang the bell, I noticed that the door was ajar, so I went in. The sound of Mozart was coming from the floor above. I went up into a large, dark, mutely lit drawing room and Michael rose from a distant sofa to greet me. 'I'm taking you out to dinner,' he said, 'but I thought we'd have a tiny drink first.' He poured us martinis and as he held out the glass to me I realized, with a shock, I was physically attracted to him. It made me extremely shy and breathless.

He took me to the Étoile in Charlotte Street, in those days a modest, well-run French restaurant with hard chairs and little hanging lamps shrouded in red silk. The food was delicious, but I couldn't eat much. I'd fallen in love.

One admirable consequence of meeting Michael was that I found a much better home for Nicola. When I spoke of my anxieties for her, he told me that his cousin, Josie Baird, who lived next door to him, had just had her third child and wanted a nanny, but was worried about the expense. They had a daughter, Julia, of Nicola's age and he thought they might be pleased to have her live with them and share Nanny Buss. I went to tea with Josie in her beautiful drawing room overlooking Regent's Park. I felt she didn't like me very much, but she agreed to see Nanny and Nic and to discuss the finances with Pete, who was by then at Slimbridge having founded the Wild Fowl Trust. Everything was arranged, and Nic, Nanny and Bushy went to live with the Bairds.

This was an enormous relief to me. Nicola was now ten minutes away from Blandford Street by bus, in a beautiful house with a park nearby and two other children to play with, while Nanny had a baby to look after, her dearest wish. I visited every week, miserably aware of how unsatisfactory this was, and I felt guilty. Nicola and Julia went to a school a short bus ride away, and Josie and I embarked upon a cautious friendship that has ripened and warmed to this day.

Josie was tiny, with a complexion like the best porcelain and a face that Gainsborough might have painted. Aside from the high forehead and fashionably neat, rosy lips, she had wit and intelligence that sparked from her eyes. Her husband, whose name was Michael but was invariably called Bumbo, was a lawyer working in a bank. He had a passion for architecture, looked like the nicest kind of bear and had, as Josie described to me later, 'a well-furnished mind'. But at first all I noticed about them was that he was kind and extremely courteous and that she was also generously kind and very highly strung. The only stipulation that Michael Behrens made about this arrangement was that Josie and Bumbo weren't to know anything about our affair.

In March, just before my twenty-sixth birthday, *The Beautiful Visit* was published. I was in Paris when I read my first review – a cool, but friendly piece by Francis Wyndham in the *Sunday Times*. I also had a very good review from Antonia White, best known for her lovely novel *Frost in May*. I'd started by then on my next novel, the construction of which I'd thought about far more carefully than I had with the first. It was to be about a marriage, told backwards, from the time when it broke up, to the couple's first meeting. The idea of stripping people down to their raw beginnings seemed to me to have interesting possibilities.

That spring I went to my first Cape party. I didn't know any other writers, and I felt they would all know one another. I dressed carefully for the occasion in a black skirt and stiff satin shirt of duck-egg blue that had been made for me out of a piece of material I'd bought in an antiques shop. It buttoned all the way up in small satin-covered buttons the size of peas. Jonathan Cape conducted me up the large first-floor room to the far end where, grouped around a piano were Rosamond Lehmann, Cecil Day-Lewis and Cyril

Connolly. I was introduced, and Cyril said, 'Do all those buttons actually do *up*?' I was so dazzled by this group, all of whom I knew by sight from the jackets of their books, that I was virtually speechless. I've always found walking into a room full of people, known or unknown, slightly nerve-racking, but William Plomer and Daniel George, both editors whom I'd met, looked after me.

At some time during the late spring, Jill Balcon invited me to a drinks party in her flat in Pimlico. It was very jolly – Siriol was there – and I ended up making corned beef hash for the late stayers. A small, fair girl called Audrey Dunlop and I took to each other. As Joanna was leaving Blandford Street to live with her mother, I invited Audrey back. She'd been in Paris for several years, and had left, I came to know, largely because of an unhappy love affair. She was a designer, looking for somewhere to live, and soon afterwards she moved in. She wanted to occupy the top floor, so we moved the kitchen and dining room down to the first floor where Joanna had lived. She also wanted to redecorate. This inspired me to do the like. We went off to Coles together, as they made easily the best wallpapers. I turned my bedroom into a dressing room and put a divan in the sitting room. Audrey chose a dignified grey paper with a gold pattern on it. I went for stripes, two different reds, like the passages in the Royal Opera House, for the dressing room, and the same width of stripe in a yellow and cinnamon brown – a terrible mistake: it dazzled. Coles recommended the Beswick brothers to hang the paper. They came to measure, two jolly little men, quite young. Len was very quiet and Stan rather noisy, with a laugh exactly like an empty tin can tumbling down uncarpeted stairs. On the day they started work, they brought a very old man with them. He was almost bald, with large protuberant red-rimmed eyes, like a bulldog. 'We've brought Mr Edwards,' they said. 'It's just the right-sized job for him. Now, Dad, sit down and have a cup of tea before you start.' Mr Edwards was panting heavily with excitement. 'You won't have to worry,' they said. 'He's taught us all we know. Been at it nearly fifty years.'

He was incredible. He would take one look at a mantelpiece, slash the paper, and it would fit exactly: he never measured anything. My walls were still bulging with weak old plaster, but he managed to give the impression that the stripes were straight. There is a peculiar joy in watching someone do anything as well as that. Mr Edwards kept a book, the brothers told me, that recorded every single paper he'd ever hung, and included several palaces, they said with pride. The brothers came back at midday to see that he wasn't overdoing it. It was the beginning of a long association with them: they hung papers for me in four subsequent houses. Eventually Stan left to become a greengrocer, Len told me with quiet contempt. It was Len I got to know best. He always wore white overalls with white shoes, and always brought a packed lunch. He never played a radio while he worked.

In August, the IWA staged a Festival and Rally of Boats at Market Harborough. By now Tom Rolt and Angela had parted and Tom was very much in love with a girl called Sonia Smith, who'd been an actress and then married a boatman. Tom had resigned from the council, so the main effort of staging the event fell to Robert, and he did it very well. A play was to be performed in the Assembly Rooms. Robert wanted the piece to be light entertainment, and chose Benn Levy's *Spring Time for Henry*. The cast of four were Barry Morse, Nicolette Bernard, Carla Lehman and, surprisingly, Pete, who decided he would like to have a go. He was very good in it. The farce was on the short side, and it was decided to have a curtain raiser. I'd written a two-hander called *Illusion* and showed it to Nicolette and Barry, who both said they'd like to do it. But Robert couldn't bear the idea that a play of mine would be performed. He was adamant, and decided upon Schnitzler's *A Marriage Has Been Arranged* instead. It went very well, but I was desperately disappointed not to have this chance of seeing my play performed by professionals. Eventually it was consigned to oblivion.

The festival was a great success, largely because it put the idea of waterways as a recreation on the map. The IWA ceased to be a small society of cranks with wild bees in their bonnets and became a body whose influence is still felt today. It's interesting that this began just as its core was splitting. A civil war had started, with Robert and Tom vying with each other for the claim that *he* had started the whole enterprise.

The ghost stories were published by Cape that autumn, and were fairly well received. Reviewers speculated on who had written which story, and usually got it wrong. That autumn I told Robert I was leaving him: I couldn't deal with the constant rows, scenes, the general exigency that he imposed. I told Ray first, said I was afraid that I was letting her down. I'd earlier told her I'd fallen in love with someone else, and I couldn't love two men at the same time. She said she completely understood: Robert *was* impossible – she wasn't sure how much more she herself could stand of him. Yes, she agreed, he would be very angry and resentful when I told him, and she would have a bad time, but it couldn't be helped. We agreed to keep in some sort of touch when possible, and I faced Robert.

He was as angry as I'd expected, of course, but I couldn't help noticing that there was more anger than grief: he felt utterly betrayed, he said. I didn't retort that philandering hardly went with a deep lifelong romantic love because I realized that I didn't care enough to justify myself to him. It was a relief to recognize that he'd only loved me in relation to himself. Then I wondered if that was how I was. Could I only see myself in the reflection of other people's eyes? This was an uncomfortable thought, but I was twenty-seven, and wasn't able to harbour uncomfortable thoughts for very long. I was better at justifying things to myself than I was to other people. I *had* tried to be what Robert wanted; I'd tried, but I couldn't keep it up.

I walked home from Gower Street to Blandford Street slightly dizzy with the sense of freedom. I'd lost my job with the IWA and would have to find something else, but I could wear what I liked, go to bed when I pleased, would no longer have the continual apprehension about Robert's state of mind when I next saw him. He'd taught me a great deal, and I'd got him published, so what credit there was seemed more or less balanced. I was amazed at how unsad I was about the whole thing. I got home to Audrey, who was drinking black coffee and designing clothes for Margaret Rutherford's part in a television play. She was delighted. 'I never liked him,' she said.

The following spring, I was invited to the party at which the John Llewellyn Rhys Prize was to be awarded. In those days it was for a novel by an author aged less than thirty, and Jonathan Cape, who was there, had entered *The Beautiful Visit*. It took place in a dusky little sitting room in a house in Maida Avenue. The contenders had been narrowed down to three of which I was one, but I was none the less dumbfounded when they said I'd won, and I was handed a cheque for fifty pounds amid many kind congratulations. 'I suppose you realize I shall expect ten per cent of that,' Jonathan said, with his crocodile smile.

The ladies of the committee flew at him. 'Outrageous! Out of the question!'

He backed off, trying to imply it had been a joke, but I don't think it was. Worse was to come. Robert wrote, in his capacity as my agent, that *he* expected ten per cent of the prize. I knew by now that that *was* outrageous and wrote an angry letter back, saying at the same time that I didn't want him to be my agent any longer.

And so I kept my riches to myself. Some months later, A. D. Peters wrote to me saying that he would like to represent me. At the time, he was the most respected literary agent in London, and I felt flattered to be asked. I was invited to lunch with him at his office, an eighteenth-century house in Buckingham Street, Adelphi, near Charing Cross. We had smoked salmon, pork pie and a green salad that he dressed himself. He was a stocky man, with large, slightly protuberant blue eyes and a quiet voice. He was also extremely shy, but as I was nervous at this first encounter, I was struggling with my own shyness. Conversation was jerky and stilted, with silences during which he busied himself filling my glass or helping me to food. He asked me what I was writing, and I told him about the novel to be written backwards. He seemed doubtful about this, but said, 'You must do what you want.' This was the slow beginning of a long, affectionate relationship that lasted until his death. I still miss him. He was Danish, although his English was impeccable, and he would never use his first names, so everyone called him Peter Peters.

We are in 1951 and I'd reached the age of twenty-eight. It took me the following four years to write *The Long View*: I was still struggling with the whole business of writing a novel – its structure, its proportions, and, above all, saying what I wanted to say. But they weren't the only reasons I took so long: another was the need to earn immediate money.

I can't see now how I managed this. Audrey was also hard up, but I suppose that between us we made Blandford Street as civilized as it could ever have been. Our bills were small. There was no central heating to pay for. We didn't use the telephone as people do now and we walked everywhere or went in buses. But we managed to employ someone to clean our house once a week. Mrs Downs was large and pale with a fringe – she looked like an elderly Katherine Mansfield – and her general view was that life was awful, but had to be got on with. She began every day with ten aspirin and a cup of tea.

'But you *do* have a holiday every year,' I said once, trying to find a gleam of light or pleasure in her life.

'Oh, we 'ave '*em*.'

'Where do you go?'

'We go to Cheltenham and sit under some trees.'

It didn't sound much fun. 'What else do you do?'

''*E* goes fishing, or *reading*. They both give me the creeps.'

She was utterly good-tempered, but when I tried to imagine her happy or pleased about something, I always failed.

Another reason that my novel took so long was my pre-occupation with love. Love seemed to me the most desirable, the most important of human emotions. As far as sexual love was concerned, I was older but not much wiser. But every other aspect of love – intimacy, affection, being first in each other's lives – I wanted, as much as I wanted to write. The problem of how to combine them was far in the future. I thought that if I could get love right, everything else would follow naturally. I don't write this to imply I was unusual: most women feel the same in varying degrees, I think. *My* instincts were cowardly and I seized opportunities with a lack of discrimination, a kind of reckless bravado that, if I'd been less ashamed of my timidity, I would have ignored. Furthermore I was lazy with my writing; I'd not yet learned the kind of discipline necessary for serious work. My lack of education showed here: I'd never had to swot for exams, write essays to order, read books I found difficult, or do any of the things that university might have taught me. So I frittered away much of those four years.

Not that it felt like that at the time. I was seeing Michael four times a week. Audrey and I – thrown together by the most casual chance – lived in parallel as it were, for much of this time. Audrey was small, with very short blonde hair, a rose and white complexion, a firm little nose and mouth, and large, pale blue eyes whose habitual expression denoted both intellect and humour. She'd been properly educated. She had one brother whom I hardly ever saw. Her father had been a master at Eton during the war, and Audrey, who was rather in awe of him, depicted him as extraordinary, witty and fascinating. Her mother had weathered, from his eccentricity and brilliance, into a wanly smiling cypher. They came occasionally to tea bringing with them Audrey's dog, a corgi called the Little Lion because, her father said, he always tried to look like one of the lions in Trafalgar Square. Audrey was scraping a living as I was. She seemed able to make anything with her hands, and was particularly good at designing simple, ingenious clothes, and this got her a job doing one garment a week for a daily newspaper.

Shortly after she came to Blandford Street, Michael introduced her to his cousin Jeremy Harris with whom she began going out. This graduated quickly to an affair, so there we were: both in love, both trying to make enough money from designing and writing to live, both about the same age, and both unsure of what we wanted out of life. We'd get up rather late in the mornings – at about nine a.m. – drink coffee in our identical grey silk pyjamas and earnestly discuss our feelings for Michael and Jeremy and theirs for us. Then we'd separate for the rest of the morning to work. The Margaret Rutherford play fell through, and Audrey was living more or less on her earnings from the newspaper.

I'd struggle with the novel. I'd graduated, if one can call it that, from writing with great energy and ease and little apparent thought, to a painstaking crawl, where every sentence was examined, found wanting and cast again. We had a sort of lunch. Audrey was always dieting but as I was very thin I didn't bother. I ate what, if anything, came to hand. We spent hours every evening getting ourselves ready for our dates, washing our hair, doing our faces, choosing and discarding clothes. Audrey, after her *séjour* in Paris, took clothes very seriously, and taught me that one couldn't take too much trouble. At about seven thirty, what the North Brothers downstairs used to call 'the Boys' would arrive in their Bristols.

Other adventures sometimes happened. Nancy Spain read my first novel, and took me up. At the time she was – apart from her job on the *Daily Express* – editing a small magazine that featured book reviews, and she employed me to write some from time to time. She also used to ask me to lunch at Wheeler's in Old Compton Street where we invariably had oysters and Krug champagne. Nancy was insanely generous, gave food and drink to anybody she met. She was lesbian, and in appearance rather like a large friendly blackish bird – this was augmented by a long black cloak that she wore over her trouser suits. She once took me to lunch at Rebecca West's house – somewhere in Berkshire, I think. Rebecca was married to a man who collected Sung pottery, much of which was displayed in wall cabinets with museum-like lighting.

After I'd known Nancy for several months, she came back to Blandford Street after one of our Wheeler's lunches and asked me to go to bed with her. 'I don't think I'd be any good at it,' I said. I'd read *The Well of Loneliness* and was very anxious not to hurt her feelings. 'Oh, come on, darling. Just pop into bed with me and let's see how we feel.' So I did.

'Well?' The bright brown bird's eye was fixed on me. Eventually she said, 'Well, it doesn't seem to be any good. Never mind.' We got out of bed and put on our clothes. And that was that. She continued to employ me, to ask me to lunch, and never referred to the incident again. In the summer, she invited me to go to Ireland with her to stay with Elizabeth Bowen. I admired Bowen very much, but was still anxious of staying with people I didn't know, and refused. How stupid that was. When I got to know Elizabeth later, I realized I'd have enjoyed that visit very much.

11

That summer in 1951 I came out of the Underground at Notting Hill Gate to read on an *Evening Standard* poster 'Peter Scott Divorces Actress Wife'. So I was divorced, and Pete would be able to marry Phil, which he did a month later. Phil was the quiet girl whom Kit and Freddie had brought to the dinner party in Mon Debris before I'd married Pete, and who had become his secretary after Liz had married Wayland. It really was past history; I wasn't even an actress any more. I was hardly a novelist; I wasn't anything.

Also that year, my friend Jill Balcon and Cecil Day-Lewis fell in love. He left his wife, and Rosamond Lehmann with whom he'd had a long-standing affair, to go to Jill. She told me that Rosamond had exacted a promise from him that he and Jill wouldn't see each other for three months. This they did, but Jill asked if I'd have lunch with Cecil so that she might have news of him.

I don't remember much about that lunch. It took place at Antoine's in Charlotte Street and Cecil was there when I arrived. I remember thinking that he really did look like everyone's idea of a poet. He combined good looks with urbanity and romanticism, plus a beautiful voice with a beguiling Anglo-Irish accent. We talked, of course, about Jill and how much he was in love with her and his anxiety that her parents wouldn't approve of their marriage. It wasn't, honestly, possible to reassure him on this point. I felt too constrained to ask why he'd agreed to Rosamond's three months – neither a stipulation nor a length of time likely to decrease any lover's passion. The best thing I discovered during that meeting was that he loved to laugh: his beautiful craggy face would break into volcanic fissures of amusement and, as I later discovered, he was also wonderful at telling stories. I could go back to Jill and say that he certainly loved her and how much I liked him. Three months wasn't so long, I said, and then they'd be together. She'd had a long affair with a married man whom she could hardly ever see. I had a sharp recollection of her at her twenty-first birthday party at her parents' home in Sussex, ravishing in an ice duck-egg-coloured satin dress, glittering and unhappy, because the person she most wanted there couldn't come.

She once asked me if I wanted to marry Michael, and I said – truthfully – that I didn't. 'I couldn't anyway. He *is* married – he doesn't want to change. He's always had mistresses. I seem cut out for that post.' But I did love him. I find it difficult to project myself accurately into the past, to *know* with any honest certainty the extent and quality of enjoyed, endured past love. I certainly believed I loved him. I wanted to be with him, thought about him, desperately wanted him to love *me*: I was still at the stage when my sense of self rested almost entirely upon how somebody else saw me. I wanted his affection and interest more than anything else in the world.

Shortly before I knew him, he'd become – rather suddenly – rich and was enjoying it very much. The disparity in this respect in our lives was extreme: he had two large houses and servants, and in the summer took a large villa in the South of France to which he repaired for a month's holiday. I enjoyed being taken out to good restaurants for dinner, indeed it kept me going physically, but I refused to be helped in any other way – with one exception. He would take me to buy everyone Christmas presents, but not for me, and I minded. It didn't last: the third Christmas after we'd met he gave me a very pretty seventeenth-century crystal and enamel ring that I still have and love. He also gave me a cat – a Siamese – to whom I became devoted. But that was all. He tried to lure me into a more salubrious flat, pretending that the rent was much lower than it really was, but even the fictitious reduced rent was almost twice that of Blandford Street. I knew he'd be paying the difference, and refused. The *patron* at the Étoile once asked me why I didn't lunch there on my own, and on hearing I couldn't afford it, offered me a table in the window and a free lunch whenever I wanted. I smelt a rat there, too, so that never happened.

But I did find hard the month that Michael went away in the summer. I imagined him swimming and sunbathing and having delicious drinks with friends in beautiful places, while I baked in my hot little house in London where I couldn't even see a tree from my window.

The second summer in Blandford Street in 1953, after I'd been ill for some time, my father suddenly suggested I should go to the South of France to stay with friends of Ursula called Zunz. They lived outside Marseille and would love to have me. 'They've had a rough time in the war,' my father said, 'and Ursula says they are very hard up. So if you go and I pay a decent amount of board money for you it would help them.' I found that Wayland and Liz were taking a car and going down there and thence to Italy: they'd give me a lift. There'd only be the fare home, twenty-one pounds in those days by air. Before I went, when I'd dined with Ursula and my father, she said, rather mysteriously, 'I wonder how you will get on with René.'

The journey with Liz and Wayland was very enjoyable. We stopped for a night in Paris, went to a nightclub where we danced. I found a partner to dance with who I thought was a friend of Wayland. We stayed in a wonderfully cheap and basic hotel for five shillings, and the next morning we set out for Chartres. Now there were four in the car, as the 'friend' had joined us. It wasn't until we reached Chartres that it was revealed that he was no friend of Wayland, who'd thought him a friend of mine: he'd simply attached himself to us and remained silent. He vanished as unobtrusively as he'd arrived.

Liz and Wayland were inveterate sightseers, particularly addicted to churches. I discovered on that trip that while I didn't mind looking at churches – I preferred the small simple ones – what I really enjoyed was looking at the countryside. By the time we reached Provence, I was entranced. In Arles we shared a room meant for a couple and their child, after we had sat drinking *fine à l'eau* to the sound of a thousand frogs. I noticed how beautifully the French kept their trees – avenues of planes bordering long, narrow roads, geometrically planted poplars, terraces of vines, and further south, the elegant pines.

In Marseille Wayland said we should have a serious lunch before they dropped me at the Zunzes. That, too, was a revelation to me, the first time I had *oursins*, sea urchins. We watched French families going through course after course and particularly a pale, very pregnant girl with her family and the waiter's solicitude about what she would like to eat and drink. She drank Vichy water and toyed with a small piece of fish.

The Zunzes lived in a suburb east of Marseille in a small house with a pretty garden. Doreen Zunz was English, a tall blonde with a face that, when she wasn't animated, was set in a kind of dramatic despair. René was short and dark with mournful brown eyes. He was Jewish and I was too ignorant then to know how dangerous and difficult his life must have been during the war. It was never mentioned, although he did say how hard he was finding his work – some kind of import business. They were both very welcoming, asked after Ursula and my father. The first thing I learned was that their only daughter, Betty, had died of meningitis when she was barely twenty. This had wrecked them. Doreen spoke of her constantly, saying how happy, how full of life, how clever and gifted she was – 'It has made the end of my life.' She'd taken refuge in chronic ill health, was often in bed, or simply lying down on a sofa. I asked René about her illness. He muttered something about heart trouble, but then said, 'She will make no effort – that is what is wrong.'

The Zunzes were generous hosts: rich, nourishing meals

appeared at regular intervals cooked by someone who came in every morning and evening. However, I couldn't eat them. In those days, I had bouts of being unable to eat that sometimes lasted for weeks. This seemed to be one of them. I was very tired from my illness, but encouragement to build up my strength by these kindly people was of no avail. I'd sit before an immense juicy steak and delicious salad, trying to swallow the first pieces of meat, my stomach heaving, and wanting to cry from embarrassment. 'I'm so sorry. I don't eat much,' I had to say. But at least, I thought, *they* were eating it. It was obvious that they didn't usually have steak or many of the other things with which they tempted me. Doreen didn't drink, but René enjoyed wine and brandy. He invented a drink of brandy and red Cinzano that I liked. It became a ritual every evening.

They wanted to take me out, to sightsee, to bathe, but I was an apathetic guest, didn't want to go anywhere or do anything except sit in the garden and read and write long letters to Michael. I was missing him, and almost as soon as I got back to England he would be leaving for his summer holiday. I told Doreen and René about him and they immediately suggested I ask him to come and stay. René drove me to Marseille where I sent a telegram to Michael, inviting him, although I knew he wouldn't come. Then René took me to a shoe shop, as I needed a pair of sandals. We stopped at a bar on the way home and he said how much they liked having me to stay and how good it was for Doreen to have someone new to talk to. 'And I,' he continued, 'I very much mind talking to you. You're someone who makes life worth living for.' That was the beginning, although I'd no idea of it then.

Generally, they treated me in a parental way, indulgent and affectionate: they desperately wanted me to have a good time. They gave a dinner party for me, invited four or five friends, all French, to meet 'an English author'. I was amazed at the general respect that my being a writer incurred, completely unlike England. The trouble was my wretched – or rather, non-existent – French. Nobody in the

223

party was any better at English. Doreen and René were forced to do a lot of wearisome translating. From all the fuss about preparations beforehand I realized it had been an unusual occasion for them. I think they couldn't, in the ordinary way, afford to entertain.

Doreen never left the villa, although René sometimes took me for drives. We'd drive along the coast further east, until we could look down from the road on to small rocky coves with water the colour of Quink. My first sight of one of these was so beautiful in its distant intensity – the absence of people, the pale pristine sand that edged the astonishing sea, I can see it now – that it became a treasure imprinted in my mind's eye. René had stopped the car as I wanted to look, and after a while he asked if I wanted to go to a beach and swim. It seems astonishing to me now, but I didn't. I simply wanted to look at it. There was a lovely scent of hot pines – far out the sea was glass, the sky was milk.

I was only staying for a fortnight, but half-way through the atmosphere slowly became charged with undercurrents that felt dangerous before they became explicit. Doreen became spiky; she constantly snubbed René and was rather ceremoniously polite to me. One evening when he'd brought me a drink in the garden where I was writing, he asked if he might stay and smoke a cigarette. When he had lit our Gauloises, I asked him what was the matter.

'What matter?'

'Doreen seems rather upset about something. I feel she is angry.'

'She is unhappy because she *knows*.'

'Knows? What?'

'That I am in love with you. Desperate. As *you* must know,' he added.

I'd no idea of it. And then I realized that wasn't entirely true. I *had* noticed he paid me a great deal of attention. I knew he admired me – he'd become rather jokingly gallant. I'd rather basked in his evident approval of everything I said. I'd flirted with him. I took, I can see it now, the usual line that people who don't reciprocate love do. 'You don't really love me,' I said. 'It's simply that you're bored and don't see people much.'

'Oh, no. It's not like that.' He smiled at me with wounded eyes.

'Anyway, I am in love with Michael. You know that. Doreen knows that.'

'And to either of us it makes no difference.'

There was much, much more of this, until eventually I began to feel quite angry, and said we should both go and talk to Doreen, have it out. She was lying on her bed. A scene that might have been out of a bad play followed, in which each one of us became – more awfully – ourselves: Doreen the martyr, René the tragic romantic, and I the self-righteous prig. Repetition congealed these attitudes until they made us nothing but what we said, or retorted, or moaned, or sneered. The room became airless with exaggeration, lies, recriminations, excuses and self-justification. Round and round we went. I lost my temper in the end and told Doreen to stop being sorry for herself, to get up and *do* something – anything. I said if I had to live with someone who behaved as she did to René, *I'd* want someone else in my life. There was much more, all in the same bracing, brutal vein. At the end of it, Doreen said, 'You come here, you ruin our lives and then you speak to me like that.'

'It's all right. I'm going. I'll go tonight. I'm sorry. It's all been the most awful mistake. I shouldn't have come.'

There was a short, shocked silence. Then, 'Oh, no!' They united at once in insisting I stay. Of *course* I must stay till the end of my holiday. René said he would make a nice cup of English tea and we'd have it cosily in Doreen' s bedroom. No, no, she would get up and come down, and perhaps she would find something I might like to eat . . .

The scene was over: I was being placated. We drank tea and brandy in the hot, dark sitting room and Doreen chatted as she had on the day I arrived. She asked more about my father and Ursula, and I understood that she didn't want them to know anything about the bad play. René drank a great deal of brandy and backed her up in a spiritless manner.

That night in bed I was haunted by their inexplicable *volte-face*, but contempt was quickly quenched by thoughts of what I'd actually have done if they'd agreed I should leave. Where would I have gone? I had almost no money. I didn't even know how far the airport was. The craven extent of my fears extended to my terror of even trying to use a French telephone. This sort of thing has bedevilled my life – it still does – but this was the first time that I recognized it. In many practical matters I am singularly both craven and inept.

They each gave me a book on parting. Doreen's was inscribed in French, 'Pour Jane, amour toujours, Doreen', and René gave me a copy of Stendhal's novel of Napoleonic mythology, *La Chartreuse de Parme*, in French inscribed in English, 'For Jane who makes life worth living it'.

Back in England, Ursula was unexpectedly curious to know how I'd got on. After a bit, I looked her straight in the eye and said, 'Did you have an affair with René?' And she answered, 'Not for very long.' It made some matters, at least, clear. Doreen hadn't been crying wolf. There had been wolves before.

'A slice of life,' Audrey said, when I told her about it.

René wrote me two or three letters after I got back to England, love letters of a resigned, depressed kind: he never expected us to meet again, but his feelings would never change. He did not mention Doreen, and asked me to reply to his office address. I wrote back once to them both, thanking them for having me to stay, and that was that.

12

In term time I continued to go to Hanover Terrace to see Nicola and to look after her on Nanny's day out. Every week I took her to the Mercury Theatre in Notting Hill Gate for ballet lessons. She'd reached the age when she was mad about dancing. I never knew how good she was at it because minders weren't allowed to watch the class, so week after week I used to sit in the little changing room that smelt of damp overcoats and hot little girls. It was odd to be there again. When I'd been Nic's age, my mother and Mimi Rambert had started ballet classes for children there, before the Gothic chapel became a theatre. Walking about Notting Hill Gate with Nic to and from buses, I half expected to hear Mimi's parrot shriek, 'Hold yourself straight, child!' which so frequently assailed me whenever I'd gone out alone in those streets.

Looking back on this time, it's easy for me to see that I'd got into a rut. The same things happened week after week: I struggled with the novel, which seemed interminable. Writing had become an anxious challenge that I dreaded and frequently evaded. I still hadn't learned how to work, didn't write regularly, or for regular amounts of time. When I reviewed what I'd written I was both besotted and defensively critical. The book had to be marvellous — otherwise why go through all this agonizing effort — but it wasn't, was it? It was nothing like as marvellous as it ought to be because, I told myself, I was simply too lazy and preoccupied to put it first. And, of course, the sneaking feeling that it might be no good *anyway*, however hard I worked at it, recurred in the night and left me with nothing – back to square one: no good at anything I'd tried to do and no good at what I wanted to do most. One thing spurred me on. I sent Peter Peters some of the novel and he wrote back a long letter saying that, although he liked the characters and the writing, one simply couldn't write a novel backwards: it was an impossible way to trap the reader into wanting to know more. I'd have to turn it round and it would work. This I absolutely refused to do. But the disagreement was profitable: I became determined to prove it could be done.

On top of this, other parts of my life weren't going well. I spent five evenings a week with Michael when he wasn't away, which meant I saw few other people. Our relationship hadn't altered from what it had become in the first few weeks after we met, but *I* had changed. I loved him more than he loved me and I wanted more time with him – in the day, when we could do things together. He did take me, about twice a year, to Paris, which was wonderful. We'd spend all the mornings walking and looking at pictures, and then a splendid lunch, more pictures, and a kip before going out in the evening. Occasionally, there, we met other people – a young financier once, who wanted Mike to invest in some project of his. He dined with us, said he was far from well, and could hardly eat anything. He and Mike discussed this project during dinner, while he sipped Vichy and crumbled a piece of bread. He was very quiet, courteous and withdrawn, seemed uninterested in whether Mike joined him in his enterprise or not. When he'd finished his consommé, he excused himself and left. 'What did you think of him?' Mike asked me.

'He seemed very nice.'

'Would you trust him?'

'Yes,' I said, rather startled. 'Why?'

'He wants a lot of money. I thought that as a girl, not to speak of a *brilliant* novelist [he always teased me about that], you would have deeper perception than I.'

'He seemed perfectly honest to me,' I said, flattered to be asked.

Mike trusted him and he turned out to be a first-class con-man, the first I ever met.

On another occasion we met Pat, a business friend of Mike who lived in Paris with his Hungarian wife Edith, and we all had dinner. Edith was tiny, dressed by Dior, with masses of expensive bracelets on her little stick arms. She ate an enormous dinner, then disappeared for a long time. Eventually, Mike wondered where she was, and I said I'd go to the ladies' and see if she was all right. She was being prodigiously sick. She was quite cheerful about this, repaired her face and returned with me to our table where she started with gusto upon her second *terrine de canard*. 'My wife is something of an Old Roman,' Pat said, wryly, as she went through the whole dinner again.

Nicola was having sore throats too often. I didn't want her to go through my medical experience as a child and took her to our family doctor, who agreed that her tonsils should come out. The afternoon before she went into the nursing-home I took her for a walk in Regent's Park. She was rather silent. I asked her if she was worrying about having her tonsils out and added that there would be ice cream afterwards and no more sore throats. We were walking on grass by the lake, which was crowded with ducks, and she interrupted me saying, 'I wouldn't mind *anything* if only I could find an egg.' I started to say that ducks didn't lay eggs in the open grass when she found one. Everything went well after that and the operation was a great success. But I still felt out of my depth as a mother. One day Josie, with whom Nic was living, said, 'I notice that you do all the dull things that mothers have to do for their children, but you never have any fun with her.'

This was quite true, and I could hardly bear it. 'Why do you say that?'

She looked at me very kindly. 'It just seemed to me rather sad for you both.'

I wanted to throw myself on her, to tell her how unnatural and bad I felt, to confess everything, and somehow be comforted, or advised, or even absolved. But I didn't: our relationship had progressed only so far as good manners and propinquity allowed. Another bar between us was my affair with her cousin Michael, of which she knew nothing as he had told me not to tell her.

And then one day I went to Hanover Terrace to find Josie wasn't there. She'd been taken to hospital. She had TB; she was very ill. Better go and see her, I thought. I bought a bunch of flowers and went.

It was an awkward visit. She was lying in bed propped up by pillows, looking like a small, fragile bird in a nest, rosy and comfortable. She didn't seem pleased to see me, and wasn't very forthcoming about her condition. She'd been feeling increasingly tired, and turned out to have lost an alarming amount of weight. Eventually she'd have to have an operation, but she had to put on some weight first. I didn't stay long, but when I went over to the bed to say goodbye I got a shock. She was terrified: she was so filled with fear that she could hardly deal with ordinary intercourse. She was cut off, isolated. I'd never encountered anyone so frightened, and my first instinct was to do all the wrong things – put my arms round her, ask her about it, do anything to minimize her feelings – all really to make *me* feel better. For once, I didn't do any of that. 'I might come and see you tomorrow,' I said, as casually as I could manage.

'If you want to,' she replied. The studied indifference, ungraciousness even, was unlike her.

Walking back from the hospital I tried to think about what she needed. She must have friends far closer than me: indeed, she probably didn't count me as a friend at all. We'd not thought of each other in that way. But, then, if she *did* have such friends, she wouldn't have been so locked in with her fear. I'd go tomorrow.

I saw her every day for three months. Fortunately, they moved her to a branch of the hospital that was ten minutes' walk from Blandford Street, so it was very easy. And that is how I got to know and love Josie, who has remained a wonderful friend ever since.

While they were fattening her, before she went to hospital in Midhurst where she was to have a series of horrendous operations, she *did* talk to me. It began with a letter, and went on to conversation. When she went to Midhurst, Michael lent me a car and a chauffeur so I could go once a week. The whole business took the best part of a year and she ended up with one lung after a great deal of pain. But she lived, is still living; her nature, like Jane Bennet's in *Pride and Prejudice*, her integrity and taste are second to no one else's and her kindness illimitable. A friend of mine once remarked that one could throw one's bread on the waters and get back cake, and that is what happened to me with Josie.

Mike had a friend, Roy, with whom he did business and we occasionally dined with him and his girl. Roy's affair with her broke up and Mike said he was distraught about it. 'He has to go to Monte Carlo to do Onassis's deal with the casino, and I thought you might like to go with him – lovely hotel, nice place and a little holiday for you.' So I went. We stayed in the Hôtel de Paris in adjoining suites. The manager was solicitous and accompanied us to the rooms. There was a door that joined the suites; he tried to open it with a flourish and found it locked. He sent for a key: there was none to be found. I'd said several times it didn't matter, we didn't need the door to open, but he put this down to English inhibition and took not the slightest notice. I enlisted Roy to back me up – it made no difference. A locksmith was sent for, and after some skilful fiddling, the door was opened. *'Voilà!'* The manager disappeared, wreathed in broad-minded smiles.

In the daytime, I walked about Monte Carlo while Roy had his meetings with Prince Rainier and Aristotle Onassis or their representatives. In the evening we dined in the hotel, and Roy sat, hardly eating, telling me how unhappy he was. Once, at my request, he took me to the casino, where I lost a few francs. 'I can't stand gambling,' Roy said.

'I thought you did it all the time,' I said.

'That's why.'

By now I'd got to know several of the people who worked with Mike. He'd bought a bank, and they all seemed to be doing very well, although there was a blip when everything went wrong and Mike said we couldn't afford to go out to dinner as rigid economy must set in. For weeks I made dinner – I wasn't an experienced cook, but he never complained and I enjoyed the increased domesticity.

The regime at Hanover Terrace had come to an end; Nanny went to look after the Sutherlands' baby, and Nic went to a small boarding-school called St David's near Egham. I'd have liked her to go to St Paul's where she would have been a day girl, but the travelling every day and the fairly heavy schedule the school imposed seemed too much for her at that age. I remembered my brief and awful time at Graham Street, and didn't want her to spend two hours in buses every day. Pete and Phil – with whom all these decisions were made – agreed that St David's seemed a good choice. It was small, and each child had a room of its own. Pete had given Nic a pony that was kept at Slimbridge with him and this was the love of her life.

I was much less sure than she about the love of *my* life. My relationship with Michael was the same – he rang me often, and occasionally wrote me notes in his tiny beetle writing. He never said he loved me, and I never asked him. But I *wanted* him to love me, hoarded the slightest sign of affection or interest, and I told myself – and others – that I loved him. However, although I thought ceaselessly about him, I don't think I thought honestly. I saw it all through a romantic haze, where I, the good mistress, was being short-changed on love.

To some extent, this might have been true. Michael didn't find it easy to talk about anything that he felt. Like so many public-school boys, he'd learned the hard way to keep his feelings to himself, and by the time he was forty, lack of practice had taken its toll. Although a glamorous figure, dark, very handsome with bright brown eyes that could gleam conspiratorially when he was amused

— which was often — or become like flat pebbles when he was angry, and in spite of a great deal of charm, I think he was basically unsure of himself. Perhaps he felt that he wasn't what he wished to be.

He loved good writing, particularly poetry, and used to try his hand at it, in a rather jokey way to ensure that no one thought he took himself seriously. He loved painting and bought both pictures and sculptures, and he loved the company of artists and often helped beginners when he thought well of them. He had a very low boredom threshold and had no interest in sport or games. He loved food and wine, and although I didn't notice it when I first knew him, he came to enjoy music.

I'd been with Michael for three years and had begun to feel that things might remain the same for ever. This implies that I was dissatisfied, and although I found it difficult to define exactly what was wrong, I knew that something was. The restrictions that almost all affairs with married people impose were there. I couldn't have holidays with him. I couldn't be in more than a very small part of his life. The partial secrecy was very trying, as I was cut off from a great deal else of ordinary social life. 'Do you want to marry?' Audrey asked me — her mind was very much running upon marriage.

'I don't know,' I said. 'In any case, I can't. He *is* married.' But the question, and my answer, nagged me.

I was thirty in the spring of 1953 when my older brother invited me to go with him to France and Italy in his Lotus car, the fifteenth to be built.

Back in 1946, Robin and his wife had returned from Arizona where their efforts to make a living had failed. Robin had rejoined the family firm and they had had a daughter, Claire. Then Robin's wife left him, with the three-year-old child, whom my mother took on. He badly needed a holiday, and I was delighted to go with him. Michael then suggested that, after two weeks with Robin, I should join one of his partners in the South of France for a further two weeks. 'Paul is having a bad time with his marriage. He needs cheering up.' I'd got to know Paul Bowman over the years, as I'd gradually got to know most of the partners. Like Michael, he was an old Etonian, but he'd led a starry life there – a member of Pop, or the Etonian equivalent of being a prefect, and good at everything. He'd had a distinguished war, been made a colonel at twenty-one and soon afterwards he married an actress far older than he and had a daughter with her. Paul was charming, extremely attractive, and I sensed Michael admired him very much. This was all I knew about him. It didn't strike me as odd that Michael should make this suggestion – after all, he'd sent me to Monte Carlo with Roy – so I agreed. It was a wonderful thought that I was to have a really long holiday.

The holiday with Robin was tremendously enjoyable. The little Lotus, silver and open, was an exciting car. Robin was running it in, which meant it wasn't to exceed seventy miles an hour, but it did that everywhere. We had one or two adventures. One late afternoon, when we were in France and on our way to Italy, we realized there was a strike and that the petrol stations were all shut. Robin wasn't daunted. There *might* turn out to be one that was open, on the other hand we *might* just have enough petrol to get into Italy where we could fill up. There wasn't, and we didn't. We ground to a halt at about ten o'clock that evening on a very minor country road – nowhere.

As we got out to survey the scene, another car drew up behind us, out of which climbed a charming man who asked if he could help. Robin's French wasn't much better than mine, but he managed to explain our problem. 'Come with me,' the man said. He would put us up for the night, bring us petrol in the morning and all would be well. Somehow, he assumed that we were married, and Robin and I – very tired and feeble – failed to disillusion him in time. We drove up to what we could see, even in the dark, was a large house – a château. We were offered food and drink, and a room with a very small double bed, in which we spent a fairly restless night.

In the morning, we found ourselves sitting round an enormous dining-room table, with Monsieur and Madame and eight children of different sizes but otherwise identical – like a set of ring spanners. Our enjoyment of all this was spoiled by the lie we'd let by. I felt if we had admitted to not being married and said we were siblings they'd simply not believe us. Silly, no doubt, but there was a strong Catholic atmosphere. They were charmingly generous, refused to let us pay for the petrol that Monsieur transported in a can the next day. All we could do was thank them and take their name and address. Later we both wrote to thank them again for their great kindness.

The Italians adored the Lotus. Everywhere we stopped, a crowd of people seemed to come from nowhere to stroke it and exclaim at its beauty. We had one row in the car when we lost our way in Milan. I read the map wrongly and argued about it, and for half an hour we were back in our childhood, but we got over it.

We ended up in St-Tropez, and in the village street I met a lady I'd known slightly in London – Ruth de Lichtenburg. She had a house there, she said, and invited us to have a drink with her family that evening. We went. Ruth, whose husband, a painter, had died rescuing his two daughters from a fire, had lived in their house throughout the war with her mother-in-law and her two daughters. She'd worked for the Resistance. The daughters were there: the fair one a scientist, the dark younger one a ballet dancer. Robin fell at once for the dancer, whose name was Nadia. The next day, however, he had to drive back to London, having deposited me at the hotel where I was to meet Paul.

Two weeks ensued, which, looking back on them, were the most sybaritic of my life. The coast had not then been built up and populated as it is now. There were plenty of little coves where we could bathe, without other people, in a clear, clean, warm sea. There were restaurants by the beaches, with mattresses and umbrellas for hire, and delicious *hors d'oeuvres* lunches were available. I, used to English summers in London and English food that was uniformly dull, was intoxicated by these continuous pleasures. At night we showered and dressed and went out to dine and dance in the warm velvet air. To be asked what I wanted to do, to choose equally with Paul where we'd go and what we'd do, was also a new and delightful experience. His consideration charmed me, but I was altogether charmed, was completely absorbed by our mutual enjoyment, and the fast-growing consciousness of mutual attraction. To begin with, I had qualms of guilt and anxiety about Michael.

And then, half-way through the first week, lying sleepless in my room, wishing that Paul was there and telling myself I shouldn't, I remembered the earlier trip to Monte Carlo with Roy. Michael had sent me on that. Roy's affair had broken down. And now Michael had sent me on this holiday with Paul whose marriage was breaking – had already broken – down. Perhaps he wanted rid of me, but couldn't face it unless I was hitched up with someone else. At that moment, there was a tap on the door. It was Paul, asking if he might come in. Yes, he might. Much later, when we were lying in the narrow bed, he said, 'You can't imagine how long I've wanted to do this.'

'Before this holiday?'

'Long before.'

So there we were. Everything went our way. Paul had a rich, rather shady acquaintance, who had a large villa in the hills above Nice. We were invited for lunch and a swim in his pool, and at the end of the afternoon he offered us a small house in his garden for as long as we liked.

Trying to look back on those short, heady ten days, I can't honestly recall my true feelings. Again I certainly thought I was in love with Paul, and I was entranced that he should be in love with me. He was, or he seemed at the time, to be deeply affectionate in a way that I hadn't encountered for years. He was honourable – he never once said anything bad about his wife. He was devoted to his daughter, who was then about five. He was wonderfully unconscious about his appearance and the effect it made. So we spent ten hot, golden days as though they would go on for ever, as though there was no life outside or beyond them. It wasn't until our last evening that we began to face reality. Tomorrow we'd see Michael and would have to tell him.

'Perhaps he won't really mind,' I said.

'I rather think he will. You realize, don't you, that I won't be able to marry you for some time?' I hadn't thought that he wanted to marry me. 'Of course that plan is slightly dependent on how you feel about it. All I want to do is influence you unduly.'

'You have,' I said. 'I should love to marry you.'

13

Michael met us at the airport. Neither of us had expected him. He was in very good spirits, and said he'd drop Paul off at his house then take me on.

As soon as we got to Blandford Street, I told him, and saw his eyes become like pebbles in a face blanched with anger. He was furiously angry, at first inveighing against Paul for playing such a dirty trick. I said I was in it too, that it was more serious than a dirty trick, and that we were going to marry. 'I'll put a stop to *that*,' he said. 'That's the last thing you'll do.' There was a good deal more of this before he slammed out of the house. I said all the hopeless things: I was sorry, there'd been no planning, but of course it was useless.

The next evening Paul came to see me. 'We need two rather large gin and tonics,' he said. 'I've got some bad news.' Michael had sacked him – he had been out of the firm from eleven that morning. I could see that this was bad, but not how bad. I supposed it might have been difficult to go on working with Michael and he answered that it might be marginally more difficult not having a job. Later, I asked if he wanted to change his mind. 'Good Lord, *no*! Nothing would make me want to do that.' I asked him if he wanted to come and live at Blandford Street, and he said, no, he thought that would be unwise. He would stay with friends, and another friend would lend him a flat where we could meet. 'Rather an extraordinary place,' he added.

It was. It was in a mews off Park Lane, pitch dark and packed with gnomes. There were imitation pools made with mirror glass round which these grinning dwarfs eternally fished. There were very small ones on every shelf and large ones that sat in chairs. The lamps were dim and coloured red or green and filled the place with an unearthly glow. Paul referred to the owner as 'he', but I think it was some high-class prostitute's flat. Paul's connection with tarts wasn't known to me then. It didn't even dawn on me when, mysteriously, we both got crabs. This horrified me – I'd never even heard of them before, but when I asked how on earth I could have got them he said he couldn't imagine. We got over that.

Audrey told me that Michael had asked his cousin Jeremy to reason with me to leave Paul, but that he'd refused. Michael then sent his partner along, a man packed with unreliable charm who had a reputation for getting anyone to do anything. He failed. Paul's financial troubles had simply stiffened my resolve to stay with him. He was trying to get another job and not succeeding. He'd been to lawyers, who said I'd have to be cited in the divorce. Paul took me to see them. There were two of them. They chose a hotel in Brighton, and deliberated with each other.

'The third floor has been found to be reliable, hasn't it, Mr Smith?'

'We've never had any trouble with it. It would be helpful if the lady would draw *attention* to herself. Like spilling the coffee-pot over the bedclothes . . . '

'Or dropping a vase full of blooms on the carpet,' said the other. 'Something of that nature.'

'Would you rather drop or spill?' Paul said when we'd rid ourselves of hysterical laughter in the taxi. 'Oh, darling, I feel awful dragging you through all this.'

'Well, it's true, isn't it? It is what we're doing.' So we went through it all.

Sometimes, at weekends, we went to stay with Michael Ayrton, the neo-Romantic artist and sculptor, and Elisabeth, his wife, in their house in Essex. Michael was an old friend, he liked Paul and it was lovely to be with friends who accepted us without any fuss.

All these things happened over a period of about three months during which I discovered I was pregnant. Paul was clearly confounded by this, and said he'd fix it. 'We can have children when we're married,' he said, 'lots of them.' This comforted me and I was surprised that it did. My feelings about having children had changed. I still felt inadequate, afraid I wouldn't make a good job of it, but now I wanted another chance. This was clearly not the moment.

Paul took me to a doctor, and in no time I was on a table, unconscious, then conscious again. 'Please get on with it.'

'It's done.'

I felt weak and weepy and not at all relieved. Paul was very kind to me. He said we must look for a flat, somewhere to live together. He was still without a job, and although he was reluctant to talk about it, his daughter's school fees had to be paid and he didn't have the money to pay them. Could I lend him anything? I'd no money, so I sold my jewellery for a few hundred pounds. I also had my beautiful piano that the artist Robin Darwin, a friend, had been housing for me in his flat. I sold that for four hundred pounds.

Audrey and Jeremy were now engaged, and the marriage was to take place quite soon. It seemed that Blandford Street was coming to an end, and I wasn't sorry. The lack of garden and not being able to see a tree from any of the windows was cumulatively depressing.

And then, one morning, Audrey came down to my room to say she was terribly sorry to hear the news.

'What news?'

She looked aghast. 'About Paul. Surely you know. He's gone back to his wife.'

I hadn't known. It was a complete shock, so much so that I didn't believe it, but then things Audrey told me made me. Paul was back in his job, everyone in the office knew about it. I knew then that although he'd made a date for six that evening, he'd no intention of turning up, and I felt furiously angry. I rang him at the office. He sounded uncomfortable. 'I was going to write you a letter.'

'No,' I said. 'I want you to come round this evening and tell me yourself to my face what you've decided to do.'

He agreed, and he came. I can remember little about that last meeting except his discomfort, his forays into boyish charm to lighten the occasion, and his embarrassed attempts to comfort me. The distance between us – the chasm that had opened – now seemed to stretch back over the whole affair. I do remember at one point that I said, with a stab of perspicacious hostility, I supposed he'd got crabs at the Bag of Nails, a venue for prostitutes, and hadn't liked to tell me that either. He shrugged and said he couldn't deny it. Two drinks and he left. He was sorry, but he had to be going. He sounded as sorry about having to go then as he'd earlier said he was about going for ever.

I listened to his steps on the stairs, the first and then the second door slamming, and resisted the illogical temptation to go to the window and watch him walk up the street. He must have been lying to me for weeks, I thought drearily. I'd not asked him what had made him change his mind; humiliation always provokes salvaged pride, and now I didn't even want to know. To be so easily taken in implies dishonesty to oneself, but I didn't recognize it then. For the ensuing weeks, I cried a good deal, was sorry for myself and either bad company or none at all.

I think now that somewhere inside me I knew that marriage to Paul would have been disastrous; that really we had very little if anything in common. If I'd been able to see the South of France interlude as simply a light-hearted affair I shouldn't have been so miserable. I was unwilling to accept that I was the sort of woman who had light-hearted affairs: it didn't fit with my grandiose and romantic view of myself. And so, I lied to myself.

About a week after Paul left, Michael rang me and asked me if I'd have dinner at his house. I was hesitant, not sure that I wanted to see him, but he was very persuasive – gentle and persuasive.

That evening I saw a side of him I'd never seen before. He was almost delicately tactful, didn't attempt to puncture my shaky dignity, and seemed to know instinctively how much and in what way to talk about what had happened. At one point he said, very quietly, 'I know you've had a rotten time,' and I realized he knew about the abortion, which I couldn't bear to talk about. Before I could say anything, he said, 'Pick up the cushion beside you.' There was a large cushion lying flat on the sofa. I picked it up, and under it was my jewellery. 'I couldn't get it all back,' he said, 'but most of it's there.'

It was so unexpected; I put my hands over my face to stop myself crying and failed. It wasn't that I had the jewellery back, it was what he'd gone through. I started to say this and he said, 'I know. It's not so much that you're glad to have it back, it's the trouble I've taken to get it.' And gave me one of his large white handkerchiefs, with a gentle sardonic smile. And so, a short while later, I was back with him. It wasn't the same. I felt differently.

At first I didn't even recognize this, I was bruised and humili-ated, and was pretty slow on self-awareness anyway. But two things happened that forced me to understand my situation. The first was that, her marriage to Jeremy imminent, Audrey made it clear to me that I wasn't to be asked to the wedding. She was quite cold about it, said simply that with Michael's wife there and Jeremy's father and stepmother, it would be too embarrassing. I was very hurt. I was supposed to be Audrey's best friend, but she was becoming respectable, and I wasn't.

When I told Michael how I felt about this, he became evasive, but finally admitted that my presence would make things awkward – it wouldn't really 'do'. We had a scene, and I said bitterly that I supposed I'd always be excluded whenever he, and people like him, thought fit. 'Oh, no, Jenny darling, but really you'll always be *there.*' On your terms, I thought, and afterwards, when he'd gone home, I thought that really everything was on his terms. He saw as much of me as he wanted, and otherwise I didn't affect his life in any way. But mine *was* affected.

I grasped then what the idea of marriage with Paul had been.

I'd been caught by the idea of total commitment, although in the case of Paul that would clearly not have worked. It struck me again that I saw things as I wanted them to be rather than how they actually were. My relationship with Michael was predicated upon some future unspecified change – that he would love me more, that he might marry me. What evidence did I have for either of those notions? He hardly ever said he loved me, and only seldom threw out an odd hint that one day things might be different. I'd clung to those odd moments, and had regarded them as secret truths. Now I saw that they were nothing of the kind.

14

My first novel, though well received, hadn't made me any money. Jonathan Cape, who had a profound distrust of paperback publishing, had refused to allow me to be published by Penguin. I'd earned out my advance of fifty pounds, and that would seem to be that. As for *The Long View*, I seemed to have been struggling with it for ever. I simply didn't work hard or consistently enough. Lack of money forced me to do any odd jobs that came to hand, so work was constantly interrupted, but it wasn't really a valid excuse. I was lazy, locked up in my emotional life. Above all, I was afraid I couldn't actually write well at all. I was worried that I wasn't, after all, going to be the greatest living novelist, and this, at my age, meant I was no good. Such extreme notions are commonplace in the young – the vast spectrum between being great and being no good tends to get ignored. There is a great difference between wanting to be a writer and wanting to write, and this isn't always obvious in the salad days of a writer's creative life, and sometimes never.

For the rest, Audrey was leaving Blandford Street shortly so I needed to find a new lodger. I hadn't the energy or heart for it. If only I had a garden, I thought, I should be happier. Then one turned up. Michael told me that Roy – with whom I'd gone to Monte Carlo – had found a maisonette for his girl in Blomfield Road by the Grand Union Canal, and another was going next door. The rent was two hundred pounds a year, which was very low. I went to see it. It consisted of four rooms, a large sitting room looking out on to the garden, and a smaller one, with a minute kitchen carved out of what once must have been the wine cellar. Upstairs there were two bedrooms and a bathroom. The garden was large, about the size of a tennis court, and unkempt. Although I knew I'd have to find a lodger to help with the rent, I was utterly entranced by the prospect of my own piece of ground.

The flat had no heating, but there was an open fire in the sitting room and I brought my trusty gas fires for the bedrooms and dining room. Len Beswick papered the walls and I painted the woodwork. The garden was a weed-ridden jungle and Michael paid for the entire plot to be ploughed as a moving-in present. This was wonderful, as I couldn't have dealt with the initial stage myself. I knew little about gardening and had no idea about design, so my garden ended up with a rectangular lawn, a wide bed running down the sunny side and a narrow one opposite. The bottom of the garden was dominated by lime trees – then, I didn't know their nasty little ways. I bought two camellias, white and deep rose, a white may tree and a forsythia bush. Friends gave me bits and pieces from their gardens.

I am hazy about dates, but I think I moved to Maida Vale in the winter of 1953 when I was thirty. It was clear that if I didn't have a lodger, I must get some sort of job that meant a regular income. Cecil Day-Lewis suggested I should work at Chatto where he was an editor.

'I don't know how to be an editor,' I said.

'You'll learn soon enough.'

In those days Chatto & Windus operated rather like an old-fashioned family firm, presided over by Norah Smallwood and Ian Parsons. The office was an immensely tall old building off St Martin's Lane, with very few rooms on each floor and an ancient lift. Cecil's office was at the top of the house, on the sunny side – it was baking hot in summer – and there was a parapet outside where pigeons ate the duller pieces of the innumerable buns that Cecil and I consumed.

The work involved reading new scripts that flooded steadily in every day, marking up accepted ones, and sometimes reading and making notes where any changes seemed desirable or necessary. Each new manuscript had to be sent to Norah's or Ian's office, accompanied by a report summarizing the book and recording whether the reader thought it should be published. Cecil was very good at sifting the real dross from the possible gold. The shortest report I ever saw from him read, 'Pah!' Four times a year we spent two or three awful days simply writing jacket blurbs for forthcoming books. One of my first jobs was to edit a very long and immensely dull book about travels in Africa. 'What's it like?' Cecil asked, after a day or two. I said it was like being trapped in a train with someone who told you every single thing that had happened to them for the last six months. 'Plough on,' he said. 'He's under contract and Norah is quite keen on him.' Once I'd got the hang of things, Cecil and I worked alternate weeks, although sometimes we'd overlap if there was a deadline on getting a book to the printers.

Cecil was an exceptionally beautiful man with a marvellous forehead creased and mapped like the tributaries of a river. He had a well-shaped head with thin iron-grey hair, and blue eyes. The rest of his face was full of mobility, amusement and concern – it was a very lived-in face and the more handsome for it. He dressed to suit his persona – he was more than debonair, he was glamorous. He had one trick that was unique to him: he could purr continuously, like a cat.

From time to time Norah would burst into the room without warning. Sometimes she had an author in tow to whom she was proudly showing the offices. On these occasions she was gracious, introducing us to them – this is Elspeth Huxley, or Iris Murdoch. When she was unaccompanied she worried at us like a small terrier. 'Eating *again!*' she would accuse, looking at the greasy paper bags held down by doughnuts like paperweights.

'It's all the frightful books you make us read,' Cecil would reply, in his weariest, most polite voice. He always managed to make her laugh, and eventually I did the same. It was the passport to being in her good books. She bullied people who were afraid of her, but underneath it all she was an extraordinarily kind woman. Her husband had been killed in the war, and she subsequently gave all her considerable energy, loyalty and devotion to Chatto.

That winter I was ill: it started as flu but went on and on, and eventually I had to stop work and stay in bed. It took weeks to recover and when I did it was with a deep depression. I had no energy for writing, I didn't like living alone, and I could hardly drag myself to the office every other week to earn the six pounds that barely kept the wolf from the door. I was also going through another bout of not eating and I remember the misery of sitting in restaurants faced with enormous menus and finally asking for something like a piece of cold chicken only some of which I managed to force down.

My relationship with Michael had become hopelessly static. It was clearer and clearer to me that I ought to leave him, but I'd not the strength or courage to do it. Someone I'd met at a party with Audrey before she married said he'd fallen in love with me. He was married – as, it seemed to me, every personable man was – and, although I liked him, he wasn't for me. I told him I was with someone else, but that didn't deter him. He asked if he might take me to my office in his car every morning on the days I went there. I agreed – ungraciously, I'm afraid – largely because it got me out of going on the Underground in the rush-hour.

And then, out of the blue, I was invited by my friend Lorna to go to America with her and stay in her family's house in Connecticut. Lorna Mackintosh came into my life indirectly through Michael whose friend, Roger St Aubyn, was her lover – she later married him. Her mother, Loelia, was an American heiress who'd married Ali Mackintosh, a 1920s playboy, very charming but not wildly responsible about money. She eventually divorced him and took her two daughters to France where she married a French duke. He was short of money and she liked the idea of being a duchess. There was a house in America, a flat in Rome and a house at St-Brice, outside Paris, which had once belonged to Edith Wharton. Lorna had spent much of her childhood in Connecticut. The house there had a farm and it was the place she loved best. In spite of this, she'd had an unhappy childhood. She was small and blonde, with a fair skin and blue eyes and features that would have suited Holbein. We became friends immediately.

When I approached Chatto to ask for two weeks off, Norah was unexpectedly kind. Of course I could go, it would do me good. It was agreed I should look for some American books for Chatto while I was there. They paid my air fare and I'd saved about fifty pounds for general expenses.

Michael and Roger saw us off at Heathrow and pinned particularly vulgar, vast orchids to our winter coats. As soon as we took off Lorna said, 'Horses' Necks.'

'What?'

'Whisky and ginger ale. It's my airplane drink.'

We had two each, then tried to sleep. Flying across the Atlantic took far longer in those days: the plane stopped at Shannon to pick up passengers, and again at Gander in Newfoundland to refuel. We staggered off the plane in Boston eighteen hours later to face disgruntled Customs men who tore the orchids from us with much accusatory comment.

The house was called Gwyn Careg. I remember little about it, except the vast kitchen that was engulfed in a hygienic pandemonium after every meal. The family fascinated me. When we arrived it was to find Lorna's sister, Sheila, who'd recently married a French count, Jean de Rochembeau. They were still on honeymoon. When I first met her, Sheila was wearing a sea-green dressing-gown made for her by Dior. It trailed behind her on the ground and it was undoubtedly the most glamorous dressing-gown I'd ever seen. Jean hovered in her wake: he was small and dark with a constantly mournful expression. His English was poor, but as the girls spoke impeccable French he'd little incentive to learn.

Their mother didn't arrive until some hours later. She was

accompanied by her best friend, Aline, who lived in Rome, where they'd both just been. After the briefest of acknowledgements, they flopped down on two sofas with a small table between them and continued the game of Scrabble that they'd started on their plane. Loelia de Talleyrand was very tall and, though not exactly beautiful, had an air of majesty. She always sat with her back straight enough to satisfy the most exacting Victorian; her iron-grey hair was always beautifully dressed and her clothes were glamorous and impeccable at any time of day or night. She was always very nice to me, but I sensed that relations with both her daughters were enigmatic and unsatisfactory. Lorna certainly didn't feel loved by her, and both girls disliked Heli, their stepfather.

We spent only a few days there and I remember nothing of it except that we experienced the tail end of a hurricane called Flora. It was my only experience of a hurricane and I remember the extraordinary hush that descended before it reached us – a sort of dead stillness of a kind that happens in a theatre sometimes when the house lights go down before the curtain rises.

Lorna and I went to New York, she to stay with relations and visit friends, I to visit publishers and agents in my search for books for Chatto. Reality struck me at this point. When I'd been there with Pete, I'd been the much spoiled and protected guest of his friends. Now I was on my own, with hardly any money and knowing practically nobody. I had kept in touch with Robert Linscott: we'd written to each other steadily for the last five or six years. I rang him at Random House and asked if I could stay with him. He agreed, and I met him that afternoon and he took me back to his apartment. It was very small, and he said I'd have to sleep on the sofa in his sitting room.

I stayed with him all the time I was in New York and he was unfailingly kind and patient with me. I'd brought my three-quarters finished novel, *The Long View*, with me for him to read. I'd expected that he'd be full of encouraging – even flattering – remarks, but he was curiously silent, only suggesting that he should give the script to Robert Haas, the vice-president whom I'd met in the elevator on my first night so many years before. Meanwhile, I trudged all over the city seeing people. I longed to take back some wonderful work for Chatto to publish. I had dreams of being so successful that they'd send me over every year. Everyone was courteous – Chatto had a good name – but it was long after I got home that it dawned on me I'd been fobbed off with all the scripts they'd despaired of selling to anyone.

I was always hungry. A sandwich cost the equivalent of ten shillings, and I couldn't afford many of those. Bob fed me in the evenings, and once took me out to dinner with William Faulkner and a pretty, dark girl called Jean Stein. Faulkner was small and quiet. He lit up only when he spoke to Jean with whom he was clearly much enamoured. He treated her as though she was a young princess out of a magic dream. Otherwise he seemed shy and withdrawn. Afterwards, Bob told me that once a year he came to New York for six to eight weeks, turned up at Random House every single morning and sat in Reception until one of the editors or senior officials took him out to lunch. It was fine for a week or two, but after that, Bob said, they drew lots for who should lunch him. Occasionally, he sat and wrote a story, but this didn't happen very often.

At the weekend, Bob took me to his house in Massachusetts. We went by train to Williamsburg and then he drove into the country. His house was beautiful, clapboard, with bare wooden floors and little furniture except books. There were woods round the house, and he took me to see the beavers. It was early evening and, while we waited quietly, we saw a raccoon eating frogs on top of the beavers' dam. Presently a beaver swam from his island nest and drifted slowly along the dam. He was testing it for leaks, Bob said. The beaver's expression implied that a leak was unlikely. While we were watching there was a sound like a rifle shot and the beaver swam – much faster – back to his island. The sound had been other beavers' tails slapping the water as a danger warning. I remember that evening with pure delight.

Robert Haas asked me to lunch to tell me that they really didn't feel they could publish my new novel. This was a shock. Haas said they were worried about the order of it: a novel couldn't be written backwards – all the tension of the story was lost as the reader always knew the ending. Perhaps with my second draft I'd rearrange it and do it the right way round? I wouldn't. Then he suddenly gave me a hundred dollars 'to buy yourself a nice dress'. He was a kind man, and I knew he felt I'd come down in the world and that turning down my book was – among other things – a financial blow. It was, of course, but the money was much less of a disappointment than the rejection. I left lunch in a trance of gloom, bought myself a black velveteen coat for exactly a hundred dollars, and wrote to thank him and tell him.

Back home I started work again at Chatto. Norah was very nice about the quantities of scripts that deluged them from New York. I think one or two were published, but made little mark. Meanwhile, I'd been given another job. Cecil handed me a typescript one morning and asked me to make a report on it. It was a biography of Bettina von Arnim – an early nineteenth-century romantic; both she and her mother had been girlfriends of Goethe. The material, of course had been in German, and Arthur Helps was a brilliant translator, but his well-stocked mind rambled over time and place with nomadic abandon and the book was like an immense heap of sand. When I reported this, Cecil and Norah said they agreed, but they thought, with considerable sorting out, there could be a good book. Would I like to collaborate with Mr Helps to this end?

Sometime during the months after my return from New York, I left Michael. Of the evening when I told him, I remember just a feeling of despairing unhappiness. Michael was very good about it. After he'd asked me if there was anyone else and I'd replied that there wasn't, he didn't argue or try to change my mind. 'I haven't a leg to stand on,' was the only thing I recall him saying. I think it was a shock to him; Michael's feelings normally only appeared momentarily on his face before he became closed, stoic, or bland or debonair. I know that he was sad – '*Oh*! I shall miss you, Jenny' – but I don't know whether he was as sad as I was. Come to that, *I* didn't know how unhappy this separation was going to make me. After he'd gone and I'd cried myself out, I felt simply a general kind of despair. I thought I was cut out just to be a kind of extra for people. There would never be anyone who would take me seriously or put me first in his life. I wanted much the same as everyone else – to love one person, to live with them, to have their children. But I also wanted to be a writer, and it was here that the most serious difference between the sexes revealed itself to me. Men could be novelists, prime ministers, doctors, lawyers *and* fathers. It was a much trickier combination for women. None the less, tricky or not, it was what I wanted.

But as the working days and empty evenings went by I began to miss Michael. 'If you want me for anything, just ring up,' he'd said. It would have been so easy. But somehow I knew I'd made the right decision, and having made it, I couldn't go back on it. I worked in the office, but had no energy to write.

There were some distractions. Jill and Cecil had moved to a house on Campden Hill. My goddaughter, Tamasin, was born. I used to go to supper with them, sometimes *à trois*, sometimes with their friends. Once or twice the poet Henry Reed was there. He told wonderfully funny stories of his war: arriving in some Midland digs, unpacking his case – almost entirely full of books – watched by his landlady who looked at them with great distaste and finally said, 'Books are a thing I *never* read.' And later, taking him down to the narrow kitchen, where the family were having their tea, and down the back garden, where she remarked, 'There is the privy. *If* you should ever care to use it.'

Cecil and Jill were both good laughers, and I saved any jokes or stories that came my way for them. The only time I met Robert Frost was at dinner there. Cecil had edited a collection of Frost's poetry, and he gave me a copy. Frost started to inscribe it to me, with lines from *The Road Not Taken*, got it wrong and insisted on a piece of paper to be pasted over the mistake and inscribed afresh. He and Cecil were very good together. Both had craggy faces crowded with incident. Their foreheads were like Clapham Junction – indeed, both of their faces looked thoroughly lived-in. I wish I could remember more about that evening, but a disagreeable feature of being unhappy is an incapacity to live in the present, which subsequently means a patchy memory of the past.

I have very little memory of the rest of that year. Robin married Nadia, the dancer he'd met in St-Tropez. Ray had left Robert, and now had a new flat in Paddington and was far happier. I'd begun collaborating with Arthur Helps on his book.

This wasn't made easier by the fact that he was incomparably ancient, and lived in the west of Ireland. He would turn up at Blomfield Road at eight thirty a.m., saying, 'I thought we might have a happy day at the British Museum.' Each time I had to explain I had to go to the office and couldn't. His mind was like a vast cupboard, presided over by an enterprising jackdaw. Facts of every kind tumbled out whenever the door opened. My job was to assemble this material into some sort of comprehensible order, and this often meant excising his ruminations about the state of Europe in Bettina's day. Once, having discovered that she had paid a long visit to Vienna, I wrote to ask him if she'd met Beethoven. A postcard came back that said simply, 'Not interested in music.' Never mind, I wrote back, *did* she meet Beethoven? Then half a dozen letters arrived that they'd written to each other. I knew a little about music and was therefore able to exploit this small seam of information, but I reflected gloomily about all the things I didn't know that Mr Helps might not have been interested in. Oh well, I thought, I must just do the best I can. My novel lay untouched for months.

At Christmas Michael sent me a case of brandy. I opened it and burst into tears.

PART THREE

I

One morning – it must have been a blurb-writing day – I noticed that Cecil seemed unusually absorbed by a proof copy he was reading. When I asked what it was, he said it was a travel book by Laurie Lee. 'It's his first prose work.'

'Is it good?'

Cecil said it was a bit purple in parts but, yes, it was good. 'He's written some very good poetry,' he added. Later, when Cecil had gone out to lunch, I looked at the book. It was called *A Rose For Winter*, and I was enthralled by it. He could write about anything – a sunrise, a city – in a manner that was both fresh and familiar. His language flowed as naturally as a spring of water whose depths are never obscured by muddy uncertainty – a revelation to me then, and an enduring pleasure now.

I can't remember where I first met Cathy and Laurie, almost certainly at a party somewhere. They were enormously popular, I soon discovered, and it was easy to see why. Laurie, when he chose, was a natural entertainer and a natural musician. He usually brought his guitar to parties and he and Cathy sang – Spanish songs, folk songs from either England or America. This might have been awful, but with them it wasn't. They never did it unless it was clearly wanted, and they never did too much. He was always wonderful company, funny, dry, and perceptive. Cathy, far younger, was beautiful and tall, and had thick, rich corn-coloured hair and very large cornflower-blue eyes that sparkled. There was something majestic about her, but her manner – she was a very humble person – was both frank and self-deprecating. She loved Laurie and had learned how to be his first lieutenant. I loved them both on sight.

Soon we were going to supper with each other. When she was staying with me Nicola, who at that time was very fond of dancing and wonderfully unselfconscious about it, danced *sardanas* with Cathy. Laurie was always very sensitive to the young. He'd ask them questions in a grave and gentle manner that always got a response. In *A Rose For Winter* he goes up to a Spanish child standing by the sea and asks her, 'What would you like most in the world?' She answers, 'To go in a boat on the sea to find my father.' I quote this as it illustrates so exactly how Laurie was with children. He always seemed to know precisely what to ask them, could reach their heart's desire in seconds.

In those days Laurie was frequently ill – had chest infections, fevers and epilepsy. Sometimes we'd have supper in their bedroom, with Laurie propped up on pillows, playing his guitar quietly. When he was better he played his fiddle. Music wasn't a random entertainment or special-occasion pleasure with him: it was an essential continuous background to his life. In spite of his delicate health, he had a profound distrust of doctors. 'They came for me last week, but I hid,' he said to me once, with a shrewd look of stealthy triumph.

If I had to think of one word that encapsulated Laurie, it would be 'discrimination'. One expects a poet to be discriminating about words, but Laurie was discriminating about absolutely everything, his surroundings, his friends, what he ate or drank, other artists' work, and how he treated other people generally. Discrimination informed all of his life. It took me years to understand how weak I was in this respect, but I could recognize it in him. He could be a prima donna, sometimes a bully, but he was never unkind or insensitive to anyone who was vulnerable.

He loved to tell jokes – sometimes I suspected he'd invented them. He once told me that when he went to the opening of the 1951 Festival of Britain the invitation said, 'Medals may be worn.'

'I hadn't any, so I pinned a catherine wheel to my jacket.' Then he was introduced to an actress in a strapless gown called Sabrina, whose reputation rested largely upon her breasts. 'Something came over me. I took off the catherine wheel and pinned it to her front.'

'What did she say?' I asked, fascinated.

'Fency!' he said gloomily.

Some time during these two years my brother Colin came to stay at Blomfield Road. He'd left Cambridge and was in the throes of a breakdown. He didn't want to tell me what was the matter, and I never asked him. He was seeing a psychiatrist three times a week and the rest of the time he was remote, withdrawn and sometimes in tears. I became more and more worried about having to leave him to go to the office every morning, and eventually asked him if I might see his doctor. He didn't mind, so I rang to make an appointment.

When I saw this man I found him thoroughly hostile. He seemed to think I'd come to try to worm out of him my brother's problem. When I said I hadn't, he was offensively incredulous. Why *had* I come, then? I'd come because I was increasingly anxious that my brother might kill himself and I wanted to know if there was anything I could do. His reply was that, on the whole, he thought it unlikely, that *he* knew what he was doing, and it really wasn't my business. It was all very well for him: he saw my brother for three hours a week; all the other hours Colin was in my house. We parted with mutual aggression, but I couldn't feel either respect or trust thereafter. Eventually, my brother recovered enough to find a dilapidated house in Kensal Road that he rented and started his business of making hi-fi sets.

Colin's leaving our mother and coming to me did nothing for my relationship with her. She *did* try to find out from me what was the matter, and I don't think she believed me when I said I didn't know. Of course, she missed him – poor thing. Great-aunt May, who'd been living with her, became senile and she had to put her in a nursing-home. I went to see May there, and the spectacle of her poor mind revolving in a smaller and smaller circle was shocking. My mother was now alone, bitter and unhappy. I knew that all the feelings I'd had for her when I was a child had gone, replaced or overwhelmed by a fog of boredom and impatience.

Why, I wondered, as I waited for a bus home after caring for her one evening when she was ill, were these feelings so strong and hardly ever lightened by love or concern for her? She was very unhappy – perhaps had always been so – but she was an intelligent, gifted woman. She had, when it was allowed to surface, a good sense of humour and she could be very generous. It was just that she was so continually sorry for herself. And then I saw that a good deal of the time *I* was exceedingly sorry for myself. I recognized that the faults we most dislike in others are the ones we fear in ourselves. So began a battle within myself to eradicate this nauseating characteristic, a battle that lasted – with brief false summits of premature triumph – for the next thirty years.

Insights are inspiring but, practically speaking, they are of no more use than a sign that says, 'To the North'. It may be where you want to go, but it doesn't tell you how to get there. I made a shaky start on my self-pity.

That autumn I took Nicola to see Lorna's lover who was a GP. As we left the block of flats where he lived, Michael emerged from a car. We couldn't avoid each other. He looked stricken, and I was hardly able to stand. We said something, a taxi mercifully arrived, and I bundled Nic into it, following her as fast as I could. In the taxi tears began pouring down my face and I saw dimly that Nic was regarding me with impartial curiosity. 'Sorry, darling, I just feel a bit sad.'

'Poor you,' she said.

Sometime after Christmas, James Sutherland's sister, Moira, asked me to a drinks party. 'Sorry it's such short notice, but it would be lovely if you could come.' I accepted. Moira had been married to Humphrey Slater and subsequently to Derek Verschoyle. She lived in a smart little house off Montpelier Square. The room was full of people but, except Moira, I knew none of them. I've never been good at parties and can never think of things to say to strangers.

I was just beginning to wish I'd not come when a man, whose back had been turned to me, suddenly whirled round, saw my empty glass and seized it. 'You need more drink,' he said. He was no taller than I, with a bullet-shaped head and thick brindled hair brushed straight back from his forehead with a parting so low on one side that at first it was hardly visible. He had high cheekbones and eyes that were now sparkling with flirtatious curiosity. 'Let us begin at the beginning,' he said. 'Tell me your name.' He had a heavy accent – not Russian, Polish perhaps? Then I remembered my grandfather's friends, the d'Aranyi sisters, brilliant violinsts both, and thought that maybe he was Hungarian. I told him my name, and waited.

'And what do you do?'

I said I worked as an editor at Chatto & Windus, and that I wrote novels. He went on asking me questions of an innocuous nature, but what struck me was his energy. He positively crackled with it; it was as though if you touched him you would get an electric shock.

'Shall we go out to dinner?' he said, not as if it was a question. I agreed: I felt drawn to him and intrigued. 'Find your coat and we will say goodbye to Moira.' As I was putting it on, I said, more out of politeness than anything else, 'Do you write?'

'Dar*leeng*! Don't you know who I am?'

'No.'

'I am Koestler. Arthur Koestler.'

I must have looked blank, for he suddenly burst out into torrents of laughter. 'She doesn't know who I am!' he shouted across the room to Moira. 'Do you *really* not know? You're not pretending?'

'I'm sorry, but I'm not.' I noticed that several people in the room were looking at me with indulgent contempt. Then I remembered Bob Linscott writing to me about *Darkness At Noon* and the impact it had made in America. 'Oh, yes. You wrote *Darkness At Noon*.'

'*Vich*, of course, you have not read.'

'Which I'm afraid I've not read.'

In the street, as we walked to a restaurant, I apologized for not knowing him.

'It was very shocking,' he said, and I noticed how lightly he wore his fame; he was neither pompous nor arrogant and he took an almost childish pleasure in his success. But, I realized later, it hadn't shifted the bedrock of his nature.

At dinner, we learned a few more facts about each other. That we had the same agent: 'Oh, if Peters has you, you may be some good.' That I'd been married and had a child: 'Good, darling, that is out of the way.' And that he also had been married but his wife had died. 'But I still see Celia of whom I am extremely devoted.' Celia? Celia was Mamaine's twin, he said impatiently, the Paget twins, surely I'd heard of them? No. He looked at me pityingly. They weren't only beautiful, they were very clever and everybody loved them. Celia was now married to another Arthur. 'A very good man, which I am not.' Many of his remarks ended upon this slightly challenging note. As he talked, seldom drawing breath, he ate and drank a surprising amount speedily, and all the time I felt his intelligent eyes – grey, sardonic, faintly mocking us both – appraising me. It was a little like sitting opposite a box of indoor fireworks.

'Now we go to my house,' he said. There was no question of a question this time.

His house, on the corner of Montpelier Square, was tall and painted grey inside and out.

'How pretty you are!' he exclaimed, as I sat shivering on the floor in front of his ineffectual gas fire. I'd never been called pretty before, and it made me feel neat and charming.

'I will drive you home in the morning, but we must be out of the house before nine. Mrs Watson comes at nine, and we must not shock her.'

This anxiety proved so important that we were up, dressed, had consumed a cup of excellent coffee and were speeding across Hyde Park in his open two-seater by eight forty-five.

'I will not stay, darling, I must get back to Mrs Watson. But I shall call you later when she has gone.'

It was Saturday and I didn't have to go to work. I had a bath and fell into bed to sleep till midday when he called.

The next evening he said, 'I have decided that we should get married, darling. I think that would be a very good thing to do.'

I was mesmerized. I wasn't in love – though much disposed to the idea of it – and I made one of the very few sensible decisions of my life. 'I won't marry you now, but I will come and live with you for three months and see how we both feel.'

'*Vary* sensible, Janee. That is what we will do.'

So that is what we did. Mrs Watson mysteriously disappeared, and Mrs Bridgeman came to Montpelier Square. I moved in with some clothes and a small inlaid dressing table, all of which was kept in Arthur's dressing room. I continued to work every other week at Chatto. Life became rich but incredibly exhausting. Arthur had boundless energy. His regime was to write all morning – he was deep into his book about Kepler – to eat a snack lunch of salami and cheese, to sleep for twenty minutes after it, and then to spend the afternoon arranging the rest of his life.

He wrote articles; people came to see him from all over the world. He adored parties and going out to dine with friends. I was quickly introduced to a number of them. The most important were Celia and her husband, both of whom I loved on sight. Celia, like her sister, was asthmatic; her health was generally delicate. Arthur, who'd been a prisoner of war in Japan, had joined the Foreign Office afterwards, from where he had gone to Japan with his first wife, a Polish war heroine. They had a daughter called Cecilia. His wife died, very suddenly of acute diabetes, and later he married Celia. He left the Foreign Office and they bought a house at Crondall in Hampshire, where Arthur and I used to go and stay. Celia was very musical and Arthur loved music. She was the only woman with whom he was never in the least irritable or impatient, and for someone of his volcanic nature this was an accolade.

There were other friends, sometimes we went out to restaurants – I remember an evening with Stephen Spender for whom Arthur was writing a piece. They had some kind of argument, and then Stephen suddenly leaned forward across the tale and said, in his soft, pedantic voice, 'But, then, Arthur, you're sometimes a very stupid man.' The intent was mischievous and fortunately taken so. He took me to dinner with Louis and Grizelda Kentner, warning me that our hostess was a superb cook. He always said something of the kind about the hostess – she dressed impeccably, she knew how to entertain. All this was to put me on my mettle when we returned the hospitality.

Those occasions were an ordeal for me. They frequently took place on weekday nights when I'd been working all day. I'd get home just before six, with a three-course dinner to produce, the table to lay, and I had to change appropriately for the evening. Arthur's obsession with perfection and his capacity for bullying began to emerge. In those days, I wasn't an experienced cook. I became terrified of making mistakes, dreaded being openly snubbed by Arthur in front of his friends. I remember with gratitude Laurens Van der Post defending me one night when Arthur hadn't liked a pâté I'd made. 'It seemed to me delicious,' he said, in such a way that Arthur subsided.

Arthur had written his four volumes of autobiography, and when I'd finished *Darkness At Noon* Celia advised me to read them next. She was quite right: I learned a great deal about Arthur that would otherwise have remained unknown to me – chiefly his astonishing courage, moral and physical, equally matched, a rare, remarkable combination I'd never encountered before.

Somebody told me that *Darkness At Noon*, which had sold four hundred thousand copies in France, had been the single most powerful influence that had stopped the French voting Communist after the war. Arthur was then a lone but influential voice against the Soviets and constituted a real menace to their regime. I began to understand why he had an intercom on his front-door bell — unusual, in those days — and he said he'd always answer the door. The possibility of assassination *was* present, although the only time he referred to it was a mention of the gun he kept in his bedroom — but it was said with a kind of goblin gleam of secret ownership. Arthur could dramatize an unsuccessful piece of salami or the lack of coffee spoons on a tray but, to me, he never dramatized his own life.

There began to be a pattern about our living — a gradual accumulation of small rituals that he particularly enjoyed. Part of him wanted a cosy — a word he often used — life of regular domesticity, but a far larger part was quickly, irritably driven mad by the prospect. He embraced the ordinary as some do a bank holiday. Real life was a moody, tempestuous business hardly to be borne.

One of the rituals was that he would lock me into the freezing drawing room to write while he worked upstairs. On Saturday mornings we'd stop at noon and go to the pub to meet Henry Green and sometimes Dig, his wife. These occasions were always enjoyable, indeed they verged on 'cosy', since Arthur and Henry were very fond of each other. Any propensity of Arthur's to turn an argument into a row met with the massive wall of Henry's innate courtesy and understanding of Arthur's uncontrollably volatile temperament.

One morning, when I was unlocked, I complained I couldn't finish my wretched novel. It had been going on for too long and I could see no end to it. Perhaps I'd better ditch it, and start again? 'I will read it for you,' Arthur said. He did. He described my writing as a cross between Nancy Mitford and Evelyn Waugh — an opinion that has both flattered and mystified me ever since. But the good news was that he told me I *had* finished the book — fifty pages back from where I was struggling, and he was quite right. Oh, the *relief*!

Sometimes my friends came to dinner — always an anxious

occasion for me: Jill and Cecil, Liz and Wayland, Lorna and Roger. On the whole, Arthur tended to dismiss women, unless he was pursuing them or they'd graduated over the years to being old friends. Of these six friends, he took to Roger St Aubyn the most, although later he 'chummed up', as he would put it, with Liz and Wayland. He also liked my brother Colin, who built him a gramophone, and once invited my mother to tea because, he said, if we were to be married, he ought to meet her. 'What about *your* mother?' I knew that she lived in Swiss Cottage, and that he visited her occasionally, often accompanied by Margaret Stevens, A. D. Peters' stalwart partner in the business. 'My mother is *hell*,' he said. Margaret told me that he was quite frightened of her.

Arthur was charming to my mother, who in turn was at her best; she was funny, fascinated by him, and she didn't produce a single snubbing remark.

He got drunk with alarming ease. He disapproved of himself about this, but often to no avail. One hot dusty evening when we had been dining with Martyn and Pinky Beckett, great friends of Arthur's of whom I became very fond, he said, 'I am vary, vary drunk, Janee, but you will see. I drive the car so slowly that nobody will know that.' The car was ricocheting gently, at about five miles an hour, from kerb to opposite kerb across the immense width of a fortunately empty Brompton Road. It was about two a.m. He wasn't caught.

He was the first man I'd ever met who noticed and appreciated what clothes I wore. Shortly before I met him, I'd gone to Paris with Lorna to stay with the Talleyrands at St-Brice, and from there we had spent a delirious morning on the top floor of Christian Dior where they sold off models very cheaply. I'd bought two dresses, both grey, one in silk organza with a wide dead-white satin sash, and one of wool and silk that he admired every time I wore it. 'Vary pretty, darling,' he would purr, walking slowly round me. I also had a few things made by Mrs Grodzicka that met with approval.

He loved England. He once told me that when he finally reached these shores and was interned as an alien, he'd written to the Home Office saying that the prison was like the Ritz compared to the prisons in Spain and in France.

He had – I suppose it wasn't surprising – an enormous vocabulary in English, that made no concession to accent. '*Vy* do you do this? Becose you are eenfantile!' he would say. He was irascible, obsessive, infinitely courageous, a manic depressive, and an idealist. Above all, he possessed an energy whose voltage would have served at least five ordinary people. Energy is always charming to those who encounter it in someone else, but to possess his degree of it was an agonizing burden, at times almost insupportable. Whatever he was, there was too much of it for anyone near him, with the striking and marvellous exception of Cynthia Jefferies, his secretary, whom he was eventually to marry and who died with him tragically in a joint suicide pact in 1983.

I can't help writing about him with hindsight: at the time, I was too raw, too inexperienced, and too *stupid* to understand much of this. In any case, I was a small incident in his life. He pursued and enjoyed or endured many encounters with women. He loved Mamaine, and I was always told that they could not bear to live with or without each other.

So where was I in all this? I was dazzled: I'd always been attracted to men older than myself. I admired him – his integrity, his discipline with work, and his lack of any pretension. I learned a few things about him that enabled me to join his life. Often when he became suddenly irritable, it was because, like some racing engine, he needed fuel. I'd post pieces of salami into his mouth to some effect.

But I couldn't deal with the bully. I reacted in the worst possible way – became silent, apathetic and, worst of all, a martyr. *He* was behaving badly, but I would not – resentment, so commonly the weapon of defence, didn't count as bad behaviour, which of course it is. I could have learned more about that. Once, when we were staying in a hotel, visiting Celia and Arthur in Lincolnshire, he began a bullying session in our bedroom. Suddenly, beside myself, I threw a full water carafe at him, narrowly missing his head. He stopped at once, laughed affectionately. 'Janee! I didn't know you had it in you!' I didn't have it in me very often, and manufactured rage wouldn't have produced the same result.

In the spring, Arthur acquired a canoe, a blue craft capable of holding two paddlers. He couldn't think what to call it, and I suggested *Blue Arrow*: it had a connection with his first volume of autobiography, *Arrow in the Blue*. He was very pleased with me.

I think we found this craft at Gamages – a store now defunct – which was in High Holborn. Having bought the canoe, he became possessed with the desire to buy more things. As we passed through the garden-furniture department, fraught with gnomes of various sizes, he cried, 'Gnomes!' pronouncing the G. 'Janee! I could have many of them on my roof terrace, don't you think?'

'No,' I said.

He persisted, bouncing about the place, picking one up and trying to cajole me in a studiedly wilful manner, and I sensed I was meant to disapprove. He gave in quite suddenly and never referred to gnomes again.

The boat could be loaded into the car in canvas bags, and at weekends we went to the river Wey, where she was put together. I have remarked earlier that men are often at their worst in boats, and Arthur was another example. In spite of trying very hard, I couldn't do anything right. I paddled too hard, or not hard enough; I was lazy, stupid and altogether a hopeless crew. These tirades were interspersed with sunny periods, when we ate our picnic and he had a brief nap, when peace and silence soothed him and he would invite me to extol it with him. But they were brief, and by the end of the day I was exhausted, frightened and withdrawn, and I expect the ghastly martyr put in her appearance.

Once we boated on a lake beside which was a hotel where we could stay the night. It had been a hot day, and Arthur's temper was in tatters by the end of it. We packed up the boat and trudged back to the hotel in silence. After one or two drinks, dinner was relatively calm, and after it, he proposed an early night. In bed he became very affectionate, and apologized for how fierce he'd been all day. 'It's simply that you madden me sometimes, but not always – not now . . .' I mentioned that I'd better to do something about birth control and the storm broke. There was no need. When would I *ever* learn? It was the wrong time of the month for me, I always thought I was right about everything, it was the one thing he couldn't bear about me.

He won, of course. He was a gracious winner, full of gentle, persuasive charm once he'd gained his point. The next few days were comparatively calm. The following weekend we went to stay with Celia and Arthur. Celia was having a baby – much wanted – but both Arthurs were worried about the delicate state of her health. Celia told me that she'd told my Arthur that if he and I broke up it would make no difference to her friendship with me, and she wanted to make that plain to him. That touched me. Things were beginning to feel very crumbly, and I think I knew it wasn't going to last.

I was still working at Chatto every other week. Cape had accepted *The Long View*, and Peter Peters wrote to me very handsomely admitting that he'd been wrong about its structure. An enthusiastic French fan had translated *The Beautiful Visit*, and Éditions Gallimard had accepted the second novel too. All this was reassuring, but didn't impinge upon my situation with Arthur. Sometimes I dreaded being alone with him. Sometimes I loved him very much. Always I felt spellbound.

There were good moments: sitting in an armchair, Arthur perched on the arm, looking at a book we had just bought together – 'Janee! *Zis* is what I really like. So cosy – domestic bliss. *Vy* don't we have it every day?' I didn't answer because there was nothing that Arthur wanted every day, and I recognized sadly that this was true then. There were also bad moments: a whole day spent rehanging his pictures in the drawing room. The bullying that this provoked was as bad as being in the boat, but more exhausting. I'd stand for hours holding a heavy picture and trying to adjust its position to his command. 'To the *right! No!* Zat is too far – now, up a little – not *enough – far* too much. Are you an *idiot*? Or are you simply trying to make me angry?' And so on for hours. Occasionally a picture was actually hung, and possibly two or three more, but then something was found wrong with one and they had all to be taken down and the whole business would start again.

And then, about two months after our last canoe trip, I realized I must be pregnant. Arthur had always made it very clear to me that he didn't want any children. He told me that he did have a child, by a French girlfriend who'd insisted on keeping it, but that was that. It was never to happen again. When I told him, he was unwilling to believe it at first, but as another week went by, it was impossible not to. Never mind, he said. He would fix it. Abortion was still illegal then. He would ring his friends, and someone would know somebody who would do it. He'd drive me to the place and it would all be over in a moment.

I thought about what had happened last time, and said I wasn't prepared to go to just anyone, they must be a doctor: it was my insides, and I'd be responsible for them. This made him angry, but indecisive. How would I find such a person? I thought again about the last time: he had been a Polish doctor and had done me no harm. I'd go to him. This was agreed, but there was a delay: I had to wait until I'd reached three months. This interim period became the last straw in our relationship.

My last evening with Arthur was spent dining in an hotel in Kensington with Henry Green and Norah Sayre – a young woman who'd come over from New York with an introduction to Arthur. I arrived at Montpelier Square a few minutes late, and could tell at once that I'd incurred displeasure. Arthur didn't offer me a drink, and it was Henry who offered me one. Throughout that awful evening – when most of the time Arthur pretended I wasn't there – it was Henry who kept me going, pouring wine for me and including me in the conversation. I don't know how much he knew but he seemed aware that the three of us were beside an unexploded bomb, and he kept it unexploded.

When the evening was over and Norah and Henry had gone, the storm broke. Why was I late? Why had I walked into the room as though I owned it? Why had I looked so gloomy – like a tragedy queen?

I said I wanted to go home. I was due to go into the nursing-home the following morning anyway, and I could neither argue nor defend myself any more. I wanted two things: to be alone and to go to sleep.

Everything went smoothly at the nursing-home, where officially I had a D and C – a respectable euphemism for abortion. But – and I don't know how this happened – my mother rang me there soon after I was back in bed. Somehow – I think she'd rung Arthur – she cottoned on to the idea I'd had an abortion and proceeded to talk about it. She didn't suggest coming to see me, but asked a lot of questions that I found difficult to stop. Very soon after this call, the Matron arrived, apologized and said I'd have to leave. It was the beginning of a bank holiday. I knew that there was nothing in my flat – not even a pint of milk – and that I'd be alone. She said I could find a friend to look after me, surely. I rang Arthur to tell him I was going back to my flat. When? At once. Well, he was going to spend the weekend with Arthur and Celia, but he would drop round before he went. I packed up, a nurse got me a taxi and I went back to Blomfield Road.

Arthur came. He seemed very uneasy. He, too, suggested that surely I could find a friend. I felt so feeble in every way that I was unable to think of anyone. At this moment I heard a voice calling me from my back garden. I looked out, and it was Wayland. I must have told him what was happening, but his arrival at that moment seemed miraculous. 'You can look after her,' Arthur said with relief.

'Well, someone's got to, haven't they?' Wayland returned, with some asperity.

'I'll tell Liz and I'll come back for you,' he said when Arthur had gone.

I stayed three or four days with Liz and Wayland, who were unfailingly kind and calm. Arthur wrote a short note in which he said it would be better if we didn't meet for a while. I wrote one letter to him.

2

I spent that summer in a kind of dazed apathy of despair. How clearly I can see now how these repetitive mistakes came about. But then I thought in extreme and simplistic terms: either a relationship was my responsibility, and its failure was my fault, or the other person was solely responsible, in which case it was his. Generally, I veered between the two. I didn't understand that relationships are a mutually responsible affair. I'd been brought up in the critical, judgemental ethos of my mother, and had neither understood nor escaped from it.

I suppose one reason for the blackness that descended upon me was the subconscious knowledge that I wasn't learning from my mistakes. Ignorance – at any level of consciousness – is usually painful. The first thing that made me smile was when I went to Peter Peters' office with some work, and saw Margaret Stevens who, knowing Arthur well, was aware of everything. She looked at me with great kindness and said, 'Never mind. We'll soon have you signing books at Harrods.' The kindness and the absurdity let in a little chink of reality and light.

And here I have to write a bit about my appearance. I find this embarrassing and difficult, but in trying to be truthful, I can't leave it out. It had dawned on me – rather slowly, as I'd been raised to feel plain and clumsy – that I wasn't considered plain. There were two reasons for this. The first was that I'd also been brought up to dismiss flattering remarks as bad for one's character: a bad character would accept them, a good character wouldn't. The second reason was that I'd never much *liked* my appearance.

Since I was quite young I'd had visions of a smaller, elegant creature with luxuriant auburn hair, sea-green eyes and a dazzlingly white skin. I think now this started with the fairy tales when I was small. I'd paint pictures of princesses in the books, whose hair was golden or dark auburn, and I'd change their invariably blue eyes to green. I didn't have a single one of these desirable attributes, so when told I was beautiful I neither believed nor agreed with anyone.

This didn't stop me trying to do the best I could with myself. I was quite capable of spending what time and money I had in efforts to look more attractive. I remember Wayland, who'd been talking to me while I was dressing for a party, saying, 'I say, Jenny, you don't get any plainer, do you?' And my thinking, I should hope not. I knew by now that a number of people regarded me as beautiful. But much in the way that rich people don't want to be loved simply because they are rich, I didn't want to be loved simply for my appearance. People need to be loved for themselves, whatever that might mean. I was certainly far from sure what it meant then. I simply felt I was making a hash of it, and underlying that foggy conclusion lay the dread that I *wasn't* anything else. I still had the desire to write, but depression leaks energy – like pain – and all that summer I couldn't write. This has always been a downward spiral for me: I couldn't write because I was depressed, and not being able to write confirmed and strengthened the depression. Repetitive experience can be brutalizing: the less I understood my experiences, the more I repeated them, each time becoming less aware of what I was doing.

One hot day, Colin said he knew I was unhappy, and why didn't I ask Laurie and Cathy to supper? 'They'll cheer you up.' So I did.

My affair with Arthur had never been secret. I'd never mentioned it to Laurie, but I knew that evening that he understood. He asked me what I was doing in the summer. Nothing – working at Chatto every other week. He was going to stay with the Devas' on Jersey in September, would I like to come

with him? 'You look as though you need a holiday.' I would, but
would they want me? He said he'd find out.

A few days later, he rang to say that the Devas' didn't have room
for me, and before I could say never mind, in as undisappointed a
voice as I could manage, he said, 'So I'm going to take you to Spain
for two weeks.'

'With Cathy?'

'No. Just the two of us.'

'Won't she mind?'

'Of course she won't.'

I have to say here that it never crossed my mind that this trip
would result in my loving Laurie. I loved him, of course, but I
thought of him as a friend, as indeed I did Cathy. I believed, which
was true, that Laurie had planned the trip to help me get over
Arthur and the consequences. I'd never been to Spain and to go
with someone who spoke the language and knew the country so
well made it both an adventure and reassuring.

We travelled third class. We sat opposite each other on hard
slatted wooden seats on the night train from Paris in a packed
carriage with companions who proved more silent awake than
asleep, when most of them snored. Laurie put his feet up on the
side of my seat. He had taken off his shoes and his socks smelt of
hot Stilton cheese. He closed his eyes and I did the same, but it was
too uncomfortable and I was too excited to sleep. The train
stopped once or twice during the night and by the time we
reached Gerona our carriage was more than half empty. Out on
the platform, blinded by the rich golden light, I saw Laurie greet a
group of people – Rodrigo Moynihan being the only one I knew.
'Bang goes our hideout.' He always pronounced the E in hideout
making three syllables of it. When I asked him why, he said that that
was how he'd read it when he was a child.

We walked from the station, carrying our bags for what seemed
like miles. It was nearing noon, and the sun was like a scorching
searchlight. Just as I felt I couldn't walk any more, we stopped and

went into the small hotel, whose hall was as cool and dark as a cave. Minutes later we were ensconced in two little rooms on the top floor. We'd sleep now, Laurie said, and go out later.

I remember feeling very thirsty, but there was no water in the room. I began to undress, but in the middle of that was overcome with the desire for sleep, and fell on to the hard white bed, straight to oblivion.

When Laurie woke me it was dusk. We walked through streets, some narrow and dark with fleeting cats and old women knitting in doorways, and some wide, lined with shops and yellow lights and crowds of people drifting slowly along as though in a dream. There were young men together, and girls linking arms – shirts and dresses dazzling white – and small children in starched frocks. There were babies, heads covered with little damp curls, decorated with tiny gold earrings and crosses on spidery chains.

We stopped when Laurie found the bar he wanted. It was large, dark and cavernous and smelt of spilt wine on wood. Laurie introduced me as Isabel – 'They wouldn't be able to say your name' – and I was looked at with courteous approval. There were no other women in the bar. I asked for a glass of water, which Laurie watched me drinking with impatient distrust. 'You don't want to drink too much of that.' Then we had wonderful light aromatic sherry – glasses filled to the brim slapped down quivering on the bar before us. Little thick white saucers with prawns, or glistening olives appeared. I was content to eat and drink and listen to Laurie deep in conversation with the barman and other customers. For the first time in months I felt completely carefree: everything was new – wonderfully foreign – the present filled me with joy.

I only remember fragments of the next two weeks. After one night in the hot little rooms, we left Gerona, went in a bus to Estartit by the sea. Then it was a simple fishing village with one small *pension*. Outside the doors of the fishermen's cottages were one or two, three or four large stones. Laurie said they showed the night-watchman the hour in the morning that the fishermen wished to be called. On the beach where we swam we were suddenly surrounded by a cloud of young girls who descended upon Laurie like butterflies, chattering to each other and to Laurie, and laughing at everything he said. Whenever we went out of doors, they would always find us. They sang Spanish songs with Laurie, and we danced *sardanas* in our bare feet on the sand.

We didn't stay very long. The morning that we left – perhaps it was *why* we left – the dining room at the *pension* was suddenly flooded with a busload of British. They were subdued, and talked to each other so quietly that the room resounded with people saying 'podden' to each other. 'Oh these poddens!' Laurie said, 'Dropped all over the place like little trench mortars.' We left when the bus came, accompanied by a stream of girls and their younger brothers and sisters.

I hadn't known we were going, and I didn't know where we were bound. I didn't care. I was enclosed in a magic capsule with Laurie. A continuous happiness possessed me. I fell steadily in love and there was nothing dire about it, no anxious speculation about the future and no agonizing about my past – particularly the preceding months with Arthur. It all fell away, leaving me light and free to enjoy each day. Laurie never mentioned Arthur. He had the most sensitive discretion about my failings or unhappiness. Although he could be brutally dictatorial when he felt like it, he was gentle, tender and discerning to those who were more accustomed to being dismissed as dull or shy.

In Gerona again we stayed in a hotel frequented by the picadors from the local bullring. It was a warren, much larger than it looked from its modest façade, with a restaurant on the ground floor that spilled out on to the pavement where the picadors sat for hours with friends and a drink on the table before them. Laurie procured for us what he described as a simple room and we dumped our baggage and spent the evening in the bar we'd been to before and ate out somewhere afterwards. We returned late, but the café and restaurant were still crammed with people. The harsh fluorescent light made their faces dramatically pallid and their enlarged eyes clashed with the glint on rings and gold fillings. We threaded our way through the tables – populated entirely by men – to a door to the right of which was the restaurant, visible through its own glazed entrance. In front of us a dark staircase rose steeply.

We climbed up three floors on each of which was a narrow landing with a row of doors each side. On the third floor Laurie led the way down the landing and stopped at a door. 'We are going to share a room tonight. Because it's *cheaper.*' He'd described it as simple, and indeed it was, with four walls, the door we had entered by and a small double bed. There was no window, but a naked bulb hung from the ceiling distributing a weak yellow light. None of this mattered in the least. Laurie produced a bottle of brandy from his bag: I hadn't seen him buy it. 'We haven't any glasses.' He unscrewed the cap, took a swig and handed it to me. 'Go on, my typical Kurd.' He'd earlier joked about how tired he was of travel books with pictures of swarthy natives robed in blankets, squinting at the camera, and usually captioned 'A typical Kurd'. It had become a term of affection.

I'd become, suddenly, desperately nervous. This brink – this, by now, familiar brink that had so many times simply ended in a slow slide of isolation and disappointment – was before me now and the thought of repeating it was paralysing. I began to try to say I wasn't – I couldn't – but he interrupted, 'Don't say any of that. I'll find you.' And so he did.

That night, which was so amazing for me in so many ways, also contained comedy of a frenzied kind. I woke some time later with a desperate need for a lavatory. 'You'll have to go and find one,' Laurie said. I got up, put on my long white cotton nightdress and went on to the landing, lit by another ailing bulb. I walked up and down the corridor: all the doors were identical. In desperation, I tried one. Instantly an enormous man in a string vest sat bolt upright in bed, saw me and held out his arms. I shut the door quickly and ran down the stairs, but the other two landings were the same. Just doors with nothing to indicate that large men in string vests weren't inside. The restaurant, I thought, there *must* be one adjoining it. I opened the glass door, half expecting it to be deserted by now, but no, it seemed as full as ever with people eating and drinking, and now staring at me. I saw a waiter passing: '*Toiletta?*' He indicated with his shoulder – he was carrying a large tray – towards the centre of the room where there was a sort of barricaded hexagon whose walls stopped a foot from the floor. To this I went.

I suppose the sight of someone in a nightdress with long hair streaming down her back and bare feet wasn't usual, for conversation had all but ceased as I stumbled into what turned out to be a kind of *pissoir* clearly designed for men. It served, but then I had to face the return journey. This time there was a collective display of good manners: people continued to talk and ceased to stare as I practically ran through the place and up the stairs back to Laurie.

The next day Laurie took me to the bullfight. It was very hot, and the stands round the arena were full. I have never seen another, or in the least wanted to, but the elements of elegance, cruelty, courage and skill, the squawking circus music, the dramatic ritual, the informed appreciation of the crowd, all combined to lift it to something more than a spectacle of simple crude and brutal bloodshed. Although the bull, however strong his courage, is doomed, he has a fighting chance of inflicting damage on his opponent. For his part the matador, in his rich, stiff, Goya–like attire, has grace and skill added to his courage. That afternoon, a young matador was carried out of the ring having been gored, though not fatally. The final bullfighter, kept to the last as he was the most experienced and famous, gauged his passes with the cloak to a hair's breadth.

Later that evening, I sensed that all wasn't well with Laurie: that he was in danger of having an epileptic fit. The prospect was alarming: I wasn't sure I knew how to help him. I suggested that we buy him a guitar, and playing it seemed to do the trick. The guitar store was also the workshop where the instruments were made. When Laurie had tested and chosen the one he wanted, he tried to commission a much better one for a friend of his. They only made guitars for real, professional musicians, they said, and Laurie confirmed that the recipient would be a worthy owner. 'It's for Julian Bream,' he said. He'd bring the owner to collect the guitar, and they wouldn't be disappointed.

We went back to the coast after that, ending in Port Bou where we swam. I remember one day we talked about writing and Laurie said that nobody who looked as I did could be any good at it. I was so incensed by this that I knocked him off the rock he was sitting on into the sea.

I was so entirely immersed in the present of each day that I didn't notice how many we'd spent together, until one morning Laurie said, 'We have a train to catch in an hour. We must go back and pack.' We did this, and an hour later we were on the train travelling north. We had each bought a large flagon covered in basketry that held the equivalent of fourteen bottles of wonderful sherry. Laurie had his guitar, and I'd bought two white embroidered shirts – one for Cathy and one for myself. We were far more encumbered than when we had set out.

Hours went by on the train. We sat opposite each other, and I began to lose the present, to think with a kind of desperate sadness of the future when this idyll would end. I longed to be lying with Laurie – ached with wanting him. He knew this, although I said nothing. 'We'll get off at the next station.' It was Orléans. We spent a night in a hotel there, and the next morning went on to Paris where we spent our final night. We had been careful with money and I had a little left. I remembered a small, excellent restaurant in the rue du Cherche Midi where Michael and I used sometimes to lunch. They specialized in *raie*, skate, with a delectable light sauce. I took Laurie to lunch there – the first time I'd ever taken anyone to a restaurant – and he was suitably impressed. The *patron* was the chef, a huge tall man who spoke in a very quiet, greedy voice, as though his culinary art and our appreciation of it were sacred.

We went back in the train, the ferry and the train again to Victoria Station. There, Laurie stopped at a slot machine from which you could tap out a luggage label on to thin metal. 'Isabel I love y' he wrote before the tape ran out. I have it still. After I'd dropped him in Elm Park Gardens, I sat clutching it. I'd had two weeks of unalloyed happiness, so why should I cry? It had been lovely and it was over. I wanted to write to Cathy, thanking her for her part in this, but I knew that Laurie would have been incensed. Taking me away had been *his* decision; he wouldn't allow her a role in it. I did write to Laurie, to thank him.

It wasn't the end of our friendship. We continued to meet, the three of us, and Cathy, whom I grew to love and appreciate more and more, never changed her attitude to me. In all the years after this I only had one row with Laurie, when he kicked my cat out of his way, and took offence when I objected. Eventually I said sorry. Years later, I got a postcard of a Mathew Smith painting on the back of which he'd written, 'I still think of you with rapture.' I have that as well. In fact, we continued to write to each other, though often after long intervals of silence, for the rest of Laurie's life.

3

In the autumn I began writing again.

For some time I'd had the idea of writing a novel whose theme was to be what people could change about themselves and what was immutable. I'd put this notion on the back of an envelope and shoved it into my desk, where it had sat for months like a fuse waiting to be ignited by thought. I have never been much good at thinking about *how* to set about structure or plot, or indeed the people who are to inhabit it. But I'd begun to discover that if an idea lay in the back of my mind little by little some flesh started to cover its bones.

Meanwhile there was still work to be done on *Bettina*, and I was still working every other week at Chatto. I was also doing a certain amount of television; book programmes were more plentiful in those days. On one I was asked to interview Laurie, and he was asked to recite his poem 'Apples': he got it wrong and got stuck and I had to prompt him. I was worried he'd be cross about this – when we had played dominoes in Spain and he lost I never heard the end of it – but he chose to be flattered that I knew the poem by heart. I was also asked to appear on *Table Talk*, a political programme, where we all had lunch, then listened to the one o'clock news and proceeded to discuss its content. I am only mildly a political animal and was picked because the producer wanted one woman on the programme who wasn't left wing.

The Long View was published in the spring of 1956. It was a Book Society Choice, which boosted its sales. I also got a number of good reviews. Jonathan Cape was so pleased that he said he wanted to give a party for me. I told him I hated drinks parties. What kind of party would I like? A party with food and if possible dancing. I should have it. Would my friends be able to come? They would. How many? As many as I liked.

The party started at nine and my friends did come, and there was food, and I remember one incident. A tall, good-looking man came up to me and said, 'I suppose you know that this party is as much for me as it is for you.' I said I was sorry, I hadn't known that, and asked his name. It was Ian Fleming.

Having a book published that was a modest success changed several things. I had more money, and all sorts of people began asking me to dinner. I think it was at Stephen and Natasha Spender's that I got to know Cyril Connolly much better, but I can't remember how I met John Davenport, a critic and friend of many in the artistic community. I'd heard about him from Michael Ayrton, who said he combined great physical strength with a phenomenally active and well-informed mind. He'd once seen John pinning two six-foot American soldiers to the ground, a gigantic hand on each throat, while he growled, '*Never* let me hear you say, "Who the hell is Henry James?" again.' Michael also told me that John had a passion for music and that when he'd come into some money he'd spent it all on hiring a string quartet to play privately for him in his house. I didn't see very much of John, although he used to ring up quite a lot, chiefly to discover whether Cyril was there. They took to playing a kind of game, having recently fallen out because John had given Cyril's fragment of a new novel, published in *Horizon*, a bad review. 'I suppose *he*'s there,' John would say, 'wasting your time when you ought to be writing. Indolence is very infectious, you know – you could easily catch it.' I saw more of Cyril. He was at a loose end having divorced Barbara Skelton – whom I think he still loved – and was not getting on with the fragment. He was writing a piece every week in the *Sunday Times* in which he reviewed a non-fiction book, and he used to give me meals in very posh restaurants, and some-times came to Blomfield Road. Once he brought his ring-tailed lemur to stay. She was an enchanting creature. She roamed the garden eating all the buds off my lilac, but her beauty and agility made up for her depredations. She had a benign expression and looked slightly surprised at whatever happened to her. She seemed fond of Cyril, but I balked at the idea of his leaving her with me for the night. Her habit of sitting on the back of a sofa to shit, even though Cyril explained that, to her, the sofa was really a branch of a high tree, wasn't reassuring. In the end he took her off in a taxi.

Cyril was the most wonderful company. Norman Douglas's remark that everything was worth talking about certainly applied to him. He made me laugh and I loved him for that. We were both slightly anxious with each other – I because I felt I must bore him with my ignorance. But he was definitely uneasy with me. This might have been partly because Stephen Spender had told Cyril that he thought I'd make him a suitable wife – a prospect that he might well have found disturbing, but it also had to do with his chronic sense of insecurity, I think. He must have known that he was exceptionally gifted, but I think his hatred of his own appearance obscured much else.

He once took me to stay for a weekend with a friend of his, a farmer who lived in a large house in Kent. The house is shadowy to me now, but I do remember being struck dumb at the sight, in a small study, of a portrait that my host said was of Jane Austen. Cyril's friend said he was a relative of hers. At dinner the first night, a young couple who lived on the estate were the only guests. It transpired that Edward, our farmer host, was romantically in love with the wife but could only see her with guests and her husband. The evening was a sticky one, and after the girl and her husband had gone, Edward and Cyril spent ages plotting how Edward could contrive to be alone with her. They sounded like two characters in a Shakespearean comedy, and at any moment I expected one of them to suggest exchanging clothes so that *nobody* in the ensuing drama would recognize them.

I think in Cyril I encountered yet another man whose brilliance of mind, whose sophistication of taste was balanced – perhaps *un*balanced would be more accurate – by some essential immaturity that caused him both confusion and pain, and often confounded the people who crossed his path. I had yet to learn that this wasn't unusual: I still expected people to be of a piece. In the time I knew him well I enjoyed his company with its rich mixture of information and entertainment.

However, I was sometimes taken aback by his taste – he wrote off Mozart with the exception of the operas – and I found other aspects of him unnerving. He was a sybarite – liked whenever possible to eat and drink beyond his means. He was a romantic and was acutely sensitive. He *was* indolent, as John had suggested, and used his great capacity for writing as little as he could get away with. He could be peevish and malicious, when his face would become that of a fat, angry baby.

But he also possessed the gift of serious appreciation of the arts and particularly of good writing. This last doesn't sound particularly striking, but in fact it's much rarer than generally it's presumed to be. Our relationship gently ground to an unpainful halt after several months.

There was one final incident at the Jane Austen house in Kent. Edward, our smitten host, flirted a good deal with me on the evening before we left and finally blurted out, 'I'd do anything in the world for you. Just say what you want.'

That kind of remark always made me want to tease. I thought quickly. He was a farmer. 'I should like a whole lorryload of farm manure delivered to my house.' And I watched his face for shock or at least chagrin. But he simply said, 'It shall be done.'

And it was. The following week a lorry arrived and I became the proud owner of a steaming heap of nourishment for my garden.

I'd got my next novel into some sort of shape in my mind. But again I left it. Reading and editing, television, radio and writing short pieces for various magazines ate up my time.

I went to parties that Olivia Manning gave, lunches mainly for writers, where I met such luminaries as Stevie Smith and Ivy Compton-Burnett. I once shared a taxi with Ivy, and as Olivia lived in St John's Wood and I in Maida Vale, Ivy conceded I should be dropped first. She spent the entire ride we had together calculating what would be a fair division of the cab fare. I was quite frightened by her. In appearance she looked and dressed like an old-fashioned nanny on her day off. She had bird's nest hair in an invisible hair net, and she wore a flannel skirt and jacket with white blouse, and double-strap black shoes. There was something steely about her that made me feel extremely shy.

Olivia introduced me to old-fashioned roses, and she had a Siamese cat called Faro whom she adored. I was also regularly asked to Hamish Hamilton's dinner parties. He was one of Jonathan Cape's great publishing rivals. His friends called him Jamie. These dinners were generally star-studded and I met there, among others, Princess Marina of Kent, Somerset Maugham, who was extremely nice to me, writing me a letter about *The Long View*, which he had bought and read, and Cass and his son, Michael Canfield, the latter then married to Lee Bouvier. Cass was running Harper & Row in New York, and for several years after I met him, he used to take me out to dinner and dancing at the Four Hundred Club. He was a famous wit and raconteur and was hugely entertaining.

I had one or two followers, none of whom affected me except with the unease that unreciprocated feelings seem to induce. It always brought out the worst in me – a combination of guilt and irritation, often turning me into a sulky bully, followed by disastrous lapses when, ashamed of myself, I tried to be kind. Once this involved actually getting into bed, which just made matters worse. I learned not to do that again, at least. One day, I suppose I thought, someone wonderful will turn up. Meanwhile I had many friends and I was earning enough to keep myself, if I was careful. I saw a lot of Colin. I loved the way he used language. 'When Uncle Ronnie turned a Catholic, he became wilfully broad-minded' –

that sort of thing. But in general I was neither happy nor unhappy, I was arranging my life in such a way as to shut out the possibility of starting the next novel; a prospect I dreaded since I knew now the toil and anxiety involved.

Then, on a Sunday morning in midwinter, the telephone rang. It was Romain Gary, a French novelist with whom I'd once dined with Arthur. He looked like a character from a Russian novel – dark hair, dark moustache and mournful eyes set in a face of faintly olive-skinned pallor. He and Arthur had discussed French literature and politics, and I'd eaten my dinner quietly as Arthur liked me to do – 'seen and not heard'. In the middle of the meal Arthur had suddenly cried out irritably, '*Vy* do you stare at her like that? *Vy?*' and Romain, clearly embarrassed, denied that he'd been staring – not at all.

Now he was saying that he had something he particularly wanted to tell me – could he come to my house?

There wasn't much to eat but, having told him that, I said he was welcome to what lunch there was.

Half an hour later he arrived. I took him into my sitting room and sat down, assuming that he would too. But he stood, leaning against the mantelpiece, looking down at me. Then, in a matter-of-fact manner, he said he'd been madly in love with me since the first moment he saw me. He'd not approached me earlier because he'd known that the affair with Arthur had caused me much unhappiness, but he'd been told I was over it now. 'You may not know, but I am to be posted by the Quai d'Orsay to be consul in Los Angeles and I desire you to come with me. Don't worry – the Quai d'Orsay, who would much prefer me to have a regular mistress, are prepared to ship your furniture and anything else you want over there. I think you would be very happy with me and we should have a good life together. Now, let us not speak of this any more for the present. Let us have lunch.'

We had lunch. I managed to ask when he was going to Los Angeles and he said in two months. Otherwise he talked about his new book, *The Roots of Heaven*, which had just come out in England and been well reviewed. He was married, he said, to Lesley Blanch and that would never change, but she lived in Menton and wasn't coming to the States. I knew of her books too. *The Wilder Shores of Love* had been the latest.

We had coffee back in the sitting room, and as soon as he'd finished it, he stood up. 'I have to go. I have very much to do before I go back to Paris tomorrow. Will you consider what I have said and call me at my hotel this evening? I am sincerely in love with you and pray that you will come.'

He kissed my hand and went. I sat at my desk and tried to think. I recollected several things Arthur had told me about him. He was Lithuanian. Gary wasn't his real name. He'd had an amazingly brave war as a fighter pilot, bringing his plane – seriously on fire – back to England, landing it and escaping before it blew up. He'd been badly wounded. He had the Légion d'Honneur. But all this was really beside the point. The point was that someone I hardly knew was inviting me to change my life utterly – go and live in another country and become a recognized mistress in a diplomatic life . . . Why had he chosen me? He said he was in love with me. How could he be? He knew me no more than I knew him.

On the other hand, I'd always believed that one day someone would come along and sweep me off my feet. Romain might be the one, and if I was feeble about it I would never know. The thought of leaving my house and living somewhere foreign did, in truth, terrify me, and my terror was the clincher. I *had* to do things that frightened me, to rid myself of that weakness. It was sheer madness to up sticks and go and live thousands of miles from my home with a man I'd only met twice in my life. Of course it was. He was attractive and looked both intelligent and gentle. I liked him for not attempting to pounce on me.

That evening I rang him and said that before I made up my mind I'd like to spend a week with him in Paris to see how we got on. That was an excellent idea. The next morning he rang to say that if I caught the train for the two p.m. ferry the following Friday, he would meet me at the Gare du Nord.

So I packed my best clothes and set off for Paris. By the time I had paid for the taxi to Victoria, I realized I had very little money, far less than I thought I had. I had, in fact, exactly ten shillings and no francs. Perhaps I could buy a sandwich? But supposing he didn't meet me, I'd need the ten shillings – and actually ten shillings wouldn't be enough anyway. I searched my bag again for the three pounds I'd thought was there, but it wasn't.

'How amazing to see you here!'

A tall man was standing over me whom I didn't immediately recognize, until he said, 'We met in Paris with Michael Behrens.'

'Of course I remember.' He was the man with the tiny wife who had eaten two dinners.

'I was just going along for a spot of lunch. How about you?'

'No, thanks. I think I'm going to skip lunch.'

'Oh, no! Please let me give you some. I shall be so bored by myself.'

So I had lunch with him. He was obviously very curious about why I was going to Paris. As he didn't mention Mike again, I guessed that he knew that we weren't seeing each other. In which case . . . I could see him speculating.

'Is anyone meeting you?'

'Yes, at the Gare du Nord.'

Much later he said, 'Well, if you don't mind, I'll just make sure that you *are* met. I have a feeling that you haven't got much money on you.'

'I haven't, as a matter of fact. I left it at home by mistake.'

'Ten quid?' he suggested.

'Ten shillings actually.'

'Good God! Let me lend you some.'

I refused – although he seemed kind, I didn't trust him. 'I must say, you're an extraordinary girl. Supposing you *aren't* met?'

'I'm sure I shall be.' But I began to feel anxious about that.

289

It was dark when we arrived, but I could see Romain – he looked dashing and romantic in a fur hat – standing on the platform.

'It's all right,' I said, 'I am being met.' I didn't much want to have to introduce the men to each other, and managed to avoid this by not attracting Romain's attention until my train companion had gone.

'You look very beautiful.'

'You look like someone in a Russian novel.'

He smiled; he liked that idea.

The week wasn't a success: it wasn't awful, but it lacked momentum. I didn't fall in the least in love with him and, for his part, I think I must have disappointed. My inability to speak, yet again, came into it. It made me awkward and dull with many of his friends. He took me about a great deal – I suspect to get other people's opinion of his plan. He took me to his tiny attic room office at Éditions Gallimard, his publisher. It contained a bed, a chair, and a battered open suitcase full of the manuscript of *Racines du Ciel*. He gave me sheets to read, but his writing was of the kind that, though large, was illegible. Then, as we went down a flight of stairs, he said, 'I want to show you something.' He opened a door. 'Look!' It was a large and beautifully furnished room, with a grand piano and rugs on the polished wooden floor. 'Camus,' he said bitterly. 'Camus gets this room, and I get an attic.'

We met Camus later in the week, at Les Deux Magots, the famous literary café: he was sitting against a wall, with newspapers spread all over his table. In spite of Romain's feelings about their rooms, they seemed to get on well and plunged at once into an animated discussion of French politics. This was disappointing to me, as I'd naïvely imagined that when writers got together they talked about writing. Camus was a very beautiful man – one of the few I have ever met – and I watched him, unnoticed, while he and Romain had an explosive argument about some minister or other. At the end of it they were completely amicable, almost as though the argument had been simply a violent game that had run its course and ended in a tie.

At the end of the week, Romain asked me to go home and think about his proposition. I said I didn't think it would work, but he was insistent I go home to think about it that I agreed. I went home with some relief; it had been a small adventure, but nothing more. I think he must have been relieved when I said I didn't want to join him. He went to LA, met Jean Seberg and eventually married her.

I come now to one of the worst things I did in my life. I fell in love with Cecil Day-Lewis, and when he made advances to me, I succumbed. The affair was, in fact, a very brief one, because I felt so awful about betraying Jill. It would be easy to make excuses – I was essentially lonely. I longed for a mutual love, and particularly the affection that goes with being in love with somebody whom I'd had time to get to know and who I felt knew me. I didn't want someone to whom I just looked good and was worth making a pass at. But none of that, I very soon realized, excused me. I had to put an end to it, and I did do my best to do that in the right way. I thought that if I told him I couldn't go on with it because of Jill, he might take it out on her. So I thought I had to lie, and tell him it simply wasn't working for me. I did this, not taking into account that almost any man dislikes being turned down in that way. He was bitterly hurt, resentful, called me a whore – which I suppose I was – and wrote letters long afterwards to this effect. I left Chatto and didn't see either Jill or Cecil for a long time. I am trying to write this without hindsight; I thought at the time I was giving up someone I could truly have loved, but with whom I'd never expected any future. I was extremely unhappy, and I think I felt I'd done the most I could do by going; it expiated at least some of my guilt about the affair at the time. I wasn't able, then, to recognize that such things need not happen if they are resisted in the first place; I thought that they simply struck one – like lightning – and that one had no choice.

4

It was 1958. I had to find another job as lack of money was pressing again – just as well, really, as it forced me to get work. I went to Weidenfeld & Nicolson, and was hired as a deputy fiction editor working under Barley Alison. We worked in a small office in Cork Street, whose space was considerably reduced by the tottering piles of manuscripts that occupied the major part of it. Barley was tiny, dark, courteous and often extremely funny. Australian by birth, she'd been for some years at the Foreign Office. I don't know how she moved to being a publisher, but the life clearly suited her. She loved writing and writers, and she was always kind to me.

Occasionally, George Weidenfeld would hold meetings in a room further down the house that was so dark he was frequently holding pieces of paper at different angles to catch enough of the musty light to read them. One afternoon he took me to tea at the Ritz and intimated that we might get married. Before I declined this kind offer I had a wicked urge to accept – simply to see the look of horror on his face.

Once, Barley went on holiday for two weeks and I was left alone with the scripts. Haunted by the countless authors starving in basements and bed-sits while they waited for fame and fortune from their uniquely important contributions to literature, I worked longer and longer hours trying to clear the formidable backlog.

But then one day, I went to have lunch with Peter Peters and he asked me how my book was going and I said it wasn't because by the time I got home in the evening I was too tired to write. There was a pause. 'How much do you need to live on while you're writing it?'

I looked blankly at him. I never knew how long any writing would take me. 'Just a rough idea,' he urged.

'Three hundred pounds?' It seemed an awful lot, but surely I could finish the book with that. 'Right,' he said. 'Give in your notice to Weidenfeld and I will send you a cheque.'

And so my few months with Weidenfeld came to an end, and I settled down to serious work. I'd discovered that working every day in the mornings made the process dynamic, and that after a few weeks, I didn't exactly look forward to but began to live in the book when I wasn't writing it. Things I hadn't consciously thought about fell into place, almost as though they were somewhere I had really been.

I can't remember much about the rest of that year. I wrote a couple of short stories. I wasn't short of money and could, when I had friends to dinner, buy a leg of lamb instead of a shoulder. Mrs Grodzicka still made nearly all my clothes. I know that later that year while outwardly, on a practical scale, things appeared to be going quite well, inside I felt rotten. My new-found energy for work drained away. I felt the success of *The Long View* had simply raised expectations from my publisher and agent that I'd certainly be unable to fulfil. The two completed novels had been a fluke. I'd flip through them despairingly, wondering how on earth I'd managed to do even that. Anything more that I attempted to do would prove me a fraud.

The rest of my life was equally hopeless. I couldn't find anyone with whom I could irreproachably fall in love – someone with whom I could share my life. I reflected again that I was simply the kind of person who was designed to be a second string. The more I thought about this, the more inescapably true it seemed to be. Looking back now, I can see that I was dangerously unaware and the few things I did know about myself were neither consoling nor inspiring. I was lazy, and where writing was concerned this was inexcusable. I was also a coward: the only way to discover whether I'd be any good at writing was to go on doing it, and I was terrified of taking that risk.

I also felt overwhelmed by a series of misconceptions – like a small range of mountains that blocked the view. Some of these I might well have been born with; some were inculcated by my parents and nannies; some I no doubt painstakingly fabricated for myself. 'Boys are better than girls' was an early one – my mother, nannies and even our cook, Emily, made plain their preference. 'You're a remarkably stupid little girl,' a music mistress had once said to me when she was trying to teach me key signatures. An elderly cousin I overheard rhapsodizing about Robin ended by saying, 'Jane's a plain little thing, but she seems to have a nice nature.' At eight years old I didn't care in the least about my nature, I wanted to be as beautiful as the day, like in *The Five Children and It*.

At least at that age – and for some years afterwards – I'd thought I knew what I was going to *do*, how I was going to spend my life. Marriage and the war had deflected my desire to work in the theatre. That little flame of ambition guttered quietly for years and finally went out. I'd failed both at marriage and motherhood, and writing had assumed a different hold on me. There was none of the excitement and fun of working with other people, of playing to an audience, of being applauded, and setting about the next play. Writing was solitary, difficult work, where self-criticism had to be constantly alert. A day or a week's work was merely a few more drops in the bucket, and the end of the story shifted maddeningly a little further out of reach, like false summits on a mountain, or a mirage in the desert.

I knew my life was neither happy nor productive, but I'd no idea how to change it. How could one change, and how much? This dilemma sparked the idea for my next novel. I wanted to write about what people could change in themselves, and what was immutable. There were to be four main characters: an ageing, successful not-quite-first-flight playwright, much older than his neurotic wife. He was to be the offspring of an unhappy mixed marriage: an Irish Catholic father and a Jewish mother. I called him Emmanuel Joyce. He was to be married to a woman from a more privileged background, and they would have had a child who died in infancy. She, unable to have another and distraught by her loss, takes refuge in chronic ill-health. She was to be called Lillian. Emmanuel should have a faithful lieutenant, a much younger man who admires him, and who acts as a manager. Jimmy knows that Emmanuel is periodically unfaithful to Lillian. The novel should open with the attempted suicide of Emmanuel's secretary and her departure. The final character was to be a girl they hire to replace her. She was to be nineteen years old, the daughter of a West Country clergyman, and it would be her first job. She would become the catalyst. I wrote the novel from the four points of view of these characters, enabling the reader to know more about them than any of them knew of themselves.

I wrote half of the first chapter, and then the offer of some small job intervened. I was still too afraid of running out of money to turn things down. And also, at that point, I was asked to a party by the Tynans in their pitch-black flat in Mount Street. Shortly after this, Ken rang me up and asked me to go to the theatre with him. It transpired that Elaine Dundy, his first wife, was going to America for three months and Ken asked me to be his evening companion during that time. It was a welcome and distracting proposition, and I thought, Why not? Only, I decided, as he was married, I'd not fall in love with him: I'd behave more as men did about these situations. I'd enjoy three months, and when Elaine came back I'd disappear – unpainfully – from the scene.

At that time Ken was a most successful and rightly acclaimed theatre critic. He worked for the *Observer*, and had a good deal to do with that paper's circulation. He was tall and good-looking with light brown hair that fell in a lock over the side of his large, high forehead, and large blue-grey eyes – all of his features were large.

He was a creature of self-constructed layers. At first sight he looked like most people's notion of a privileged, handsome undergraduate with the assurance and the continuous flow of asides designed to shock. He also gave the impression that, as people would say nowadays, he was cool, that he would never be out of his depth and that nothing could happen that he didn't expect and could deal with. There was an air of indolence about him, but this was underlaid by a sharp and perceptive intelligence. He looked much of the time as though he were waiting for something to amuse or excite him at any moment. He dressed flamboyantly in beetroot-coloured suits, white jackets and shirts of various brilliant colours. There was another layer to him – more childish – that could emerge. He adored glamour of almost any description: famous names, exotic food, dressing up, late-night parties. The core of him was his genius as a spectator and the way in which he could communicate with pithy brilliance what he saw and heard. He was also, however, an unconfident, uncontrollable romantic who was constantly warding off disappointment lest it should turn into despair. This much I learned of him during the three months, which were, indeed, both distracting and enjoyable. We went to the theatre every night and then out to a variety of restaurants for dinner. He took to sleeping at my flat, using his own only for writing his copy and collecting clothes. One Sunday night he took me to a jazz concert – I think at Earl's Court – and we went to see Louis Armstrong afterwards. He was sitting in his dressing room, majestically benign, putting little pieces of soaked cotton wool on his mouth where he'd split his lip playing. Ken wanted to learn to play the trumpet and had a stab at it for a while.

We went to bed very late. Ken had little use for mornings. He would go off about midday having arranged where we were to meet in the evening. We weren't compatible lovers: both of us, I think, were shy in this respect. I never gave him what he wanted, because I never knew what that was, and my sex life had become so confused and muddled by guilt, and general failure – Laurie now seemed like a distant oasis long lost in the desert – that I didn't consider it. I *liked* Ken, enjoyed his marvellous company, his affection and his funniness and left it at that. One of the most affectionate memories I have of him is his dancing and singing 'The Rain In Spain Stays Mainly On The Plain' stark naked. The only time Elaine was mentioned was when he said that on her return they were going to Spain to see some bullfights – another spectacle he loved. He gave me his book *Bull Fever* to enthuse me, but it didn't.

Our parting was easy and amiable. Some months later he wrote me a long letter saying that he was going to visit Gordon Craig, Isadora Duncan's former lover and a pioneer of stage design, in the South of France, and would I accompany him? He *did* love me, he went on to say, but I was too splendid for him. And much else: it was a very good letter, full of – I was going to say himself, but what I mean is full of what he was. I didn't see him for a long time after that. I missed life with Ken, but mildly. On the whole I was pleased with myself for not minding more. If I was to be doomed to play second fiddle in the lives of the men I encountered I need not fall miserably in love with them. This seemed a realistic and sensible conclusion, and perhaps it would enable me to concentrate upon my work as Peter Peters was constantly urging me to do. Sense and realism don't enthrall. It seemed that I must settle down to hard work, and fewer, smaller pleasures.

It was somewhere about then that I got to know Victor Stiebel. Judy Campbell, the lovely actress whom I'd first met with Pete during the war, invited me to a party at her house. Victor wasn't then smitten with the multiple sclerosis that would eventually kill him, and was at that time making the most beautiful romantic clothes in London. He was small, with thick white hair, brilliant blue eyes and the charm that comes with a sincerely passionate interest in other people. He treated me as though I was the most interesting person he'd ever met. This, of course, made me more interesting, as it did everyone he talked to. After we had been chatting for some time, about theatre, books, music, Judy came by with a jug of martini and said, 'She's just had a great success with her last novel, Victor. You ought to read it – it's marvellous.'

'You write? And you never told me? What modesty! Sandy!'

A young man came over to us. 'This is Sandy Wilson. *Salad Days*, you know. This is Jane Howard. We are told to read her new novel.'

'I've *read* her new novel. It touched me to the core.' There was a pause, and then he said: 'Do you know a novel called *The Beautiful Visit*? Because that is the only novel I can recall having touched me as much.'

Not sure now whether he was having me on, I said I'd written it.

'*You* wrote that as well? I am staggered. How can I have forgotten your name? Oh, Victor, what a *treat* you're in for.'

'*Was* he having me on?' I asked Victor, when he'd gone.

'Of course not. Can't you accept a glorious coincidence when it comes your way?'

From then on we were friends. It transpired that Victor wanted a new hi-fi and I told him that Colin would do it for him. They got on extremely well, and then, when it came to Victor paying him, Colin said, 'I think my sister is the kind of person who should wear your clothes. Could I have a dress instead of money?' Victor was very touched by this, agreed immediately, and shortly afterwards Colin and I went to Cavendish Square and sat on tiny gilt chairs while various models were shown us. Colin, in his best dark trousers, looked like a benevolent spider.

I soon discovered that while I passionately wanted a little black dress, Colin envisaged me in a full-blown ball gown. Victor told the *vendeuse* to bring out the Wedgwood-blue silk for me to try. Dresses of that sort were built upon an elaborate structure of stiffened coarse net, whalebone and layers of underskirts. It wasn't the kind of dress that anyone could have got into by themselves – it reeked of ladies' maids. 'That's just what I mean,' Colin said, and then, 'You do like it, don't you, Jinny? It does suit her, doesn't it?' to Victor. I realized I couldn't disappoint him. I was going to have to take a dress I'd probably never get a chance to wear.

Victor said we should also try some of the black dresses. The third was of soft corded silk, very simple with a low round neck, a neat waist and a bell-shaped skirt. 'I think,' Victor said, 'that you should have them both.' I knew then that he'd been aware of exactly what Colin and I had been thinking and had chosen this generous path to suit both parties. Everybody was delighted.

I did wear the ball dress once – at a dinner in the Guildhall for the Arts and Sciences to which I was invited. A friend had to dress me, but I was deeply grateful I had it as the dinner was very grand and fellow writers were wearing their orders; I had none. The first person I met before dinner was Rosamond Lehmann. She looked at me with cool distaste then pointed out that I had a shoulder strap showing.

I still hadn't come to terms fully with living alone. Since writing is necessarily a solitary business, I succumbed to almost any distraction that involved being with people. Evenings, in particular, weren't for writing, but parties or concerts, theatres or cinemas – or simply going out to dinner with men who asked me. On one such occasion, I was asked by a man I knew very slightly, a lawyer, who, I found, had invited a friend of his to make a third. For reasons that will become clear later, I shall change both their names. They were both Jewish, and as dinner progressed, it became clear to all three of us that my host's friend, whom I shall call Sam, and I were immediately attracted to one another. Sam had been one of the people to whom Romain had dedicated a book. He was full of energy and intelligence, and he clearly liked the company of women. The next morning he rang me and asked me to have dinner with him, and to come to his flat for a drink beforehand.

He lived in Onslow Square. The flat was beautifully furnished and decorated: it was clear he had very good taste. He told me he was married, to a Swiss girl who wanted English nationality. They were friends, but it wasn't a serious marriage. Suzanne was away – she worked for a producer of art books and her work took her to Switzerland, Germany and France a good deal. In a short time we became lovers, and when – with friends – I rented my brother's mother-in-law's, Ruth de Lichtenburg's house in St-Tropez, Sam came too. The party consisted of Pinky and Martyn Beckett, friends of Arthur Koestler's of whom I'd become very fond, and Celia and Arthur Goodman, the same Celia who had told Arthur that if our affair came to an end, she would still regard me as a friend. On arrival Martyn, exclaiming that the journey had exhausted him, threw himself on the double bed in their room, and shot up at once with a cry. A black cat and several kittens emerged from under the quilt – unharmed, thank God, said Martyn.

The first week was wonderful. St-Tropez wasn't spoiled then. The villagers still fished. There was a shop where you could have sandals – exactly as the Romans had worn – made for two pounds. There was Senquier, the café and pâtisserie that sold the best nougat in the world, made to an old and secret family recipe. Our house was outside the village near rocky coves and the great sandy beach of Pampalone. It was deserted in those days, except once when we saw Brigitte Bardot covered only partly by her tawny mane and more efficiently by a bronzed young man. Round their ecstatic writhing bodies, two children walked, solemnly collecting shells. Daringly, we tore off the tops of our bikinis, and browned ourselves. The Becketts and the Goodmans knew each other through Arthur, but Sam, the only newcomer, was a great success. He got on with everyone. A pleasurable routine was quickly established: the mornings on a beach, a picnic lunch, home for a siesta and then an excursion into the village for drinks on the harbour front. I remember one evening seeing the Windsors at one of the grander restaurants, she looking like the wrath of God, he like a miserable little boy. Augusta, the de Lichtenburgs' faithful housekeeper, made us dinner and at night Sam and I – and, I imagine, all of us – made love under ancient mosquito nets through which experienced mosquitoes frequently found their way.

Sam had one of those faces most accustomed to animation – telling jokes, laughing at other people's; even listening was an animated process with him, as his face would reflect his responses. Sometimes, I'd catch him when we were alone or there was a silence and, looking at him, I saw nothing but despair. 'Are you all right?' I asked one day in the car. 'Are you happy?'

'Of course I'm happy, my little darling. How could I be anything else?' A strangely unsatisfactory reply, but the next moment he was singing and making plans about the evening.

Ten days into the holiday Celia had a bad attack of asthma. She'd always been fragile, and after a night and a day spent by her bed as she fought for breath, Arthur felt he must drive her home. She preferred to fly and be home faster, and went on the earliest available plane. Arthur had to drive his car back, and it was arranged I should go with him, as Sam was also leaving a few days before the end of the holiday. 'Back to making suits for lunatics,' he remarked.

Arthur's marriage to Celia was very happy for both of them. I went down to their house in Crondall to help with their first baby, Ariane. Some years later, and not very many, Arthur was killed by his dog, which tripped over his gun when Arthur was resting during a shoot.

During the following autumn and winter it became clear to me that Sam's relationship with his wife Suzanne was nothing like as simple as he'd told me. He reiterated that he felt responsible for her. I took this to mean that she was in love with him but it wasn't reciprocated. It seemed likely that an arrangement that had been made in good faith had, on her part, at least, turned into something else. Whenever she returned from one of her trips abroad, he'd explain that he couldn't see me much because he felt guilty about her.

Gradually, during those months, more information about him trickled out. His family had a tailoring business in the East End.

They were Orthodox. His parents had wanted him to become a rabbi. He'd been in the Army during the war, I think in intelligence, and he'd been an examiner of Nazi war criminals at Nuremberg. When I asked him about this, he merely said, 'It had its moments.' But his face became implacable – closed. After conversations of this kind, he'd revert to a kind of frenzied gaiety.

Slowly I realized that he was leading a completely double life. His family never came to his flat, he went back to them at intervals, and they knew nothing of his marriage – they'd have gone through the roof if they had found out about it. Suzanne wasn't a Jew, 'Any more than you are, my little darling.' I had some Jewish blood way back from a liaison between Leopold II and a Rebecca Goldschmidt: he laughed, 'A very few drops of your blood.' The manic gaiety began to be hedged in by fits of melancholy. In January he said he had to take Suzanne for a holiday in Mexico. She wasn't happy and he'd always promised to take her there. 'And then I shall come back to see you.' While he was away I tried to work, but I felt suspended. I loved Sam and he said he loved me, but I was no longer sure what either of us meant. I told myself that when Mexico was over, he would come back and everything would be as it had been in the summer. It wasn't.

He returned on a Sunday morning, straight off the plane. He looked dreadful, haggard, with blue circles under his eyes. He was dead tired, he said. I put him to bed to sleep, and set about cooking. In the evening we had some food and talked. He told me then that Suzanne *did* love him, he'd not realized how much. 'And you love her?' I asked.

'I don't know. Not enough. I'm in no state to love anyone. I feel as though I'm going off my head. I'm no use to you. I'm no use to anyone. I'm in a mess I can never get out of,' he replied. I thought he needed help, and asked if I found someone for him to talk to would he agree to it? He'd think about it, but meanwhile, he was going back to his flat: Suzanne was going away again, and he would be on his own.

I'd been doing a certain amount of TV on panels with David Stafford-Clark, a psychiatrist. He and his wife had been to dinner with me and I felt I knew him well enough to approach him. I rang him up and he made an appointment for me to go and see him. I went. This was the third time in my life I'd approached a doctor of this kind on behalf of somebody else: for Robert Aickman, and for my brother Colin, and both times I'd been offensively rebuffed. So it was with some trepidation that I went to see David.

He was extremely kind. He listened to what I could tell him of Sam, and said if Sam would agree to it, he'd be glad to see him. This happened. For some weeks or perhaps months, Sam went to David, and I saw less and less of him, and my feelings about him changed from wanting to *be* with him, to simply wanting him to feel better at any cost. Occasionally, Sam rang me up to see how I was. I never asked him about how he was getting on with David, as the whole process seemed too fragile for me to intrude. I did ask him how he was and the replies were always, 'Simply splendid, much the same.' In the end I stopped asking. I knew the affair was over, but I was resigned to feeling more anxious about him than unhappy.

A hot summer, and Nicola was staying with me at Blomfield Road. It was Sunday evening, and Nic and I were just wondering what we could do that wouldn't make us any hotter when the telephone rang. It was Ingaret Van der Post. Would I come round for a drink? When? Well, now – this evening. I said I must bring my daughter with me and she said of course. 'Round' meant two longish bus rides, as the Van der Posts lived between South Kensington and King's Road. There was only one other guest, Jim Douglas-Henry, whom I found charming and I could see that he was interested in me. We arranged to meet again. We had our drink and went back on our buses. The next morning I saw Nic off at Paddington to go back to Slimbridge and her beloved pony and Pete.

Lorna Mackintosh asked me to stay for a couple of weeks that summer in the new house she'd bought in Cornwall. She was now married to Roger St Aubyn and the marriage was already full of dangerous rocks. It wasn't a happy visit and half-way through it the telephone rang at midday. It was Sam – for me. 'How are *you* then?' he asked. I'd told him about Jim, and after I'd asked how he was and received the usual sardonic reply, 'Marvellous!', he said, 'Well, I hope you will be very, *very* happy,' and rang off.

Later that day there was a call from David Stafford-Clark. I don't know how he found me, but he did. Sam had been found dead in a garage – he'd killed himself. The police had found a note from me on him, as well as evidence that he was seeing, or knew David, and David was warning me. He said he would deal with the matter, but perhaps I'd better come back to London.

I remember sitting on the train unable to stop crying – not continuously, but in endless sudden bursts. Trying to imagine the degree of desperation that had driven him to this dreadful end was too much – I couldn't. The shock of it recurred, each time as though I'd just heard it, and his last words on the telephone now seemed unbearable. *Why* hadn't I realized how desperate he was, and what could I have done to prevent it? I wept and wept until I was dry.

Suicide is the angriest death – a way of telling those who loved and cared for you most how useless they have been. In the successive nights I grieved for his father, his mother, his other unknown family; also, and far from least, the wretched Suzanne. I couldn't write or ring her up, since she might not know of my existence and discovering it might make things worse for her. The man through whom I'd met Sam rang me and very gently told me about the funeral and where Sam was buried.

About a week later I went to see David. After we had talked about Sam and he'd attempted to absolve me of guilt, I said I seemed to do nothing but make dreadful mistakes with people and that perhaps there was something wrong with me and I needed help. Would he help me? No. Why not? 'Because I should fall in love with you.' He then said that if I wanted it he would find someone else. I said I'd think about it, and tell him if I did, but my innate suspicion of the experience I'd had with other psychiatrists intervened and I didn't ask him. Afterwards I thought it was very honourable of him to say what he did. It was then that I grasped how much I wanted to stop being men's mistress. And I realized that for years I'd wanted to marry Michael; then I'd wanted to marry Paul, and even – briefly – Arthur. I'd repressed my feelings about Michael because somewhere I knew that he wanted to stay married to Felicity, with whom he settled to a happy old age. And I was certainly glad I hadn't married the other two. But still the idea persisted that what was wrong was that I hadn't found a man for whom I'd be the central person and he for me. And I now wanted children. I felt I'd grown up enough at least to be a decent mother.

5

Some time earlier in 1958, Natasha and Stephen Spender asked me to dinner. It must have been spring, because I remember a large flowering cherry in their back garden. Oona and Charlie Chaplin were there. I sat next to Charlie at dinner, and he told me that they were in England for some months as he was making *A King in New York*, in which his eldest son was also to star. We got on very well, and I asked him if they'd like to come to dinner at Blomfield Road. To my surprise they were both enthusiastic and I remember a second very enjoyable evening. During it I said how much I should like to come to the studios and watch the film being made. Charlie not only agreed to this but – I suppose on impulse – said if I wanted to write about him making the film, I might; he would give me the world scoop on doing it, as he wasn't allowing any journalists on the set. Naturally, I felt very flattered, and when I met Terry Kilmartin, who'd succeeded my friend Jim Rose as literary editor of the *Observer*, he agreed to publish the article. My vision of Charlie, prior to knowing him, had been of an emaciated little man, with a white face and his eyes, below his bowler hat, ringed with black like a lemur. His film image included the little square black moustache that you might buy in joke shops stuck on with glue, and a face that could change from pantomime yearning to a dazzling smile of the most airy dismay. A beautiful mover, his elegant hobble with his stick was all part of that early persona. Now, his body had filled out, his hair was white, but his lovely hands were as expressive as ever. His movements still possessed that neat, charming agility that had endeared him to so many.

Charlie was directing his film, as well as playing in it, and watching him show other actors what he wanted was endlessly fascinating. When he talked to them, he never seemed to get what he wanted, but when he showed them, by saying their lines to the appropriate movement, it was clear as day. I particularly remember his struggling with Dawn Addams, whose appearance reminded me of Paulette Goddard – one of his earlier wives. She had a line to deliver, and half-way through it he wanted her to do a 90-degree turn. They shot it several times without success, and then Charlie leaped on to the set: 'Watch me. Just watch me.' He delivered the line spinning on one heel and was in just the right position as the line came to an end. 'Easy! See?' But everything he did seemed that. I went day after day because it was so fascinating.

Oona was almost always there, and I got to know her better during those weeks. In spite of having – I think – six children by then, she had a kind of changeless beauty: slim and dark, with her hair simply knotted into a loose bun at the nape of her neck, her face a pale oval, expressive and very intelligent eyes, and a wide mouth. She gave the impression of complete serenity and although she looked remarkably young for her age, she knew exactly how to handle Charlie's mercurial moods. She adored him, and it was clearly mutual. He would constantly turn to her for reassurance. He'd not made a film for a long time, and I think somewhere inside he was anxious whether he could produce something that would do well in a new era and was afraid of it.

Later, I went to stay with them in Vevey in Switzerland, at their large rectangular house, with gardens and views of snow-covered mountains and a wide glacier. The children were all present at supper and since, that first night, the cook was off, Oona had made a Mexican meal that Charlie particularly liked. I sat next to five-year-old Victoria who, the moment the meal began, turned to me and said, 'Do you know what I quite thought?'

'No.'

'When I was inside Mummy's tummy, I quite thought Daddy was Spanish.' I asked her when she stopped thinking that. 'The moment I came out. I could see he wasn't.'

I went to sleep that night in a beautiful room with a view of the glacier, and a sweet-smelling log fire – one of the greatest luxuries in the world.

One morning Oona showed me her quarters: a suite of rooms, bedroom, dressing room, bathroom and a small study, the walls lined with books including a complete set of the works of Eugene O'Neill, her father. She was eager to show me everything: her collection of Fortuni dresses, sea-coloured greys and blues and greens, the silk so finely pleated that you could twist the dress into a rope for packing and not harm it. She also had the largest collection of lipsticks, I should think, in the world. She told me she hunted down every shade of every make. She was very proud of them. It was during that morning I realized that, in spite of loving Charlie and having a large family and anything she wanted, she was essentially lonely. When she showed me the engagement ring Charlie had given her, a very large jewel, she said, 'It was what I asked for. The largest topaz in the world.' During that morning she intimated that she wanted me as a friend. I loved her. One night, Charlie said he was taking us all out to dinner. 'All', however, didn't include the three-year-old Eugene, who sat in the middle of the hall floor, scarlet with rage, and uttering his ultimate threat. 'If you don't take me, I shall *read* in *bed.*'

I used to battle on with the first part of my novel, which I was now calling *The Sea Change*, working in my bedroom. In the late morning, Oona would come in for a chat and sometimes I'd read to her.

Several times, after dinner, Charlie ran some of his early, silent films. The children would be entranced: 'Look out, Daddy! You'll fall over that!' and shrieks of laughter if he did, or *just* didn't. The dance of the bread rolls was rerun, because they – and I – enjoyed it so much. Once I looked across the room at Oona, wondering how many times she'd seen these films. Her expression was serene, pleasure at the children's amusement and watchful that Charlie, too, was happy. He was: he was at his most gentle and expansive when surrounded by his family. Then they were still very young. Oona told me one day that Geraldine, the oldest, had said to her, 'Never mind, Mummy, when I'm old enough, I'll have the baby every year.'

I flew back to London with them, and began to understand why they lived in the comparative isolation of Vevey. Charlie was recognized wherever we went, stared at, commented upon, and often besieged for autographs. Sometimes he took it amiably, sometimes not. He, like many others, had been a victim of the McCarthy witch-hunts and had left America. He told me that Oona once went back incognito to fetch 'various things' but he never did.

During the shooting of the film, we sometimes went on Sundays to lunch with the Ogden Stewarts, who, also exiled, lived in a beautiful house in Hampstead. Donald Ogden Stewart was one of the best scriptwriters of his day. *The Philadelphia Story* was a notable example of his work – the first version, with Katharine Hepburn. The house was full of Paul Klees. They also kept a monkey in a very large cage, and my brother asked whether the monkey had recognized Donald after he'd been away for some weeks. Donald said, 'No. But he pretended to.'

Once, Oona and Charlie invited me to Paris for the weekend. I was to fly to Paris and stay at the Georges V hotel. The next day, Charlie said he wanted to go to Versailles. We set off in a chauffeur-driven car, but as soon as we arrived and got out, Charlie was besieged. It was quite frightening: people surged round him until he was almost invisible. Oona and the chauffeur pushed their way through, and hustled him back into the car. He was very cross: 'People have no *manners*.' Back in the car he cheered up, and talked of an early visit to Paris when he was much poorer and less well known. He said, 'I stayed in a small hotel, an awful little place – the bedroom had terrible wallpaper that kept me awake.' Suddenly he, magically, became the wallpaper, twisting his body into wild zigzags and at the same time being himself in bed watching it. There is no way to describe this – it was simply very, very funny.

Once we were all back in London, I went with them to a showing of *A King in New York* in Leicester Square. There were crowds and crowds of fans, but they were orderly. The film wasn't a success. I don't remember the Chaplins saying anything about it at the time, but it didn't get a good press, although much of that was respectful about past achievements.

During these times I asked Charlie about himself. I could only do this in brief snatches, as I sensed it bored him. He must have been asked many of my questions hundreds of times. Once, in the South of France, he showed me the beginning of the auto-biography he'd started to write. All I can remember was his description as a child of seeing the sea for the first time. He went down a steep hill, and there was a wide strip of blue before him, like a wall, and he thought it was going to knock him over. He asked me what I thought of the few pages, and, honestly thinking they were good, I made respectfully encouraging noises. I asked him if he would like to see what I'd written so far about him, and he said, 'Read it to me.' So I did. 'It's almost too flattering,' he said, but he had a purring expression, and the 'almost' was exactly what he meant. 'Are you in love?' he asked suddenly one day. I said I wasn't sure. 'Find out. Love is the most important thing in life.'

That winter, Oona wrote to me, asking Nicola and me to come for Christmas. For some reason, we couldn't go. Letters passed between us, then suddenly stopped. I wrote twice to her and she didn't answer. Somebody told me that Charlie got jealous if she had close friends – even a woman – and that was the end of our relationship.

There was an unfortunate coda to all this. When I sent in my piece to Terry Kilmartin, he rang to say it wasn't what he'd expected. He came to see me about it, and his complaint was that I hadn't written about Charlie's political opinions. I hadn't because I thought that was the dullest part of him. What *was* interesting, and what I'd written about, was the way in which he worked, how he dealt with his immense notoriety and his large family life.

Terry absolutely disagreed. We had a long argument. 'Put the political part in,' he said. I refused. He was seriously angry. 'Well, I shall see to it that you never write for this paper again.' I never did write for the *Observer* again. The piece, which I still think was a good portrait, was lost. I was inveigled into sending it to some magazine that was starting in an Indian ashram: they published it, then refused to pay me, and I never saw it. In those days I was careless about copies.

I think it must have been the same summer that I went to Greece for the first time – spent four or five weeks on the island of Hydra. It was a quiet, simple place, inhabited – apart from its small Greek population – only by a few writers, mainly Australian. It had been the island where prosperous Greek captains had retired and there were some fine houses. The painter Ghika had a house there about a mile from the port, and there was a monastery high up on the mountain above the harbour. The agora – the port – was paved with pink marble. There wasn't much to eat: a grocer sold macaroni and tins of corned beef, sardines, rice and tinned milk. Occasionally I'd see small goats being driven to the abattoir and everybody rushed to it for a share of the carcass. There were wonderful tomatoes, olives, feta cheese and onions, and sometimes the grocer provided thick slices of streaky, very fat bacon that was delicious.

Bathing wasn't easy, but there was one rocky inlet near the port. Old men, crippled from sponge diving, sat on hard wooden chairs outside the grocer's shop with a can of retsina and pieces of bread. The whole village was built on a vertiginous slope as the mountains rose straight out of the sea. From a distance in a boat, the houses looked like handfuls of sugar lumps.

I fell in love with Greece in those weeks on Hydra. I'd hardly travelled anywhere – a few visits to France, to Spain, and the two trips to America – so the impact of Greece was intoxicating, and the effect much like that of a first love affair. The sheer, continuous beauty, the purity of the light, the air, the amazing clear, clean sea and the long heroic sunsets were mesmerizing. The perfume of hot thyme, the excitement of finding small pink cyclamen growing out of the rocks, the absence of cars, the sound of little tapping donkeys' feet, the generous courtesy of the Hydriots – all of this seized my heart.

Two small pieces of chance or coincidence occurred. One morning, when I was bathing, I'd noticed that a ship had moored offshore, and shortly afterwards a group of people came to bathe among whom was Cecil. He seemed both unsurprised and unpleased to see me. It was like meeting a familiar stranger. Then, some weeks later, Laurie suddenly turned up. He was on his own, but he said he had been with a very young girl who had got too attached to him. Could he stay until he caught the next boat to Athens? He had a fever, and an epileptic fit followed. I was rather frightened as I'd never been with him during a proper fit, but I managed to stop him falling off the bed. Afterwards we had a friendly, quiet evening and the next morning he was gone.

On Hydra I'd been working on the New York section of *The Sea Change*, but I decided that the next part of it should take place in Greece. I know now I am not a true traveller, but I like going to a place – preferably not a city – and living there. I could set some of my novel in Hydra, because I felt I'd got to know it a little.

Back in London in the spring of 1958 I got jaundice – not the terminal kind, clearly, but the next worst. I was taken with a very high fever in an ambulance to a hospital. Nobody seemed to know what was the matter with me, until my own doctor, John Allison, who was also a friend, told me. The moment he left, a nurse arrived with a tray on which was a fried egg and chips. 'I don't think I'm meant to eat that,' I said. I couldn't face food of any kind.

'Don't think we can do special diets in *this* hospital,' she said, and flounced out.

Nor did they. For three weeks I lived on grapefruit brought by friends and water. When I was through the yellow stage, I was allowed to go home, feeling weaker than ever before in my life.

While I was in hospital, my father wrote me one of his rare letters. Wasn't it funny, he said, that the whole family should be laid low at once? My mother had broken her sternum, Robin was having his tonsils removed, and he was himself in hospital having examinations because he'd been feeling rather rotten lately. The last time I'd had him and Ursula to dinner, I'd made a great effort to produce a rich three-course meal, I remembered, and I saw my father, suddenly rather grey in the face, saying that my pâté was delicious, but he couldn't eat any more of it.

It took me weeks to recover. At first I felt so tired that if a fly landed on my forehead I was too feeble to brush it off. Anthea and James Sutherland kindly lent me their cottage in the Isle of Wight to convalesce. My father wrote to me again there. This time he was in King Edward VII's Hospital for Officers, having treatment. Treatment for what, I wondered. It was a shaky little note, but cheerful. He said Myra Hess had come to visit him, and that Matron had been most impressed. As soon as I got back I went to see him there. My aunt Ruth turned up, and when we left together, I asked her what *was* wrong with him as he didn't seem to want to talk about it. 'Cancer,' she said. He was having radiology. 'They told me that they couldn't save his life, but they could save him a lot of pain.'

When he came out of hospital he went to stay in a friend's house in London, because he and Ursula had moved to a house in Hawkhurst in Kent. I remember looking up Mrs Beeton and making him beef tea, and taking it in milk bottles to Chelsea. It looked awful, a thin browny liquid, but he seemed pleased. Then he was well enough to go home, which he longed to do. I rang at intervals, but always spoke to Ursula as he seemed to be asleep or resting whenever I telephoned. He was doing very well, she said. I thought then that whatever my aunt had said, perhaps he was going to get better.

I was short of money again, so when Beatrix Miller, editor of a newish magazine called *Queen*, offered me the job of book reviewer I was grateful. I went to Peter Peters to tell him about this: he didn't think it a good idea. 'You should be writing your novel.' I said I'd go on writing it; the magazine was published fortnightly and they only wanted about 1,200 words. 'Well, don't do it for less than a thousand a year,' he said. That seemed like a fortune. It was agreed: my first proper job with a decent salary.

Then, my aunt rang up suddenly one day and said she and my uncle John were going to drive me down to see my father: they'd fetch me after lunch. In the car they explained that my father had been asking for me. 'Is my daughter in the house?' he'd said, and the nurse had gone to the housekeeper and asked if Mr Howard *had* a daughter and once told, my aunt was called to fetch me.

I asked if he was very ill. '*Very* ill, poor old boy.' There was a long – interminable – silence, while my uncle drove with my aunt beside him. Desperate to break it, I made one of the two most crass remarks of my life. 'I'm earning a thousand a year,' I said. I saw them look at each other with a kind of weary distaste. They didn't reply. The moment the words were out of my mouth I knew what an awful thing I'd said. I felt bitterly ashamed and wondered why on earth I'd blurted it out. Now, I think I was trying to prove defiantly to my family that I could manage my life since they'd ignored me for so long, but that was no excuse. It just sounded as if I didn't care for my father – only for myself. This wasn't true: I *did* care about him, and I realized that he must be dying.

When we arrived I went upstairs to see him. The nurse gave me a small bowl of cotton wool soaked in cold water. 'You can moisten his lips with this,' he said. He was a kind young man, and immediately left us alone,

My father lay on his back, propped up by pillows. His hair was brushed and he'd been shaved; there was a faint hectic flush on his cheekbones that now stood out in his thin grey face. He looked at me with anxious, frightened eyes and tried to smile. 'Hello, darling.' I kissed his hot dry forehead and pulled a chair right up to the bed. 'I wasn't sure – afraid you might not—'

'I came as quickly as I could.' I took his hand – a weak, dry collection of bones. He turned his head towards me and fell asleep. For a long time we remained like that. I noticed that his mouth was so dry his lips were cracking, and I used the cotton wool. His sleep was fitful. Every now and then his eyes opened, unseeing, and his hands picked weakly at the sheets. He didn't say anything more until, what seemed like hours later, I heard people coming upstairs and Ursula and the doctor came into the room. The doctor bent over him. 'How are you feeling, old boy?'

'Bloody awful.'

'I think I can do something about that.'

Ursula motioned to me to leave the room. I picked up his hand and kissed it. He smiled then and tried to put his hand to his mouth to blow me a kiss. That was it.

Some time after that, and before my brother Robin and I left to drive to the Beacon for the night, I found my father's chauffeur, McNaughton, hanging about in the hall. He was absolutely devoted to my father, driving him to and from London every day, carrying his guns on shoots, cleaning his shoes, and generally looking after him 'I've cleaned all his guns,' he said. 'Last week he wanted his medals cleaned. He said the King was coming to tea with him.' Tears were streaming down his face.

I can't remember much more about that day. I know Robin and I had a good cry in the car. We spent the night at the Beacon where our aunt Helen now lived and she was very kind to us. But I lay in bed that night thinking about that almost silent vigil with my father, and wondering if I'd let him down by my silence. I might have talked to him, told him I loved him, given him some affection and reassurance. I knew that he passionately didn't want to die: that he'd endured months of pain and illness and fear of death in silence. He was certainly too ill to talk to me by then, but he might have *heard* me, and I'd said nothing. This feeling, that I'd somehow failed him, had let him down when he was dying, was to recur for me with other people. I was recognizing another fault, a weakness, and resolving to learn from it yet not learning.

6

Going back a little, I worked throughout the winter of 1957 on *The Sea Change*, able at last to live every day for it. It's a strange life. Many writers go through these reclusive periods. I'd wake very early each morning, sweating with fear that whatever had made me able to work the day before would have vanished, and that I'd go to my desk and find myself paralysed. And occasionally, after weeks of steady work I'd suddenly see the whole book as though it was already finished, and then when I wrote I felt wonderfully free of *myself*, as though I was simply translating to paper something that was already there, outside me. There is no experience to beat that – it's like a celestial visit that can't be predicted or sustained. For me it's a rare occurrence, but the desire for it is what makes me want to go on trying to write.

Working at that pitch precluded social life. Once or twice I went to parties, but found I had nothing to say, and would end the evening lying on someone's bed asleep, apparently drunk: not so, I was as empty of drink as I was of everything else.

I reviewed books for *Queen* in tandem with finishing my novel. I was working under Francis Wyndham who was the literary editor. He was a very easy boss and gave me complete freedom to choose what I reviewed. It was overwhelming. The limited space I had meant that I couldn't review more than three or four books per issue, yet I was supposed to cover everything the readers might want to read. I'd go to the office every week or so to look through and choose books to take home. I read far more than I reviewed, but it was impossible to keep up with the steady stream of new publications. I never reviewed a book without having read all of it. I worked on the principle that there was little point in writing about any book I thought bad – it would be like telling people how not to get to the post office. Reviewing is not literary criticism: a reviewer is there to tell people what they might like to read and why.

It was during these early months of 1958 that my brother Colin brought a new friend of his back to Blomfield Road. Sargy Mann was at that time working in Oxford. He and Colin had met through a mutual love of jazz – I think Sargy was playing drums even then. He was a tall, immensely thin young man, with reddish hair and thick glasses. He was mostly very serious, but also the only person I have ever met who actually shouted with laughter. We didn't talk much then, he says now I always had my nose in a book, but he and Colin talked a great deal about jazz in which I'd no interest. But he was to become a very great friend.

Francis Wyndham and I became friends too. He adored cats and came to see mine. He introduced me to several writers, including Muriel Spark whom he brought to dinner one night with a very angry Jamaican writer whose name I now forget. I remember that Francis had a fairly violent row with him and I noticed with interest how Muriel watched them expressionlessly – like a bird witnessing a road accident. She had me to supper in her house in Camberwell – it was the time of *The Bachelors* and *Memento Mori* – both of which I reviewed. I loved her murky funniness and her wonderful economy with dialogue, but I always felt vaguely frightened of her.

During the early months of 1958, Peter Peters invited me to a lunch party he was giving at the Caprice. The other guests were Jack and Margaret Huntingdon and Alec Waugh, brother of Evelyn and author, in his own right, of fairly popular novels. It was a very enjoyable party as a result of which I got to know the Huntingdons well and went to dinner several times at their house in Roehampton, where they lived with two small daughters and two responsible corgis. I'm not sure I ever saw Alec again, but he used to write to me and send me small, intricate scarves from North Africa or wherever he happened to be.

Margaret Lane, Margaret Huntingdon's professional name, had been a novelist and a journalist – she'd had a world scoop by interviewing Al Capone, but later became a biographer and a novelist. Jack, apart from being an earl, was a mural painter and a Labout politician. They also had a house in Beaulieu in the New Forest, and a sailing yacht.

For about a year, I'd been involved in the Ouspensky Society, introduced by Jim Douglas-Henry, whose mother was also a member, and whom I'd been seeing ever since the drink with the Van der Posts. It was a movement based on the teachings of Gurdjieff, and originally put into practice by P. D. Ouspensky. Meetings were held every week in small groups, when the whole membership got together in a house bought specifically for the purpose. I was informed that this philosophy of life was a unique way of becoming a better person, something I was anxious to achieve. It is a philosophy based on the life of civilizations and on the convergence of science, philosophy, art and religion in the search for ultimate truth. On a more practical level it looks for simple methods of finding an inner stillness. Although I liked and became friends with some of the members, I soon found the secrecy of it rather silly and self-regarding. There were all kinds of rules about this. If you met another member in the street when either of you was with someone outside the society, you had to treat him or her as a stranger. As the months went by, I sensed it wasn't popular to have friends *outside*.

Matters came to some sort of head in the spring of 1958, when the leader of the sect announced that he didn't care for members living together outside marriage. And so, in April, I got married with another pair of dissolute members.

Why did I marry my second husband, Jim? There was no single reason, rather a collection, not one of which, by itself, would have swayed me. But, put together, they became a formidable reason for marriage.

He was an attractive man and, like all con-men, he was possessed of a considerable charm that he knew exactly how to use. I wanted children, and Jim said he did too. I was tired of being taken to dinner by a series of men who, baldly speaking, seemed to expect me to pay for my dinner by going to bed with them. I was sick of the inevitable scenes and longed – as Mrs Patrick Campbell said – for the 'deep, deep peace of the double bed after the hurly-burly of the chaise-longue'. My mother had known his, and although she told me that Jim's father had been regarded in her family as something of a black sheep, this did nothing to nullify the fact that I knew very little about him. Apart from the Van der Posts, who introduced us, he also knew Dosia slightly, and I'd met and liked several of his friends. He was unattached and he was extremely interested in the Ouspensky Society. All this was reassuring, and I wanted to be assured. I was charmed, and when I fell in love I became more credulous. The fact that he had no visible means of support did not present itself as any kind of warning. He said he loved me? Then of course he did.

A few weeks before the wedding, Jack and Margaret suggested that we might like to take their boat across the Channel and down the rivers and canals to Marseille, as they wanted to do some cruising in the Mediterranean. It was agreed that we should go, with a friend of the Huntingdons who was a very experienced sailor and a young boy, called Kip, to whom they wished to give a holiday. Kip Asquith was tenuously related to the Huntingdons since his stepfather, Peter Cameron, was Jack's cousin.

The yacht, *Sharavogue*, was built for Atlantic racing, so the rather rough crossing to Le Havre, though exciting, wasn't spoiled by terror. She drew six feet below the water, which made for stability. Her draught, however, became a serious problem when we reached the first canal. French working boats – *péniches* – are far larger than English narrow boats, even when fully laden.

At Lyon, we were told that the Rhône was so dry that year that no boat drawing six feet could hope to get down it. Eventually, we managed – loaded inside a *péniche* that was returning, empty, to Marseille. The *Sharavogue* had to be chocked up inside the hold of the working boat, and this meant that we had to creep about in her with the utmost caution, lest we disturb the chocking. When the captain of the *péniche* finally invited us into his cabin for a drink, it was the best part of the trip. We took off our shoes – working-boat cabins are impeccably clean. What fascinated me was the similarity to the interiors of English narrow boats: the same wooden walls, scratch-combed and hung with pieces of coarse white lace, on top of which perched china plates with lacy edges. Like old gypsy wagons, the decorations in the boat were international. It was as a result of this trip that my daughter met Kip, in London at Blomfield Road.

I worked for *Queen* magazine until 1960, when I was fired suddenly, with no notice. I was desperate: the salary had been keeping several heads above water, and I panicked, as so many people fired summarily must do. I went to Francis Wyndham to ask him why. Francis was very uncomfortable – no, no, it was nothing to do with my writing. Somehow, that day, I discovered that Penelope Gilliatt, who wrote the theatre column, had seen the salary book and found that I was being paid more than she. I asked for an interview with Jocelyn Stevens, the editor. By now, fear had made me reckless. I told him that he simply couldn't sack me without due notice unless he'd some cogent reason for doing so. He muttered something about magazines needing a change, so I said all right, but I needed three months' notice in order to find another job. He agreed to this: a respite.

Marriage hadn't lightened any of my financial responsibilities, which were heavier than I'd envisaged. About six weeks after we were married, Jim had handed me an account for handmade shirts from a firm in Jermyn Street. The sum was ninety pounds. 'Goodness, Jim,' I said, 'how are you going to pay that?'

He replied, 'You've got a private income. You can pay it.'

I couldn't afford simply 'to get on with another novel' as Peter Peters and others advised: I had to have some part-time job for a regular salary. Earlier, I'd been offered a reviewing job on the *Sunday Times*, and had turned it down, as it seemed wrong to review in more than one paper. The regular spot was no longer free, but I was offered some novels from time to time. This, like the odd television job, was too chancy. I'd imagined that if I wrote a novel that was well reviewed, Cape would sell a great many copies, I'd earn my advance and then, twice a year, royalties would be there. I'd published five books in all, and nothing of the sort had occurred. I earned my advances, and sometimes a little more. I'd earned nothing more, and hadn't expected to, from the short stories or the biography with Arthur Helps. But the novels! I'd certainly had hopes and dreams about them.

My contemporaries, and those younger than I, were being published in paperback, which in those days meant Penguin. But Jonathan Cape wouldn't allow me this, and the terms of my contract with him – unsurprisingly – gave him the whip hand. It was hopeless, therefore, to keep counting on being able to earn my living as a writer, even though that was all I wanted to be.

I wanted to write, but my next novel was just a vague notion, set nowhere, uninhabited by people, and often quite difficult to discern in the densely unhappy climate of my life that provoked a kind of paralysis in me. I'd got myself into a marriage I didn't in the least understand, and I'd no idea how to get out of it. Indeed, I thought I shouldn't even *have* such a notion. I had to trust that prolonged association with the Ouspensky Society would enlighten and generally improve me, but something there, too, was deterring me. When I'd finished *The Sea Change*, the man running the society had insisted upon the novel being read by his secretary to vet it for 'leaks'. I couldn't respect this, but as I'd written nothing that had anything to do with them or their views, I handed the manuscript over and got it back with some sententiously irrelevant cuts. At the time I let this pass, but even the idea of a recurrence made me feel a good deal of contempt for both myself and the society. At any rate it wasn't a good place to start the long business of a new novel. Jim had got a job with Harlech Television and had a flat in Bristol where he spent most of his time.

And then one of the kindest men I have known came to my rescue. Cyril Frankel was a member of the Ouspensky Society. I'd first met him when he and his friend, Stephen Andrews, a Canadian painter, were living with John Allison, my doctor, in Eccleston Square. Cyril had now moved and had bought a short lease on two houses in Wilton Place because, he said, he wanted the fun of living somewhere both large and grand if only for a while. He was a film director and, like so many of them, was looking and waiting for something to turn up. When it did he asked me to go and see him with a view to our working together. An American producer, Raymond Stross, who looked as if he'd been very badly carved in wood, had recently married Anne Heywood and wanted to star her in a film. He had got hold of some newspaper cutting about a young woman being stalked. He wanted Cyril to direct it if a scriptwriter could be found.

I became the scriptwriter. The work had to be completed within six weeks and I'd be paid six hundred pounds. Every morning I went to Cyril's house, was given a cup of real coffee and was shut into a large bare room that contained only a table, a chair and a typewriter. I didn't know how to deal with where the camera was while people were talking or doing things. Cyril said don't worry about that, just make the people and write the story and he'd turn it into a shooting script.

There were a few strictures. First, Anne Heywood insisted that she should be called Tracy in the film. She wasn't really Anne Heywood. She'd been born with the enchanting name of Violet Pretty and from there it was only possible, nomenically speaking, to go downhill. Second, her husband in the film was to be Richard Todd. Time was the third.

I managed to write a script that they eventually used. Cyril was extremely kind. He had a way of making sudden treats, taking me out to a meal, or to a film, or inviting people to lunch whom he thought I'd enjoy. I think he knew how confused and unhappy I was and wanted to cheer me up. He was gentle and discreet and had a very warm heart. I also found I enjoyed writing scenes for people to act: when I am writing a scene in a novel, I always envisage where the people concerned are – when they move and generally how they dispose themselves – and now I'd actually watch them doing it.

The film was shot at the studios in Bray outside Dublin, and I went there to rewrite the chase sequence at the end as it was now to be shot on the roof of a block of flats, which altered the whole thing. I spent two days there and saw nothing of the city.

Raymond Stross, Anne's husband, was all set for doing another film, again derived from a newspaper cutting, and again with Cyril and me. This time, Mr Stross said, he would pay me much better: I should have six thousand pounds for a script. The new film was to star Anne as a good girl gone to the bad. After a long spell in prison she forms a friendship with an older girl, and together they escape. In the train going north, the older woman goes to a lavatory while the train is stopped and when she comes back Angel – for so she is called – has vanished and is never seen again. The fact that this was a 'true' story impressed everyone greatly, except me. Readers, and particularly would-be writers, always place undue significance on 'the true story', 'the real character' – usually an elderly relative – that they know would be the making of your next novel. These characters are always packed with eccentricity and wit and are bound, their owners feel, to prop up the shaky structure of make-believe.

Researching Angel entailed a visit to Holloway prison where she'd been an inmate. It also, more surprisingly, included several visits to the journalist Godfrey Winn, who'd written the original piece about her. I went to lunch in his perfect little Regency lodge outside Brighton. Godfrey was one of those people who are presented by others as caricatures of themselves. He was gay (madly gay, they would say), keen on interesting people (a howling snob, they would say), and emotional (wildly sentimental, they would say). Actually, he was all of these things in moderation, had been extremely courageous in the war and was good company. There was some kind of deal going on between him and Raymond Stross, and his brief was to tell me as much as he knew of Angel. He did all of that, and I wrote the script. I showed it to Cyril, of course, indeed I was still writing in his house, and he seemed pleased. But Messrs Stross and Winn thought nothing of it: it wasn't merely not quite right, it was utterly and mysteriously wrong, since none of them could say what it was that they didn't like. It gradually became clear that Mr Stross, while he wanted his wife to be a prostitute and go to prison, expected none of it really to be her fault. She was to be the innocent victim of circumstances always out of her control. Anyway, they not only didn't want a second draft, but also refused to pay any of the money promised. Eventually, through Peter Peters, I went to law and was awarded the six thousand pounds, whereupon Mr Stross proved to be bankrupt. The first film, entitled *The Very Edge*, came out. I went to the press show with Cyril and, seeing the uneasy smiles of the critics, knew it was no-go. Some of them apparently called it 'The Very End', but actually it was a decent little film, earning no superlatives in either direction. It turns up on television from time to time.

During these eighteen months or so, I began *After Julius*. In this novel, Julius leaves his wife and daughters and publishing business to go and take men off the beaches at Dunkirk. The novel is about what happens to all of them and its theme is the distinction between public and private responsibility. I was also doing a television programme in Manchester every three weeks called *Something to Read*, compèred by Brian Redhead and directed by Olive Shapley.

This was a good old-fashioned programme of the sort they

don't do any more. Every week, I had to review three or four novels straight to camera – no autocue – with the floor manager holding up his fingers to show me how many minutes, or seconds, I had left. I also interviewed one author for each programme and it was there that I met Elizabeth Taylor whose new novel, *In A Summer Season*, was just out. Naturally, I'd read it before the interview, and had prepared about twenty questions to ask its author. The novel was of a kind that at the time you enjoy very much, and afterwards still find yourself impressed by. It had such ease, such simplicity, and was so deliciously funny and sharp in its perception. Her economy of expression reminded me of Austen with whom far too many novelists are carelessly compared, but here it seemed really apposite. I looked forward to the interview with confidence and interest.

Elizabeth sat quietly opposite me, her large, extremely beautiful hazel eyes fixed attentively on me each time I asked her a question, to which she answered either yes or no. In less than a minute I had none left. I hadn't had the sense to realize that my questions had to be framed in such a way that they couldn't be dealt with by monosyllables, and there were five more minutes to fill. Later we sat under fluorescent lighting at a Formica table with cardboard cups of rotten grey instant coffee and her shyness remained impenetrable. After that I read everything she'd written and, much later, got to know and love her, but then it was all courtesy and embarrassment.

Meanwhile a hard core of misery that was my marriage was settling in my life like an Ice Age. It was so continuous, and as far as I could see so endless, that the only way I could manage to endure it was by pretending it wasn't there. This convinced others on the whole, and gradually even myself. The moment I began to think about it, I was overwhelmed by self-criticism, and as it just made me feel worse, I did everything I could not to think of it at all. But one incident did bring it home to me for a while.

I was trying to begin *After Julius* and life alone in my flat was extremely difficult. Michael Howard, a director at Jonathan Cape, invited me to stay with him and his wife Pat in their house near Farnham. Pat was a painter and Michael went to the Cape office in London every weekday; the idea was that I should work there and we'd all have supper together. This arrangement was ideal for me: I have always liked working in a house where others are also working and I loved company in the evenings that didn't have to be arranged. So I went there for about three weeks.

Michael's first wife had drowned in France after a picnic by a river. Pat was his second and they were very happy together, living in a brightly painted house with two Siamese cats. For a time, all went well. I worked hard, only leaving the house once for my television stint in Manchester, and an hour each day after lunch when I went for biting winter walks. At weekends, Michael and Pat would spend the afternoons in bed, and after my walk I'd lie in mine and wish I wasn't alone in it. Whoever woke up first would make tea and take it to the others. I remember carrying a tray into their bedroom and seeing them in their cosy, sensual *déshabille* and feeling acute pangs of envy. During those weeks it became clear to both Michael and Pat that all wasn't well in my life. Michael was particularly kind to me and as a result we fell a little in love with each other. It was mentioned but that was all. Michael decided to tell Pat, and at once, the *ménage* came to an end: I went back to London the next day, and they went to Marrakech for a holiday to forget it all. Pat, of course, did the right thing: the romance was nipped in the bud, but for months afterwards I couldn't help dwelling on what I wanted and didn't have. I might have recognized by now that three wasn't a good number, but at the time, I simply felt stuck – unable to see the trees for the wood.

The Ouspensky Society, membership of which was supposed to improve me, didn't seem to be doing much good for me. My friend Ray Aickman, Robert's wife, left to become a nun in an Anglican community, and invited me to go to attend the ceremony where she would take the vows of a novitiate. I was allowed to see her for a little while the evening before the service. She looked exhausted, and her ugly novice's dress was rather dirty, but she seemed happy. I asked her if she prayed a great deal. 'Oh, there is hardly any time for prayer,' she answered. 'Prayer is a luxury.' On a later visit, she told me that her Reverend Mother had asked her what she missed most of what she'd left and she had said intelligent conversation. It became slowly impossible to have that with her, since so many subjects were barred: anything about our earlier life together, the books we'd read, people we had known, the state of the world, or how she spent her life in the convent – all of it was banned, until finally we were reduced to smiling sadly at each other, full of difficult goodwill.

Then Maharishi Yogi came to London. He appeared at one of the big meetings of the society, and sat motionless on a large chair dressed in white silk and a camel cashmere shawl, surveying us all with a watchful and serene intelligence while our leader introduced us to him and he to us.

Maharishi is now an established figure, and transcendental meditation widely used and known, but this was, I think, his first semi-public appearance in England. That evening he introduced us to the idea that meditation – thought for so long to be the property of mystics and recluses – was a tool for what he called the householder, the ordinary person living in the world. The practice of it was simple, twenty minutes twice a day would suffice, and peace, happiness, health and virtue would flourish.

He spoke volubly and well, although there was a disconcerting high-pitched giggle when he made a sharp or amusing point. I think that everyone in the room was moved and uplifted by the prospect he laid before us, and we were all eager to be initiated into the rite of meditation. Focusing on a mantra – a word or a sound – and emptying the mind of all extraneous thought is at once so easy and so difficult that it can't but be absorbing to those who try it.

The one thing that was certain was that it required practice.

Forty minutes in twenty-four hours doesn't sound much, but that time varied – could expand or contract itself from a kind of fidgeting eternity to some nameless dimension where it was nothing at all. Eventually, I was taught to 'check' or help new initiates, but I never felt worthy of the responsibility, although people with glowing eyes who felt the great benefits and surges of benevolent energy surrounded me.

On one occasion Maharishi decided to conduct a course in Austria high in the Alps, and many of us went. This was the only time I ever went abroad with my mother, who'd taken to meditation. We all stayed in a hotel that was used for winter sports in season, but was now given over to us. Maharishi announced that he was embarking upon a translation of the *Bhagavadgita* and asked for volunteers – writers or people interested in language – to help him. There was a forest of hands. My mother nudged me. 'Go on. You could do that.' I said I didn't think so.

Later that day Maharishi sent for me and asked me to help him, so of course I did. As there were lectures and meditation all through the day, the translation work had to be done at night. This didn't seem to worry Maharishi as he seemed hardly ever to need sleep, but I remember sitting on the floor of his room until well after midnight wrestling with the difficulties of translating one word of Sanskrit into intelligible English. Sanskrit – of which I knew nothing – turned out to be a kind of portmanteau language: one word could have a dozen different meanings. Maharishi would explain the sense he was after, and I'd have to try to find a choice of possible English words that might fit, then he'd deliberate and decide.

It was a slow and arduous business: one verse could take nights. There were also frequent interruptions. I remember particularly how a woman burst into his room at about two a.m. She was clearly in deep distress. Before she could speak, Maharishi said, 'You must not be so anxious. Your daughter was in great danger, but she is getting well now and she will be all right.' And the next morning

329

she had a telephone call saying that her daughter had suddenly turned the corner and was out of danger. 'How did you know, Maharishi?' someone braver than I asked him. 'I went,' he said. 'Travel can be conducted in different ways.' Other things happened that made it plain to me that he was no ordinary man. For one thing he was the only person I have ever met – for me, at least – who had an aura around his head. One day someone asked him about saints, and he said in a matter-of-fact voice that the trouble with many of them was they were so happy that they wouldn't take the trouble to go on to become angels.

One day he expressed the wish that we should all go several miles up the mountain to the top of the pass to meditate. There was deep snow and ice on the rocks, and someone suggested that we might get rather cold – by now meditations were a matter of hours rather than minutes. Maharishi looked across the room and smiled. 'It will not be cold.'

It was about half an hour in a bus to the top of the pass, from where the view stretched down for miles into Italy. The air was sharp as a knife, the pale yellow sun without heat, but when we were enjoined to sit on the ground – it was *warm*. I remember looking at John Allison, my friend and doctor, amazed, and he simply smiled with a shrug. The ground remained warm during the hour that we sat there, but nothing was said.

While I was there I managed to meditate for up to four hours a day, but back home it all seemed difficult again. And then, gradually, as I listened to the lectures it dawned on me that meditation *was* for recluses or people inclined that way. Prolonged practice could only result in a detachment from life that, although it might be better, I didn't want. I didn't want to become indifferent to *anything*, and as I watched those closest to Maharishi it seemed to me that they had this desire, gift, need – however you want to put it. I wanted to be in the middle of ordinary life trying to make the best of it even if – I could see more clearly now – it entailed my making the same mistakes many times. I didn't want to give my life to anyone, I wanted to have it and use it and be an ordinary householder. So gradually I stopped. I think of Maharishi with great respect and affection, and I am sure that there is a spiritual hierarchy in which I am merely on the lower rungs. That was it.

7

In February 1962 I was invited to a meeting of the Arts Council to discuss what was to become of the forthcoming Cheltenham Festival of Literature. John Moore, who'd directed it for some years and had always been a leading light in its affairs, wanted to retire, and a new director was required. At the meeting it transpired that they thought I'd be a suitable candidate. I was amazed, flattered that anyone thought I could do such a thing and said I'd think about it. 'We need an answer rather quickly,' John said. 'There is only eight months to go.' He knew I was going to accept.

Cheltenham's festival was a very much smaller affair then than it is now. It had almost no money, very little sponsorship, and most of the local inhabitants were totally uninterested in such an event, but it had been quietly plodding along for years. I'd attended it as one of a group of young writers sometime in the 1950s. Running it would be a challenge in every sort of way, and my present life made me long for distraction, something that would use up energy and crowd out the lethargy of despair.

I started to make lists of ideas for events. I have always been the kind of person who has many impracticable ideas, one or two of which work. We had the first meeting with the festival's council in the town hall. It came to my turn to speak and I produced my list. It included an exhibition of portraits of living writers, a literary zoo, cheap train tickets for the festival, courtesy of British Rail, three schools' events, and a bookshop in the town hall for people to buy the works of writers they'd heard and have a glass of wine.

I thought we might arrange for messages from all the most ancient and established writers throughout the world to be sent wishing the festival well, and possibly an auction of manuscripts. I also suggested about a dozen events: one with playwrights, one of biographers, several of novelists, lectures by Peter Scott and Laurens Van der Post and so forth. I also planned to seek sponsorship from a major newspaper. Schweppes already sponsored the programme and, having a friend who was a professional designer, I resolved upon something glossy and illustrated.

The council listened to all this with silent, amazed incredulity. Only John said he was sure they'd made the right choice in choosing me, and good luck. I was allowed money for writing paper, stamps, and travelling expenses to and from Cheltenham, otherwise the appointment was strictly honorary.

I went home and started to implement my pipe dreams. I went to the Arts Council with the idea of the exhibition, hoping they'd help me, but they'd thought of it years ago and there simply weren't enough works to mount one. I didn't believe them. British Rail was unprepared to do anything about train tickets. The zoo was equally adamant about the impossibility of the literary zoo. On the credit side, the *Sunday Telegraph* agreed to sponsor one evening for £1,500. I wrote letters: to writers asking them to come; to people who owned paintings or drawings or pieces of sculpture; to advertisers to take space in the programme; to yet more writers for manuscripts they felt they could donate; to schools offering events; and to the Publishers' Association for agreement about the bookshop. This last was a hard struggle. It had never been done before, the bookshops in Cheltenham wouldn't like it, and we wouldn't sell any books anyway. I persisted with this for the entire eight months, and in the end they grudgingly agreed to give it a try.

Organizing just one event required about twelve letters. I'd decided to rent a house in Cheltenham and bring down my lovely and capable Irish daily to act as housekeeper. The council didn't see the point of this at first, but financial argument won them round: it would be far cheaper than putting writers up in the hotel. From the writers' point of view it was better to be somewhere they could have a drink and sandwiches late at night after their show and talk to each other if they wanted to. I was allowed a part-time secretary and John Moore eventually suggested Jackie Gomme, who had been his secretary. She was perfect: funny, literate and full of good-will. We've been friends ever since.

After about six months, I went back to the Arts Council with my list of exhibits. Oh, they said, if we'd realized there was as much as that about, *we* could have mounted the exhibition for you, but it's too late now. The least they could do was to pay for the carriage and insurance of the pieces, I said. They agreed.

The *Sunday Telegraph* evening was also having a bumpy ride. The paper wanted a symposium on 'Sex in Literature' to be chaired by their editor Donald McClaughlan. I'd managed to persuade Joseph Heller to come from New York, Romain Gary from Paris and – a great coup – Carson McCullers, also from the US.

Then they announced that they'd invited Kingsley Amis to take part. I was furious. They hadn't consulted me and I thought four people would be too many for the programme. They were ada-mant, and even hinted that they mightn't sponsor the event after all. I went to my cousin, Peregrine Worsthorne, then assistant editor, and he agreed that they couldn't go back on their word. I wrote to Amis, inviting him and his wife to stay a night in the house. No reply. I wrote again. I felt slightly frightened at the prospect of him coming: I thought he would be an 'Angry Young Man' who would think the whole thing was silly. I got a very nice letter back enclosing a copy of the earlier one he'd sent and accepting in a cordial manner.

By now I had a fair amount of generously donated manuscripts and took them one summer evening to my friend Anthony Hobson who had been the book auctioneer at Sotheby's and who had kindly consented to conduct the festival auction. Anthony had married Tanya Winagradoff, whom I'd known slightly when she was a girl, and they now lived at Whitsbury near Salisbury. Tanya was away the night I went there, but their firstborn, Emma, aged about two, received me in her bath. It was a beautiful sunlit summer evening and the house, with its exquisite domestic view of small church and meadow rich with buttercups and Queen Anne's Lace, made me suddenly long to live in the country. I'd brought the manuscripts for Anthony to see and catalogue; they weren't a remarkable collection, but he was very nice about it.

By August, the events were more or less organized. The festival programme, a sixty–page affair with reproductions of some of the paintings, would be printed just on time. I'd found a house not far from the town hall. Tickets were beginning to sell and, except for the fact that I couldn't galvanize the town council to advertise adequately, things seemed to be going well. Then, about a week before we were due to start, I got a cable from the US: 'McCullers requires full-time SRN. Please provide.' I didn't even know what an SRN *was*. Jackie did. 'A State Registered Nurse,' she said. There was a short silence, and then she added, 'My sister is one.' Would she? She might. She did.

The *Telegraph* had agreed to put Carson in Claridges Hotel for a few days before the festival began, and I went to see her there to make sure that Jackie's sister, Jo, had arrived and was looking after her.

I'd no idea then how extremely ill Carson had been and still was. A few months before she came to England, she had undergone an eight-hour operation on all the tendons in her left hand, and at the same time, cancer had been discovered and she'd had a breast removed. They'd given her a suite, and I waited in the sitting room among the carnations and grapes until Jo wheeled her in, small and frail, holding a glass of bourbon at an experienced tilt.

Her hair was cut very short with something of a fringe and her rather round face was entirely white with a compressed mouth and large grey eyes. She had the appearance of a decadent waif, vulnerable but at the same time full of presence. I was in awe of her, and stammered a greeting, saying how honoured and delighted we were that she'd made the journey for Cheltenham. She smiled, which utterly changed her face – it became irradiated with some inner happiness, joy even – transforming it with a kind of ethereal beauty, endearing to the point of love. I'd only ever seen this before with Jessie, the crippled girl who'd come to stay at Clifton Hill.

Carson's left arm was in plaster. She was in constant pain, although she never mentioned it, and though the bourbon and painkillers helped her, I think her love for and friendship with Mary Mercer sustained her. She frequently referred to her. Once, later in her stay, she said she'd like to take a present back for Mary, and I suggested going to Cameo Corner, a shop that sold antique jewellery. Oh, yes, she'd love me to take her. So, one afternoon we went in a taxi, with Jo. Antique jewellery was plentiful and inexpensive in those days, and Carson spent a good hour making her choice and was very excited when it was made and we were going back to her hotel. 'I want to give it to her *now*!'

She wanted me to have supper with her for all three nights before Cheltenham began but it was impossible, I'd so much to do. I said I'd ring her every day, and I'd send my brother to have supper with her because I thought she'd like him. He went, and she did. 'She stays the same, whatever she's talking about,' he said after-wards.

The BBC wanted me to do an hour-long interview with her for *Bookstand* on television. It took place in a strange room on the ground floor of Claridges. It had no windows and several doors, and it quickly became clear that one of them led to what sounded like the washing-up headquarters. At intervals there were noises that sounded like 365 fish forks falling from a great height into a metallic sink. I'd prepared my questions as far as I could and all went well, until I'd finished. The BBC had only brought one camera and they wanted me to ask all the questions again so they could shoot me asking them. The snag was that I had no list, and as it's possible to ask a great many questions in an hour, I had little or no idea of their order, or of what I'd actually asked. They played bits back to me and I made frantic notes, and the fish forks continued to plunge while the room got hotter and hotter and more and more airless. I made them let Carson go, at least, as she was exhausted, and I spent a frightful half-hour trying to cover the old ground.

I went down to Cheltenham the day before the festival began. The exhibition had to be hung, and the local gallery owner was now saying he'd have nothing to do with it. There were many other last-minute hitches, not least of which was that driving through the town there was no sense of an impending festival. I didn't feel the council was putting much effort into it. By now, the whole thing had attracted a good deal of media attention, and I'd unwisely let slip to one journalist my disappointment at local interest, saying I might just as well have left the whole thing alone as it was nearly impossible without local support. The one o'clock news announced that I was about to resign, and I was visited by some of the council to ask me to do no such thing. Of course I wouldn't, but I didn't have the guts to add that they could have helped more. Many local people *did* help and were enthusiastic, but arts festivals of any kind weren't regarded then as possible money spinners for the local community, and so many things that run easily now were difficult then.

Once it got started, the festival went well. There were three events a day in the town hall – three especially for schools. Pete, who had always remained a friend, was loyal and helpful, and gave a lecture on whales with one of the first recordings of their amazing voices. Laurens Van der Post lectured, I think, on Kalahari bushmen. There was an event with playwrights and another on autobiography, to which Laurie contributed. On the Thursday evening, 4 October 1962, we had the *Sunday Telegraph's* event on 'Sex in Literature'. Tom Maschler escorted Joseph Heller, Colin drove Carson and Jo down, Romain Gary arrived alone in a dark overcoat with a high stiff collar in which he looked romantically foreign, and Kingsley Amis came with his wife Hilly. The event wasn't a great success: the chairman didn't know how to draw out any of the writers, and it was rather stilted and uncertain.

I do remember Kingsley saying at one point how much he disliked what he called 'hairy-chested' sex in novels, but there weren't many light moments. Afterwards we all drove to a hotel in the country for dinner, and I sat next to Kingsley. Afterwards we went back to the house I'd rented, where the Amises were to stay: Carson had gone back to London and the others had also dispersed. Hilly said she was tired and wanted to go to bed. Kingsley wanted to stay up and drink. I didn't feel I could leave him to drink alone so I stayed up with him. What had begun as a duty turned, during the ensuing hours, into something quite different.

We talked and talked until four a.m. – about our work, our lives, our marriages and each other. I was going to spend a week with Cyril Frankel and Stephen, his friend, in the South of France. Kingsley was going to Majorca with his family to see Robert Graves and have a holiday. 'If I ring you up, will you see me in London?' Yes. When he kissed me, I felt as though I could fly.

The next morning, after breakfast, they left, and I struggled through the day hardly able to keep my eyes open. I missed one of the events – and fell into a stupor on my bed.

On the last night of the festival there was a supper in the Pump Room, with a cabaret and the auction, and – a great concession – a display of fireworks over the lake. It turned out to be the first festival that made a profit, and I was awarded three hundred pounds for my work as an honorary gift.

8

I spent the week in France with Cyril and Stephen, sleeping a lot because I felt incredibly tired, and telling myself it was no good falling in love with Kingsley, who was married with three children. I'd simply be back in the familiar peripheral position, waiting for phone calls: surely I'd learned enough about what that was like to know it deflected me from writing and made me miserable. Surely by now I'd learned *that*. When I got back to London, and was winding up festival business, Kingsley rang me. And I found myself instantly agreeing to meet him in a bar in Leicester Square.

If I try to think now about the first thing that attracted me to him so much it was his honesty with himself. During our evening in Cheltenham he'd been describing his background in rather extreme terms. I'd said, 'But you don't talk like that,' and he'd said he'd changed how he talked. 'How *did* you talk?' and he'd looked at me very steadily and said, 'Like this,' and reproduced it. 'I'm not posh – like you.' I didn't feel posh and told him, and I couldn't see how he talked mattering in the least, but I loved him for telling me, although I didn't admit it at the time.

Falling in love is an imperceptible business and I was afraid of it. It was also clear to me that, although he made it plain that he wanted an affair with me, he said nothing about love. When I met him in the bar he said, 'Before we even have a drink I have to tell you something.' He'd booked a room in a nearby hotel. He knew it was presumptuous, but he'd done it anyway and he needed to know at once how I felt about that. If I didn't want to spend the night with him, he must cancel the room or it wouldn't be fair on the hotel. I spent the night with him.

So there I was, having yet another affair with a married man. He told me he'd decided to live in Majorca – had rented a house in Soller and was going there to write. They were all going. 'I shall only be able to get back here two or three times a year, so I shouldn't see much of you.' He went on to say that we'd have to be very discreet. 'If it came out, I will blacken you – I want you to know that.' It all sounded unpropitious – and yet somehow relieving. How could I be in love with somebody I saw three times a year? But three times a year was better than nothing, and I'd had nothing for a long time.

I decided I'd accept what came. Perhaps I wouldn't be in love with him, would manage to enjoy a light-hearted affair with no strings attached. I asked him about the thing that mattered to me most. Should I be able to write to him? Oh, yes, he would arrange that. 'And I shall want to write to you. All the time.' They weren't going for some months because he had to continue his teaching at Peterhouse College in Cambridge until Easter. Easter seemed far away.

That winter he had various pretexts for coming to London. Tom Maschler, who had taken over at Jonathan Cape, lent us his house and was utterly discreet and kind. This was good because if we went about London in the daytime we kept encountering people, such as Violet Powell, Anthony Powell's wife, on a railway platform very early in the morning. We met V. S. Pritchett in a restaurant that we'd thought safe until Kingsley said, 'Hello, Victor!' and he was sitting in the next banquette. We had to conduct a feverishly unreal 'jolly good pals' conversation for the rest of the meal. In the end we only went out in the evening when it was dark.

During that winter, he met Cyril Frankel, with whom I was still working, and my brother Colin, whom he liked at once as they made each other laugh. I met Bill Rukeyser whom *I* liked at once.

He'd been a student at Princeton when Kingsley was teaching there and approached him in the library saying that he'd heard Kingsley had done an imitation of President Roosevelt on short-wave radio during the war, would he do it for him? Kingsley obliged, whereupon forty-one teachers from Iowa surged in to see the library. This was one of Kingsley's party pieces and I never tired of it. He was marvellous at making sounds, noises of anything – motorbikes, anti-aircraft guns, destroyers whooping, atmospheric radio interruptions – anything at all, and he could do any voice that came to his mind. He was particularly convincing as a robot, and used to write messages to me as one.

BLEEZE AGGZEBT GREEDINGS AND ZINZERE AVVEGZUN

and,

ZENDREZBEGDVUL GREEDINGS AND ABOLOGIES VOR REZENT BREAGDOWN BROMIZZ DO AVOID REGURRENZ

We wrote to each other whenever we couldn't meet. I'd read all three of his novels and his poetry, but I knew that he hadn't read anything of mine, and eventually I gave him a piece I'd written for *Encounter* magazine about my grandfathers. 'That's a dear little piece,' he said, when he'd read it. I didn't dare ask him to read one of my novels.

That winter of 1962 we fell seriously in love but, beyond the island we created and on which we intermittently and perilously lived, our situations were very different. When I met him, Kingsley's marriage was in turmoil with mutual recriminations and infidelity. But he had three children and wanted – expected – to hold it together because of them. Knowing this, I didn't ask questions about his relationship with Hilly, and he once wrote to me saying he was grateful for this. My situation, on the other hand, was different. I had no guilt to contend with, having tried and failed to make anything of my marriage. Jim turned up at intervals in Blomfield Road from his flat in Bristol, which meant I never dared to have Kingsley there. Except for a few trusted friends, it seemed essential to keep things secret. The only thing I knew was that, sometime after Easter, Kingsley was going to Majorca with his family.

Now I need to backtrack a year or two to write about Nicola. As soon as she left school, she said she wanted to go to a drama school, not to act but to learn to be a stage manager. Michael MacOwan, whom I knew, was teaching at LAMDA, and there they taught stage management. But Nic was a year too young to go there, and I wanted her to learn French, to make her own clothes, and to cook. I felt that whatever she did in her life these skills would come in handy. Pete found a French family who lived in the country with a large number of children, none of whom could speak English, and she spent three months with them. She'd not wanted to go, but she came back with passable French saying it was the best holiday she'd ever had. I found her a cooking school in Kensington, and classes for clothes-making that sounded sufficiently professional and she learned there to make her own toiles.

During the terms that she did this she lived with me for the first time since I'd left her father. Colin was also living with me, and they became great friends. She often went as his helper on hi-fi installations. I'd hoped that this arrangement would bring us closer, but it didn't. She was breezy and indifferent, and I was nervous and unnaturally conciliatory.

I began to realize how much I'd failed her, and that by my neglect she'd come to distrust and resent me. I couldn't blame her in the least: she'd had a hard time as a child. Pete, admirable though he was in many ways, wasn't cut out to be a parent, and it had been her stepmother, Phil, who'd provided stability. Love had been lost between us. I resolved then that I'd try to make amends, but I didn't realize – perhaps mercifully – how very long that would take. She

After my daughter Nicola's christening on HMS *Discovery*. From left to right:
Nina Milkina, Marny Tuck, Colin, Uncle Hubert, my mother, me with Nicola,
Pete, Lady K, Anthony Craxton, unknown.

Nicola aged three.

On the *Queen Mary*, returning from New York with Pete (1946).

A. D. Peters (c.1972). I still miss him. He was Danish, although his English was impeccable, and he would never use his first names, so everyone called him Peter Peters.

Jill Balcon and Cecil
Day-Lewis, and me,
at the christening of
their daughter, Tamasin.

Romain Gary and
his second wife
Jean Seberg.

Arthur Koestler.
He possessed an energy
the voltage of which
would have served at
least five ordinary
people.

Laurie Lee (c.1955) When he chose, Laurie was a natural entertainer
and a natural musician.

At Blomfield Road with Katsika, whom I'd criminally smuggled from Greece.

Kingsley Amis. If I try to think now about the first thing that attracted me to him so much it was his honesty with himself.

With Charlie Chaplin on the set of *A King in New York* (c.1956).

Nicola watching a rider.

In my study at Maida Vale.

With Kingsley at Maida Vale (1964). At last, I thought, life was everything
I could ever have hoped for.

With the Fussells and the Keeleys in Greece.

With Rosie Plush,
my first cavalier spaniel.

Sargy Man painting.

Lemmons,
Hadley Common
(1968).

Kingsley in his study at Lemmons (1974). He was one of the most disciplined workers I've ever known.

Colin, my brother, known as Monkey.

Kingsley at Lemmons (c.1972).

Catalogue for the sale of Gardnor House (1976).

In the garden at Delancey Street (1983).

Bridge House (c.1990). I bought the house in about ten minutes.

Bridge House garden in winter (c.1995).

was also going through her teenage years when mothers aren't right about anything. I was glad that there was so much affection between her and Colin, but I sometimes felt ganged-up against – excluded from their jokes and interests. I was too ashamed of myself as a mother to talk to anyone about it.

Several things, large and small, highlighted this unhappy condition. Nic went on a holiday to Scotland with Colin, and when they returned she was clearly very unhappy, and spent most of the time in her room. When I asked Colin what was the matter – I suspected that she'd fallen unhappily in love – he was evasive and only said she didn't want to talk to me about it. Later when she was at LAMDA, she wanted to invite friends to supper but would I please be out? Of course I would – I could see the point of that. I made a supper of cold roast leg of lamb, baked potatoes and salads. When she got home she said none of her friends would touch the lamb as they were all vegetarian, so I rushed out and bought two dozen eggs for them to have omelettes. Nic did very well at LAMDA, and on leaving the school immediately got a job as assistant stage manager for the opening of the Chichester theatre.

It was while she was staying with me that she'd met Kip Asquith. I remember I got them seats for a matinée, and when they came back they both said it had been marvellous, but neither of them was able tell me anything about it. After that they kept in touch and saw each other when possible. Kip had decided that he wanted to see the world and he joined the Merchant Navy and spent at least a year on oil tankers. But he'd inherited a farm in Gloucestershire, and when he came home he decided to go to agricultural college at Cirencester so he could run it.

In early 1963 Nic and Kip announced that they wanted to get married. She was nineteen, the same age I'd been when I'd married her father. I felt anxious about her age and lack of experience generally, as did Pete and Phil. Kip was also very young, but he knew what he wanted to do and was able to do it. They'd been going out for nearly five years. Nic had always loved the country and would have hated to live in a city, so there were no valid objections, really.

They were married on 12 May 1963 at Stanway, in Gloucester, where Guy Benson, the artist, and his wife, Violet, lived. I was invited to stay for the wedding and for lunch beforehand. Nic seemed excited, but more unapproachable than ever. She turned more to her new mother-in-law than she did to me, and after lunch when she went up to dress I wasn't allowed to help her. I remember that night writing a sad letter to Kingsley about it. But the wedding went off well, although there was a rather swollen line of parents since both the bride and groom had double sets. It was an unpretentious country wedding with a party in the barn afterwards, and Nic and Kip left for their honeymoon in Venice. I remember little about it, as it was one of those occasions occluded by sadness for me.

In the spring of 1963, Kingsley went with Hilly to a science-fiction conference in Trieste in Italy. Relations between them weren't good: by then she'd found some of my letters to Kingsley and had promptly sent them to a lawyer. So Kingsley decided he and I were to spend a fortnight in Spain before he went to Majorca. In the meantime, I'd agreed to go to Cap d'Antibes to stay with the Behrens' for a week, and to visit Lorna St Aubyn in her house in Provence.

My relationship with Michael had petered into a kind of wary friendship, and from time to time I was invited to dinner with them or to stay at Culham near Abingdon. It was on this holiday that Felicity rather bravely asked me whether I thought it would have been better if I'd married Michael. I was able to say, quite truthfully, that I didn't think so. I knew he'd moved on, that there had been other people after me, but I could also see much affection between them, and indeed this increased until his death many years later. I took a train along the coast to Marseille where Lorna met me. I'd been going to spend two or three nights with her, but as a train strike was starting the next day this proved impossible. If I wanted to get back to England, I had to leave by the night train.

Kingsley and I spent the night of 20 July before our journey in a friend's flat in South Kensington. We were both encumbered by a ridiculous amount of luggage, clothes, books and our typewriters – we intended working. The next morning there were no taxis, and we were reduced to lugging it all, in relays, to the Underground, where eventually we found a cab. We were both extremely anxious – that we'd be seen, that we'd miss the train, that something, somehow would go wrong. But we were also so buoyed up by love and excitement that our travel *Angst* – his far worse than mine, as I was to learn later – was contained and even transformed into a deliciously exciting adventure.

'Where are we going?' I asked, when we were safely seated in the boat train for Dover.

'Barcelona. Then we'll find somewhere quiet by the sea.' Kingsley wouldn't fly anywhere. He'd once as a boy had a five-shilling trip in an aeroplane at a seaside resort and that was it – for the rest of his life.

After the ferry, and two more trains, we reached Barcelona in the evening. It was stiflingly hot. We found a hotel and I remember drinking so much Vichy Catalan that the next day I felt ill. Kingsley said we must go to the tourist office to find somewhere to go, so we did. Uncharacteristically Kingsley was in charge of the expedition – something that was never to happen again.

He settled on Sitges where he'd been before. 'It'll be full of package tours,' he said. 'We'll be completely lost in the crowd.' We went to Sitges on a very modern little train, so ferociously air-conditioned that we emerged shaking with cold. We'd been told to go to the tourist agency when we arrived, where a Mrs Brandt would find us a flat. So, accompanied still by our seven pieces of unwieldy luggage – Kingsley had begun to say, 'What have you *got* in there?' – we went, and the very efficient and nice lady allotted us a flat, on the first floor of a small block in a quiet street. It was a studio flat: one large room with a double bed, a table and two chairs, a balcony, a kitchenette and a small bathroom.

Kingsley spent the first two days on the beach where, after a token bathe – he never liked it, really – he read my novel, *The Sea Change*. He'd asked me to bring it and I felt both frightened and glad. He said nothing at all during the two days and I hadn't the nerve to ask him how he was getting on. The second evening, he shut the book and said, 'That's a very good novel indeed. I am *so* relieved. I was afraid you wouldn't be any good. It's really *good*, Min.'

We fell quickly into a routine that suited us both. In the mornings we wrote sitting opposite each other at the table, our typewriters almost touching in the small space. Then we went to the beach where I bathed and Kingsley had a dip, then read. After lunch at one of the many, but identical, restaurants where we got near-English food, with a few concessions to Spain, like *gazpacho* or tiny fried fish, we went back to the studio for a siesta. More writing, then drinks. Kingsley quickly amassed an incredible collection of them, including frightful liqueurs such as *crème de bananes* or Parfait Amour, which tasted like old ladies doused in violet-scented talc. We went out to dinner at another restaurant, and then on to play clock golf by floodlight, which we both enormously enjoyed. I'd never felt so enclosed by affection.

I'd been waking frequently in the night with terrifying dreams. Kingsley always woke and consoled me, and they were becoming fewer. I was marvellously happy and amazed to be so. I think now that we'd both been slightly nervous of each other, he because he thought I was posh and might be, as he put it, queenly, I because I didn't hold his political opinions and thought he would despise me for that. But people in early love are generally hell-bent on finding the best in each other. I loved being with someone who made me laugh so much and who was, as I've said before, so stalwart and steady in his honesty about his taste, or lack of it. One day, thinking he might prefer it, I made him a tomato soup. I spent hours on it, wanting it to be perfect. 'Bit authentic for me, darling,' he said, and after that we reverted to the *gazpacho*.

One morning we decided to write a few pages of each other's novel in progress. This meant reading enough of each work to know what was going on, and then a careful briefing as to what each of us wanted to happen. In both cases they were party scenes: his from *One Fat Englishman* and mine from *After Julius*. Our very different writing behaviour was reversed. Normally I'd sit groaning and biting my nails, staring into space, and Kingsley would think for a moment, and then, suddenly charged up, would tap away at a steady rate, sometimes laughing aloud at his characters. So now while I was laughing and typing away, he was groaning and staring into space. The results, however, were pretty good for both of us, and the only person who spotted the changeover in each novel was my brother, Colin.

One afternoon, our peace was disturbed. We were in bed and the doorbell rang. 'I'll get it,' I said. 'It'll be our laundry.' I wrapped myself in a sheet and started to open the door. A huge boot was put into the crack and an Australian voice said, 'Is that Elizabeth Jane Howard?' The possessor of the boot was very strong, and I knew I couldn't hold the door against him. 'Have you got Kingsley Amis with you?'

Kingsley had got up by now and was dressing. 'If you go downstairs and wait, we'll see you in the garden.'

The man, an Australian, turned out to be a stringer for the *Daily Express*. Our names had been passed to him by, presumably, either the hotel or the tourist agency in Barcelona. After some argument, the man whined, 'I don't *like* doing this job,' and Kingsley said, 'But you *are* doing it, aren't you?' He said he wanted to get his photographer for a picture and Kingsley agreed. The moment he'd gone, we went to Mrs Brandt, explained we hadn't given her our real names and that we had to move at once, within the hour. 'I'll find you somewhere else, and register you as Mr and Mrs Friend.' We rushed back and packed. Mrs Brandt sent a cab and we were installed in a ground-floor studio at the other end of town. By now I'd acquired a white kitten we called Victor, after Victor Pritchett. Victor had to be put into a carrier-bag, which he intensely disliked. Kingsley called his friend, George Gale at the *Express*, to ask him to try to suppress the story, and George did his best. But the facts were published, and we knew that our unofficial elopement was common knowledge.

We got back to England, and Kingsley got the news that Hilly had gone to Majorca with the children. As Jim was still unpredictably in and out of my flat, we rented one in a mansion block in Basil Street for the enormous sum of fifteen pounds a week. Divorce was in the air.

9

A few weeks after we'd been in Basil Street, it was past midnight and we were reading peacefully in bed, when the doorbell rang. Ever since Sitges, we'd been nervous of being doorstepped. Kingsley said he'd go, but I got up as well and followed him. Ours was a flat where all the rooms led off a long passage with the front door at one end. Kingsley was now walking back from it followed by two blond-headed boys. 'This is Philip and this is Martin,' he said, 'and this is Jane.' They looked at me, impassive, too weary even for the brink of hostility, and I looked warily back. We were all trying to conceal our shock – they hadn't known I'd be there, and we'd had no warning of their arrival. I cooked bacon and eggs and left them with their father while I made up beds.

There followed a week of grandiose treats, punctuated by long and often tearful sessions spent by the boys alone with Kingsley while he attempted to explain the situation to them. But you can't do that, really. They didn't want their loyalties to be torn and any efforts to explain why he'd left their mother to live with me could only do that. Emotional protocol dictated that they should distrust and even dislike me. They were in their early teens: they'd lost their home in Cambridge and now, they feared, their father. In this situation everyone behaves in a younger manner than his or her age, reverts to an earlier period of childhood. The boys wanted scenes that would hopefully lead to Kingsley recanting, possibly returning with them when they went back to Majorca. Kingsley wanted them to love him, to forgive him – even to love me, whom they'd known for barely a week. And I wanted us all to be happy and understanding and kind to one another. One can see at once that none of these reactions could ever have been appropriate or, at least, if any of them were to be achieved it would take time.

Later, Kingsley's daughter Sally came for a week, very merry and self-possessed. She was twelve years old and seemed more curious about the situation than anything else, but she was also keen on having as many treats as Philip and Martin had had.

It was about then that I realized Kingsley's complete indifference to money, and his natural and chronic generosity, meant that he preferred not to consider finances. He'd stopped teaching and was now living purely by writing. Hilly would need money to live, and the children to be paid for. It was clear to me that I had to sell Blomfield Road to buy somewhere larger. Monkey – from now onwards I shall call my brother Colin by that name – loved looking at houses, as much as Kingsley hated it, so it was with him that I found an Edwardian villa on Maida Vale. The lease was a short one of about fourteen years, but it only cost two thousand pounds, which left me with six thousand from Blomfield Road. We needed this to rewire, plumb and regenerate what had become a near wreck – it had been occupied for years by an old lady who had finally lived in just one of the rooms with her cats. It had five bedrooms, a double drawing room and a study for Kingsley, plus a bathroom, and a kitchen in the basement. There was an octagonal conservatory at the back of the house and a large garden with fruit trees that backed on to Hamilton Terrace. Monkey and I both fell in love with it and when I took Kingsley to see it he was so enchanted by the sight of a defunct fridge in what was to be his study – 'I could make *any* drink in here!' – that he was all for it.

Peter Peters rang up one day to say that his client, Evelyn Waugh, had agreed to be interviewed on television. This had happened only once before with John Freeman. Since then he'd refused all offers, but now, approaching sixty, he'd consented to one more interview provided a woman conducted it. The BBC had suggested me, and Waugh had rung Peter to ask if he knew anything about me. 'I said you would've read his books and wrote novels yourself, and were altogether a suitable candidate.'

We met, with Christopher Burstall, the producer, at Browns Hotel. I admired Waugh deeply, but had been warned that he could be difficult.

'Ah, Miss Howard. And have you had anything to do with literature?'

'Only spasmodically, Mr Waugh.'

At lunch, he explained to Mr Burstall that one used one's knives and forks beginning at the outside. He produced a piece of paper on which were written, he said, the questions he was prepared to be asked. The interview was to start the next day and was to take two afternoons, as they wanted to shoot enough to edit for an hour-long programme. The questions were very run-of-the-mill, and unlikely to elicit much. I asked some of them, and then I decided, when I knew that a reel was coming to an end, to put in one of my own. Waugh was still playing games. During each interval when they reloaded the camera he asked things like, 'When is Miss Howard going to take off all her clothes?'

At the end of the second afternoon, I was asked to 'amuse' Mr Waugh while they took reaction shots of him. Amuse him! How on earth could I do that? In the end I told him in some detail about my lack of education which he seemed to enjoy, or at any rate he remained benign throughout. But the reply that most interested me was when I asked whether he preferred to be anxious or bored. 'Oh, bored every time is the answer.'

I've observed writers many times – particularly poets – who are in that state. They don't *like* boredom, but the alternative is too fearful for them. Kingsley, I was to discover, was no exception. The chief and most arresting feature of Waugh's face was his beautiful eyes: of a clear blue they were marvellously alive, *seeing* eyes that sparkled with intelligence and perception. Even Kingsley, when he did his very funny impersonation of Waugh's face – with its apoplectic edge of congested rage – couldn't manage the eyes.

The interview was transmitted later that spring and I was disappointed with my part in it, but fascinated by Waugh. There were many stories of his trying, and usually succeeding, to discomfort people. I remember Kingsley asking Anthony Powell, who knew Waugh very well, what it was about him that made him do this. Tony said he would think about it, and came back at teatime having solved the problem. 'He's *mad*, you see.' Not a complete solution.

In the late summer of 1963 we went to Majorca. Hilly and the children had come back to London, where she rented a house in the Fulham Road. I'd sold Blomfield Road with vacant possession in June, and had bought Maida Vale. Kingsley had rented the house in Soller for a year so it seemed best to go and make use of it.

Monkey came with us to Majorca in his car. Our house was about a mile inland. It stood by itself, surrounded by cultivated fields. It wasn't a prepossessing place but there was a charming lady who did everything for us. At that time I'd have been happy anywhere with Kingsley, but with the beautiful island, the impeccable summer, with Monkey and Kingsley liking each other, it was entirely cloudless. People came to stay with us, including Robert Conquest and his wife Caroleen. They stayed the longest because Bob and Kingsley were working together on a project that was to become *The Egyptologist* – the idea was Bob's – an elaborate satire. They enjoyed talking about it, egging each other on.

Bob was the most completely intellectual man I've ever met. When he wasn't talking to Kingsley he would walk up and down with a book in his hand, oblivious to anyone in his way. Caroleen said he did this up and down the passage of their mansion flat in Battersea, and therefore opening a door on to the passage was hazardous. Words, and word play, were his recreation. His more serious side was devoted to political history. After Koestler, he was the man who had pointed out the evils of Communism in Russia at the time when it was fashionable to do the opposite.

We went to Deya to see Robert Graves, whom I'd met before on a book programme. Robert took me down to the beach to bathe and somebody there was playing music very loudly on a transistor. Robert went over to him and told him to turn it off. He refused, whereupon Robert seized the machine, stalked into the sea and threw it powerfully into the waves. There was no reaction from the owner. When we'd bathed we lay above the beach – pine needles in the sand – and he asked me if I was in love. I said, 'Completely,' and he smiled and said one should always be in love.

I thought then how many poets feel that – so many of them doing their best work when they are young. A satisfactory or comfortable marriage is beside the point: they crave the frenzied ecstasy, the obsession. Then I thought, Kingsley's a poet – and I had a fleeting chill. We always think when we're in love that it is like nobody else's love, but I suspect we're more like everybody else at those times than at any other.

I'd been asked to chair six television programmes through that summer and had turned them down because I wanted to be with Kingsley. The producer asked me if I'd do the first programme at least, and I agreed. Afterwards she took me to a restaurant in Kensington Church Street and sitting opposite us were Gavin Maxwell and his bride whom he'd married that day. After my host left, they asked me to come and sit with them. I remember that half hour particularly, because we were all three so exhilarated: we were all – if only temporarily – in love with our lives.

Some years before I'd stayed a couple of nights with Gavin at Glenelg with two otters and an otter keeper. In the morning I went for a walk with one of the otters. Tekko rambled about, picking a few dandelions, which he carried for a while, until we got to the seashore where he concentrated upon tearing limpets off rocks. After a while, he clearly saw I wasn't joining in and gave me one – a gesture I shall never forget. Gavin's temperament was much like his otter's: generous, exuberant, highly strung, inquisitive and, above all, charming.

I went back to spend my last night at Blomfield Road lit up by all the warmth and excitement. At last, I thought, life was everything I could ever have hoped for and it had come about in a situation that had seemed to have no chance of any permanence. As my bad dreams decreased I was more able to enjoy and trust Kingsley's love, to take in his affection and approval, to enjoy doing anything for him that added to his comfort. Being away from him for thirty-six hours simply afforded the luxury of a joyful return. I lay awake that night for a long time, thinking how miserable I'd been in this place and how wonderful it was to be starting again in Majorca and Maida Vale.

In the autumn we left Soller and went to live in a hotel in Pollenza in the north of the island. It was a modern building that could have been anywhere. There was a small beach nearby, but it was getting too cold to bathe. Kingsley was deep into *The Anti-Death League* and I was nearly done with *After Julius*. Monkey had gone home and was going to try to find us somewhere to live while Maida Vale was being done up. We lived for several weeks at Pollenza – working all the morning in the small bedroom, going down in the claustrophobic lift to the huge dining room for lunch. Afterwards we'd read, sometimes go for a walk, and then work again until seven when we'd read the day's work to each other over a drink. This was the only time I rewrote a piece of a novel: Kingsley thought my first version of Julius's trip to France wasn't quite right, so I did it again. After the reading we'd go out to a bar where they had a jukebox and we could play the Beatles' records. We'd also made friends with a Jewish honeymoon couple with whom we used to drink green chartreuse. The hotel was emptying and seeing Sondra night after night in different stunning outfits, I felt sorry that she hadn't a larger and more interested audience.

In London we went back to a small top-floor flat in Keats Grove. Squirrels came in and rummaged irritably through saucers of nuts or biscuits, slid down drainpipes if we approached them, then racketed off through the dead plane leaves below. I was cooking for us by now. Kingsley was eating more and drinking less and said he'd never felt so well: 'It's my lovely life!'

I finished *After Julius* on a dark grey evening in November. The feeling after completing a novel is for me like no other. It's as though with the last sentence, I have released a great weight that falls away, leaving me so empty and light that I can float out of myself and look down at the pattern of the work I've made. I can see all at once what I have been pursuing in fragments for so long. It's a timeless moment, a kind of ecstasy – a state of unconditional love – that has nothing whatever to do with merit or criticism. Of course it goes, dissolves into melancholy and a sense of loss. Parting with people one has been living with for so long and know so intimately is poignant: they are more lost to you than anyone you meet in life. They remain crystallized exactly where you left them. Altogether, it's an occasion that makes one feel very strange for some time afterwards.

I remember I finished about five o'clock, and Kingsley was working in another room, but he was deeply engaged, so I started making supper – Joanna and Terry Kilmartin were coming. When we were eating I mentioned I'd finished my novel. Terry said, 'That must be a good thing,' and immediately turned to Kingsley to talk about him reviewing for the *Observer*.

While my novel was being typed, I concentrated upon furnishing Maida Vale. Apart from clothes and books, Kingsley had nothing, and the contents of my four-roomed flat weren't going to go very far. Kingsley was totally uninterested in anything to do with the house, which left me in control, and I enjoyed it all. Junk shops were very rewarding in those days and after the builder had finished there was just enough money left from the sale of Blomfield Road for decoration and equipment. My brother Robin was often travelling the world to buy timber, and he formed an association with a silk dealer in Rangoon that meant we could have yards of beautiful material for our drawing-room curtains. Monkey and I saw builders on Primrose Hill throwing slabs of black and white marble into a skip. We asked if we could have it, and they said yes, if we carted it away. Somehow we did that, and two art students laid us a marvellous floor for the conservatory. Monkey's friend Max Fordham was a heating engineer but had kindly undertaken to oversee our builders. He installed two factory gas heaters in the conservatory, which kept it warm, and I had staging on stilts built with zinc trays for plant pots. Monkey was going to live with us, and apart from his bedroom, he had a work-shop under the conservatory. Kingsley got a new little fridge for his study, which greatly pleased him.

Shortly after we moved in, we realized that all wasn't well with Philip and Martin. They were at schools in South London where they were miserable and truanting. I suggested to Kingsley that perhaps they'd be better off with us, and after some consultation with Hilly, it was decided that they would.

And so I embarked upon the extraordinarily difficult business of being a stepmother. I'd had experience of this already, having had my father's second wife ranged against me, but I hadn't been ultimately vulnerable. My daughter had a stepmother who'd always behaved impeccably, being direct, supportive and friendly to me. You might have thought that these different experiences would have taught me enough. They hadn't.

The boys arrived, but hostility was very apparent. They were pleased to be with their father, but it was clear that they felt I was the cause of their parents' break-up. I decided that all I could do to begin with was to feed them well, and regularly, and to be in every other practical way as reliable as I could manage. I thought that even if they continued to dislike me, some kind of trust might come about. What I didn't do was make any attempt to form any kind of relationship with Hilly. Our feelings then for each other were of mutual fear and dislike, but it might have been possible to lay these aside and put the boys first. Kingsley was no help in this.

A salient characteristic in the Amis family was passivity. They weren't initiators; they let things happen and resented or regretted them; they didn't acknowledge that the consequences were their responsibility. I think Kingsley, when he thought about it, was assailed by guilt. He distanced himself from Hilly, and he gave the boys money to appease them. He simply wanted everybody to settle down so that he could write his books in peace and enjoy himself when he wasn't working.

The trouble about bringing up children is that it doesn't begin and end by making things nice for them. Some sort of moral direction has to be given. It wasn't long before I found myself in the unenviable position of being the irritating killjoy, the tiresome prig. We acquired , for example, a second-hand bar-billiards table for the conservatory, the kind where we had to put a shilling in a slot to play a game. I suggested this money should be for a charity, and everyone agreed, but quite soon I found that there never seemed to be any money in it. Of course the boys had found a way to take it. Not important, but they had to stop. When I approached Kingsley about it, he simply said, 'Well, it isn't very much money,' as though the amount was the point. This was in front of the boys, so they *knew* I was a prig, and their father was a good sort.

These sorts of things kept hostility flourishing. They sulked with me, were nasty behind my back, and I minded very much. Fortunately, both the boys really liked Monkey, who was very good with them and, indeed, became a kind of uncle. They teased him with affection, and he taught them to play games. They both had their father's sense of humour – Phil, particularly, was a brilliant mimic – and these things lightened the atmosphere.

They had been, by then, to so many different schools that it was decided a crammer might be the best way to ensure they passed the statutory exams. So they went to Davis, Laing and Dick in Holland Park. It was a long time before I realized that they weren't actually *going*. It was the time of Mods and Rockers, and the boys were mods – winkle-pickers and all. On Saturdays they used to go out on the town in search of girls. Once, having got stuck with a couple they didn't like, they gave us an insight to their world. 'What did you do?' I asked, and Phil answered casually, 'Oh, we threw water at them down some stairs.' I made a sitting room for them with their hi-fi in a room adjoining our kitchen–dining room. There was a lot of pop music and it smelt of hot socks.

Things came to a head one Christmas, their first with us, and I'd tried to make it a good one. I'd bought them each a gold wrist-watch with their initials on the back, and they also had money from Dad and stockings. Black faces. 'All we want are the presents,' Phil said. I lost my nerve and went away to cry.

When I came back, Phil said, 'We've been rotten to you,' and Mart said, 'Yes, we have.' I think this time Kingsley *had* talked to them, and it showed me how much talking was needed between us.

Occasionally things worked. We were going to the film of *Othello*, and I discovered that neither of the boys knew the play. I suggested we should all read it aloud together first. Kingsley was keen, so they agreed.

This was about the time when, finding Martin lounging in a disaffected way, boredom seeping from every pore, I asked him what he wanted to do when he was older. 'Be a writer,' he said.

'You – a *writer*? But you never read anything. If you're so interested in writing, why don't you read?'

He looked at me and said, 'Give me a book to read then.' I gave him *Pride and Prejudice*. A little later he came to me and said, 'Jane, you've got to tell me how it ends.'

'Of course I won't. You find out for yourself.' He argued with persuasive charm, but I felt on firm ground: he was obviously enjoying it. That was when he started to read properly – a very good moment for me.

This was also a halcyon time for Kingsley and me. He was clearly happy – hardly anxious at all. He got drunk occasionally, but was always friendly. 'I have such a lovely life with you!' he would say repeatedly. He'd bring me back presents when he'd been out to lunch with the Conquests and other luminaries – a bunch of flowers, two collages he bought at Heywood Hill, the bookseller, or a complete edition of George Eliot. He would take me out to lunch suddenly, to the Étoile, which he knew I loved. He quite liked going to dinner parties then, and having them. He hated boring dark socks, so I knitted him eight or nine pairs in brilliant colours. He was incredibly disciplined about his work and was a marvellous example for me, although I didn't have the same time to do it.

We had two cats: a black one, Katsika, whom I'd criminally smuggled from Greece years before, and a blue Burmese called Malfi, who became Monkey's cat and lived in his room. There used to be advertisements for puppies on sale in the Sunday papers. On Sundays the boys used to come and have breakfast in our bedroom, and one morning I said how much and for how long I'd wanted a cavalier spaniel – a brown and white one. 'Let's go and get one then,' Kingsley said. By then I'd learned to drive a second-hand Mini – Kingsley didn't drive – and we set off for a vicarage in North London. The vicar's wife had a litter of red ones – rubies. I chose one, a bitch, and we drove home with her sitting, tiny and dignified, on Kingsley's knee. We called her Rosie Plush and we all loved her. Mart took her for her first walk on a lead down Edgware Road – 'She greeted every bus!'

In the summer Kingsley and I went to Greece. At Princeton he'd become friends with Mike and Mary Keeley. Mike, whose real name was Edmund, was a novelist, a professor of English, and the translator with Philip Sherrard of Cavafy. Mary was Greek and they spent every summer in Greece. We arranged to meet in Athens.

Kingsley's fear of flying made travelling far longer, but much more interesting too. We went by train, boat and train to Paris, then caught the night train to Venice – a lovely old-fashioned service that provided an excellent dinner and was famous for its *eau de vie de framboise*. Arriving at Venice at six a.m. on a hot, misty summer morning was magic: the city rose slowly from the sea like a disparate collection of mirages, hazy, sharply delineated, shimmering, glittering, pale and dazzling. A first sight I shall never forget.

Our boat left in the evening, so I parked Kingsley in a bar with newspapers and walked. Kingsley didn't like sightseeing then, and I was no hand at it. I liked simply to walk and be there. The canals fascinated me, and I longed to go in a gondola, but we only had enough Italian money for lunch. The boat took two nights to get to Piraeus where Mary Keeley met us. Mike was at a meeting, she said. We'd have dinner and he'd appear in due course. Mary was wonderfully welcoming, and took us up on to a terrace where we drank, and Kingsley and Mary talked about friends at Princeton and we waited for Mike.

That was the start of several long, hedonistic holidays with the Keeleys. We spent one of them on their friend Alekko's *caïque* visiting islands, most of which were still unspoiled. I particularly remember Naxos, with its lemon groves and wide village streets. In all of the few shops there were dusty bottles of Quitro, a lemon liqueur hardly known even in Athens. It was cheap – it cost about five shillings – and good and powerful. The captain of the *caïque* was keen on Naxos because his fiancée came from there. We invited her on board for a swim and lunch, and she wore a flowered dress, white shoes and a handbag, and was accompanied by two brothers as chaperones. She couldn't swim, as her future husband should not see her in a bathing dress, even though they were – unknown to her family – lovers. She sat on deck – it was intolerably hot – and watched us rather sadly. One of the captain's brothers was there too, a boy of about ten, who swam like an otter and was, the captain said, the Scourge of Athens. I bought him a knife, and when he opened it, he gave a fierce little scream of pure joy.

One summer, the Keeleys hired a house on Spetses for a month. It was the hottest summer for years. Spetses was reputed to be the hottest island in Greece, and we were told we'd chosen the hottest house on the island. I'd stand under the cold shower until my long hair was soaked, then type until it was almost dry, and then I'd repeat the process. In the evenings we'd walk through the small town beset with rubble – the Greeks always seemed to be building – with the seductive scent of unseen jasmine filling the warm dark air, and then up a small hill on the crest of which was a restaurant much loved by us all. It served tomato salad and cheese with thick slices of bread, and it was the best tomato salad I've ever eaten. The smallest waiter in the world, the owner's heir, staggered from table to table in his nappy, laying glasses and plates. Sometimes service was slow because, we were told, the owner had beaten his wife too much for her to work. There were many and varied reasons for not being a Greek wife.

We spent one summer on Rhodes with the Keeleys and the historian and literary critic Paul Fussell and his wife Betty, herself a historian and food writer. We went to Cos and found there were no available hotels or *pensions*. Suddenly a smiling man appeared and said, 'Come with me,' and we all stayed in his house. He and his wife slept in their double bed in the garden. I slept on a wooden chest. We weren't allowed to pay.

We found a small boat willing to take us to Turkey and landed at Bodrum, then a small village with no hotels. We stayed with a farmer who seemed to have one or two of every kind of vociferous animal all proclaiming their identity at night. The lavatory was an inexpressibly deep and murky hole in the ground into which Paul dropped his expensive leather wallet containing all his money and credit cards. In the morning we went to a café for coffee and bread, and hanging near its doorway were three or four Turkish robes of satin and velvet; Betty and I each bought one.

We went to Kalimnos – the sponge divers' island – and stayed in a curious place whose owners seemed to be trying to live up to a mysterious standard. We knew, unprepossessing as the place was, that it would have been worse if they'd succeeded. Part of one summer we spent on the shores of Skyros where George Seferis was staying. He was ill, but wasn't allowed to leave the country to get the medical attention he needed. He and his wife had a house by the sea, and we stayed in the oldest villa, Xenia, a lovely small place a few yards from the sea. I wrote the first chapter of *Odd Girl Out* there. We used to spend the evenings with George and his wife, for whom the fishermen used to procure lobsters. I went to see the memorial to Rupert Brooke for whom I'd had a passion when I was about fourteen, but we never went to the village at the top of the mountain. I never saw the little Skyriot horses which lived in the mountains all the winter and came down to do farm work and be raced on the sands in the summer. They weren't ponies, I was told, but real little horses – the strain being of great antiquity.

One evening Kingsley did the Offenbach can-can piece in fits of uncontrollable laughter and I have a picture of Mike laughing at him. We worked and swam in the daytime, and had long suppers in the open air, drinking a lot. Once Mary and I put candles in a church to ask that we might both have children. Neither of us managed that. Kingsley had said that if I wanted children he would be delighted. We even named them. At one point I thought I was pregnant, but I was wrong. I went to a doctor but nothing happened. He said the next thing would be to examine Kingsley, but this Kingsley refused.

I've compressed the Greek holidays. They continued for several years. I remember them as times of particular happiness. Kingsley enjoyed the company of Mike and Mary and subsequently Paul Fussell. They were also, more importantly, times when we could be alone together, an ingredient vital for middle-aged marriages. During many of those summers the boys went to Spain with their mother. When they didn't, Monkey, with his friend Sargy, looked after them. Sargy had decided to give up his job in Oxford, and become a painter. He found himself a room off Tottenham Court Road and sent himself to Camberwell School of Art. I bought him a heavy pot and taught him to make stew. But he was often with us, and gradually became a part of the family.

Very soon after we moved to Maida Vale we were invited to

dine with Stephen Potter and his new wife, and it was there that we met Dolly and Bobby Burns. He'd been a distinguished surgeon, now retired, and she was the only daughter of Lord Duveen and, as my brother put it, 'uncontrollably rich'. Parties were her life's blood and we instantly began to be invited to them. There were usually twelve or fourteen people to dinner in Chesterfield Hill, all in full evening dress, and everybody whom Dolly could possibly collect went to them.

10

Kingsley and I got married in the late spring of 1965 after we'd been at Maida Vale for a year and a few months. The boys brought us breakfast in bed on the wedding morning – clearly a gesture of peace. We were married at Marylebone town hall in the presence of my brother and daughter, Cyril Frankel, Bill Rukeyser and Tom Maschler. Cape gave a party for us, and then we had a dinner in a private room at Prunier. Afterwards we took a train to Brighton for a two-day honeymoon. The first morning there when we walked out on the pier, the sideshow men offered us free turns at everything because they'd seen our pictures in the papers. One afternoon, we went to watch the wrestling, and a huge man who got into difficulties shouted to Kingsley, 'Help me, Lord Jim.' Kingsley said he'd never been confused with Conrad before.

Dolly Burns invited us to stay with them in France, at the Hôtel du Cap Eden Roc on Cap d'Antibes. In those days Kingsley was happy to travel with me. He got on very well with Bobby and was fascinated by Dolly's flamboyant behaviour. He also enjoyed grand hotel life. The first evening we sat in the bar in extremely comfortable chairs drinking Paradis, a champagne cocktail laced with raspberry juice. After a short while Bobby said, 'Well, what shall we talk about?' and Dolly immediately answered, 'Sex is the most interesting subject in the world.' Bobby sat urbanely smiling while little pecks were made at this subject.

Dolly, I suppose, was in her early seventies. She'd lost her figure, but still had elegant little legs. Her hair was impeccably dressed, and her makeup operatically applied. She looked like a luscious, slightly overripe fruit. She was bossy, used to getting her own way in everything. She'd brought her chauffeur and the Rolls which he was only allowed to drive at fifteen miles an hour while she shouted at him to go slower. But she also had an endearing side: she was a romantic, vulnerable, naïve, and generous, as well as being extremely shrewd about money matters. She only read the *Financial Times* and *The Economist*: the arts in general meant nothing to her. One afternoon she took us to see Chagall who received her, I think, out of respect for her father, whom he knew. It was an uneasy afternoon. She went only because he was famous. She had no interest in his work. He was courteous and bored. Kingsley was also bored. In those days he had no interest in pictures, either. None of us spoke French and I sat looking at the pictures like illustrations of dreams in fairy stories, too shy to attempt any conversation.

Dolly had a passion for collecting people who were famous or good at something. Her dream was to be the hostess of the most desirable salon in London, in the South of France or in Jamaica where they had a house and went regularly. But she was also conducting a sort of affair with a Russian who composed music – I can't now remember his name. He 'happened' to be staying in Nice and she used to visit him in the afternoons. She was also genuinely devoted to Bobby, who seemed impervious to her bossiness, the endless dinner parties and her ruling of the various roosts.

She invited us to spend three weeks with them in Jamaica – all expenses paid. We went in a banana boat, one of the most enjoyable experiences of travelling for me. The boat, besides its cargo, carried about 120 passengers, among them Princess Alice, Duchess of Gloucester, and a lady-in-waiting. The captain, a Northern Irishman, whom we liked very much, told us that she loved the trip and came on his boat every year. The first two days it was rough, but after that it was marvellous. I saw my first flying fish. The captain ran the ship with admirable attention to every detail. Each week he made a complete tour of everything. Once a wardrobe door in our cabin was sticking. He noticed it, and it was mended within an hour.

We stopped for a few hours at Trinidad – no time to see anything of the island, but I do remember the largest blue butterfly I'd ever seen, which took to the air with the heavy difficulty of a bomber. In the far distance it was just possible to see the coast of Venezuela, and the sea in that direction was a gamboge yellow from the silt of the Orinoco. It was a deeply glamorous sight.

We disembarked at Kingston, and took a train across the island to Montego Bay where Dolly had her house.

Neither of us had been to the Caribbean, and if we hadn't gone on the train we'd have thought that Jamaica consisted of beaches of bleached sand and palm trees. The centre of the island had landscape like the north country in Britain: dry-stone walls and fields with sheep. Only the villages were truly Jamaican: houses made of wood and corrugated iron, red dirt roads, busy women and indolent men.

Life with Dolly there was exigent. Every morning we had all to repair to Doctor's Cave, the smart place to swim. We lunched at home, after which there was a siesta. Every evening there was a full-dress dinner party, either in Dolly's house or in the houses of her guests. The same people rotated in different dresses in different places. Despite being frowned upon, I managed two small sorties from this regime. One was to visit an old lady who lived on the hillside and attracted hundreds of humming birds by dint of innumerable honey feeders. It was wonderful to see these bejewelled, belligerent little birds so close. The second escape was with someone I met at a party. I'd been asking about the Lookback Lands, a remote and wooded part of the island where lived people who hadn't anything to do with the rest of the island. The man said he had access to a helicopter and would show them to me if I liked. So he did, but all I could see were mysterious little paths winding through the forest. After a while I remarked that I'd never been in a helicopter before. 'Neither have I,' he replied. He must, I suppose, have been having me on but I didn't think so at the time. I sat silent after that, trying to comfort myself with the thought that if he'd got the machine into the air, he must be able to get it down.

After about ten days, Kingsley grew restive, and in the end had a row with Dolly. I can't remember what it was about, but he came storming into our room saying that we'd have to leave, he couldn't stay after what had gone on between him and Dolly. I pointed out that as he wouldn't fly, we'd have to wait until the banana boat came back to fetch us. Impasse. Then Dolly *and* Bobby came into the room, Dolly apologized with tears in her eyes, and a lot of making up went on. We ended our time there staying a night with John Hearne, the Jamaican novelist.

Kingsley said he'd never stay with them again and I agreed with him. When we got home he said we must send the money for our boat tickets, which we did.

We made two journeys that had a profound effect on me. The first was to Nashville, Tennessee, where Kingsley had been invited to lecture at Vanderbilt University by the professor of English, Russell Fraser, whom he had met and very much liked when they were both teaching at Princeton. We went over in the *Queen Mary*, and stayed a week with the Keeleys at Princeton. Why on earth were we going to Nashville, they kept asking, when Kingsley had been asked to go to several other universities in the North? We had discussed this, and decided that as we'd never been to the South, this was a good opportunity. I was also anxious to see some of the Ambrose Bierce country, as I very much admired his stories of the Civil War.

Russell met us at the railway station. He'd been lucky, he'd found us a house, he said. A member of the faculty was on sabbatical, and her house had been rented for us. The moment I walked into it, I knew it was going to be awful, but Kingsley didn't seem to notice. I was tired after the long train journey, and hadn't the guts to say at once that we didn't want to live there. 'There' was a small detached house, chiefly on one floor, with two attics that we could never have used since they were stuffed with the owner's belongings. The owner was there to hand over, and so was the black lady who cleaned the house. 'You'll have to give her something at Christmas,' she said as the maid was standing by. 'Just something cheap and gaudy – anything will do.' Deeply ashamed, I glanced at the maid. Her expression was impassive, and she didn't meet my eye. We were shown how the appliances worked, and they left.

It was a drab and tasteless little place, and I was soon to find out that almost nothing worked – the fridge, the cooker, the deep freeze, the television hardly waited for the sounds of their owner's departing car to break down. The house was about two miles from the campus, and the first thing I had to do was to hire a car. It was one of those chrome-trimmed cars that give off an electric shock when you open any of the doors. However, apart from driving Kingsley there and back twice a day, I had to shop with it, since the only time I tried going for a walk, the police stopped me as a suspicious character. Apparently respectable people no long walked anywhere, they drove. I'd been put forward to lecture at Finch University, one of the then two black universities in the US, and I went to be interviewed.

My generation in England hadn't had much to do with black people. We'd seen black US soldiers in London during the war and actors in American films, so it was a revelation to see countless young, beautifully groomed black students. They said they'd have me and I desperately wanted to teach there, but it proved impossible, as I couldn't combine it with driving Kingsley at arbitrary times of the day. I regretted this more and more, as the rest of our life there was entirely confined to the whites, whose attitude and behaviour to blacks was uniformly horrible. So I drove Kingsley in the mornings, went back and worked on my novel – *Something in Disguise* – fetched him home for lunch, drove him back to work, then went to the supermarket before fetching him again.

The main part of Nashville reminded me of the Edgware Road

in London, and the rest was an endless suburb. We had to drive miles for any real country. We were asked out a lot in the evenings. There were stringent rules about alcohol left over from the Prohibition and engendered by the Baptist culture of the South. 'Liquor by the drink', or being able to buy a drink in a restaurant, came in just before we left. But there were very tiresome rules about where and how we could buy or drink alcohol. At dinners, caterers were generally used, except by us, the Frasers and another couple we met and liked; *boeuf Stroganoff* with iced tea is refreshment I still can't face today. Desperate for some exercise, I joined a gym, and after a few weeks the German wife of the other self-catering couple said she'd like to join me. When I said I had a friend who would like to join the club, the secretary asked me whether this person was – well – *coloured*? Because, if so . . . I wanted to say, 'No, she's possibly the daughter of an SS general, but she's not black,' but of course I didn't.

There was heavy snow that winter. Kingsley had very little time after his university work to write; we hated the awful little house more and more, and both of us became homesick and depressed. When we went to parties where drink was available we both drank too much. The Frasers provided relief, but otherwise we lived on letters from Monkey and Mart.

We'd made a plan with the Keeleys to go to Mexico for two weeks when Kingsley's semester finished, and we decided to stay longer, if we could find a good place to hole up and finish our novels. I wished, afterwards, that I'd asked to go to Kingsley's lectures, as I knew he was a wonderful teacher, but it didn't occur to me at the time. We spent one weekend with the Frasers in a log cabin in woods about two hours' drive from Nashville that I enjoyed, including a visit for lunch to a beautiful house owned by a couple the Frasers knew. It was an untouched early nineteenth-century building: even the wallpaper, faded and beautiful, was original. There was talk of puff adders lurking in the corn. But otherwise there was no country in our lives.

What depressed and partly isolated us most was the racism, and the realization that the North and the South were deeply and frighteningly divided. The last straw came when we gave a small party in our house for Kingsley's class. He spoke to one of the girls – an eighteen-year-old – about the fact that in the North black people were educated, were doctors and lawyers, and she replied, 'Ah, but, you see, *here* we know how to keep them in their place.'

'*Eighteen*! And she thinks that,' Kingsley said despairingly. After that evening, we just wanted to get the hell out.

There was no shortage of country in Mexico. We took a train from Nashville to St Louis, and then the splendid train from there to Mexico City – two nights and three days – where we met up with the Keeleys and spent a couple of days. My chief memories are of a fragment of an Aztec cloak made of feathers in the museum, and an earthquake when both Kingsley and I thought we'd had a stroke. We played with some lion cubs that were carelessly enclosed in the middle of a public park – they were boisterously friendly, but with truly awful claws.

Then we hired a car and drove about for two weeks. The only ugly part was Acapulco, a Hollywood film-style film resort where a suitcase was stolen off our roof rack within thirty seconds. We decided to stay on in San Miguel de Allende, a small, beautiful town thousands of feet above sea level, where we lived richly at low cost in a small hotel kept by a Spanish grandee whose English was peppered with 1920s slang – 'By Jove! It's jolly to meet some English chums.' There were innumerable servants, but as each person's job consisted of watering the geraniums, or laying the wood fires in bedrooms, or fetching the bread from the market, or feeding the birds, nobody was being ground down by their work.

The town was full of what Kingsley called 'very, very naughty little boys who, unshod and with minimal ragged clothes, none the less looked and were the picture of health'. They scrambled about, laughing, teasing us and each other, and running away in mock fright if noticed. The best bar sold tequila with a large worm in each bottle and there was a stone trough beneath the drinkers' feet into which they could piss without having to leave their barstool. There was a cathedral, whose architect, a Frenchman, had included every decorative device known to architecture. It was like a monstrous white wedding cake.

The market sold everything one could imagine wanting, and some unimagined. When we stood at the edge of town the distant mountains seemed to be the land and the hundreds of miles of country before them like an ocean. I loved it there. We stayed six weeks, and when we left, we were accompanied to the station by the Spanish proprietor and many of his staff. Kingsley had finished his book, but I hadn't finished mine.

While we'd been away, Sargy Mann had moved in to help Monkey look after the boys, and on our return, having cooked us a delicious dinner, he said he thought he ought to be leaving. 'Don't go,' I said, so he didn't. In fact he lived with us for about eight years more, until he married.

Before we'd left on this journey, I'd searched for and found a crammer in Brighton, whose tutor struck me as right for Martin. The crammer in London had been a total failure: neither of the boys had learned much and had truanted for a good part of the terms there. I explained to Mr Ardagh at Sussex Tutors in Brighton that Martin was almost totally uneducated but none the less extremely bright and, if decently taught, was scholarship material for university. I added that he wasn't my son and therefore he had to believe I wasn't saying this out of maternal blindness.

Mart went to see him, and agreed to go. In that one year he shot ahead, and while we were in America the news came that he'd got a scholarship for St John's, Oxford. I felt as pleased as if I *had* been his mother, and Kingsley was delighted. We had tried sending Philip to another tutor elsewhere, but he left after a few hours. Eventually he went to Camberwell School of Art where Sargy was now teaching.

The short lease on Maida Vale was beginning to worry me. The house belonged to the Eyre Estate, but when I asked them whether we'd be able to renew, they wouldn't agree. They said they didn't know what they were going to do with the property – it might be sold for redevelopment. In short they'd guarantee us nothing. Kingsley thought it might be good to live somewhere in the country, so we looked at various houses, none of which appealed to us.

Then I saw an advertisement in *Country Life* for a house on Hadley Common, outside Barnet, that was up for auction. Colin, Sargy and Martin came with us to look at it. It was a late-Georgian house facing the common on one side, and at its back had a large sloping garden with magnificent cedar woods and a meadow – nearly nine acres in all. There was a cottage, a derelict barn, garages and an enclosed sunny courtyard. There were eight bedrooms, three reception rooms and various offices. We looked at it, and went home for a family conference. Everybody was mad about it, including me, but I realized we couldn't afford more than token help, and it would take a great deal of work to run. I said this: the rest of the family looked at me pityingly – what a spoilsport. They'd all help and we must try to buy it. After a satisfactory survey, I rang our accountants and told them, also asking how much we could afford to bid for it. They said it sounded a cinch; they'd arrange a mortgage, and I might bid up to £57,000 in the auction. I decided that our best hope of getting the house at as low a price as possible was to employ an extremely experienced bidder, and we went to Humbert & Flint. I couldn't face going to the auction and we stayed at the end of the telephone, and duly received a call from our man saying he'd waited through early bidding, then made one bid and got the house for £48,000. Overjoyed, I rang our accountant. He replied that he was afraid the mortgage had fallen through, and he was off on holiday. We had bid, paid 10 per cent of the price, and in three weeks were bound to produce the balance.

I don't think any of the family realized how serious the situation had become. Kingsley's attitude to any family or financial crisis was to go on writing and take no notice. I rang our publisher, Tom Maschler, and it was through him that I met Anton Felton. He appeared that evening at Maida Vale and listened quietly to me while we ate vegetable soup in the kitchen. 'You *are* in a mess.'

'I know. I feel so angry with our accountants I want to sue them.'

'You could, but I shouldn't. Leave it to me and I'll see what I can do.'

Anton was also an accountant. He specialized in clients who were writers, and this was the beginning of a long and affectionate association with him as an accountant and a friend that has lasted until the present day. He found us a mortgage and from then on took over our affairs until he retired some fifteen years later.

The house needed rewiring, among much else, and Monkey undertook this with Martin as his assistant.

11

We moved in on 28 November 1968 to the usual confusion of bare boards, the hunt for a kettle and mugs and bedding among the daunting array of tea chests, and an abusive call from the new owner of Maida Vale saying how disgustingly dirty we'd left the house. When I said I'd had it especially cleaned after we left, she retorted there were marks on the walls where pictures had been – even in the kitchen. 'Perhaps she just doesn't go in for pictures,' Monkey said.

As we fell into bed that first night, Kingsley reminded me that we were due at the Bruces next day for a Thanksgiving lunch. David Bruce was the US ambassador then, and Evangeline was a wonderful hostess who gave enormous parties. But we had to dress up for them. I hadn't unpacked any clothes because there was nowhere clean to put them, and anyway I was longing to get the house workably straight. But Kingsley really wanted to go and so, of course we went.

The house had been called Gladsmuir, but we hated this name and I found among early papers that it had once been called Lemmons – presumably it had once been a farm owned by some-one of that name. So we reverted to Lemmons. We were to live there for the next eight years.

Lemmons was a large enterprise that very nearly succeeded. When we arrived, we were extremely short of help and the house needed a lot doing to it, and I, responsible for the family finances, was in a state of chronic anxiety about them. Writers don't get paid a regular wage. They have little or no idea what they will earn from one year to the next, but the basic expenses of a large house and jungloid garden are always there.

The help that had been promised by the family amounted to some lawn-mowing and occasional help with unpacking the enormous cheap bulk shopping that I did from time to time. I told them all at the outset that I couldn't iron, an arrant lie that was received calmly without criticism, but I found myself doing everything else.

I remember feeling constantly tired during those eight years; I used to fall asleep sitting upright in an armchair after dinner. However carefully I made lists and planned things, however hard I worked, I never caught up. Kingsley being unable to drive, and having absolutely nothing to do with our finances, meant I was a part-time secretary and chauffeur, as well as getting in food, cooking it and clearing it up.

Kingsley liked to have people to stay at weekends; the boys brought their girls and other friends so there would quite often be twelve or more round the table. After about two years my mother, no longer able to deal with living alone, came to live with us. Kingsley was very nice about this when I asked him, and even wrote her a letter saying how glad he was that she was coming, which pleased her enormously. I had a bathroom made adjoining a ground-floor bedroom that looked on to the courtyard.

We acquired a wonderful help in this house. To begin with, whenever we went away, whatever help we had defaulted, packed up, and disappeared on the day after they'd been paid. On one such occasion, Monkey found an ad in the local paper and answered it. Lilly Uniacke arrived. My brother had never interviewed anyone in his life, and his opening gambit wasn't promising: 'Mrs Uniacke, I hope you're not an old slag, because we've had enough of them.' She burst out laughing and assured him that she wasn't.

She was wonderful in every way, and particularly good with my mother who was becoming frail and needed more attention than I had time to give her. She moved into the cottage in the courtyard. We also found a very genteel person who ironed shirts twice a week, and a very nice gardener called Mr Mayhew, who came for three hours a week. Having this amazing garden, derelict when we arrived but showing signs of good Edwardian planting, rekindled my pleasure in gardening, and I made an old-fashioned rose garden, planted a number of trees and shrubs, and resuscitated the long south-east herbaceous border.

Gardening became a secret vice for me, a vice because I always felt guilty when I indulged in it, knowing that there were many other things I ought to be doing. It was increasingly difficult to find any time to write, and after I'd struggled through *Odd Girl Out* I found myself blocked. I was writing a piece each month for *Brides* magazine, working for Drusilla Beyfus who was a friend, but any serious writing seemed beyond me. I'd lost confidence as many of us do during the course of our writing lives. This had nothing directly to do with Kingsley, who was always attentive, honourably critical and encouraging. But indirectly it *did* have something to do with him. He'd joined both my agents and my publishers, whereupon I felt I had drifted into a position of second fiddle with both. My dear Peter Peters died very shortly after his eightieth birthday party, and in him I lost the only professional associate who really believed in me.

These feelings didn't break upon me suddenly, they seeped imperceptibly into my consciousness through a number of small things. For instance, we used to stay with a couple who'd been friends of mine and whenever we arrived there would be a small pile of books and articles Kingsley had written that our host wanted him to sign. But never, during the eighteen years I was with Kingsley, did he refer to the fact that I was also a writer. I concluded, of course, that this was because he thought nothing of me. There were a number of things like that that neither conferred nor even sustained confidence.

Eventually, I began trying to write short stories because as a medium they seemed suited to my lack of time and it wouldn't be such a big deal if I failed. But living, at times, with five men, and one woman who didn't much like me, left me feeling isolated. An aspect of feeling isolated is that one also feels responsible for it. Of course I was encouraged, even expected to be responsible, but conversely nobody finds responsible people entertaining or desirable. Kingsley wanted someone to lean on, to run all the boring parts of his life, but he found it difficult to like them. He'd been in love with me, and now he wasn't. Or perhaps it would be truer to say that he was beginning not to be.

I had two people to whom I could – at least, to some extent – talk about my difficulties. The first was Anton, who by chance happened to have a house on Hadley Green round the corner from us. He would come when I asked him. We'd go through whatever the current problems were about money or tax, and then he'd sit most patiently while I unloaded my anxieties or grievances or difficulties about the boys or their sister, Sally, who was inter-mittently back with us. He was utterly discreet, tactful and realistically sensible, always clear about when some particular problem could be solved, and when it couldn't. We were spending a phenomenal amount of money on drink, and this was Kingsley's sole responsibility in the household. He was drinking fairly heavily, although never until he'd finished his work. But still he was fairly often very drunk in the evenings – the only times that we were indisputably alone together. I didn't talk to Anton about that, but I dimly recognized that it was eroding all intimacy and affection.

The other supportive friend I had then was Victor Stiebel. Victor had reached the stage in his illness where he couldn't any longer go out. He was confined to his flat in Hyde Park Gardens, except once or twice a year when he was driven down to Brighton to stay with Dick Addinsell, a theatre and film composer famous for 'The Warsaw Concerto' in the film *Dangerous Moonlight*. He used to have a friend to lunch practically every day, and I was asked about every three weeks.

The routine was always the same. I'd drive there to arrive

punctually at one o'clock; we'd have one drink, and then his enormous Austrian housekeeper would produce our lunch, on two trays, usually consisting of poached fish followed by stewed apple and coffee. But visiting Victor was like going into the sun: he had an endless kindly curiosity about my life and family, and I always felt, if I wanted to, that I could confide in him.

I do remember one particular occasion when I was saying how difficult it was catering at weekends, as I never knew whether either or both of the boys were coming and, if so, who or how many they were bringing with them. He asked what Kingsley had to say about this.

'He said, "Why don't you simply cook enough food for twelve and stop bothering about it?"'

'And do you do that?'

I looked at him and shrugged. 'Sometimes.'

'Darling Jane, you could simply leave them to get their own food if they don't tell you when they're coming. But you always want to do things in the most difficult way, don't you?' It was so affectionately said that it really hit home. I realized that I saw these altercations as a challenge from which I had to emerge the hero. It was the first time I looked at myself from the outside and saw how much I colluded in, even encouraged these situations.

Victor never complained of his condition. He read, he listened to music, he had long telephone chats with friends. We used to talk about books and music and sometimes mutual friends. He wrote a book about his childhood in South Africa that occupied his attention and energy, and he was very excited when it was published. I look back now in some shame to think how much more I might have encouraged him with this. Only twice did I get a glimpse of the confines and misery of his life. Once he was staying with Dick and he said, 'You can't imagine how wonderful it was to see daffodils *growing* in the Park.' More poignantly he said on another occasion, not looking at me, 'Sometimes, at night, I *fall* out of bed and just have to stay there until morning when Miss Brandt comes in with my tea.' I felt so paralysed, so appalled by this sudden vision of his helplessness with all the concomitant discomfort – cold, stiffness and sheer bloody frustration – that I couldn't speak. He gave me a quick look and changed the subject. Why did I not have the kindness to say something so that he could speak of it further, as I now think he wanted to? I didn't know then that it isn't pity that people in such distress want, it's understanding. It felt like a repetition of my behaviour when my father died. I am still haunted by that lost opportunity.

We went to Prague after Dubček's fall, at the instigation of the British Council, to meet other writers, and Kingsley was to give a lecture. We took the train, as usual, and were met and installed in a hotel in the city centre. We were appointed a guide and a car with a chauffeur. The first intimation of conditions occurred when our guide said hurriedly as we left the hotel for the car, 'Please don't ask me any questions that are political.' Of course we didn't.

At home, Kingsley was one of the most disciplined workers I've ever known. No matter how bad a hangover he had in the morning, he would come down in his dressing-gown and eat breakfast – which he often made himself. He went through a stage of enormous fry-ups of almost anything he could find in the fridge or the larder. I remember Mart eyeing one of these one morning and saying, 'Dad! Your breakfasts are just a cry for help.'

The household was full of family jokes, imitations of people, fantastic stories of what had happened to them. Monkey's use of language and his eccentricity were deeply appreciated by Kingsley. He once came across Monkey in the bath doing a frightful caricaturish impression of a Glaswegian businessman, murmuring to himself, 'I strrrike a verrrry harrrd barrrgain.' Kingsley's faces – 'Sex life in Ancient Rome', Evelyn Waugh, Lord Halifax acknowledging the rather muted cheers of the crowd – were always being added to. Even my mother got marks for her impression of our genteel ironing lady, who managed to mince while she was ironing.

Kingsley loved sitting at the large table in our coach-house kitchen, arguing with his sons – he'd become wilfully right wing, nearly turning me into a socialist – and with Sargy, who loved arguments of almost any kind. Certain people set him off. Colin Welch, the journalist and critic, was one. One day, without warning, he and Kingsley improvised a Somerset Maugham radio play about tea planters in Malaysia. Colin's quiet, lugubrious voice was the isolated tea-planter's wife and Kingsley supplied all the explosive jungle noises that punctuated her ruminations on the native girl standing at the end of the garden with a baby in her arms – 'Who is that girl? I wish I was at home in dear old Cheltenham.' One day, when we were staying with Bruce Montgomery, who wrote music and thrillers and eventually died of drink, Kingsley suddenly enacted a whole B-feature wartime movie. It included a destroyer coming up the Thames directed by its Nazi captain, an air raid with anti-aircraft guns and bombs dropping, a refugee waiter letting off carrier pigeons from his window-sill, and triumphant German newscasts of the event. It went on for about twenty minutes and was a masterpiece – we cried with laughter. Sadly it was never repeated and there is no recording, as there is of his Roosevelt one.

Every Sunday, the boys and whatever guests were staying would go to the pub and come back for a late lunch, which I'd made. Kingsley never liked food with the exception, sometimes, of curry, so I made a good many of those. He disliked the authentic. 'This isn't very nice' would often be the pronouncement on any dish that had a homemade sauce as opposed to a bottled one.

His dislike of food, I learned, was largely because his mother had piled his plate when he was a child and made him eat everything on it. I began to see the dangerous frontiers he was forcing me to cross. Mum had made the food; he didn't want it. I made food and was imperceptibly turning into someone unnervingly like her. I noticed that as he drank more he ate less, and this worried me. Giving him presents was difficult as well. Drink, of course, was always acceptable and, for a time, records, but gradually he listened to less and less music. He told me that when he was about twelve and going to the City of London School, his parents gave him a satchel as their joint Christmas present, and he cried. 'It's *useful*,' he wept. I did once hit the jackpot when I gave him the Longer Oxford Dictionary, secondhand, but volumes and volumes. 'It's like being given a yacht!' he cried – delighted for once. He'd long stopped getting any pleasure out of giving me presents – usually asked Jack Ogden, a jeweller we knew, to find something for me. One was a little ring set with one cut garnet that I still wear.

Kingsley and I had both known John Betjeman separately and when we were at Lemmons he used to come and stay. He and 'good old Kingers', as he called Kingsley, made each other laugh all the time, and we – Sargy, Monkey, sometimes Mart and I – all got the benefit. 'I *am* enjoying myself!' was a habitual cry from John. Although this was true to some extent, he was someone who acted a role. He enlarged and dramatized the sunny aspect of his nature to conceal his intense anxiety of the other, always present, darker side. He and Kingsley used to do mock television interviews, with Kingsley asking earnest, daft questions. John invented a fictional neighbour of ours who had a downtrodden wife called Avril, and many notes and postcards were sent from and to her. I once spent two or three days with John while he filmed a documentary about Norfolk churches – I'd been commissioned to write a piece about it for the *Radio Times*. It was fascinating to see how quickly he got the unit working with him to feel amused, respectful and protective. The impression he gave was faintly clerical, sometimes raffish. He had a watchful melancholic eye and a beautiful voice, which might erupt suddenly into eldritch laughter.

When he'd started to be incapacitated by Parkinson's, I took him once to the Tate Gallery to look at the Turners. A wheelchair was waiting for him on arrival, and the gallery staff clearly knew and loved him. After we'd had our fill of pictures, he said he'd take me to lunch in the restaurant there. We went down to it in the lift, but as I wheeled him into the restaurant he suddenly said, rather loudly, 'Look at that disgusting old man in that chair! They shouldn't let them out when they're like that – really they shouldn't!' The whole room stopped eating and talking, and stared. 'Put me with my back to the wall, Avril, won't you?' It was a kind of pre-emptive strike against what I suppose he felt people thought of him.

The last time I saw him was when I went to tea with Elizabeth Cavendish, his companion and lover since 1951. He sat in an armchair and looked at me and murmured, 'No pain, no pain.' He was entirely, sometimes wildly, generous in spirit and heart as well as in ordinary practical ways. 'My greatest sin is guilt,' he remarked during our Norfolk sojourn.

More and more people came for weekends to Lemmons. Pat Kavanagh, our new literary agent at A. D. Peters, was a frequent visitor, and her partner at the time, Jim Durham, an Australian psychiatrist, came very often. The Welches, the Conquests, Paul Johnson and his wife, Marigold, Huw and Jay Wheldon, the Keeleys, and for one night Elizabeth Bowen. I remember taking her up breakfast in bed, and with one swift look at the tray, she said, 'You've forgotten the marmalade spoon.' Much in awe of her, I rushed down and got it. The Fussells and their children, Tucky and Sam, came – I remember one Christmas when we were twenty-five and overflowed into the cottage. Sam got chickenpox and sped about the upstairs landing like a small white greater-spotted ghost.

12

I don't know when, exactly, the premonition that all this was going to come to an end – was in some way doomed – came to me. The situation was masked in a way by drugs. Our doctor discovered me crying one Sunday morning when everybody else had gone to the pub and I was peeling innumerable potatoes. He prescribed Tryptosil and Valium in what today would be regarded as over-generous quantities. I stopped crying and slept heavily at night.

In the spring of 1972, still unable to start a novel, I went to interview Cecil Day-Lewis for a piece that Beatrix Miller had commissioned for *Queen*. I knew he hadn't been well, but I was horrified when I met him. He was sitting in an armchair in his study with a rug wrapped over his knees. He looked gaunt, had lost a lot of weight, and his face was grey. In short, he looked very ill. Jill brought us some coffee, then left us for the interview. This was long – I think two sides of a tape – and chiefly uneasy, because his illness so predominated in my mind that I could hardly think of anything else. He was a professional so we got through it, asking and answering questions about his work. I had lunch with them. He said he'd felt rotten for some time, had been in and out of hospital, but they didn't seem to know what was wrong.

I went home really worried. It was clear to me that if he got any worse the situation for Jill was going to become very difficult, if not impossible. Their house was all stairs, with the bedroom two flights up from the kitchen and a lavatory on a half-landing. If, therefore, he couldn't be nursed at home, he'd have to go to a hospital ward. I worried about him all the time I was getting supper, and when it was over, I went to my study and looked up the number of his GP in Greenwich – I knew his name because it had been mentioned several times that day. My mother, who'd recently broken her hip, had been nursed afterwards by Dosia's eldest daughter, Tessa. She was now well on the mend. I could move Cecil into her room. There would be a bathroom *en suite* and Tessa to hand if she agreed.

Which she did. I rang up the doctor, explained who I was and asked what he thought about Jill and Cecil coming to stay with us. 'If you can manage it, it would be the best possible thing for them both,' he said. I went to Kingsley and explained what I wanted to do. Kingsley had never been particularly fond of Cecil, but he was always generous about people in need of help, and he agreed readily. So did my mother. How to get Cecil and Jill there? Luck was on my side. When I rang Jill to thank her for the lunch, and ask how Cecil was, she said she'd been offered a week's work at Elstree, very near us, but she was worried about leaving Cecil all day. I asked her if they'd like to come to Lemmons so conveniently near her job. She'd ask him. He was delighted. The next day, we moved my mother upstairs, and prepared the room. Monkey installed a record player, and we put in flowers and books.

They came on a fine April day and he settled, taking to Tessa at once, as I had known he would. Here is something I wrote about him afterwards:

Nobody was better at getting the utmost pleasure from the simplest things as Cecil: a bunch of flowers, a toasted bun, a gramophone record (we left our catalogue with him so that he could order his records each evening for the following day), a piece of cherry cake, a new thriller that he'd not read before, various ice creams that Monkey kept in a deep freeze, the bird table outside his window, a chocolate, a piece of sweet-smelling soap, a herb pillow, being read to – Jill excelled at that, but if she was working or cooking him something he sometimes fell back on me. One of the few really fine days he went round the garden in my mother's electric chair: magic, he said. On reasonably sunny days, he would bask in the courtyard, watching the trees, that were beginning to leaf and flower.

After a week, I asked him if he would like to stay longer. 'I should like to stay for months, and I'm very anxious to give Jill a rest,' he said. It was agreed then that he should stay as long as he liked. During the second week he asked Jill to get him a cheap notebook, as he said he wanted to write a poem for the household.

I asked him after a day or two how it was going, and he said it was difficult to work on a quarter of a cylinder. When it was finished Jill gave us each a copy. When I showed it to Kingsley, he wept, but apart from what it seemed to tell him, he said objectively that it was a bloody good poem.

AT LEMMONS

Above my table three magnolia flowers
Utter their silent requiems.
Through the window I see your elms
In labour with the racking storm
Giving it shape in April's shifty airs.

Up there sky boils from a brew of cloud
To blue gleam, sunblast, then darkens again.
No respite is allowed
The watching eye, the natural agony.

Below is the calm a loved house breeds
Where four have come together to dwell
– Two write, one paints, the fourth invents –
Each pursuing a natural bent

But less through nature's formative travail
Than each in his own humour finding the self he needs.

Round me all is amenity, a bloom of
Magnolia uttering its requiems,
A climate of acceptance. Very well
I accept my weakness with my friends'
Good natures sweetening every day in my sick room.

C. Day Lewis. For Jane, Kingsley, Colin and Sargy
with much love.

Kingsley had become increasingly fond and admiring of Cecil, and used to drop in to have an evening drink with him. Cecil would implore him not to do or tell one more funny thing as Kingsley made him laugh so much he thought he'd have a heart attack. We celebrated three birthdays in his room: first Kingsley's, then Cecil's and then his son, Daniel's. I think his own gave him pleasure. He sat, beautifully dressed as always – he had the looks and presence to carry this off until the end – and we piled his bed with presents. He opened each one with either gallantly feigned, or perhaps true and simple, excitement.

He saw nearly all of his oldest and closest friends during the last six weeks. He grew visibly weaker and at times had periods of great melancholy, almost despair, but he always tried to conceal them and his spirit remained undimmed. He never complained and he never lost his courtesy and consideration for those around him. He did not discuss his illness and we all felt that if he wanted us to talk about it, he would have asked. One day, when I'd finished reading to him, he said, 'You've been remarkably kind to me.' And not looking up from the book I said, 'I do love you, you know.' There was a silence, and when I did look up I saw he was regarding me steadily. 'I know,' he said. And at once, all the guilt, the bitterness, the folly fell away, and we became – as really we should always have been – loving friends.

There came a weekend when Tessa was off for two days, when Mrs Uniacke was having *her* weekend off, the local doctor who'd been looking after Cecil was having *his* weekend off, and Jill and I were on our own. On Friday, he was very low and ill, but when Jill put him to bed he said, 'I've had a *lovely* day.' By Saturday morning things were certainly no better, and Tessa said she'd come back at once. With a burst of inspiration I rang up Ursula Vaughan Williams. I didn't know her then, but I knew that Jill loved her and that she had a unique reputation for being the right person for anyone in dire need. She came at once, and she was.

My daughter, her then husband and their three children were coming to Sunday lunch from Gloucestershire. By the time I had realized that this wasn't going to be the best day for it, they were already on their way.

I saw very little of Cecil on Sunday, but after my family had gone I went in to him and asked him if he would like some tea. 'It would be bliss.' He drank from a small mug with a bendy straw and lay back and closed his eyes. As Jill was snatching a few moments of much-needed rest and we weren't leaving him alone by then, I settled down to read. He said, 'When are you going to begin?' We'd abandoned *Emma* for *Pride and Prejudice*. I read him a chapter, and I thought he'd gone to sleep. 'Read me one more chapter.' When I'd read this, he said, 'Marvellous stuff,' and then slept a little. Tessa came back. Tamasin was there. Monkey fetched Dan from the station. Sean, Cecil's eldest son, arrived. During that long night's vigil, we held his hand in turn and loved him through his dying. He slipped so quietly away from us that we hardly knew. He said once that he didn't fear death but rather the act of dying, and I hope that in return for all his courage and endurance, that night, at any rate, he was spared the fear.

He was buried near Thomas Hardy at Stinsford in Dorset. It was a quiet and private funeral. Jill gave him a chaplet of laurels made of leaves from our garden, and so he was left, crowned, beside one of the poets he'd loved most.

For some days after that, none of us wanted the outside world. Ursula went home, Dan went back to school, and Tammy, I think, to Cambridge, but for the rest, the house enclosed us kindly while we absorbed the shock.

A week or two later, the Spenders invited Jill and me to stay for two weeks in their house in France. It was an uneasy two weeks, although I felt that the Spenders were kind in just the right way. For Jill, I think it was a very hard time. She was physically and emotionally exhausted, and for her I can only imagine that it used up some of the agonizing time to be got through. Shock is not always something that happens suddenly to people, it's more often the actuality of something they have long dreaded. It was the first time I'd been away without Kingsley since we married. Harold Evans asked me to write a piece about Cecil for the *Sunday Times* and I agreed, largely because one or two people had written spitefully about his work during the months before he died, and I wanted to set the record straight. Jill agreed to this, and I finished it while we were in France. It was well received and got many letters – including a bitter missive from Rosamond Lehmann, accusing me, amongst other things, of deliberately choosing the worst possible picture of Cecil. It was taken when he was already ill – a family group with Jill and the children. I wrote back briefly saying I was sorry the piece had upset her, and that I'd no control over what pictures the paper used for the piece.

All that summer, apart from writing a few short stories and doing my stint for *Brides* magazine, I was working on the programme for a festival in Salisbury. My friend Geraint Jones was to do the music, and I the rest. It was the first festival of arts to take place there, and it meant that the problems of mounting it were ten times as difficult as they had been in Cheltenham. For some reason, the slightest whiff of any festival brings all the amateurs out of the woodwork. Geraint and I had to remain firm about this.

If there was to be a festival that people would come any distance to visit, it had to have professional – even international – artists in its programme. As Geraint repeatedly and patiently said, there was nothing to stop the local amateur societies from organizing opportunities for their performances at other times of the year. If we were to get Arts Council backing, or indeed any outside backing, we had to produce a programme that would interest them enough to help finance it.

Geraint did marvellously well. He conducted Handel's oratorio, *Jephtha*, which had first been performed in Salisbury Cathedral and which Handel had written in the gatehouse to the cathedral. I got a friend to collect and arrange an exhibition of Handeliana in the gatehouse. Walter Klein gave a Mozart recital. I got Angus Wilson to give a lecture on Dickens. Geraint imported Paco Peña, a wonderful Spanish group who played and danced. Robin Ray produced a theatre programme, aided by Colin Welch's wife, Sybil, in the Playhouse. Princess Alexandra agreed to be our patron and to come and open the festival.

I arranged that Sargy Mann should have his first exhibition, a joint one with Patrick Procktor, a friend of Cecil Beaton, with whom I went to stay to talk about the programme. Ralph Kirkpatrick was to give a recital of Scarlatti sonatas in the double cube room at Wilton.

We arranged a Festival Club, and our kind wine merchant, Christopher Leaver, organized a hogshead of decent red wine. Geraint, Winnie, his wife and a marvellous violinist, and I took a cottage at Broadchalke where we and Ralph would stay. It was very hard work, but in spite of some setbacks, the festival had its high points, chief of which was Ralph's recital which was magical. He said afterwards it was the best room for sound that he'd ever played in. When it came to an encore, he played my favourite sonata of all in my honour, one of the nicest compliments I've had in my life.

The Salisbury Festival is now a large and very successful event, but that was the beginning of it. I became very attached to Ralph. It was said that when he met the Pope and was kissing his hand, he had an uncontrollable desire to bite it as he suddenly saw the interesting headline 'Man Bites Pope' as a welcome change from 'Man Bites Dog'.

Kingsley became very fond of Geraint and Winnie. Geraint had all the Welsh love of language and, besides being a very good organist and harpsichord player, he was a conductor for the Kirkman concerts for many years. Winnie, a fine musician in her own right, had, and still has that bewitching charm that comes from being directly and always herself. They lived near us, in Arkley, and we saw them regularly while we were at Lemmons. Once we went with them to Normandy for a short holiday. They had a caravan in which they slept and Kingsley and I slept in various hotels along the way. This was one of the last few holidays we had abroad together: Kingsley said he didn't like travelling, or abroad, and preferred to stay at home.

And then, shortly after her eightieth birthday, my mother died. She'd been slowly diminishing for months and hardly ever left her room or, eventually, her bed. It became increasingly difficult for me to communicate with her, because an awful artificiality had set in. When I went into her room, she'd turn off her radio and smile – a rictus – displaying a pleasure that she, poor thing, evidently didn't feel in the least. She talked a good deal about her death, but in a way that I found it hard to respond to – my death talk on her terms quickly ran out. I felt pity for her, for her bitterly unsatisfactory life, and for her – she thought hidden – resentment. She resented any time I didn't spend with her, feeling neglected. She told my older visiting brother that I never gave her lunch, which was nonsense, but she was convincing enough for him to confront me seriously. She read a great deal, had taught herself Russian when she was about seventy in order to read the great novelists in that language. She was too rheumatic to use her hands much, but she crocheted vast lovely blankets and shawls. Her memory was, I thought sometimes, wilfully selective. She'd say, 'I haven't seen you for *days*,' when I brought her lunch, having brought her breakfast earlier the same day and sat with her the evening before. She resented all the people coming to the house, who she rightly thought deflected attention from her, and she often said, 'Why do you *do* it?' When I said Kingsley liked them to come, she changed the subject. Kingsley resented the amount of time I spent with her, so whatever I did someone was displeased.

My mother had few friends. She'd really always preferred the family – particularly her own – although she was also fond of many of the Howards. But she had only one remaining brother now who lived in Westmorland. He used to come down about once a year to stay a few days, and one or two faithful old cousins made the journey too. She was terrified of Philip and Martin, and though she enjoyed Kingsley's company when he dropped in for an evening drink with her, she felt she bored him and I'm afraid she was right. Self-pity was her stumbling block. It was as though she was coated in it, like flypaper, we got stuck on the outside, and were paralysed – like flies – unable to penetrate further. Sometimes I used to feel unbearably sorry for her, and the next minute exasperated, repelled. Monkey bore his half of the brunt, and although she loved him, it was never enough. Her chief consolation was my old Siamese cat, Hugo, who had a good deal of time to spare, and spent it all with her. He sat on her bed all day in the attitude of a roast chicken and love passed easily between them – she had only to touch him and his purr, like the starting up of a distant lorry, would gratifyingly begin.

Then, one weekend, when half a dozen people were staying with us, and Mrs Uniacke was having her weekend off, and I had taken her breakfast, I discovered she'd been incontinent – something that had never happened before. It caused her agonizing shame and disgust. Monkey and I lifted her into a chair, and remade her bed, saying that it didn't matter, it happened to lots of people, it was just a piece of bad luck, but I could see that she wasn't comforted. We stayed with her while she had breakfast and she cheered up a bit.

Outside her room when the door was shut, Monkey and I looked at each other. Monkey said, '*Poor* Mum.'

'I know. She always said the two things she dreaded most were senility and incontinence. She's far from senile.'

'I should think that would simply make her mind the other thing more.' We decided that we ought to tell her doctor because, apart from anything else, she *looked* so ill.

I'd never liked my mother's doctor, but she did, so it had been pointless to say so. She didn't turn up until about seven in the evening, and then she was in no good mood.

'What's all this I hear?' She bent over my mother and listened to her heart for a minute or two. 'There's nothing wrong with you. You've got a perfectly good commode. Why on earth didn't you use that?' My mother didn't reply, simply gazed up at the doctor with frightened eyes. 'Let's see you get on it now. Go on. You know you can jolly well do it if you try.'

Speechless, my mother began to struggle out of bed. I began, 'Doctor, I really don't think—'

She interrupted me. 'Leave it to me.' Then, to my mother, 'You see? You can, when you can be bothered to try.'

It's to my eternal shame that I didn't turn on the doctor then – why didn't I? I didn't want to have a row with her in front of my mother, who was distressed enough. But I suspect that cowardice came into it as well. There must have been a way of shutting her up *without* a row but I didn't know how to.

The doctor told my mother to take a Valium and left. She had other calls to make, she said, and it was supposed to be her Saturday off. My mother murmured an apology, but she was breathless from her efforts. As soon as she'd gone, I helped my mother get back into bed, and rearranged her pillow so that she could sit upright, which she preferred. I got her the Valium and kissed her when she'd taken it. She was still trembling. 'She shouldn't have made you do that. If you want another pee, you ring your bell and *I'll* come,' I said, and then that I was going to get her evening whisky, and that when I'd cut the meat and served dinner, I'd make her a hot milky drink and stay with her while she drank it.

'You're a good little nurse,' she said. It was the nicest thing she'd said to me for – oh, years, and tears were hot in my eyes. I got the whisky, served dinner, then heated some milk with Horlicks. When I took it in to her, she was dead. I picked up her small frail wrist, there was no pulse – but, anyway, I *knew* she was dead.

The knowledge that she'd died entirely alone, that I hadn't been there to hold her hand, to comfort her, was one of the most painful experiences of my life. I picked up her barely warm hand again to hold it now. Countless fragments of her life – or, rather, what I knew of it – flitted through my mind with soundless speed. I thought of her lying on the sofa at Lansdowne Road, crying from the pain and shock of having all her teeth out; of her dancing to me suddenly in the drawing room – pent-up frustration translated into an amazing grace and beauty. I remembered her reading aloud to me from Austen and Dickens, of being her lady's maid when she dressed up for parties. She told me once – how did she manage to speak of it? – of seeing a man undo his trousers when he met her as a little girl in the street. Diaghilev had told her once that the ugliest part of a woman was her knees but that hers were beautiful. I thought of her gentleness and care when she dressed my six-year-old cousin Robert's hand after it was shut in a car door, of her making me jump small jumps bareback on the pony with my arms folded, and falling off and having to do it again. I thought, too, of her teaching me bar exercises with a riding whip, how different she looked when she laughed, and the smell of her skin – Earl Grey tea with a touch of lemon. I remembered her voice when Nana had her stroke and she knelt on the floor with her in her arms – the tenderness, the love. I'd never heard her speak like that before – 'You're a good little nurse . . .' I had that. She'd not known then that I was going to fail her when she said it. I kissed her hand and laid it back where it had been on her breast, and went to ring the doctor.

The undertaker asked me whether I wished Mother to lie in the Chapel of Peace, but I said no: I wanted her to stay in her own room until the funeral. He approved of that. 'The modern ones send them off nowadays at once.'

So for a week she lay in her coffin in a white shroud with a loose ruffle round the neck, and Mrs Uniacke and I dusted the room and put flowers in it and talked about her. Once I said something about how the room smelt of violets, when we had none to pick. 'It's your mother,' Mrs Uniacke replied. 'They always get like that.' I thought of the stories of saints smelling of violets and wondered briefly how people could distinguish between sanctity and decay. I really could not think about anything, and yet the moment my mind was empty it was filled with waves of self-recrimination. I kept trying to imagine whether she'd *known* she was dying, and if so why she hadn't rung her bell. Perhaps she didn't have time . . . It was my fault for leaving her.

I asked my aunt Helen to come to the funeral and stay the night with us, and of course she came. She'd been fond of my mother, and I wanted there to be at least someone of her own generation who'd known and cared about her. It was a comfort to me. Kingsley was kind, but I knew he felt nothing but relief. I asked Monkey what he felt and he said, 'Nothing.' He'd had the hardest time with her, as he'd lost our father when our parents separated and our mother had leaned on him to an unbearable degree. So it was with Mrs Uniacke that I went to scatter her ashes in the small churchyard at Hadley.

For months after that, I was haunted by all the small unkindnesses I'd inflicted, most by default. She, like most people confined, longed to get out, and sometimes suggested that we go for little drives in the afternoon, but there always seemed to be something else I thought I should do. How often had I staggered in with her breakfast tray, ungracious and clearly cross at having to get up so early? I think the worst time, and there is no excuse for it, was when I told her she'd been drinking too much when she fell on the fitted carpet and turned out to have broken her hip. It hadn't been her fault, Kingsley always made very strong drinks. It had been her birthday party and I'd bought her a long black velvet dress with a lace collar in which she looked very distinguished. The Maudlings had come to dinner, Reginald was Home Secretary at the time; they were nice to her and, enjoying herself, she can't have noticed how much she had drunk. But that is what I said when she asked me how on earth she could have fallen down. I remember her stricken look and her silence, and also her courage when my brother and I lifted her into bed, which clearly gave her agonizing pain. She simply gave a little gasp and didn't cry out. All those years, when I was a child, I'd loved her, and when she became old and needed my love, I'd failed her.

I began to understand that love is neither a conditional business nor an ever-fixed mark by arrangement. People always know somewhere inside them if they are not loved. No gestures, talk, conciliation, pronouncements can prevail over that deep instinctual knowledge. So she'd known that of me, and to some extent I think it must have been mutual. After her death when I was clearing up her papers, I found that she'd kept many letters from both of my brothers, but not one from me.

This was the time when I began to know that Kingsley no longer loved me and, curiously, I think this failure on his part was as painful for him as it was for me. He needed me, but he no longer wanted me. There were still calmly comfortable times together, but they were increasingly dependent upon the company of other people. Alone, he hadn't much to say to me, and his discomfort led to endless criticism. It was my fault that he no longer wanted to go to bed with me, my fault if we were late arriving somewhere, and my fault if I wanted to go home from a party before he did. Once, driving back at about two a.m., he suddenly said, 'You're driving on the *wrong* side of the road.' I said I wasn't. The drink and driving laws were dangerously lax in those days, but I didn't like getting drunk, and was always careful when I knew I had to drive back.

'You *are*. You *always* have to be right, don't you?' Before I could say anything, he seized the wheel and wrenched the car to the right-hand side of the road. I'd braked, but the car spun round so that we were facing the right-hand ditch. If a car had come round the corner it wouldn't have been able to avoid hitting us.

I took his hand off the wheel. 'Shut up or I won't drive at all.'

I had to reverse back to the left-hand side of the road and we proceeded in silence until he said, 'Perhaps you're right.'

It was this sort of thing I dreaded. Then something else happened that dominated the next several months.

13

Kingsley had met Elizabeth Taylor as briefly as I had, but he appreciated and admired her writing as much as I did. The Taylors invited us over to Penn in Buckinghamshire where they lived. We were to go to lunch. We had drinks in their garden, and John, Kingsley remarked approvingly, was very good at making them. John had been a sweet manufacturer but was now retired. He was a bluff, totally unintellectual man whose favourite occupation was felling trees and chopping them up. They had two grown-up children. Kingsley also got on with Elizabeth. I have always felt shy with artists whom I very much admired – Sybille Bedford and Peggy Ashcroft are two who come to mind – and this made me alternate between silence and banality. None the less, it was a very pleasant day. They told us that they always went to separate pubs in the evening, as Elizabeth liked to sit quietly listening to the pub talk.

Quite soon after this they came to spend the day with us. Elizabeth and I went blackberrying in our meadow, which she loved – she'd not done it for years. Later in the year, they came to lunch. Kingsley took Elizabeth into the drawing room for drinks, but John followed me into the kitchen. 'Liz has got cancer. I just thought you ought to know,' he said. His tone was matter-of-fact. 'Now. Are you going to join us for drinks?' In a minute, I said. I felt faint with anxiety. Nothing more was said.

They had lunch and went home at about five o'clock. As soon as they'd gone I told Kingsley, who was horrified. I couldn't imagine how John would manage to look after her when she got really ill and what could we do? Kingsley put his arms round me, and said, 'Anything you like.' There were tears in his eyes. Most of us then thought that cancer spelled death.

I started writing to her. She loved overheard sayings – anything faintly ridiculous. We had an old builder who suddenly said to me one day, 'I had a friend who accidentally had a letter from Poland.' She loved that kind of thing. She was in hospital for a time, and when she came out I asked if they'd like to come for a weekend. I spoke to John, who said she was better but still weak from the treatment and would need to spend a lot of time in bed. We agreed that I should put her in the room on the ground floor. I remember hunting in antiques shops for the right jug to put flowers in her room. I found it: a pale lavender blue embossed with white china feathers. During that weekend she told me that she'd had a breast off. 'Imagine if it'd been the other Elizabeth Taylor's breast,' she said. 'It would be headline news.' The weekend went well; they didn't have to think about food and Liz rested and said it had been lovely. A repeat visit was arranged, but half an hour after they were due, John rang me: 'I'm afraid the weekend is off. We got as far as your drive, but then Liz was frightfully sick.'

After that, I used to go over to see her. She had a remission, and John was taking her for a trip abroad. They'd drive: she adored his old Bristol and was looking forward to it.

I'd just published my collection of short stories *Mr Wrong,* which I'd dedicated to her. I posted her the first copy, which she got just before they left. She wrote me a long letter about it, and John said she burst into tears when she saw the dedication. But she wrote again from France, saying that she'd had to give up the holiday. Her back hurt so much that she could hardly walk or enjoy anything. They were starting back that evening.

The last time I saw her she was in bed, very pale but her beautiful eyes sparkled with a wry amusement at the slightest sign of a joke. While I was there, the window cleaner came to do the windows of her bedroom. 'You look nice and cosy in there.' 'Why don't you pop in with me?' She'd knitted me an enormous beige muffler. 'Not a very interesting present, but there is love in every stitch,' she said. Not long before, when she'd still been able to get up, she made me a risotto for lunch, and as I ate it I realized what a heroic effort it must have been.

She died soon after that. John rang me to tell us, and asked if Kingsley would say something at her funeral. This he did extremely well: it was, indeed, the best thing about the service. Afterwards there was tea and drinks at their house, but I found I couldn't bear to be with people, and went upstairs and sat on her bed.

She'd struggled during that last year to finish her last novel, *Blaming*, and Kingsley reviewed it for the *Observer*. Here is something he wrote about her:

> Outside her family and friends her death wasn't much noticed except among the smallish band who care for our literature. Her genuine distaste for any kind of publicity – that rarest of qualities in a writer – and her deeply unsensational style and subject matter saw to it, that in life, she never received her due as one of the best English novelists born in this century. I hope she will in the future.

Soon after her death John asked me if I'd write her biography. I refused because – among many of her Austen traits – she led a life that contained very little incident. She'd asked Robert Liddell, the great friend of Barbara Pym and expert on the novels of Ivy Compton-Burnett, with whom she had corresponded most, to destroy the correspondence. I miss her still, and in particular feel deprived of all the novels she didn't have the time to write. It was after her death that I got to know her daughter, Joanna, and we can talk about her sometimes to our mutual comfort.

After *Mr Wrong*, I seemed to dry up. I still wrote my piece for Drusilla Beyfus every month, but otherwise seemed to have no capacity to write. I remember standing at the kitchen sink one day thinking, I can't really be unhappy, because I never cry nowadays. I was so full of Valium and Tryptosil that I can't now imagine how I managed to drive, especially late at night after a long day. The thought occurred again that we'd not be staying at Lemmons. I'd no particular reason to think this, but it filled me with terror. My greatest solace then was the immense, ill-kept but beautiful rambling garden. I'd planted a good many trees, and attempted to bring some order to one of the borders, and there was the rose garden and the majestic cedar; the idea that I must leave all this was more than I could bear to contemplate. I dismissed the notion as fanciful and morbid.

It was about then that we went on a short holiday to Italy with Jim Durham, who'd recently married another Australian doctor called Nita. Kingsley had become much attached to Jim whom he not only found good company, but whom – more unusually – he listened to and trusted. I'd once heard Jim remark that no woman over thirty-five was of much, if any, sexual interest and he implied that such women weren't worth having any real conversation with. He also said he never read novels written by people he knew, in case he found he didn't like them. Naturally he'd read Kingsley's as he'd been reading them before he knew us. It seemed a silly point to me but my self-esteem was at rock bottom anyway.

He'd taken his car for the journey, and when I offered to take my turn at the considerable driving involved he turned me down. He and Nita did that. I felt like an anonymous outsider. Kingsley had always said he had no interest in buildings or pictures, which we were going to Rome to see. With Jim his attitude to these pleasures changed and he became enthusiastic. Jim was only too pleased to take him round and tell him about everything he was to see.

All my life, I have never wanted to be told anything about a picture before I have seen it. I need to have my own first impression to myself. So, in galleries I left them to it, and went round on my own. I'm sure this was taken as me being contrary and sulking, but the situation was such – Kingsley spent all his time talking to Jim, and Nita was wrapped up in the new-found happiness of marriage – that to be on my own was a relief. I was also, I realize now, physically and mentally worn out when we went on this journey. But I was glad that Kingsley actually wanted to go abroad again, and knew that he wouldn't go without me: he needed, however grumpily, to take me for granted.

Jim was clearly trying to help Kingsley both with his phobias and his loss of libido. To aid the latter, he suggested that he go to a sex therapist and, to my surprise, Kingsley agreed. After he'd been three or four times, he said she'd asked to see me. I went. She was an interesting mixture of shrewdness and naivety, and after a few minutes exclaimed, 'From all I've heard about you, I thought you were going to be simply *awful*, and you're not, are you?' I said I didn't know. There were one or two more sessions with the three of us. Then she asked to see me again. She asked me what I wanted, and I heard myself saying I wanted to stop smoking. 'I know just the person for that,' she said.

And so began my experience of psychotherapy. Once a week I went to a basement flat in South Kensington to spend exactly one hour with a young woman, Kate Hopkinson, who was about the same age as my daughter. We discussed my addiction – why I wanted to smoke and what it did for me. I was fifty-three years old.

When I'd been going to her for three or four weeks, Kingsley said it had been suggested to him by his therapist that it would be a good idea if we went away for a long weekend with our dog Rosie. We found a hotel at Woodstock that was prepared to take dogs and Kingsley wrote to Iris and John Bayley to say that we should be in their neighbourhood. They asked us to dine and stay the night with them at Steeple Aston. The day before we were to set off, Victor Stiebel rang and asked if I'd lunch with him the following day, Friday. He usually arranged our meetings with some notice, and I intuited that there was some reason for this sudden invitation, nevertheless I felt I couldn't postpone the weekend and said how sorry I was I couldn't come. 'Of course you must go. Never mind, darling Jane. Goodbye.' And he rang off.

The evening with Iris and John was extremely enjoyable. They'd invited others to dine with us, of whom I only remember Tony Quinton, the philosopher – an old acquaintance of Kingsley, whom he was very glad to see again. The house was fascinating. The short drive descended to the front door. It was winter, and each time the door opened, dead leaves wafted inside. They'd reached half-way up the stairs where they lolled amongst small piles of books that were, like the leaves, presumably in transit from one floor to another. The ground-floor rooms, of which there were several, all contained trays with table legs, upon which teapots, shells of boiled eggs, intractably old pieces of toast or open copies of Dickens were propped against milk jugs. 'We don't wash up until we've used everything,' John remarked.

He took me into the garden to show me his birthday present for Iris. We entered a largish greenhouse. If you sneezed, it felt as though a piece of glass would fall discreetly to the ground. At one end there was a circular tub, about twelve feet in diameter. It was full of black, silent water. 'Iris loves swimming,' John explained, 'so I had this pool built for her.' Apart from the black, uninviting water, I worked out that if the gallant Iris got into it, she'd be able to swim precisely two strokes before she reached the other side. 'What do you think of it?' His complaisance was such that I had to admire it.

We left the following morning, installed ourselves in the hotel, and went for a beautiful winter walk in Blenheim Park.

This was my last most truly happy time with Kingsley. He was relaxed, affectionate, funny, communicative, said how much he was enjoying being alone with me, and that we should do this sort of thing regularly. It was like old times – not the breathless beginning but something that held the promise of endurance, of an honest and companionable future. I went to bed feeling lighter than I had for years.

The next morning we had breakfast in the dining room.

Kingsley had bought *The Times*, and after a few moments' reading, he handed me a page, and I read that Victor had died the night before. 'I'm so sorry, Min.'

The shock was so violent, so horribly unexpected that for a moment I felt stunned. I read the piece again, remembered I was in a public place with people all around me eating breakfast and said I'd go to our room to ring Victor's housekeeper.

I don't know why, but my first thoughts were of her. She must have gone into his room and found him.

'Oh, Miss Howard! The shock! I'd given Mr Stiebel his dinner and when I put him to bed and was going he called me back and said, "Miss Brandt, I want to thank you for all you have done for me. You have been wonderful. Wonderful," Miss Howard, and I never guessed that they would be the last words he would ever say to me. And he was so fond of you!'

When I'd reassured myself that she had people with her, and said how good she'd been, we said goodbye, and I collapsed on the floor by the bed. My dear friend! I remembered going with him to Covent Garden when they'd carried him to his seat – the last time, I think, that he was able to go – and the time before that, when he'd gone to the theatre and sat in a box with Dick to see *Hello Dolly!* and the star had sung, 'Hello, Victor, we're so glad to see you back . . .' and how it had pleased him. The extraordinary unobtrusive courage with which he'd dealt with the awful restrictions multiple sclerosis imposed so that visiting him was a gift to the visitor; his interest in people, in music and books never waned. I remembered his saying lightly, apropos of nothing that had gone before, 'One day I shall stop.' Then I realized that he'd wanted to say goodbye to me and I'd not responded.

Kingsley was kind about Victor because he knew I'd been fond of him, but I also knew that he'd no idea how much of a loss his death was to me, and I felt that our rapport was too fragile for me to express it. We went to Oxford to see Catherine and Anthony Storr, the psychiatrist and author, and nothing more was said between us about Victor.

The following week, Mrs Hopkinson opened the session by asking me how the weekend had gone. I started to tell her about the walk in Blenheim, and about Victor dying, and then without any warning, I was sobbing uncontrollably. It felt like a dam bursting – a great weight of grief pouring from the fathoms out of my heart. Present grief for Victor, past grief either unacknowledged, or only partly acknowledged until now. I cried for Liz, for my mother, for Cecil, for my father, for Sam, for Charles, for Derek, for Julian, all friends killed in the war, for my grandfather, for Margaret Jennings, the little girl who'd fallen out of the window when I was nine years old. And I cried again for my mother, for the loss of her love and mine. I must have cried for the best part of the hour, and during it Mrs Hopkinson sat quietly. She didn't try to comfort me, or make any attempt to stop me, but gradually, through this swamp of grief, I recognized her attention and was grateful to the point of love for it.

After that, smoking was no longer the main issue, although it wasn't dropped. I developed a heavy transference, turning Mrs Hopkinson into my mother or, rather, into the mother I should have liked to have. For those not cognizant of therapy, transference is a kind of primary cliché; some therapists work with it, some don't. It's a condition that people who have not suffered it tend to dismiss with a more or less kindly patronage, bordering on contempt – rather like gout or piles or hot flushes are often the subject of jokes. In fact, it is one of the most painful experiences, not least because the subject doesn't, for some time, understand what is going on. I was a slow learner in this as in almost everything else.

Transference is like being in love – hopelessly so, because it can't be reciprocated. If the therapist is of the opposite sex, sexual desire may be added to the anguish. Fortunately I was spared that. It took me weeks to recognize what was going on, and recognition didn't make it immediately easier. My self-esteem was non-existent. I realized this when Mrs Hopkinson asked me what was good about me. After a frantic mental search I said I thought I was reliable. Going home after the session I thought that even this wasn't true. I'd not written any fiction since *Mr Wrong* and had instead compiled an anthology, *A Companion for Lovers*, which didn't count as real writing to me.

Kingsley was bored by his sex therapy and became more sceptical about mine. He resented the status quo, but wasn't further prepared to make any change. This was when I recognized I *did* want to change. I wanted to understand how I'd become this abject, unfruitful creature.

While all this was going on other things were happening.

Nicola's first marriage broke up during this time. I'd realized from when I went to Condicote, her home in Gloucestershire, that all was far from well, but those were days when she didn't confide in me and I was afraid to ask her outright. But I particularly remember a time when I stayed there and she was in a state of defiant excitement. She wore the same pair of dilapidated trousers day after day, and when I said something about this she replied, 'I haven't got anything else to wear.' She was painting the kitchen with some help from all three children. There was a lot of tension in the house – and I noticed that she and Kip spoke to each other as careful strangers.

Shortly after this, Phil rang me up and said Nicola wasn't well, and that she and Pete were taking her on one of the nature cruises at which Pete used to lecture.

When she returned, having very much enjoyed the cruise, she left Kip. Eventually, he bought her a cottage very near Condicote. There was a divorce and Daniel opted to go with her, and the girls to stay with their father. But, again, it was clear that she didn't want me to be closely involved in any of this, and I reflected sadly that, after her childhood, how could I expect that she would?

One Sunday morning, after we'd seen the Fussells off to America, Kingsley shut the front door and said, 'I don't want to live here any more. It's too bloody cut off. I want to go back to London.'

I suppose it wasn't the great shock to me that it immediately seemed. I'd known that Lemmons would come to an end and that London would be the alternative. I didn't in the least want to leave the house or, even more, the garden, but I thought it wasn't fair for two people to live where one of them didn't want to. I thought also that if we *did* move, Kingsley would be happier and therefore so should I. I took the precaution of asking where precisely in London did he want to be? The answer was uncharacteristically clear. He wanted to be within five minutes' walk of Hampstead tube station – otherwise he didn't care what the place was like.

We put Lemmons on the market and Monkey came house-hunting with me in Hampstead. We had been told by estate agents that Lemmons should fetch about £125,000 and therefore must look at houses that were under £100,000. There weren't many houses within the five-minute radius of the tube, and we'd soon seen them all. They were either too expensive, or horrible. Mean-while, many people came to view Lemmons, largely out of curiosity to see where Kingsley lived. Eventually, after some false starts, somebody made the right offer. We agreed to drop the price by £15,000.

Monkey and I found what we thought would be the perfect house in Flask Walk built in the eighteenth century by a man called Gardnor, who'd managed the springs in Well Walk – Hampstead had once had the same reputation as Cheltenham and Harrogate for its health-going waters. Because of its age, I employed a well-thought-of surveyor, who said the architraves round the window on the back of the house required rebuilding but that otherwise there wasn't much that needed to be done.

So then we moved. Martin's story in his admirable book *Experience* isn't quite accurate about this, for he thought I was trying to be a martyr by not using professional movers. Actually my daughter Nicola, who knew how much I minded leaving, rallied round with the wife of a friend of Sargy's, Jane Raybould. Jane said, 'We've had a lot of pleasure staying with you, and we want to do something back.' I agreed largely because, apart from being touched by their offer, I really didn't care as I was so upset to be leaving. They took it all over – all I had to do was help pack tea chests with books and kitchen equipment. Dan Day-Lewis came to help Monkey move out of his workshop and the barn, where he'd stored quantities of strange objects he'd bought cheaply to restore one day. We hired skip after skip, and sewing machines, clocks, television sets and old speakers were hurled into it by Dan and Monkey, while Terry, Jane Raybould's husband, and Nicola filled her horsebox, which she'd driven down, with furniture. During all this, Kingsley sat in his study, surrounded by half-empty bottles that he'd been drinking up for weeks, typing his novel, only moving when we had to take his desk away.

The evening before we left I went round the garden by myself. I had little hope that the new owners would do much to look after it. The wife had twice come round the house, and while we were all in cotton and sandals, she resolutely wore her mink coat and leather boots that reached to her ritzy little knees.

It was a beautiful evening in July, the start of high summer, hot hazy dusk. The grass was tall in the meadow. The small white flowers on the blackberry bushes, where I'd picked the fruit with Liz, growing softly on their writhing briars, reminded me of medieval embroidery, and I wondered if anybody would pick them. I went round all the trees I'd planted; the cut leaf beech had died, but all the others were growing well. One more look at everything – the rose garden, the old mulberry whose main branch had rooted itself afresh in the ground where Lucy Snowe, our little white cat, had had been buried. The path led to the medlar – twisted and malevolent like an Arthur Rackman drawing – then to the ancient useless greenhouse with a gravestone marking Bonzo, some distant Edwardian pet, outside it, and finally through a door to the courtyard with its overfull skip and the sunflower-coloured lights from the kitchen windows. That was done. The next day I'd go through the empty rooms, and then that would be done too.

Monkey was moving in with us, but the others would be gone.

Sargy had married earlier that year, a beautiful girl called Frances Carey, who'd been a student of his at Camberwell. Terry, Dan and Monkey had carted everything and filled the horsebox and a van we'd hired, and early next morning we'd start the move. Mrs Uniacke, Jane, Nicola and I had packed some eighty tea chests that were filling the hall waiting to be taken in the second load. It seemed amazing that we'd got so far.

The move was over by midday, in time for a picnic lunch in the new house. It was 1978.

PART FOUR

I

Gardnor House was pretty, in fact, and must once have been a charming country residence with gardens and orchards reaching up from what is now Gayton Road to the High Street. Now it stood marooned on a small triangular piece of land that was overlooked by subsequent building.

It was reputed to be haunted by Lady Gardnor, who, I'd been told, was supposed to have disliked women, so on the first evening I stood in the drawing room and assured her I'd do my best to look after her house. Its top floor made a nice flat for Mrs Uniacke who kept a large white rabbit there with the slightly misleading name of Bunny, since he had a ferocious personality. The house possessed, among others, three particularly large, beautiful rooms, a dining room looking on to the back garden, the drawing room above it and our bedroom above that. I had a study on that floor and Monkey had a large room on the first floor over the front garden, which ended with a garage whose gates were reputed to have come from Newgate Prison.

The rebuilding of the architraves began that summer – a noisy and dust-encrusted affair. We also rebuilt the kitchen, to make it large enough to eat in and and give it a glass roof for better light. Kingsley had a study on this floor, which he seemed pleased with. The first week that we were there he announced that he was never going to use the tube as he'd decided that he hated going in any underground train. He also refused to have any kind of holiday, so I went to stay for a week in France with the Welches and then for a week in Tuscany with Woodrow and Verushka Wyatt. This wasn't a popular move. Kingsley was resentful when I got back, even though I'd arranged for friends to stay while I was away so that he shouldn't be alone, which I was beginning to realize frightened him.

I know now that these fears had always been there, but at Lemmons they'd been masked because the house was always so full of people. I'd hoped that the move to London might make our marriage better, but this didn't seem to be happening. Kingsley went to the Garrick Club fairly often, which he loved, and people came to dinner. Philip Larkin came to stay a night once or twice. Although I knew him very little, I always felt drawn to him. He had the most beautiful smile and could be majestically courteous. I'd encountered him when we were both on the literary panel of the Arts Council – an unfortunate committee that self-destructed, and I knew we'd agreed about its incompetence and futility.

Philip was one of Kingsley's oldest friends, so after we'd had dinner I used to leave them to play jazz records and drink in the drawing room. We never went to Hull where Philip was librarian at the university; there was a rumour that he didn't possess a table so that nobody could come to stay with him. We still went out to dinner with people, and Kingsley went regularly to his Monday Club lunches at Bertorelli's, where journalists, writers and economists with right-wing views gathered to gossip and enjoy each other's opinions. But he never took me out. We rarely went to restaurants and cinemas together.

Quite a lot has been written and said about his political views swinging from the left to the right. The truth was, I think, that he wasn't a political animal, it was more that he enjoyed the chappish company of people for whom politics was the social peg upon which they hung their conviviality. After the first few months in his company I never took his political views – of whatever party – seriously, although I never told him so. He loved lunching and drinking with men, and I knew by now that he had little use for women. He regarded them as intellectually inferior, and often as 'pests', hanging about, getting in the way, and interrupting men. Women were for bed and board, and he'd ceased to be interested in either. Still caught in the web of my transference, it was easy for me to concur in his views, at least as far as I had any part in them.

My sense of myself was so rocky that his estimation of me could hardly have been lower than my own. We seemed to be locked in some mysterious paralysis where his passivity about our relationship, and indeed almost everything else in his life, and my ineffectual struggle to emerge from my psychological quagmire kept us trapped. I suppose I'd started to want to change things, beginning with my perception of myself. And he did not. He preferred to grumble or be resentful. And yet, of course, life went on much as though none of this was of any consequence.

That first autumn in London Michael and Felicity Behrens invited me to spend ten days with them at a house inland of St-Maxime that they'd bought. Life there was very unexacting. We all swam in the pool, and lay in the sun and played Scrabble and boules. But I was wrestling with my writing block – apparently never-ending – and missing my sessions with Mrs Hopkinson, so I was depressed. I also had chronic backache and sometimes felt very sick. As the symptoms persisted when I got home, I went to our doctor, John Allison, who examined and then X-rayed me because he thought there was something wrong with my gall bladder. He sent me to a surgeon, who said he would take it out the following week.

Mrs Hopkinson had earlier suggested it might be good for me to do group therapy, and had found me a group that she thought suitable and I was booked into it. The operation meant I wouldn't be able to go. I was doing a broadcast with Peter Ackroyd just after I heard this news and I was devastated and can remember blurting out to Peter about the operation. 'Christ! I'd be worried,' he said. I didn't tell him that it was missing the group I minded far more than the prospect of the operation.

The night before I went into King Edward VII's Hospital for Officers, Kingsley took me up the hill to a restaurant for dinner. It was an extremely cold evening with some snow that had turned to slush. When we got back, I discovered I'd lost one of my gold leech earrings. They were the first piece of ancient gold I'd bought and I loved them. The next day, I retraced our steps up the hill, searching for it, and asked at the restaurant, but to no avail.

Kingsley took me to the hospital the following evening, saw me to my room and then left. It was eight thirty and I wasn't used to going to sleep much before midnight. I felt abandoned – and the time when Pete had left me at the nursing-home to have Nicola came back to me. I wrote a long letter to Mrs Hopkinson, during which John Allison came to see me and was kind and reassuring. Very early in the morning, someone came and gave me an injection that made me feel comfortably irresponsible and sleepy. By the time they came to take me to theatre, I didn't care about anything.

When I came to, in my own room again later, there was Susie – John's wife – sitting by the window knitting. It was immeasurably comforting to see her there and I am grateful to this day for it.

Patients in private hospitals don't usually see much of one another, but one morning, a nurse came and asked me if I'd stay with a child who was shortly going to have her tonsils out. She was about six years old, very agitated, and kept asking where her mother was. They said the mother would certainly be there when she woke up. She'd promised, they said.

They left us together. The child was restless and unhappy, although she'd had her pre-med. 'Tell me about the best day of your life,' I said. And, almost at once, she started to tell me and again, almost at once, she fell asleep. I stayed till the men came with the trolley.

About six in the evening she ran into my room, in a little white bloodied nightdress. She was crying, which clearly hurt. 'She *didn't* come. She *promised*! And she didn't.'

Later the mother, a real Knightsbridge lady, arrived in my room. 'Just to thank you for being so kind to my little girl.'

'It was you she wanted.'

'Well, I'm sure you know what they're like. I got caught up.'

'I do,' I said, wishing I was a basilisk. She smiled uneasily, and went.

The healing was slow and painful. It was impossible to turn over in bed, since I immediately felt that a rather blunt saw was grinding into action. I stayed about a fortnight in hospital. People came to see me, Monkey and Kingsley, Dosia and Jill, and even Mrs Hopkinson, bringing an avocado. John Allison said I needed to convalesce and suggested Osborne House on the Isle of Wight where patients from King Edward's were allowed to go. He said Kingsley could come with me, but Kingsley refused – saying that he wanted to have Christmas at Gardnor House with me. So in the end, kind Dosia had me for about ten days in their beautiful house by the Thames at Barnes. I slept for hours every afternoon and got up for supper with the family, but I was still very weak and my wound wouldn't heal in spite of endless salt baths. Finally, John sent me back to the surgeon, who plunged a pair of tweezers into my stomach and withdrew what looked like a piece of green electric flex. 'You'll have to do without that, I'm afraid,' he said heartily. The pain was so agonizing I couldn't reply. But after that the wound healed.

Gardnor House was another matter: it was all stairs, and I could hardly crawl up and down them once a day, let alone cook or shop. So we found a nice lady who wanted to earn money in order to go to India, and had a rather subdued and cheerless Christmas with her.

Weeks of no energy and depression followed. One strange thing happened. The kitchen had a window that looked out on to a tiny concrete yard about three feet square, perfectly flat and surrounded by the house walls and steps up to the street. I was looking out of this window one January afternoon, and thought, If only I had my earring back, that would be something, and, suddenly, there it was, in the middle of this small yard, glinting at me. I can't explain it.

There was no way in which it could have lain there all those weeks undetected, but there it was now.

Two things dominated my years at Gardnor House. One was my worsening relationship with Kingsley, who I now began to realize not only didn't love me but actually *disliked* me. In company he maintained neutrality; alone he was either surly or ceaselessly finding fault with me, until I became nervous of being alone with him. He was turning me into his mother, someone he both required and disliked.

And then the thing I'd been dreading and trying to pretend to myself would never happen did happen. Monkey decided to leave us and buy a house for himself. I could see that this was absolutely the right thing for him to do. He'd been working for some time as a director of a firm manufacturing hi-fi systems in Huntingdon, which meant that he was away all day and got back late in time for dinner. But another factor that influenced him, I'm sure, was that Kingsley had turned against him, was endlessly sniping at him, putting him down, and grumbling about him when he wasn't there. This upset him profoundly, but it also made him see that he needed, quite rightly, to lead his own life. I don't know whether I succeeded in concealing my misery and dismay at the prospect of his leaving, but knowing it was the right move for him, I did try.

We went house-hunting for him as we'd done now three times before for the whole family, and eventually he found a small Victorian house in Tufnell Park that he really liked and wanted. He put down a deposit, took out a mortgage and moved.

For the first time in our marriage we were living on our own. It was as though everything had happened the wrong way round. If we'd had more privacy in the early days, I thought, perhaps we might have forged a companionship that transcended the early 'love' part of our lives. Middle-aged marriages are more, rather than less, in need of this. But now we'd reached a point where, with the children gone and leading their own lives, with Sargy married and gone, and Monkey in his own house, we had that privacy too late.

Kingsley wanted me there all the time. He'd go to his club for the better part of a day, or spend an evening there with his friends, but he resented my going out, which I had begun to do in order to attend therapy groups.

I was desperate to get past the millstone of transference, and the groups that Mrs Hopkinson recommended might be a way out. I always tried to arrange that a friend or one of the boys would spend those evenings with Kingsley. Still, not unnaturally, he resented my having any life outside the house. But when we had evenings alone, he watched television or read, and always ended the evening drunk. He'd become quarrelsome and I learned that it didn't take two to make a scene. I took to going to bed earlier and earlier. We stopped sharing a room, because he wouldn't allow me to turn over in bed since he said it woke him up and he couldn't get back to sleep again. I couldn't spend the night completely still without being awake. He was angry about this as well.

There was one moment when all this was different. I was standing by the window of our bedroom one morning, looking out of the window and feeling very sad. He came to me, put his arms round me and gave me a long, gentle kiss, and said, 'I used to be so much in love with you.' Before I could say anything, he turned and walked out of the room. It was like meeting a loving ghost suddenly, who vanished before I could respond. I stayed by the window until I stopped crying. But that evening, after work, when I tried to talk to him, he'd retreated. Insulated by whisky, he was withdrawn and dismissive. 'I don't think so, I don't want to do that.'

During these months we were both working. Kingsley was writing *The Russian Girl* and I was writing television plays. They had started for me at Lemmons when I'd watched some of the *Upstairs Downstairs* plays, and I'd rung our agency, A. D. Peters, and said I thought I could do one. 'Oh, I don't think so,' was the dismissive response. This cowed me for a while, and then I thought again and rang and said, 'Will you ask them if they'd like me to do one?' The reply came back that they would.

I went to London Weekend Television Centre to be briefed. They were a remarkably professional bunch. Alfred Shaughnessy, John Hawksworth and Rosemary Anne Sisson had been writing most of the plays, and they were outlining the next series. I was given a play that was to take place during the first Battle of the Somme, and was told three or four things that *had* to happen in it. Their knowledge of all the characters was impressive. When I asked whether Mrs Bridges had ever had a marriage or an affair, they said no at once.

I went away and wrote the play, calling it *Our Glorious Dead*, and subsequently I went to watch some of it being shot. It went well, was broadcast in November 1974 and won an award. They asked me to write another but didn't use it. As a result, however, I was asked to contribute one of six plays about love for LWT, and wrote a play called *Sight Unseen*, the inspiration for which came to me while I was with Sargy as he had his cataract operations. I also wrote a television play that was shot in Manchester for a series about courtesans: it was about Skittles, who had had an affair with the poet Wilfrid Scawen Blunt. Then I adapted *After Julius* in three plays for Yorkshire Television.

This all gave me some returning confidence in my writing, although plays were an entirely different craft. I found that the only way *I* could do them was to make a shopping list of major events in an act, then take a running jump at it, working very fast. I developed a good sense of timing, and wrote them mostly in one draft with subsequent cuts.

Then Thames Television commissioned seven plays from my novel *Something in Disguise*, and this time I had a script editor, Richard Bates, with whom I worked. In the end the plays were cut to six and were broadcast in 1982. Moira Armstrong directed, and Richard Vernon, Ursula Howells, Elizabeth Garvie and Barry Stanton were among the wonderful cast.

Often when some treat or luxury was contemplated and not available to both of us, Kingsley would appropriate it. When I protested, 'Why should it be you?' he'd say, 'Because I'm older, richer, heavier and I earn more money.' This was true and a joke, but the fact was that neither of us was earning enough. It was Tom Maschler who introduced us to Jonathan Clowes. He had come to Lemmons, but I remember him more at Gardnor House. There were two things about him that reminded me of Peter Peters: he had a very quiet voice, and he gave the impression of being shy. We both moved to him as our literary agent, and at once our financial situation looked up.

But a good agent isn't simply a matter of money. There has to be a degree of mutual trust for integrity to have a chance to keep its head above ground. There was one occasion when I was offered the opportunity to write a biography of the Queen Mother. The money I was offered seemed astronomical to me. I thought about it and decided that I could only do it if source material was made available. To this end, a kind friend arranged for me to have lunch with Queen Elizabeth. She was one of Her Majesty's most trusted ladies-in-waiting, and was personally very keen that I should write the book. The lunch, though a cheerful occasion with the Queen Mother charming and nice to me, yielded no agreement about source material. I told Jonathan I really felt it would be a pointless exercise and he instantly agreed. He never tried to persuade me or make me feel I was making a mistake.

Kingsley would write every morning, despite what must have been the most frightful hangovers. He taught me a lot about discipline. If you were professional, you worked, whatever else was going on, whatever you felt about the rest of your life. He was drinking more heavily all the time. *Never* before working, but always after it. One of the difficult things about living with someone who drinks is that they intensely resent you not doing the same. There were several reasons why I couldn't. I hated feeling drunk. I've always had a fairly strong head and therefore getting drunk for me meant that the day afterwards was unbearable. A hangover for me might not have been as powerful as it was for

Kingsley, but I wasn't used to them. Also since the jaundice, years ago, I fell extraordinarily ill for days afterwards when I drank too much. Finally my writing would have been utterly incapacitated and I was finding the beginning of the first novel I'd attempted for some time hard enough as it was.

It's odd to think that in those desperate days of our crumbling marriage I even contemplated joining Kingsley in his drink, but I did. I'd long stopped trying to encourage him to drink less. With Monkey gone, the increasing numbers of evenings that we spent alone were more and more to be dreaded.

The night before the shooting of *Something in Disguise* was to start, I went to bed early, since I had to get to the studios in Richmond by nine o'clock. Often when I did this Kingsley – balked of the scene he felt like having – would follow me up the stairs to go on having it. This time he was past doing that. I couldn't get to sleep and lay waiting to hear him come up. My feelings for him were extremely confused. Sometimes I felt that everything was my fault, sometimes I hated him, sometimes – and this was the worst – I felt frightened of him. The dislike and anger were so potent I shrank from it, became dull and ineffectively conciliating. I didn't know then, as I do now, that conciliation makes the conciliated more aware of the effectiveness of their bad behaviour so consequently they increase it.

Anyway, as I was nearing sleep, I heard a most awful crash and knew that he must have fallen on the stairs. I found him lying on a landing. He was on his side, and he was smiling. I helped him up, and got him into his pyjamas and his bed. I asked if he hurt anywhere, and he said his shoulder. He was sitting up, and I made him stretch his arm out, flex it and clench his hand. He was able to do all that without pain and I concluded that his arm wasn't broken. I made him a cup of tea with sugar in it for the shock, and when he'd drunk it he instantly fell asleep. The next morning as he still complained of pain in his shoulder, I made an appointment for him with John Allison and arranged for a taxi to take him there.

He said I must come with him, and I said I couldn't as I had to be at the studio. When I got back in the early evening, he was enraged. He'd broken his arm very high on the shoulder where it couldn't be splinted, it just had to heal itself. 'And *you*, of course, are so taken up with your own life that you couldn't be bothered to come with me.' This went on and on. At one point I wanted to remind him of an occasion when I'd had to go to be X-rayed for TB, and he'd not come with me. Anton Felton, shocked by this, had driven me. Kingsley's shoulder did heal, but he never forgave me.

Sometime in the late spring of 1978, Mrs Hopkinson suggested I do a women's group with a colleague of hers with whom I think she'd worked in Holland. I had, by now, taken part in about three different therapy groups. They were mostly one-day affairs and I'd learned one useful thing from them. When I watched other people working on their own problems, the solutions often seemed easy to me. If this was so, others must think the same of me, so if I could understand my own nature, there *was* a way forward. I'd no idea about the length of time, or the degree of determination that this would take.

This was where I met the therapist, Jenner Roth, who arrived a bit late, because, she said, she'd just got back from a holiday in Corfu. She was wearing jeans and a dark blue sweatshirt: her hair was cut very short, and her face reminded me, in some inexplicable way, of a tulip. That first day of the group I felt, as I usually did, very much the new girl among a number of experienced people, and it took several sessions for me to feel brave enough to take part. But I perceived and respected her remarkable skill: she was the first person I had ever met who could say anything to the people with whom she worked without bruising their sensibility.

Then something awful and quite unexpected happened. Mrs Hopkinson's partner died very suddenly, and she said she couldn't work with me any more. It was an extraordinary blow at first and I felt lost and abandoned. I kept recognizing that it was incomparably worse for her, and as the weeks went by my transference fell away and, with it, the sense of abject dependence. I discovered that, beneath or beyond this painful state, I did love and care about her, and also found that there were many small practical ways I could be of use.

It took me longer to pluck up the courage to ask Jenner if she had any time for me. 'I wondered when you'd ask,' she said. When I first started working with her, I was nervous – afraid that perhaps the transference would simply move to her. When I said something about this she just replied, 'I don't work with transference,' and I felt free of it.

Kingsley was unexpectedly sympathetic about Mrs Hopkinson's tragedy, and said that of course I should help her in any way I could. I went to Ursula Vaughan Williams, who had become a great friend, and immediately offered Mrs Hopkinson, or Kate, as I now called her, a room in her house.

This seems to be the moment to say something about Ursula, who was – is – one of the most generous-hearted people I have ever known. Her generosity extends far beyond people to every living creature. She used to leave a saucer of milk and regular meals on her doorstep for a tramp cat, and one evening, returning to her house with her, we saw four slugs drinking out of the saucer. 'Plenty for all,' she murmured, and went to fetch the milk bottle. For years she cooked her cleaning lady a proper breakfast which she ate while reading the *Daily Mirror* before she started work. She bought thick woollen socks for the local fishmongers as she felt that their work entailed cold feet. She and Ralph had been in love for many years, but didn't marry until his wife died, after which there were five years of bliss. When he died, she told me that she now understood about Indian suttee. When someone was once being rather po-faced about meek people she said briskly, 'If the meek are to inherit the earth, I'm leaving it.' She knew about grief and people in need and was tirelessly kind to those who came her way.

For about a year and a half I worked with Jenner, tried to help

Kate get her life together and struggled with my hairdresser novel *Getting It Right*. Then, in the early summer, Kingsley said the Powells, Anthony and Violet, were going on a Swan cruise from Southampton, down the coast of Spain and Portugal and finishing in Nice. They suggested we should join them and Kingsley, to my surprise, seemed keen to go; I was delighted. Kingsley invited the Fussells, Paul and Betty, to join us.

It didn't start very well. I confused British time with continental time so that we reached the dockside just as they were drawing up the gangway and we nearly missed the entire trip. The ship was Greek. There were lectures on the sights we were to see, and the passengers were rather more serious than cruise passengers usually are. We ate all our meals with Violet, Tony and the Fussells – Kingsley was very fond of Tony, who was wonderful company, full of gossipy anecdotes, sometimes ironical but never malicious. The three men took charge of the conversation. The food was pretty awful, and we stopped at a number of places – Mont Saint-Michel, Oporto and Lisbon. But I can't remember much because, the moment we were alone, Kingsley's irritation with me was like the atmosphere before an impending thunderstorm, and this dominated the cruise for me.

I dreaded being alone with him. To add to my dread, a Greek steward formed a kind of farcical passion for me and Kingsley accused me of inviting it. In fact, I had to work out ingenious ways to avoid the man. We finally reached Nice where we were to part from our friends. Kingsley and I were to take a train to Brive where we were to stay with Joy and Richard Law.

Joy was a very old friend of mine from the Blandford Street days, and she'd bought a little house not far from Sarlat, in the Dordogne. The Fussells were to stay the night in Nice, and we went with them to their hotel and had a final meal together. The Powells had flown home. Kingsley was dreading the train journey; he was never a good traveller. A good deal of his anxiety had rubbed off on me, made worse at the beginning by my gaffe about timing when we'd sailed from Southampton. He deadened this by drinking steadily all afternoon, and by the time the Fussells kindly accompanied us to the railway station, he was surly drunk. I felt their relief at parting from us. We left Nice early in the evening, and Kingsley drank and slept through the journey to Brive where Joy met us. I could hardly get him off the train. The first question he asked Joy was where Richard was, and she replied that he'd not been able to get away, but she had a painter and his wife staying.

It was a difficult ten days. Kingsley was writing an account of our cruise for the *Sunday Times*, and fortunately that gave him something to do. He only worked in the mornings, and the rest of the time he made it clear that he wasn't enjoying himself. Joy behaved through it all with the utmost courtesy and good manners. She devised trips for us, took us out to lunches, and did everything in her power to make the visit a success. Although he showed brief bursts of animation at lunches, Kingsley remained obdurately determined *not* to enjoy it. He kept repeating that he wouldn't have come if he'd known Richard wasn't going to be there – to me, fortunately, not to Joy.

When we got back to London and unpacked he couldn't find his piece about the cruise. Instantly he accused me of destroying it. He was serious. This shocked me probably more than anything else that had happened between us. The idea that I'd destroy *anyone*'s writing, let alone his, made me realize how much and how thoroughly he disliked and despised me. Of course I told him I couldn't understand how he could think this, but it only made matters worse. He said I liked to think of myself as somebody who I most certainly wasn't. 'I know you, you see,' he said. I said perhaps he'd left the piece behind in France, got in touch with Joy, who after a search, said she was sure it wasn't there. In the end I got Kingsley's suitcase out and found it, in a zipped compartment. When I gave it to him, he said simply, 'Oh. You've found it, then.'

During the months before the cruise, I'd been trying to work with Jenner on my feelings about my marriage. I repeatedly told her I couldn't leave him, as he couldn't bear being alone. At one of these sessions she remarked, 'I wonder what he would do if you were run over by a bus.' And later, that night I thought, He'd be all right. He'd find someone else. But the mere thought of leaving terrified me then. Where would I go? How would I earn my living? My earnings from novels wouldn't keep me – I'd have to find another job. I was fifty-six, and unlikely to find anyone else with whom to share a life. If we parted, this would be my third failure at marriage. Also, and it seems strange now, considering the previous few years, I still loved him, or at least loved how we had been together. He never called me Min or Piney now. He was angry with me because he didn't want but needed me, and I was withering from his dislike.

Apart from Jenner, the only other person to whom I'd talked about my marriage was Ursula. She listened carefully, as she always did, and said, 'If you leave, you must come to me.' I'd not expected this kindness and, looking back, I can't think what I'd have done without it. Gone were the days of really cheap rented flats. Anyway, this offer was made before I'd taken the decision to go.

That happened in Edinburgh. Dickie and Patricia Temple-Muir had suggested that we come for a fortnight of the festival. At that time Dickie owned half of the Roxburgh Hotel and we were to stay there. Kingsley liked Dickie: he was convivial and amusing and a very good host. When we arrived in our room there was a welcoming bottle of whisky and Dickie got full marks for that. We went to one play, *Watch on the Rhine* by Lillian Hellman, which hadn't worn well: it confirmed Kingsley's view of the theatre that none of it was any good. So when another play for which we'd bought seats was on, he refused to go. He also refused to let me go. He didn't want dinner in the dining room, but wanted sandwiches and drinks in the room.

Then Gaia Mostyn-Owen, who had a charming little castle outside Edinburgh, invited the Temple-Muirs and us to lunch. Claudio Abbado, who was conducting a series of concerts at the festival, was there too. It didn't take long for Kingsley to become extremely offensive to him. The subject was Mozart, and Kingsley told him, in so many words, that he didn't know what he was talking about. It was a large lunch party, and conversation virtually stopped at this. Abbado looked at Kingsley with some curiosity, then turned to our hostess and changed the subject. After lunch Kingsley went to sleep, and I went for a walk with Dickie and Patricia. 'He's not always like this?' Dickie asked.

'No. He isn't.' It's very horrible feeling ashamed for someone else.

Later that evening, when he wasn't eating sandwiches and I wasn't drinking whisky, he said, 'I suppose I was rather offensive to that Italian chap.'

'Yes, you were.'

'Silly bugger. He'd got it all *wrong*, you see. He didn't know what he was talking about.'

'It wasn't that. You just didn't agree.'

'And what if I did? Disagree?'

'Well, it's possible to disagree more gracefully.'

This was a mistake. I was being upper class and suggesting people shouldn't say what they thought. 'Like *you* – things are always boring when you dislike them or you're afraid of them.'

This was true, and I'd learned it. 'I know,' I said, 'I'm sorry about it. I'm trying not to do it.'

'Oh, yes, of course. You're always trying to do the right thing. You always have to be *right*. You *have* to be right, don't you?'

'I expect so.'

He went back to his newspaper, and I lay on the bed and went to sleep. When I woke up, there was a half-bottle of champagne in a bucket beside the bed. 'I know you like it,' he said. But these little crests of affection had become very rare, and the troughs of accusation, resentment and plain dislike had become deeper and more frequent.

It was during the end of our time there, when these troughs became continuous, that I realized I had to go. I began to think how I could do this so it would be the least difficult for him. There is no good way of leaving someone. However you do it, you will afterwards be accused of doing it in the most heartless way possible. I decided it would be best if I went away for about ten days, then simply didn't come back. He would have had ten days to get used to my not being there. I had, over the years, been to a health farm in Suffolk twice, largely to have a bit of a rest from cooking and housekeeping. I arranged to go with Patricia Temple-Muir.

But first there were some people who had to be told. I went to our lawyers, and told them and wrote a letter for them to be delivered on the morning I was supposed to return to Gardnor House. I told Mrs Uniacke, because it didn't seem fair to walk out on her when she'd been faithfully with us for so long. She understood at once and was utterly discreet. I told Anton, who said, 'I'm amazed you haven't done it before.' I asked him what it would be like, leaving and starting again. 'Two years of hell,' he said, and then things would straighten themselves out. I told our friend and part-time secretary, Helen Benckendorf, because I wanted her to take Rosie, my dog. I was afraid that if I left her Kingsley wouldn't let me have her later. I told Jonathan Clowes and I told Monkey, because I've always told him everything.

The visit to Shrubland Hall, the health farm, was planned for the end of October to the first week in November in 1980. For some weeks before this, when Kingsley was having long lunches at the Garrick, I removed suitcases of clothes to Ursula. I decided to take my quarter-written novel and my typewriter with me to Suffolk. As usual, I arranged for Kingsley to have some company in my absence.

When the morning of my departure arrived, I came into the kitchen to say I was going. Kingsley simply said, 'I see.' He didn't look up from his newspaper.

I was driving to the Temple-Muirs' in Essex to have lunch there and pick up Patricia to go on. I'd thought that I'd feel exhilarated at actually leaving, but I didn't. I was unable to think. It felt like an escape I couldn't yet believe in.

2

When I was within a few miles of the Temple-Muirs' house, I got out of the car. There was a gate into a field, and I hung on to it to cry. *I* had gone. It was I who'd taken the decision, had planned it as best I could, but hanging on the gate, it seemed a shock. From now on, I was on my own – something I'd always dreaded, and had never really believed would happen.

The ten days at Shrubland Hall passed. I was very tired to begin with, but as I recovered, my dread of returning to London and to Kingsley's reception of my letter increased. After dropping Patricia off at her house, I drove straight to Ursula. She had a young composer occupying her two basement rooms, so I slept on the top floor next door to her, the room crammed with my belongings.

The day after my return, a letter was dropped through the letterbox. It was from Kingsley. It said that although life with me hadn't been much fun, it would be worse without me, and if I'd return he would try to drink less and be a better husband. I was tempted, but I knew from perceived experience that people who drink as much as he did can't cut it down for more than a week or two: they then simply revert. I wrote back saying that if he'd stop drinking altogether I'd come back, and that I didn't think drinking less would work. He didn't agree and divorce proceedings began their unwieldy way.

I have to say something, briefly, about money here. Kingsley had never been in the least interested in money, and I'd had to deal with it, with Anton's help. When I married Kingsley he had almost nothing after he stopped teaching. I'd only ever earned just enough to keep myself. As we became better off, I suggested to him that all our earnings should go into a joint account and that from it we should each have £1,500 in separate accounts to spend exactly as we individually pleased, on clothes or presents. This meant that the mortgage, the house bills, the money for the boys, the car and holidays were paid for from the main account, and I had some idea of what we could afford. By the time I left, Kingsley was earning about eighty thousand a year, and I was earning between three and four thousand. Clearly this was over. I now had to subsist on my private account and anything I earned. In the first six months this sum was a hundred pounds. I was told I'd eventually get half the value of the house, but I didn't want to ask for any sort of income, since it was I who had left. I'd never taken money from either of my previous marriages, except for the small amount from Pete to spend on Nicola. It meant I was immediately in trouble for money. I had two banks, and went to the first, where I'd been a client since 1946, and asked them for a loan of five thousand pounds. They refused, as I had nothing to back it as a guarantee. I went to Childs' Bank where we'd had our joint account, explained the situation and asked them for a loan. 'Yes,' they said. 'How much?' I closed the other account and banked with them.

I never used the loan, and this was entirely due to Ursula, who kept me for eighteen months, with my dog Rosie, who was an immense comfort. I'd written about half of *Getting It Right*, and all I could do was finish it as quickly as possible. At first I worked in the back basement room in Ursula's house. Later, the composer moved into a flat and I had the basement to myself. I asked, through the lawyers, if I might take a few pieces of furniture from Gardnor House, and this was agreed. Ursula bought me a second-hand gas stove that we put in the coalhole, and I cooked on that. A few days after I'd moved, I rang Jenner and Terry, her husband, and asked if I could come round. I could. I went, and when I got there and before I could say anything, I started crying and cried for a long time and then they gave me a cup of tea.

Hilly and her third husband, Allie Kilmarnock, moved into Gardnor House – Hilly was to be Kingsley's housekeeper so that he wasn't alone. I didn't have to worry about that, which strangely I'd still been doing. After about a year, they put the house on the market. I'd been advised to ask for my half of the house plus the original fourteen thousand pounds with which I'd bought Maida Vale. It was suggested I should claim the interest on it, but this seemed wrong to me. Kingsley's lawyers refused at first to believe I'd bought the house, and Anton had to produce the papers to prove that I had.

That first Christmas of 1980 was awful, and the months that followed are a dim jumble to me. I tried to work hard, but it was extremely difficult, since the moment I was alone, my situation, the future, the anxiety about how on earth I was going to make out preoccupied me. I went to stay with Nicola who was now happily married to Elliot, her second husband, and went to some sewing classes there. Paul and Marigold Johnson were kind to me, and had me for a weekend – took me to the Saville Garden at Windsor when the magnolia and tiny narcissus were out. My agent, Jonathan, married Ann Evans, and she became a friend, and I stayed with them in Sussex at Penshurst. But, generally, I felt pretty cut off from the people who'd come to Lemmons so much.

Jenner and Terry had a son, Jodie, and they made me one of his guardians, if ever they should die together, which touched me very much. Ursula was utterly staunch, took me to Covent Garden and afterwards round to meet Placido Domingo, whose huge, warm personality made me feel as though I was being enveloped by a cloud of sunshine.

Eventually, by 1983, the divorce came through, Gardnor House was sold and I could start looking for somewhere to live. Mrs Uniacke had been offered the choice of going with Kingsley to his new house or coming with me. She chose to come with me. For months, while all this was going on, I used to drive up to the corner of Flask Walk and Well Walk, and she'd bring my fresh laundry that she'd done, and take the next lot home in a bag. She did this secretly, and I was deeply grateful to her. I told her I didn't know how much money I'd earn, but that I'd try to find somewhere that had decent rooms for her, and she trusted me.

I searched and searched, and twice I thought I'd found the right place, but the first was very open to burglary and I was advised not to buy it. The second house, which I desperately wanted, I offered for and the owner raised the price by five thousand pounds. I went home and did the sums. I could *just* afford it, if I did nothing to it. It was a small three-storey house on a noisy road, but the large garden attracted me. I offered again, and the owner increased the price by yet another five thousand. I wept bitterly about this: almost anything made me cry then.

Eventually, I found a house in Delancey Street, in Camden Town, a noisy one-way bus route, but it had a small garden and looked out at the back on to a large square of gardens. It was a narrow four-storey house, with two rooms on each floor and one bathroom. I bought it, and had money left over to put in a shower and a kitchen for Mrs Uniacke in the basement, so that she had a bedroom and a sitting room. Jenner and Terry came to help me move in the spring of 1983.

I spent my first night in the house alone, as it wasn't ready for Mrs Uniacke, and lay awake for a long time in the dark. It was the third time I'd moved on my own – Blandford Street after I'd left Pete, Blomfield Road after I'd left Michael, and now here. But those moves had had a different quality about them. I'd been frightened then at each prospect, but they had also felt like an adventure, a temporary state from which something joyful would emerge. Now I felt I'd be alone for the rest of my life. Nobody would want a 'bolter' of fifty-six. I finally fell asleep just as I'd reached the uncomfortable notion that solitude was probably good for writing.

The builders arrived two days later. I found them by pure chance: Monkey and I had been looking at a pretty little house that seemed unoccupied, when two men came out of it. Monkey asked if we could see inside. They said it was sold, but they'd no objection to showing it to us. 'The new owner has ruined it,' one said. He was quite right: all the original features of the house had been torn out, and replaced with nasty alternatives. But I was impressed that they felt this and told them I was looking for a house in the area, and that when I found one, I'd like them to do the work for me. They gave me a telephone number and that was that. They were called Lennie and Jo Chapproniere. I asked them separately, at various times, whether they were French, and one said yes, and the other said of course not. They worked for me for some months, and I became very attached to them. They were real Camden Town people. When I went about with Lennie in his van looking for things like Victorian fireplaces, people would shout greetings to him in the traffic. Len Beswick came to hang the wallpapers as usual, in his tennis shoes and white overalls, his lunch carefully packed.

I'd finished *Getting It Right* and sent it to my new publisher, Christopher Sinclair-Stevenson at Hamish Hamilton. I hoped desperately that this novel would be a breakthrough for me. The idea for it had come from one small incident. At Lemmons we were always short of money, but the house needed constant renovation. Two of Monkey's friends came to help us paint some of it. They were gay, working class, and I knew they loved classical music because Monkey had got to know them when he made their hi-fi system for them. They usually came at weekends as they both had jobs, and were often at dinner or lunch with a wide variety of our other friends. They were funny, interesting, devoted to each other and wildly unfaithful: they got on, or off with everybody.

One day, a rather intellectual journalist was talking at lunch about Bach and organ music. Peter, one of Monkey's friends, who'd been listening quietly, interrupted him and disagreed on a point. He went on to give a brief, but stunningly well-informed account of early seventeenth-century organs in Germany. When he'd finished, he quietly filled his mouth with fish pie and reverted to listening to Kingsley. Afterwards I asked Peter how he knew so much about these particular organs, and he said, 'Well, it just came up in conversation, didn't it?' After that I noticed that these nuggets of esoteric information were by no means confined to organs. Architecture, pictures, gardens, houses – at any moment Peter's well-furnished mind might reveal more. So I thought it would be interesting to write about someone who, on the face of it, had no cultural or educational advantages, who got along perfectly well without any of that, but who'd acquired his interest – sometimes his passion – out of sheer curiosity and love of various subjects.

I didn't want to write about Peter and his friend directly, so I created Gavin Lamb, who lived with his parents in Barnet where his father was a builder. Every day he goes to an old-fashioned hairdresser where he cuts and dresses old ladies' hair with kindness and tact. He is thirty-one and a virgin because he's terrified of women. The novel charts his breaking through this fear and his efforts to find the right partner. Gavin is based on either of our painter friends, but they made me realize how many people there are whose multifarious interests give them another – often unacknowledged – dimension.

I was doing a gardening piece once a month, taking over from Anne Scott-James in *Good Housekeeping*, and I'd received my advance of five thousand pounds for the novel. But I needed to start something else, and had two ideas that I found paralysing.

Eventually I asked Mart to come for a drink and told him about them. One was to write a novel that was a present-day version of *Sense and Sensibility*. It had occurred to me that sensibility had become more fashionable and I'd started to block out the first six chapters from Austen's novel. The second idea was one that had lain in the back of my mind for a long time. I wanted to write a trilogy about a family going through the last war, taking the story over ten years starting in 1937. When people wrote about that time, it was largely in terms of the battles fought; family life was merely a background. I thought it would be interesting to do it the other way round. England had changed so much during the war, but this hadn't been much written about. Mart said immediately, 'Do that one.' And so I began on the 'Cazalet Chronicle' with *The Light Years* in 1982.

Getting It Right came out – pretty quietly. It got some good notices and one or two bad ones. The most cheering and maddening thing was getting a postcard from Victoria Glendinning saying what a smashing novel, and what a pity it had come out when it wasn't her week to review novels in the *Sunday Times*. It *was* a pity: I could have done with one really enthusiastic review by someone of her status.

I settled in to writing the new novel, in between making my garden, getting the house straight and having the occasional party. But to aid finances I needed a lodger. There was a large room on the top floor that had a view of St Paul's on the street side and of the square of gardens on the other, plus a small bathroom on the half-landing below. I asked friends, and one day a young man turned up, had a good look at it and moved in. His name was Jonathan Burnham, and he was working for Carmen Callil, the new publisher at Chatto & Windus. He was a natural and inspired cook, and soon we were cooking for parties we gave together. He became a great friend and has remained so.

This was a time when I renewed old friendships – I'd hardly seen Dosia Verney, for instance, who had married Andrew Verney some years after Barry died, because they didn't get on with Kingsley or he with them. They had moved from their lovely house by the river to Wandsworth and I made a supper to take them for their first night there. It was lovely to be back with Dosia. I also encountered Jack and Margaret Huntingdon's eldest daughter, Selina Hastings, whom I'd last met when she was a schoolgirl in Roehampton, and was touched and rather amazed that she remembered me. She became a close and true friend. Shirley and

Bill Letwin were also extraordinarily kind. I used to go to dinners with them when I was with Kingsley, but they didn't stop asking me when I was on my own, as some people did. It was at their house that I met Sybille Bedford.

I'd first heard of her when I was working for Weidenfeld, who published *A Visit to Don Otavio*. I was deeply impressed with that book. It was beautifully written and had the hallmark of true originality. I said how very much I should like to meet her, but George Weidenfeld looked at me and replied, rather dauntingly, 'Mrs Bedford is a *very* intelligent woman.' So awe was added to homage and nothing happened. But there she was, years later, standing by the fireplace in Shirley's drawing room. We were both very shy, and it was some time before we became the friends that we are now.

More friends have accumulated since then, but even at this early stage in my separation from Kingsley I'd begun to realize how good it was to be free to make friends without having to contend with a partner's disapproval. Fay and Tom Maschler were splitting up, and I saw a good deal of Fay while that was going on, and subsequently we attempted to liven up society by giving suppers in each other's houses. After the first, we had to ask people to bring some wine with them. We were also on the Evening Standard's Theatre Awards Committee for two years, and occasionally, when Fay was away, I did her restaurant column for her.

About two years after it was published, an American director optioned the film rights for *Getting It Right*. Eventually he and his producer, Charles Evans, arrived in London to see whether they thought I could write the script for the film. The director, Randal Kleiser, said he wanted to make the film as soon as he'd read the novel. It was a surprising film for him to want to make: hitherto he'd made *Grease* with John Travolta, *The Blue Lagoon*, and other markedly commercial movies. It was agreed I should write the script. I didn't know then the passion that everybody concerned with movies has for endless drafts – a process I've always hated, and managed to avoid when writing novels. It need not take very long, I thought, as I began on the first. I'd have to leave the novel, but would soon get back to it.

In fact, the script took the best part of two years, while we went through three producers and many rewrites. Randal was very good to work with and we became, and are, friends. I went to New York for a week to stay with him in his amazing apartment, which had an enormous flat roof on which I longed to make a garden. Randal took me to a nightclub that was all the rage. Entry to it was difficult and much prized. It contained a series of tableaux – mostly of people who were just about to start something, or had just finished whatever it was – the enigmatic fatuity of which reminds me now of elements of the Turner Prize. He took me to the theatre, too, and to private screenings of movies.

Charles Evans, the first producer, was effortlessly offensive. We had meetings in his office about the script and then were put into a fusty little room with no air-conditioning for hours to do our homework, with a plate of wizened sandwiches for lunch. He treated me like an impoverished secretary who, at any minute, he might sack. He didn't last long. The next producer was far nicer, but he went off to run the Disney enterprise in Paris. The third producer, Jonathan Krane, saw the picture through.

I spent a week in Los Angeles staying with Randal and rewriting parts of the screenplay. He had a house in the hills above town with a swimming pool and horses, dogs, and a pig he was keeping because he was going to make a circus movie that needed one, and he wanted to learn its ways. One Sunday morning, he took me to watch an audition for this film. It took place in a concrete garden lot of a studio. The audition was for minor parts, and a sad, garish crowd queued to do their turn. The most pathetic was a very old ex-clown who came on with a square yard of wooden board which he placed on the ground and proceeded to do an effortful, shambling tap dance on throughout which he fixed a smile that made me want to cry. As he was picking up his board,

Randal said to his assistant, 'We'll have to find something for him.' One of the things I loved about Randal was his tender heart.

The film was shot in England, and casting sessions began there. In the end it starred Jesse Birdsall as the hero, Lynn Redgrave, Helena Bonham-Carter and Jane Horrocks, with a strong supporting cast. Then they decided to ask John Gielgud to play the vulgar seat-belt manufacturer and, to my surprise, he accepted the part. I'd always admired him deeply, but the one thing he couldn't manage was to be vulgar. He arrived immaculately dressed, was courteous and patient during rehearsal, but his accent was definitely wide of the mark. Randal, being American, didn't notice. The film was premièred in 1986. Randal said it was a cult movie in the US but it didn't do well here, largely I think because anything extreme in the way of behaviour was cut out. Americans couldn't take more than a pastel degree of realism then, which is funny if one thinks of movies now. Violence of one kind or another seems always to get by, but Helena's part, which was an anorexic who had eating binges and was also bulimic, was pared down, and that of a heartbroken gay man who is left by his partner was also compressed so that it had no real meaning. There were some very good performances, and I, at least, learned a lot.

While this film was being set up and made, another film offer turned up. My agent rang to say that a producer called Jonathan Cavendish who ran an Irish company, would like to see me for a project they had in mind. Jonathan came to Delancey Street to tell me about this. They wanted to make a film about Somerville and Ross, the two Anglo-Irish ladies who had collaborated as writers for many years. *Experiences of an Irish RM* and *The Real Charlotte* were their best-known books, it seemed like an interesting idea and I agreed to do it. The director was to be Peter Sykes, and Jonathan took us both to Ireland to Castle Townsend where the Somervilles had had their house in Drishane. It was my first trip to the country in Ireland, and I loved it. I also got to know Jonathan, whom I have loved ever since.

3

I'd stopped having one-to-one sessions with Jenner, who had said she thought it would be useful for me to have some with Terry. This was a good move for me because I still felt anxious and unsure of myself around men.

I'd thought that once we were divorced, and Kingsley felt safe with his household arrangement with Hilly, we might become friends. I couldn't have been more wrong. He maintained an implacable resentment towards me for the rest of his life. My wanting to be friends with him, he wrote, or said, was further evidence of my gross insensibility about what I'd done to him. He was painfully open about this, in interviews and in the two novels he wrote after I'd left. For years I found that very hard to endure, because it wasn't how I felt and because he was intent on wiping out anything good that there'd been about the eighteen years we'd spent together.

Apart from that, therapy was giving me a steadier view of myself. I could see my faults and weaknesses more clearly and could forgive them, which in turn meant I was in a better position to do something about them. I learned things slowly and often I only realized I *had* learned them later. I discovered my lack of discrimination, for instance, and my neediness. 'It's no good being a bottomless pit,' Jenner said to me one day. I realized the difficulty I had with confronting anyone if I thought they were going to mind it, and my subsequent resentment when I'd not done so. And I noted my presumptions about people that rested only on what I wanted them to be. As I learned to be less critical of myself, it became easier not to make adverse judgements about other people.

Insights of this kind don't, of themselves, alter one: they merely further the possibility of change. Change was something I passionately believed in – change being movement, and movement life. I began to feel more responsible for myself, and this enormously helped the old bugbear, self-pity. This last was something I thought I'd vanquished years before, but I now recognized it would always lie in wait.

Faults are rather like weaknesses in the immune system: I found I had to work at protecting myself from them. I knew by then that I couldn't afford to stop working, there was nothing to feel smug about, but at least I was beginning to find my way around myself and could consequently deal with issues. Some people will dub all this indulgent self-absorption but, in fact, feeling good, or at least better, about yourself enables you to be of more use to other people. It also promotes the chances of living in the present – something that children are so good at and adults so poor. I'd spent a great deal of my life after childhood being an adolescent; a stage that most people think occupies a finite number of years. So I am openly and deeply grateful for the opportunity therapy has given me to grow up.

After I'd reread some of their work and also a biography of Somerville and Ross, I realized that there was no way their lives would fit into a dramatic structure needed for a film. So I suggested I did a film script that wasn't biographical and was only very loosely based on the idea of two women collaborating and living in Ireland. Jonathan Cavendish agreed.

When I'd finished a first draft that was considered promising, we went to Ireland again, this time to look for locations. By now a new director was involved, Philip Saville, who announced that he could only sit in the front of the car. Despite this – I don't much like spending most of the day in the back of a car either – it was a fascinating trip. I have always loved looking at houses anywhere, and many of those we looked at – all within a reasonable distance of Dublin – were both beautiful and romantic. They were often in varying stages of destitution: buckets in their lofty halls catching water that dripped or streamed through the exquisite plasterwork of their ceilings, drunken shutters hanging by a single screw, and walls blotched with advanced damp. Sometimes the houses were empty. Once or twice they were still inhabited by owners frantic to rent. I think we spent about three days doing this, and no certain locations came out of it, but I enjoyed it immensely, not least because I liked Jonathan so much.

Shortly after this I met his girl. Lesley was tall, with long blonde hair and a beautiful, clear-cut face. She never wore makeup, because she said she looked silly with it. She made commercials for television and she was very good at it, but she never talked about her work and didn't seem to think it mattered. I loved her at once. She had a great affinity with dogs, and my dog, Darcy, who had taken the place of dear Rosie, now dead, the longest-lived cavalier spaniel on record, often went to stay with them when I went away for weekends.

I eventually finished the final draft of the script, which I called *The Attachment*, and Jonathan's company started to raise the money to make it, but it didn't come off. Although they got most of the money, the last £250,000 eluded them.

I was also compiling a gardening anthology, which involved a lot of pleasurable reading, and was also well into *The Light Years*. I had realized fairly early on that I couldn't get everything into three volumes so it would have to be four. Jonathan Clowes had moved me to Macmillan where I met Jane Wood. Jane was my editor for the last three volumes of 'Cazalet Chronicles' and beyond, and we got on at once – another friend for life.

Meanwhile, among my friends, some bad news was that Tanya Hobson got breast cancer. She and Anthony were determinedly optimistic about it, and she came to stay with me after her operation. I'd known her a little when she was a young girl as she'd been the best friend of Dosia's stepdaughter, Ming. She married young and went to live in South Africa, but the marriage didn't work out so she returned to England and married Anthony. I was godmother to their third child, Charlotte. Tanya was half Russian, and one of the most lovable people I have ever known. She was warm-hearted, modest, funny, deeply intelligent and cultivated in the best sense of that word – interested in everything and discriminatingly appreciative of much.

She seemed to recover completely, and Anthony wanted to take her to Jordan and Israel for a holiday. He invited me to go with them, and when I told Selina Hastings this, she wanted to come too. The novelist Pauline Neville made the fifth of our party. I liked riding into Petra through the narrow, circuitous path cleft in the high rock more than I liked the city itself. I loved the desert, which we drove through to reach the top of the Red Sea, which lies beside Israeli Elat, divided by barbed wire and machine-guns, where I'd stayed with my friend Nina Milkina some years previously. Then, we'd walked into the desert and a few yards in had felt enclosed by the enormous silence. Driving, as we did now, the noise of the car obtruded and it became a more ordinary place. After Jordan, Selina and Pauline left us to go home, and Anthony, Tanya and I proceeded to Israel via the Dead Sea, where Tanya and I insisted upon bathing in the hot, grey salty soup. Thence to Jerusalem, a city more fraught with ill-will than anywhere I've ever been.

But Tanya's health didn't last: two years later she was seriously ill. I went down to Whitsbury to cook for her while Anthony was away. It was early spring and she was in remission. Her eldest daughter, Emma, was due to be married, I think, in June, and she was hopeful of lasting until that happened. I realized, during that visit, how much I loved her. But a kind of shyness had always prevailed between us so I couldn't tell her this. Two months later, she rang me in London: 'I'd hoped I might live long enough to see Emma married. Now, I'm afraid I shall not!' And then, before I could say anything, she said, 'Goodbye!' and rang off.

I couldn't bear to go to her funeral, and later, when Anthony asked me for a weekend, I found it difficult to be there without her, but at least I could cry in my bedroom. Funerals are inevitably public, and I always feel that it's unseemly that I, whose loss must be far less than the family's, should threaten their control by my lack of it. I continue to miss Tanya. I can hear her voice now saying, 'Really nice.' 'A virtuous Woman: mild and beautiful,' as Shakespeare said. Charlotte, her daughter, often reminds me of Tanya: Charlotte has written her first book, *Black Earth City*, and Tanya would have been – rightly – very proud of her for that.

Mrs Uniacke retired and went to live in a little flat quite near. The stairs had got too much for her, and in any case she was well past retirement age. I missed her dreadfully. It would have been impossible to replace her, so I had to find someone to come in and clean, which I did, unsatisfactorily, for the remainder of my time in Delancey Street.

Then Andrew Verney, who was a doctor, retired, and Dosia and he moved to the country, to Pewsey. Dosia was very unhappy about this; she loved London and her friends, but she made the best of it, and made a rather ordinary little house pretty and interesting, as all her houses had been. I missed her, but I could go to stay with them.

Another sudden blow was that Jonathan and Ann Clowes decided to live in France. Jonathan wasn't well and they decided to cut down their clients to twelve and keep a small office in London. I spent one last weekend at Penhurst with them and Ann told me the following week. She hadn't said anything to me at the weekend because she didn't want to spoil it for me. They'd bought a flat in Villefranche, where they'd been staying for long weekends, and where I'd stayed with them. But now they were going to live there and look for a house further north. Ann had gradually become a great friend and I knew I was going to miss her very much – especially as they had to stay out of England for a year before they could return to London. They were selling Penhurst, with its deer, its bluebells and its black rabbit. Ann has a genius for friendship and

I loved her, so the idea of her living in another country meant great despair to me. When you're on your own, friends become more and more important. I'd not, at that point, begun to shape up to being solitary.

But the most serious anxiety during this time was Sargy, who was gradually going blind. Since he'd married he'd had three children and Franny was clearly the perfect wife for him. Everything about his life seemed right and fruitful, and I saw them regularly at their house or mine. He'd had several operations on his eyes, starting way back when we were all at Lemmons: he had developed cataracts at an unusually early age. Then, after he married, he used to come and stay at Gardnor House for a few days after eye operations, as he had to be very careful not to get knocked or bumped afterwards. He was extraordinarily stoical about all this, although I remember him sitting one day at the kitchen table and saying, 'I could bear anything – *anything*, so long as I don't go blind.'

There had been some hope then, but there seemed to be none now. He had detached retinas and had already lost the sight in one eye, and the other seemed to be slowly failing. He used to teach at the Camden Arts Centre when I was at Delancey Street, and came sometimes for tea between his classes. His sight then was so poor I made him get a white stick. He said he could hear traffic – apart from bicycles, I pointed out, and he would be much safer if other people understood that he couldn't see well. They were heart-breaking teas. He needed to talk about it: I remember him saying that he almost wished that he *were* blind, that waiting for it to happen was perhaps the worst part. For anyone to become blind is sad: for a painter it's devastating. Being extremely ignorant, I went to ask a doctor whether it was possible to donate one's eye to somebody else, and was told that it wasn't. The cornea could be transplanted, but not the whole eye. Finally Sargy had peripheral vision in one eye and he has never clearly seen his fourth child, Michael, who was born a few months before they went to live in Suffolk.

Sargy has continued to paint; the nature of his work has

changed a great deal and it would seem that his poor sight – while it may have changed his direction – has in no way impeded his evolution. Now he paints huge, stunning pictures that ambush you suddenly when you are at the right distance from them. He and Franny have together transcended this colossal blow with all the alchemy of courage and love. I have to add a story here. His son Peter, then aged about nine, was, walking home from school one day with a friend, who was overheard to say, 'I suppose your father is the best blind painter in Peckham?' Sargy told me this. It was a good title for *his* autobiography, he thought, but Franny said it should have a subtitle, 'Do I take sugar?' He's known for finding decision, at any level, difficult.

They decided to move to the country, and spent several months searching for something that they could afford. The West Country, of which Sargy was very fond, proved too expensive, so they settled for a house in East Anglia where several of their friends lived and painted.

After Mrs Uniacke went, I spent some time refurbishing the basement flat in order to let it. My older brother Robin and his wife rented it for two or three months, but then they had to go back to their antiques business in Fareham. I put the flat on the market and got a charming young actress called Rebecca Pidgeon. She looked like a young Russian heroine, and David Mamet, her lover whom she subsequently married, spent much time there. They used to sit in my garden having tea and toast after happy afternoons in bed.

But after nearly eight years there, I decided I must move. I'd never really liked the house, and parking my car, if I'd been out in the evening, became more and more difficult – sometimes even frightening. Most of all the garden depressed me: it was small, and there wasn't anything more I could do with it. North London was full of gardens, some much better than mine, and it would be good not to be living in a noisy, dirty, one-way street. I put my house on the market and started to look for a new one.

4

The Light Years had been published to a fairly quiet reception, and I'd begun upon the second volume, *Marking Time*. I knew that moving would be totally disruptive, but the market in houses had risen enormously, and it felt like the right time to sell. Finding somewhere else proved hopeless. I wanted a flat with three bedrooms, one for a study, and a decent garden, but there was nothing in North London to be had for the price I hoped to get for Delancey Street. Eventually, I teamed up with two friends who also wanted flats and we found a large house in Dartmouth Park Avenue with about a quarter of an acre of derelict garden that seemed just right. It was on the market for £400,000. Having offered for it, we had it expensively surveyed, only to be gazumped by someone who was prepared to pay £500,000. That was that. Meanwhile my house had been offered for and completion was to be in August 1990.

One morning Sargy rang up from Suffolk and said, 'The house next door to us is going to be on the market. It would be lovely if you came and lived here.' I hadn't thought of living in the country, and I knew hardly anyone in Suffolk: it seemed a mad idea. But then Nicola rang up and said, 'Ma, you really should go and see that house.' At that time she and Elliot had thought of moving to East Anglia and had done some house-hunting. So I took one of my many goddaughters, Minky St Aubyn – who has especially good taste in houses – and we went to see it.

We went by train and Fran met us at Diss. It was a lovely

summer's day. Sargy and Fran seemed happy about their move, although everything was very new. It was sixteen miles from Diss to Bungay. 'One reason it's so nice,' Fran said.

I bought the house in about ten minutes. Nobody had told me that it was beautiful, and the moment I walked into the room that is now my study, I knew I wanted it. The affable owner, a man who, it transpired, didn't like living in any one place for long, showed us over it: three attic rooms on the top floor, five bedrooms on the first floor, and three large rooms and a kitchen on the ground floor. The house, supposedly rebuilt in 1688, was now mainly mid-eighteenth century and had even retained its lovely windows with shutters, its pretty fireplaces, its door furniture as well as the doors. A bow had been built on to the sitting room in 1840, but nothing had been spoiled. I didn't know at this point that the property included a large meadow that ran beside the river and a third of an island. I made my offer, then asked for twenty-four hours to reconsider before I clinched the deal.

When I got home I still wanted the house and the bargain was struck, subject to survey. But then I got really cold feet. What on earth was I doing, moving by myself to the country? True, I had Sargy and Fran next door, but otherwise it was a foreign land to me. I told Jenner about it, and she said she'd like to see it, so we went again. She said afterwards she was worried that I might be making the wrong move, but saw the point of the house, as my goddaughter Minky had. The survey proved to be all right, but a good deal needed doing inside to make it what I wanted. The only staircase was spiral, which meant that anyone going up or down it in a hurry would probably break their leg. The two bathrooms were awful. The kitchen needed a complete facelift. There was no sensible dining room, but I thought that could be solved if I had a conservatory built off the kitchen, big enough for people as well as plants.

Once all the plans were drawn up I went to America, supposedly to help publicize *The Light Years*, which was being published that September. This trip was a farcical failure. I was given a very nice dinner by my publishers, but they hadn't really laid on anything for me to do. I was supposed to give a reading at Brentano's bookshop at seven p.m. When I arrived there was no audience. I asked how anyone was supposed to know that it was happening, and they told me they'd put a notice in the window *that day*. Nobody came. The loyal workers in the shop said *they*'d stay to hear me. This was deeply embarrassing, but there was nothing for it but to plough on. They sent me to Boston, where I stayed with my friends Elizabeth Taylor Mead and her husband Nick Dubrul. Elizabeth had been a member of Jenner's women's group and I had been very sad when she left to live in America. I was due at a bookshop there but, again, nothing had been done to publicize the book and nobody came. The trip was bad from the point of morale, and must have cost the publishers a bomb. But I was now so excited about the new house, that I didn't care much about the publishing débâcle.

It was Martin who rang to tell me that Kingsley was dying. He was in hospital and they didn't expect him to get home again. I asked Mart if he thought Kingsley would like to see me. I asked it desperately – I knew really that he wouldn't. Mart said he was afraid not. He said that Sally, his sister, was being a wonderful support. They were all seeing him; he wasn't alone. Mart rang me later to say that Kingsley had died on 22 October 1990. The funeral was to be private. There would be a memorial service later. It was a second parting, more painful than the first since now there could never be any resolution. I realized that, until now, I'd never entirely given up hope of that – a hopeless hope. You can leave someone and still grieve for them. He'd once said in a newspaper interview that the worst thing that had happened to him was meeting me. That's not true for me: there were many things about him that I still loved – and shall always love.

The memorial service, a year later, was in St Martin in-the-

Fields. I was walking down the aisle, looking for somewhere to sit, and saw Iris Murdoch in an otherwise empty pew. As I went to sit down, she said, 'I'm afraid this pew is entirely taken. People are coming.' I realized she didn't recognize me and backed off. Then Mart came and said I should be in front with him and Isabel, his second wife. I was very touched by that.

I could take possession of Bridge House on 12 December 1990. In the meantime I stayed with my brother Monkey in Tufnell Park. It was a strange feeling to be homeless again. Monkey gave me his sitting room to sleep in, and I borrowed a dress rail on which to hang clothes. Jenner and Terry offered me a room to work in in their house, and allowed me to furnish it heavily with my books. I didn't really need them: it just seemed comforting to have them there. I was working slowly, but every day, on *Marking Time*. I felt then as though *I* was marking time until an unknown and new life began. Most days I dreaded it – dreaded being definitively lonely, cut off from so many of my friends. But another part of me looked forward very much to leaving London and waking up every day in the country. I spent hours thinking about the house and how I wanted it to be.

For the first time in my life I was moving with money to spend – about a hundred thousand pounds, which had been the difference between the sale of Delancey Street and the price of the new house – and it meant I could choose things, instead of making do. I decided that if I wanted my friends to enjoy coming to stay, I must make it extremely comfortable as well as pretty. I planned to cut the eight bedrooms down to six, and make four good bathrooms and keep the shower room, to build a new staircase and do away with the spiral one, to buy a new large boiler so that the heating and hot water would be plentiful, and finally to paint and paper all of the interior. The builders weren't able to start on all this until March 1991, and I'd have three months there with it in its present state.

On the day of the move, Minky and I and my dog, Darcy, drove down in our two cars, laden with everything I'd accumulated at Monkey's. It was a clear, sunny day: we left early, to be ready to receive the removal men who were due at two o'clock. We stopped at a pub for a sandwich but I could hardly eat for excitement.

The usual exhausting day followed, with men coming into the house asking where to put whatever they were carrying. I had two beds and getting them, and indeed anything else, up the spiral staircase was a nightmare. In the late afternoon, by which time we were very tired, I went into the town to buy essential food for Minky and me and Darcy.

Minky had to go the next day and that night would therefore be my first alone in the house. Darcy, who always slept with me, jumped on to the bed, but it was I who was dog tired. She was restive, then jumped off the bed to be violently sick – something she hadn't done since she was a young puppy. I leaped out of bed and she looked imploringly at me – she wanted desperately to go out and be sick some more. It's very difficult negotiating a new house in the dark – I fumbled about for light switches, nearly stumbling over Darcy, who in her desperation was ahead of me, but we managed it. I let her out into the garden. While she was out there, I reflected that it was a good test of the friendliness of a house if one could come downstairs in the dark and not feel in the least afraid. It augured well.

Sargy and Fran employed a cleaning lady called Dawn Fairhead for two mornings a week, but told me that she'd be interested in working for me on the other three. She and her husband David had worked for the previous owner. I interviewed them and liked them at once. It was agreed that David should do some of the gardening, and Dawn would come on the three mornings.

That first Christmas in Suffolk, Monkey, Minky and Ann de Boursac, one of the women's group, and her daughter, Claire, came down. Monkey arrived a little early. The hall was unusable as it was piled high with tea chests. We looked at the sitting room with some despair. It had been painted an unappetizing dark spinach-leaf green with ersatz panelling picked out in white. Monkey said, 'We can't stand this.' He went out and bought brushes and a huge tin of white paint. We painted everything for nearly the entire night. It did look better. We lit fires in that room and my study, but the house was cold. Christmas was jolly.

Soon after, I became ill with a fever that lasted about three weeks. Dawn and I didn't know one another well then, and I'm sure she thought I was a chronic invalid, and dreaded looking after me. She'd bring me tea and toast in the mornings, but she went promptly at twelve noon, and for the rest of the day I lay sweating or shivering, feeling too weak to go down and make myself a hot drink. Every day Fran would come in at about five with some soup, which was very cheering. I slowly got better. I felt like an old shrub that had been transplanted, doesn't like it, and only grudgingly takes to a new position.

When I was better, I went back to work on *Marking Time*. I had my desk, typewriter and a chair in the study, and camped in the rest of the house. There was no point in unpacking more than a minimum, since the whole house would become a mess when the builders came. The weeks before they did were a kind of limbo. I worked, made plans for the garden, and thought about colours for the house. Darcy loved the country; she also took a tremendous liking to Dawn, and whenever I went to London, Dawn took Darcy home with her, sitting in the bicycle basket with her paws hanging out.

It was clear to me that when the builders *did* come I'd have to get out of the house, at least for the first demolition part. The work was supposed to take three months, but I decided as soon as they'd demolished the old staircase and built the new one that I'd return and simply camp in the mess. Mr Hood was in charge of the builders: it was some time before I realized that he comprised the whole firm. He had a team of chums with different skills, including a very good electrician and an equally good plumber.

I went to London to stay with my old friend Josie Baird, who'd bought a flat in Gloucester Crescent, opposite Ursula. I went down with a bug, and was there for a week feeling too ill to do anything I'd planned – hunting for floor and wall tiles, wallpaper and carpeting. Then I stayed with Dosia and Andrew in Pewsey, taking my typewriter. They gave me a bedroom to work in, and I used to watch a rookery that was situated in a row of tall poplars. The birds looked beautiful against the winter sky, taken up with their noisy conferences and their frightful jerrybuilt nests – soothing when I got stuck.

I was about a third of the way through the novel and it was still in the sticky stage, where the scene I was writing was impossibly difficult, and the scene ahead seemed blissfully easy but when reached proved just as hard. Dosia still had furniture and china from the old days when she first married Barry and I remembered it was Barry's taste – and hers – that had first made me look at my surroundings with a critical eye. In the evenings we read and played Scrabble and I sewed. Sewing has always been a tranquil resource for me. I am making something but it's nothing like so taxing as trying to make a book. I have sewed half a dozen carpets, seat covers and cushions over the years with varying degrees of success.

But after a week or two, I had to get back to Bridge House and the builders. Of course, they hadn't done anything like as much as I'd hoped. Building work always starts with belying speed: demolition is far quicker than replacement. Also, men *like* demolishing: it goes with their love of chopping down trees and burning things. I stuck with it for a few days, then asked if I could stay with Sargy and Fran. The builders said all the dirty work would be finished in about two weeks, so for two weeks I boarded with the Manns and went to work in my study for most of the day. Of course they *weren't* finished in two weeks, but there was nothing for it but to return to the house, by then without hot water or even a working loo.

Macmillan wanted to publish *Marking Time* in November 1991, which required the manuscript to be delivered in August.

Jane Wood was a very good editor to work with. She read chunks of the book as I wrote it, which enabled me to talk about it as I went, an enormous help. I used to stay with her sometimes in London, and she'd come down to me at others. We were due to meet in Edinburgh for the festival and I managed to give her the last pages in our hotel. I had to read at the festival, and Doris Lessing was there, whom I knew slightly. I'd always been rather afraid of her, but she was utterly disarming. We went shopping together, and I wanted a rather expensive jacket, and she said, 'Go on. You've just finished your book, you can have a treat.' I loved her *unassumingness*. I also met Rosamunde Pilcher at a writers' lunch; she was most generously nice to me about my work.

Marking Time came out in November, as planned, and got a better reception than *The Light Years*. It took me the next two years to finish the third volume, *Confusion*, which was published in the autumn of 1993. This was partly because, having got the house in order, I had lots of people to stay, and partly because I spent much time getting the garden going.

I was finding living alone in the country quite difficult and longed to find a companion of either sex to share the house with me – probably another of my unrealistic notions. That sort of thing has to start far earlier in life. I was sixty-eight years old – hardly the age for amorous adventure. My contemporary friends had arranged their lives, naturally, and my younger friends would be unlikely to wish to settle down in the country with someone between twenty and thirty years older than them. And yet it's often difficult to be your age. Apart from the fact that I wasn't sure what this entailed, in many ways I didn't *feel* my age. Like one's appearance or hand-writing, one retains an earlier impression of oneself and takes it for granted, no longer *sees* what one is.

The failure of my third marriage had left me with no confidence with men, and sexual pleasure seemed now to be something that had happened a long time ago and to somebody else. Laurie wrote to me about then, asking me if I'd drive him about Spain for a book he was writing – 'Strictly business. Strictly pleasure.' But I couldn't go, another deadline was looming, and perhaps I was afraid, because I wanted to keep safe what I'd had with Laurie.

One autumn I got a letter asking me if I'd spend a Sunday in Petersfield selling and signing books in aid of Macmillan Cancer Relief. Patricia Wyndham signed the letter. I wrote back and said I would. She arranged for me to get a lift down with Philip Ziegler, the diplomat and biographer, and invited me to stay the night with her. I'd met Philip years before and had, in fact, reviewed his first book. We arrived in the dark, which I always like because you don't know where you are, and when you wake up in the morning and see, it's like a second arrival. It turned out that Patricia and her husband, Mark, loved canals and wanted to meet me because Mark had read Robert Aickman's book about the trip through Standedge Tunnel. It was the beginning of a continuing friendship. I did a second year of book signing. They came to stay in Suffolk, and I took Monkey to stay with them. For two years running we had wonderful holidays on the French canals in Mark's boat, *Wilhelmina*, a large, comfortable Dutch boat ideally suited to river and canal journeys. Most of their lives were spent running the 999 club, which provided drop-in centres for people in Deptford. But Patricia was also a keen painter, and when Fran started to teach painting for a week every year, Patricia joined the class. I'd have about eight of them to stay and it was all – still is – very jolly.

Holidays, if you're on your own and don't want to spend them by yourself, are a perennial problem. One way round this, I found, was to get a newspaper to commission me to write a piece, the place to be discussed. I've been lucky and have usually been able to choose. The *Sunday Times* employed me for several such trips: I went to Bali, to India, to China and Sicily.

The latest of these ventures was to the Seychelles with my god-daughter, Minky St Aubyn. I'd always wanted to go there, so one January, when I was still writing about the Cazalets, we went. We had a good time. It was extraordinary to drive from the airport to our first hotel amid trees I couldn't identify. There was a botanical garden in Mahé, the capital and the main island, but when we got there, though there were fine specimens there were no labels, and the only wardens were giant tortoises, who took no notice of us. We went to Praslin, the island that has the coco-de-mer and the only remaining black parrots in the world. We went to Frégate too, the best of all, since only fourteen travellers are allowed at a time, and apart from the small encampment for us the island was wild and uninhabited – except, again, for huge tortoises. For the first time since my early childish passion for desert islands, I felt I was on one. I could imagine how terribly isolated those shipwrecked in such a place might feel. There were pirates' graves on that island.

I made one more trip to tropical islands, the Maldives, with Nicola. This was the first foreign holiday we'd had together, and for me it was an idyllic time. Nicola scuba-dived for which, like Minky, she has a passion. She taught me patiently to use goggles – I've always had a terror of putting my head under water but she got me to do it, and to see all the amazingly beautiful, ethereal, jazzy tropical fish at the water's edge in their thousands. She tried to tempt me to the reef, where there were far more fish to be seen, but I still swim as if I'm riding an upright bicycle, and thought that if I got there, I'd never get back. In the evenings the stingrays came in to be fed, rubbing themselves against us if they felt we weren't doing it quickly enough. We spent a week on each of the islands we visited.

By now, my walking was not good, as I'd been diagnosed with intermittent fibrillation, which meant that after a few yards' walking I felt as though I was getting cramp. This had been coming on for some time, and was very tiresome. I'd lived in Bungay for some time. I couldn't take Darcy for proper walks, I could no longer strim – I'd been battling with ten-foot-high nettles on the right-hand side of my meadow for years, and as I don't use pesticide of any description, strimming was the only method. I was losing the battle in the meadow – had planted thousands of bulbs for naturalizing, but the grass got out of hand and the anemones, for instance, could hardly be seen. One day Mr Cundy, the farmer across the river who supplies Bungay with particularly good milk, was in the meadow which he'd just cut for hay and introduced me to a man he thought might be prepared to give me a hand.

That was the beginning of my happy partnership with David Evans. He had all the machinery ready for use; he understood land management, was a good naturalist and understood exactly how I wanted the place to be. He has revolutionized the meadow, its spinney and the long right-hand side, which is now free of nettles and is well planted with trees, shrubs, bulbs and ferns. We have twice opened the garden for charity, and this could never have happened without David. Eventually we were able to buy the rest of the island, of which previously I'd owned a third, and the piece of land beyond my meadow that marches with the river which now belongs to David. A pond on the island has been dug, and we've stocked it with fish. David has made a path that runs right round the island which in spring is covered with thick peridot-coloured moss. It's an enchanting place.

5

Casting Off came out in 1995. Macmillan gave me a wonderful party at the Ivy to which many of my friends came. Afterwards about fourteen of us went out to dinner. By now, there was more enthusiasm for the tetralogy, and some writers whom I particularly admired wrote to me and said very encouraging things. Selina, Sybille, and Roy Foster, the Irish historian, and Aisling, his wife, had always supported me with flattering interest. Jane Wood had patiently seen me through all my glooms and hiccups in just the right editorial way. I did feel very strange when I wrote the last words: it was the end of living with so many people who, for six years, had monopolized my life.

The books were selling very well: something that hadn't happened to me before. Workhouse fever receded, I actually felt rich, a most enjoyable sensation. I noticed with wry interest that as long as I published a few thousand copies of a novel and received reasonable notices I could be considered, by some, good. Now that I'd published four books that were nearer the bestseller mark, those same people tended to write me off as 'just a bestseller'. This, although many novels have been published for at least a hundred and fifty years that were both bestselling *and* good. Anyway, that didn't spoil my enjoyment. I could, for instance, buy any tree I wanted, dozens of them, without thinking of the cost. I could buy better wine, do things to my house, take taxis, give people nicer presents; there was no end to it. I've never understood people who say it must be awful to be rich – I wasn't exactly *rich*, except in comparison to the previous ten years of my life. I could easily have enjoyed being richer.

But there are other, unexpected and sometimes very moving, bonuses from being more widely read. One woman came up to me when I was signing books and said she'd recently lost her husband and that the only thing that had kept her from going mad during the weeks of insomnia after his death had been reading the Cazalets, because she could lose herself in them. When I was half-way through *Confusion*, a woman wrote to me saying how much she'd enjoyed the books, but she was dying of cancer and was afraid that she wouldn't be alive for the next volume: could I *please* tell her what was going to happen? Right until the end? This was difficult because although I know where I'm going, I like the details of my journey to be a surprise for me as well as the reader. But I had to tell her something so I wrote out a plot. Then, because she'd said nothing of her circumstances, I asked her if she had family or friends looking after her. She wrote back thanking me and said she was surrounded by love. So that was as all right as it could be.

Then I had a letter from a lady who lived in Hastings. She said she'd read the four books, and that it had taken her back to the war: she'd been one of the student nurses in my aunt's Babies' Hotel, which was evacuated to us in Sussex. Myra Hess – my aunt's great friend – had got her and a friend out of Germany, and thereby saved their lives. Her friend lived somewhere in England, but after reading the books, they'd revisited the houses where the babies had been, and where my grandmother had lived. She said my grandmother had realized how homesick she and her friend were, and used to arrange wonderful evenings when she played them music on her gramophone and they had tea and biscuits. She remembered me as a very young girl going to help with the babies. She sent two photographs; one of herself as a ravishing young girl in her nurse's uniform, and one of her and her friend, cardiganed old dears on their nostalgic visit.

In the summer of 1996 I went on a second trip with the

Wyndhams to France. Walking was no better and I felt tired all the time. I also thought I had piles – that laughable complaint, like mothers-in-law and other music-hall jokes, but deeply unfunny for the victim. When I got back to England I saw my doctor and told him about the walking and my piles. He said I'd probably need an operation to replace a bit of blocked artery in my leg, but the wait for this was up to three years. I was seventy-three: it seemed too long to wait. I asked if I could have it done privately. Certainly I could. It was also arranged that when I got notice of the appointment, I should see someone at the hospital near Lowestoft to assess the piles situation. I went to a BUPA hospital and saw the surgeon, and also had to ask about cost. He could replace the artery in a month and I'd be skipping about in no time. It would cost seven thousand pounds. I asked my new financial assistant and friend, Jean McIntyre, whether I could afford this and she said yes, it was a priority.

In November, my appointment came through for the James Paget hospital to sort out the piles. For some reason I decided to go in a cab: Jenner and Terry were staying with me, and there seemed no point in them wasting their precious rest time on driving me there, then waiting and driving me back. I set off, feeling perfectly calm about the whole thing. When I got there, I was told that the consultant I was supposed to see had flu, but there was another doctor. He examined me and then said, 'Keep still, I'm just going to do something that may hurt a bit.' There followed seconds of unspeakable pain. A kind nurse held my hand through it. Afterwards the doctor said, 'I've just taken tissue for a biopsy. We usually have people in overnight and give them an anaesthetic, but I thought I'd do it at once.'

Instantly I knew that something was very wrong. 'When will you have the results?'

'In about ten days' time. We'll inform your doctor, of course.'

I walked out into the dark where the cab was waiting. It must be cancer. And he must know it is, or he wouldn't have cut me so immediately. The cab driver was very talkative, and I tried to listen to him to stop the feeling of panic. But when I got back to Jenner and Terry I could tell them, could get rid of some of the shock. They had to go back to London the next day, and I had to wait the ten days on my own. I'd rung my doctor to tell him and found that he already knew. He was very kind, but it all felt rather ominous – a colostomy was likely. I didn't even know what that was, but of course it was easy to find out. The prospect filled me with horror.

As I waited I thought it probable that I was dying. Nearly everyone I'd known who'd had cancer had died of it in the end. It was extraordinary how all my values shifted – as though I'd shaken a kaleidoscope and all the little segments, though still there, had made a new, unrecognizable pattern. Unhappy, lonely or a failure I might have been, but even those ingredients of my life now seemed precious – even desirable. I didn't want to die. But perhaps it would all be all right; maybe I'd turn out not to have cancer. I oscillated between these emotions, but optimism lost the battle. I decided I was more likely to die than not. I thought of Victor Stiebel and the increasingly humiliating stages of his decline. I thought of Jessie in her bed for life, unable to look after herself, dependent upon others for the most intimate services. I thought of Sargy, to whom the worst had happened, and how he never, never whinged. I thought of his dignity and determination to pursue his life and work. And I remembered my father trying to blow me a kiss before he died. One thing became very clear: I couldn't prevent myself dying, but I could have some power about how I did it. I knew that this was a resolution made in ignorance: like most people I am afraid of pain and I'd no way of knowing how much of that I could stand. I had no belief in an afterlife, which might, I suppose, have made the whole thing exciting – the last great adventure. But a lot of the time I just prayed that the whole thing was a false alarm. On the ninth morning, I had to go into town to buy food, and suddenly – walking down the street to my house – I lightened completely as though, without warning, I'd emerged from a heavy fog into clear sunlight. I felt extraordinarily, irrationally happy. Whatever happened, it would be all right.

In the late afternoon, my doctor rang to say that the biopsy was positive, I had cancer, and treatment – radiotherapy – would have to begin in January. Did this mean no colostomy? Yes, for the time being anyway. That was one small relief. I had to cancel my leg operation. In the meantime, I was to have various blood tests.

Nicola offered at once to come and drive me in for the treatment, which was to take place five days a week for three weeks. She couldn't stay all the time, so my kind cousin Kay Howard offered to do the other half. It took place in the old Norwich hospital. It was hell to find a parking space, and the time in the hospital was much lengthened because the radiation machine constantly broke down. There was only one man who could fix it and he was often fixing something else. Hours would pass sitting on the artificial leather seats with rows of cancer patients, the air full of apprehension, boredom and doom. We read old – medieval – magazines until we had the sense to bring books. Nic was marvellous to me – cheerful, kind and practical. You don't feel much for the first two weeks, but after that it begins to hit you: lassitude, tiredness, positive exhaustion and discomfort. When I'd recovered from this, I was able to go ahead with the vascular operation to replace the artery in my leg at the BUPA hospital. This seemed to go well. I spent two weeks in the hospital to convalesce.

During this period of health anxieties, something quite different had been happening. In the early autumn I'd broadcast my second *Desert Island Discs* – this time with Sue Lawley. It went rather well, and I got dozens of letters, all forwarded by the BBC in packets. They were mostly friendly, saying how much they liked one piece of music but why hadn't I chosen another? There were a few obscene letters, one or two that were quite simply mad and others merely eccentric. Over the years I'd got quite good at sorting these out for replies or silence.

Among them was a brief note from a man who said he'd enjoyed the programme, and how much he would like to take me out to tea one day. I didn't receive this for some days, and when the second batch of letters arrived, about a week later, there was another note from the same man. He wondered if I'd had his first, and added that if I didn't like the idea of tea with him he would quite understand, and bother me no more. I answered, saying I'd been ill, was due for an operation and therefore couldn't do anything about tea until March. I got a letter back full of enthusiasm. At one point I wrote saying why didn't he tell me a bit about himself. He responded to this at length. Then I got one saying that he loved me. I wrote back to say that that was nonsense: he didn't know me at all. His letters about himself were rather full of misfortune. He seemed to have had a sad life. He wrote long letters about three times a week. I told him I couldn't keep up with him since I'd started to plan and write a new novel. He entirely understood that. By now I knew that he'd parted from his wife and was living on his own.

But a crucial point of this relationship had in fact occurred much earlier, after we'd exchanged no more than two or three letters. It was during my nine-day wait for the verdict on my biopsy. I was standing by my bedroom window looking at the place under the beech tree where soon the snowdrops would appear, and wondering whether this was the last year I should see them, when the telephone rang. It was him. He announced himself and said, 'I don't know what to *say* to you!' I didn't know what to say to him either. I fell back on my usual thing of asking him to tell me more about himself. No, no, he wanted to hear about *me*, he only knew what he had heard on the radio and from reading books. I can't now remember whether it was then I told him I had cancer, or whether it was later, in a letter. Anyway, there wasn't much more conversation on the telephone.

I won't write here a full account of what followed since I made a novel out of it, and being a novel it had the licence to blend fact with invention as I pleased.

In real life, the letters became more frequent – he had a talent for that and I have always been a sucker for prolonged correspondence. It was also exciting to have what, at the least, was a flirtation.

Jonathan Cavendish had once said to me, 'You never flirt, do you?' I hadn't thought of that, but when he said it I recognized rather sadly that it was true.

One of the wounds in my leg took a very long time to heal, and during that time I didn't work much, and consequently wrote more letters. By now I knew, or thought I knew, a good deal about the man and the women in his life. Apart from that, he wrote a good deal about me, had read the biographies of Peter and Kingsley, and kept telling me how beautiful I was. I wrote back saying I was no such thing: my hair was white and I was fat, and not what he'd taken to imagining from the books. This reminded me of a very young man years before, in the days of Robert Aickman, who'd stared and stared at me and finally stuttered, 'You're ageless! Ageless and shapeless!' and how much this had made me laugh. A part of me thought that perhaps I could be loved whatever my appearance – I was certainly shapeless – and his reply to that letter reinforced this.

It's commonly supposed that women of my age must, or should, have lost all interest in sex. Nature, after all, has no further requirements of women past the menopause. It may well be that a woman who has had a happy and fulfilled marriage, and has brought up her children, is able to let her sexual activity fade to be replaced by the affection and intimacy that a good marriage yields. But I wasn't one of those women: frigid throughout my first marriage and for some time after it, I hadn't understood that sex was for both partners until I met Laurie. When I did fully understand, the long-term partners weren't available, until Kingsley.

For years I went to bed with men because I wanted their affection, which is what I thought the exchange involved. By the time I met Kingsley I was in a parlous state. I was violently attracted to him. I didn't think I was going to see very much of him, but knew I wouldn't see anything if I proved to be a disappointment to him. So I cheated, pretended it was better than it was. It was only when he began to love me that it changed.

It was now sixteen years since I'd left Kingsley and there had been no sex for some years before that. Since being on my own, I'd been mildly attracted to one or two people, but I didn't expect them to be attracted to me. It was just nice for me to know that I *could* feel even a mild attraction. But this man was definitely courting me. I thought about the promised tea in March. Since he lived in Scotland and I in Suffolk, this would probably mean meeting in London in an hotel. I found this a daunting thought. So, after consultation with a friend, I decided to ask him for a weekend where others would be present. It would give not only me but also my friends a chance to see what we all thought of him.

He came on Friday evening. Jane Wood and her lover, Edward, were due on Saturday morning, so I asked my friend Nick McDowell, then the publicity director at Macmillan, whether he could come for the Friday night. He kindly agreed. When my visitor arrived, we had a glass of wine together before Nick joined us for dinner. He wasn't particularly good-looking, but it was immediately clear that he possessed enormous charm. I could see that he was very nervous – his palms were sweaty when we shook hands – but that soon wore off as we drank the wine. When we had dinner he lapsed into relative silence. Nick told Sargy the next morning that there was no need to worry about him, he was simply rather dull.

Much the same thing happened with Jane and Edward. 'I can see he's potty about you,' Jane said, when I asked her about him. Edward said he quite liked him. I was so nervous at the prospect of going to bed with him that, as is my wont when afraid of something, I plunged in and invited him to share my bed. It was clear at once that this was his element. But, less like other people I'd known, he made no sudden conquest, said we needed time – or rather, I needed time to get to know him. This remark, which had never been made to me before, enchanted me.

That was it. He went early on Monday morning. Correspondence was resumed on a more intimate level, and some weeks later I invited him to stay ten days so that we could spend more ordinary time together.

I think in all he came to stay three times, and on the second and third occasions he mentioned marriage. I told him that I didn't want to be married to anyone else in my life. He didn't accept this or, rather, he seemed to accept it, but then reverted to it as though for the first time. The second time was soon after I returned home after the vascular operation, and Nicola had come to stay with me. She knew he was coming, and fetched him from Norwich airport. I could see he was making great efforts to be nice to her, and that she wasn't impressed. At some point I fell on the wet York stone on my terrace. It was a bad fall, on the bad leg, and I was afraid I'd broken it as I couldn't get up until Fran and Susanna rescued me. I was in a good deal of pain, and he delighted in looking after me – cups of tea, and doing the shopping. He suggested coming to live in Bungay and buying a cottage. I felt what he really meant was that he wanted to live in my house with me, and something somewhere in me told me that this was a bad idea.

On the second visit, another convalescent was staying with me. Each of them came to me to say that the other was drinking too much – secretly, of course. In front of me he drank wine and beer and not a great deal of either.

It's really difficult to recall my state of mind then. I enjoyed sex with him, and we talked together very companionably. It felt extraordinary to be *having* a sex life. And yet, when he left after the second visit, I felt curiously relieved. I wondered whether – like Elizabeth Taylor's very good story about meeting someone to whom she's written for years and finding she's unable to bear him through a lunch – we might be better on paper. But no, as soon as he was away I thought of when he'd be back. 'You like me in bed,' he said one day, and it was true. What he didn't know was how unusual that was for me.

The third time he came, Selina, Monkey and Susie Allison came for the weekend. It was clear that Selina, though polite about it, didn't think much of him. Monkey had spent an evening with him in London, and hadn't liked him either. Susie, however, made one of those provocative remarks that have the opposite effect of their intention. 'He's not remotely *up* to you – different background and all that—'

'You mean, he's working class,' I interrupted. She said, well, yes, that's what she did mean. I said I didn't care a damn about his class, it made no difference to me. But in one way it did. It made me both defensive about and protective of him. I decided not to worry about the future, to enjoy being loved and cared for, to foster our mutual trust and to hell with anyone else . . .

When he left after the third visit, we'd planned that he wouldn't come again until August, as I'd been invited by the McDowells to spend two weeks with them on Ios, and then was going to spend a fortnight with Selina in Ireland.

By now I knew that he lived in a council house and he had given me to understand that he'd not got much, if any, money. As he had to do all the travelling, I paid half his fares. I also gave him some money to pay off his credit-card debt. But I was beginning to wonder why he didn't seem to have any sort of job; he was sixty-two and in good health. All he wanted to do, he said, was to look after me. This sounded both nice and not quite right. I drove him to the station and it was agreed that he would come down on 12 August – he'd already booked a seat on the plane.

About ten days later, I went to London to stay the night before going to Greece. My brother met me at the station. This was a surprise. He'd never met me before. I said I had to go to the dentist and then to Camberwell to stay the night with the McDowells, as we were leaving early. He'd take me there. After the dentist, Monkey said he'd done some alterations to his house that he would like me to see. When we got there, and he'd seated me in his new sitting room and made some tea, he said he had something rather awful to tell me.

My family had been worried by my affair and had started to make some enquiries. One monstrous lie – out of which this man had made much emotional capital – was uncovered, and this had led to more. In fact everything he'd told me, that they could verify, had been a pack of lies – some disgusting, some positively dangerous. There seemed to be nothing of the truth about him, and his reasons for making up to me became humiliatingly clear. I was too stunned at first to take it all in. There were enough verifiable lies to suggest that they were only the tip of the iceberg and, indeed, Monkey said, more and more of them were still coming out. I had to do something – put a stop to his letters before I went to Greece. I wrote a brief note to him saying I now knew things about him that made me not wish to see or hear from him again, and that I'd told all of my friends that he was *persona non grata*, and that was that. I didn't tell him what I knew: I wanted him to dread what the things might be, as it was clear now that somebody with his record of lies and destruction had reason to be afraid. I told friends I thought he might possibly ring up, and they said they wouldn't talk to him. He did ring some of them, clearly agitated about what I knew. So that was it. The next morning I went to Greece.

It's not easy to accept that somebody you thought close to you, who claimed such unconditional love, wasn't anything he'd seemed. Liars destroy the currency of all words: there was no single fragment of truth I could hang on to. Of course it was humiliating, but I wish it had been only that. In my mind, during the sleepless nights on Ios, I went back to the naïve conviction I'd had with Jim Douglas-Henry which had been my undoing: that people didn't tell lies about love. How long it had taken me to recognize that this was a fallacy! I have said earlier that I am a slow learner – and here I was, at seventy-four, having to discover this all over again. I have learned it now. It was cold comfort to say that con-men couldn't *be* con-men unless they were successful in giving the impression they chose to give. I should have known by now that any man who made up to me would be doing it for unsimple reasons. But it was a bit late to know that. I *did* constantly live in the slipstream of my experience.

In the autumn, I scrapped the novel I'd been writing and started upon *Falling*.

6

Ever since the cancer treatment I'd been going to see the oncologist to ensure there was no recurrence. I'd started to have a good deal of pain, so I asked him about it. 'You've got a couple of tiny little ulcers in there – a result of the radiation. They're very small,' he added, with a smile, meaning, I suppose, that they'd go away, or I'd get used to them.

To relieve what had been a rather black year, I decided to rent two little houses on Nevis in the Caribbean and invite friends to come on a fortnight's holiday. Jim and Pam Rose, very old friends, said they'd like to come, and the Wyndhams, Minky and Monkey. We were to go very early in January, a good month to be away, and I looked forward to it very much.

But by November the pain was so much worse that I told my doctor. He sent me to see Professor Nichols, the best consultant. I went to him privately as I couldn't bear to wait for what might have been months to see him.

My kind Nicola came all the way from Gloucestershire to meet me at the consulting room in Harley Street. When he'd examined me, he said, 'You poor thing, you must be in agony!' and rang his hospital, St Mark's at Northwick Park, for me to go in for a biopsy as soon as possible. I'd been told, I said, that I had no recurrence of cancer, and he said there was no way that anyone could know that without giving me an anaesthetic. 'I should hurt you too much if we didn't do that.'

I felt I was back at square one. Nic and I took a taxi to Liverpool

Street, but she had to leave me there to go home. I went back on the train to my empty house. I could see Nevis slipping away and had a good cry about that to relieve some of the fear.

The following week I went for the biopsy. It only meant staying in for one night. They told me the result would come in about ten days, as Professor Nichols was going to be away. I went home and thought about this, then rang the registrar and said, could I please be told as soon as *they* knew? Surprised at this whimsical suggestion, they agreed I could. The result came through five days later. I hadn't got cancer, but I had several ulcers that would have to be operated on, and this would mean a colostomy. Dates were discussed. I had the choice of going in over Christmas, 'but you won't want to do that', or the end of January. I opted for Christmas: the pain was too obtrusive for me to enjoy a holiday and I still felt anxious that cancer might be found. Losing the holiday made me feel childishly deprived. I cried about it as I had years previously over losing the house I'd wanted in North London. It was to have been a holiday with friends, something I always wanted, and this time I'd put a lot of energy into arranging it. Everyone went except me. It was a success, and I was sent kind postcards.

Selina, most loyal, staunch friend, drove me to Northwick Park, a vast hospital near Harrow. St Mark's hospital had been in Islington, and had transferred to a wing there.

The first operation was a long one. I woke up with all kinds of appliances attached to me, including a small bulb I could press to get morphine. I was in a ward with four other women in varying stages of recovery. Professor Nichols came round and said he'd only been able to stitch up two of the ulcers and I'd need a further operation in due course.

There were two wonderful nurses there, one woman and one man. To begin with I felt very uncomfortable at having a man do all the awful things to me that had to be done, but he dealt with that with extreme kindness and tact. 'I do it all the time,' he said, 'it's my profession. I love looking after people, whatever it entails.'

When I was coming round he was there. He leaned over me and said, 'I read a marvellous book last year.' What was it? '*Captain Correlli's Mandolin* by Louis de Bernières.'

'Oh, yes,' I said weakly. 'I know him.'

'I'm sure you do,' he replied soothingly. Hours later he ran into the ward and said, 'You *do* know Louis de Bernières! He's just rung up to ask after you.' He was one of those nurses who seemed to have time for everybody. He and another nurse, a woman called Jo, were totally professional and dedicated, but of course they weren't always around.

The worst thing about those weeks in the ward was other people's pain. There were at least two people far more ill than I. Sometimes when they were in agony, they made sounds I'd never heard before, sounds of a kind I imagined desperately wounded men made, hanging out on the wire during the First World War. And I couldn't get up and hold their hand or do anything.

Gradually the others began to talk to me; nobody talked much, but there were exchanges. 'You'll feel better in a day or two,' one young girl said to me. She seemed the most experienced patient in the ward, which was kept intolerably hot. One evening she went and fetched an electric fan and sat it before me. But nobody talked about what was wrong with them, and nobody asked questions. This was both interesting and a relief. I'd dreaded blow-by-blow accounts of what everybody had been through.

The best thing was that Monkey came to see me every evening. We didn't talk much – sometimes he just sat and read the paper. But he made the long journey during the rush-hour every night and the comfort of knowing he'd be there was extreme. Pam, one of my women's group, took on the task of arranging my visitors, which was wonderful, as well as being a faithful visitor herself.

The food there was pretty much the sort of awful stuff we've all been told about. One of the most bizarre dishes was scrambled eggs made, of course, with dried egg, heavily laced with sucron. Kind people brought me fruit and, sometimes, delicious sandwiches.

Efforts had clearly been made in the hospital. Each person had a miniature TV set by their bed with headphones for the sound. There was plenty of space in the wards, and several bathrooms, but only one shower. As hardly anyone could have a bath, this was the wrong way round, and there were no bidets, which would have been a most practical piece of equipment for most patients. The wards were lit from about seven a.m. until eleven p.m. and it was hard to sleep under the KGB glare, which was hardly necessary – each patient had an Anglepoise lamp that was perfectly adequate.

The worst problem, which I imagine is the same for all hospitals nowadays, was the dearth of good nurses. The ones that were any good – the more senior ones – spent most of their time on bureaucracy. On my visits there, five in all, I had to fill in a huge form with the same information.

Monkey came to drive me home after the first operation, and after that, kind nurses came in every day to dress my wound for about three months. I was still on painkillers and felt pretty ropy. Also, although I know thousands of people have colostomies, I was finding that very difficult. When I went back to hospital for a second ulcer stitching, Professor Nichols asked me how I was getting on with it. I told him and asked whether, when he'd finished with the ulcers, there'd be any chance of a reversal. He said he wasn't sure whether he wanted to do that. But if I was having trouble, why didn't I have irrigation? I'd no idea what that was until he explained. The stoma nurse would teach me when I went home.

So when I went home the wonderful, kind, warm stoma nurse came for three mornings to teach me how to do the irrigation, which took half an hour, but meant that one was trouble free for twenty-four hours. She hadn't taught me before, she said, because she'd thought I'd be certain to have a reversal. Grey thoughts of having to do this when I was eighty and had flu crossed my mind, but I was learning that if I could confine my anxiety to the present, it was far more controllable.

7

I continued to work upon *Falling*. To begin with I'd had to spend a good deal of what looked like wasting time while I made the two main protagonists for the story. Writing was very slow, partly because I didn't have enough energy, partly because summer was coming on and I wanted to be gardening.

I went back to hospital for one night for an examination with an anaesthetic as things still hurt, but all seemed to be well. People came to stay most weekends, but especially in the summer. For some years the women's group had stayed for a three-day residential: there were usually nine or ten of us, and we all felt we got a lot out of living together even for so short a time. Also, Fran had started her annual painting week, and most of the students stayed with me. They worked all morning, came home for lunch and went back to work until five o'clock. Then we had supper and lively evenings. The hard core of this group consisted of Ann Clowes, Patricia and Mark Wyndham, a friend of theirs called Elfin Ebury, Jackie Gomme, now called Hume, the old friend who'd helped me run the Cheltenham Festival, but others came too from year to year.

Also in the summers, I had children to stay. The island on the river, from which you can swim, is ideal for children, and even when they grew too old to want to have a tent and cook their supper on a bonfire they still came every year. Selina's nephew and niece came to stay with a friend each. I always asked them to invite a friend, as they enjoyed everything far more than with a sibling, who was either disastrously *young* or maddeningly *old*. Kate Hopkinson brought her two children every year. Jane Wood's grandchildren came, and there was one hilarious year when we had a paddling pool. Four-year-olds tore off their clothes and the garden was full of earthy T-shirts and minute grey socks.

Strange meals were cooked on the island bonfire – apple soup was one: it remained pieces of unripe apple floating in tepid water, and the creator of this dish was in tears because it wouldn't turn into soup. A number of faithful friends came all the year round – Jane, now married to Edward, Zach and Alice Leader, Pam and Leisha, two great friends from the women's group, sometimes my granddaughters with their progeny, Terry and Jenner, Minky, my cousin Kay, Josie Baird, Selina, Catherine Freeman, my nieces Emily and Louise Young, Dru Heinz with Inigo, her parrot. But many others came to stay from year to year.

I can't now remember when arthritis began seriously to impinge. I'd had it mildly for some years, but it hadn't prevented me doing anything. I really noticed it when I found I couldn't garden very much. As any gardener knows, three-quarters of one's time is spent on one's knees and that became steadily more difficult even with a kneeler. Although I'd got quite good at 'walking through the pain', as the professor at St Mary's had told me to do, arthritis was rather putting a stop to that. But I don't think I took in the implications of being so lame until I went to Sri Lanka with friends.

I didn't manage to finish *Falling* before we went, and this worried me because I had a date with Professor Nichols soon after our return, the outcome of which was uncertain. If all was well, he would do a reversal; if not, not. But either way I felt I *must* finish the novel before hospital, and that was an anxious feeling because I never know how long any piece of writing will take.

Anyhow, it was in Sri Lanka that I realized how feeble I'd become. I couldn't go for walks or do many of the things that such a place invited. In the first week, when we were travelling about,

I *did* see some beautiful places – the enormous statue of the dying Buddha, among the most memorable, but I couldn't, for instance, climb to the top of Sigiriya – something I'd wanted to do for years. We saw a lot of marvellous country, and we settled in a house we'd rented on the south coast by the sea with a swimming-pool. This, I thought, was going to be fine; I'd do a lot of swimming and get more mobile. But after three days I became ill: streamed and streamed and found breathing frighteningly difficult. It was only when I got home that the doctor told me I had asthma – probably a bug as well, he said, which had brought it on.

I *did* finish the novel before going off to St Mark's, where to my joy I was able to have a reversal. I came home and had a summer when I didn't do very much work.

Falling came out in the autumn of 1999. Usually after a novel, I have a great urge to write a play and I did a certain amount of research to this end, only to decide that the dramatic structure couldn't be made to work. As I feel exactly the same desire recurring as I finish this memoir, I think I shall try again, so I won't say anything more about it.

Earlier that year Verity Lambert had optioned the 'Cazalet Chronicle' for a series of plays for television. Joanna Lumley, who'd also wanted the rights, joined her friend Verity, and they agreed to co-produce. What a combination, I thought, and still think. They came down to stay for a night that was heady with champagne and all the lovely dream-like plans that occur at this stage of most dramatic enterprises. We had a marvellous time, casting and recasting, discussing what would have to be left out and what was essential.

Originally, they wanted to do six plays for each book, which would have been perfect. But then there was the BBC to reckon with. All TV set-ups are terrified of anything going on for too *long*, visualizing their audience as a crowd of grasshoppers with low IQs. They ignore the fact that the most successful drama series have been those where time had been allowed proportionate to the size of the work being adapted: *The Forsyte Saga*, *Bridehead Revisited*, *The Jewel in the Crown* are all obvious examples. The BBC instantly set about cutting. The first two novels were to be done in six plays, with a bit of the third added in because it had a wedding in it.

Verity and Joanna had commissioned an excellent and experienced adapter in Douglas Livingstone, and it was he who had to deal with the problems that the cutting involved. The Cazalet books, being a family chronicle, had an enormous cast, and the difficulties of introducing them and moving the story forward as fast the BBC wanted were nearly insurmountable. Douglas did the best he could, but none the less it was a pity. However, the BBC said that when they did the last two novels we should have twelve plays, and we all felt better about that. I collaborated a bit with Douglas on the script in an advisory capacity, and he was lovely to work with, indefatigable with his drafts.

Eventually, in the spring of 2000, the scripts were ready and casting began, and Verity and Joanna assembled a strong company. I was invited to the read-through at which sixty-two people sat round an enormous table to read, with Suri Krishnama, the director, Joanna and Verity and me at one end, and two of the BBC drama heads by our side. Shooting began the following autumn, and by December it was ready for editing.

There followed an unsuccessful battle with the BBC about when the plays should be broadcast. Verity wanted them to go out in the autumn, when people want to watch plays in the evening. But by then the head of BBC One had changed, and she was determined to put it out at the beginning of July on a Friday evening. So, apart from competing with the Wimbledon tennis finals, many people saw only the first three plays as children's holidays began and ratings dropped off. After endless procrastination and a fairly bitter meeting between Verity, Joanna and the BBC head, the further twelve plays were abandoned, on the grounds of the ratings. The series got hundreds of letters of appreciation, but this made no difference. I don't think a series of plays has been abandoned in the middle before, and we all felt very bitter about it. But Verity has become a real friend: one of the best things that has happened to me in the last twenty years is how many new and lovely friends I've acquired.

Apart from my family and friends, something that has steadily grown throughout my life has been my increasing love of the natural world. I live in a beautiful place with a meadow and an island on the river that runs beside it, which I have turned into a kind of nature reserve. There has been room to plant many trees and bushes, to naturalize wild flowers, snowdrops, bluebells, primroses, cowslips, anemones and *Fritillaria meleagris*. The island has a pond on it and is now the home of reed warblers, owls, hedgehogs, a grass snake, herons, mice of many kinds, rabbits, frogs and newts and sometimes even an otter. I am trying to get hellebore, many kinds of ferns and trillium to flourish. Roses have ramped up the very old apple trees on the island, and last year a pair of swans built a shaky mansion for their eggs. I grow wych hazel, spindle, camellia, lilac and all kinds of buddleia for butterflies, and having used no pesticide for thirteen years has paid off. There is food for everyone. The perfect thing about nature is how it's always on the move. The seasons – at least three of them – give me acute pleasure: the changing light, the bony winter trees starting to leaf, and the wild plum with its fat green-white beads that open to little fragile white stars. Every day when I walk round something new has happened and this goes on for months – goes on, of course, for ever.

When I was about eight, I remember lying in bed in Scotland one night and saying to myself, 'You have ridden on an elephant, you've worn puttees, and you've been out in a boat to catch sea trout,' and being deeply impressed with my wealth of experience. This zenith of sophistication was soon overtaken. If I were to lie in bed now with a more recent list, I would say, 'You've written twelve novels and as much again in other forms, you've travelled to seventeen countries and you've planted nearly a thousand trees.' I am less impressed, because now I know I could have done much better and more.

I couldn't even have done this without the help I have here at Bridge House. Dawn Fairhead looks after my home for me with loving care, with her husband David. David Evans, whose land management and informed love of nature have turned the island and meadow into a magical place, cares for my meadow as much as I do.

For the last two years while I have been writing this, I have been getting noticeably older. Getting old is a classic slipstream situation. It's rather like that game Grandmother's Footsteps. I stand at the end of a lawn with my back to a row of the trappings of old age whose object is to reach me before I turn round and send them back to their row. One or two of these have caught me out during the last five years: I have neither the health nor the energy that once I had. In these respects I am not as young as I feel. Arthritis is dispiriting because it's both painful and incurable, and it takes time to become reconciled to it. I can't – like my friend Penelope Lively – garden any more and that is for both of us a privation.

But on the plus side, I am able to go on writing, I can sew and cook and have friends to stay and above all read. I continue to go to my women's group; I can still learn. One of the good things about living longer is that we have more time to learn *how* to be old. It's clear to me now that inside the conspiracy of silence about age – because of the negative aspects of the condition – there is the possibility of art: that is to say that it can be made into something worth trying to do well, a challenge, an adventure. I don't want to live with any sort of retirement, with nostalgia and regret wrapped round me like a wet blanket. I want to live enquiringly, with curiosity and interest for the rest of my life.

When I do look back, as indeed I've had to do to write this book, the household accounts don't seem so bad. I've made a good many mistakes, some rather expensive, but I think I've more or less paid for them. I've slowly learned some significant things – perhaps most of all the virtue, the extreme *importance* of truth, which, it seems to me now, should be continually searched for and treasured when any piece of it is found. This book has been in search of some of that.

Index

Index

Index

Howard, Dana (cousin) 74
Howard, David (father): childhood
memories of 5, 11–12, 17–18; war
experiences 13–14, 61, 62;
appearance 14; interests 14;
character 15; marriage 15; social life
17; Christmas holidays 40–1;
relationship with daughter 66–9,
112, 116, 136, 181–2; sailing
holidays 67–8, 80; Instow visit 97;
daughter's wedding 115, 116, 117;
son Robin's marriage 173–4; affair
with Ursula 175–6, 181, 199–200;
cigars for 187; life with Ursula
195–6; relationship with Colin 200;
second marriage 201; daughter's
holiday in France 221; illness and
death 313–16, 379, 459
HOWARD, ELIZABETH JANE:
birth 17; childhood 3–12; music
11, 26, 30, 38, 47, 50, 73; riding 18,
24, 45–6, 55, 57–8, 61; Beacon
holidays 24–5, 28–9, 32–4, 40–2,
57, 73–4; pets 56–7, 62–3, 75, 220,
348, 359, 391, 427, 429, 440, 448–9;
cinema-going 61, 64–5; theatre-
going 64; sailing 67–8; acting in
student repertory 89–99; acting at
Stratford 103–7; marriage to Peter
Scott 114–17, 121–2; pregnancy
124–33; daughter's birth 133–7; air-
raid warden 143–4; at BBC 160,
162–3; film extra 167; election
campaign 170–1; in New York
183–90; IWA work 196, 203–4,
212–13; modelling 197; divorce
from Peter Scott 197, 219;
publication of *The Beautiful Visit*
210; at Chatto & Windus 245–51;
publication of *The Long View* 282; at
Weidenfeld 292–3; book reviewing
for *Queen* 314, 317–18, 321;

Ouspensky Society 319, 322–3;
marriage to Jim Douglas-Henry
320–2; film scriptwriting 323–4,
435–6; Cheltenham Festival 332–8;
Bookstand 336–7; divorce from Jim
Douglas-Henry 348; Waugh
interview 351; television work 353;
marriage to Kingsley Amis 364;
Salisbury Festival of Arts 388–9;
television writing 417–18; leaves
Kingsley Amis 427; divorce from
Kingsley Amis 428, 430; moves to
Suffolk 445–50; publication of *The
Light Years* 446–7; publication of
Marking Time 452; publication of
Casting Off 456; publication of
Falling 473
——APPEARANCE: as a child 11,
79–80, 294; beauty 273–4; dress
115, 201–2, 208, 210, 251, 266,
298–9; hair 11, 79, 202–1; in old
age, 462
——EDUCATION: Francis Holland
School 26–8, 29–31, 40; governess
43–50; Seer Green 70–2, 75–6, 78;
London Mask Theatre School 79,
84–6, 87–8, 89; Pitman typing
course 111–12
——FINANCES: allowance from father
125; allowance from husband 125–6;
extravagance in NY 187, 189; loan
on leaving Peter Scott 195; divorce
from Peter Scott 197; life in
Blandford Street 201–2, 215;
earnings from writing 244, 433,
456–7; Chatto & Windus work 245;
in NY 249, 251; money from A. D.
Peters 293; *Queen* salary 314, 321;
Jim's attitude to money 321–2;
mortgage 372–3; life with Kingsley
Amis 374–5, 419, 428–9; divorce
from Kingsley Amis 430

Index